Managing in the Information Age

Ann E. Prentice

THE SCARECROW PRESS, INC.
Lanham, Maryland • Toronto • Oxford
2005

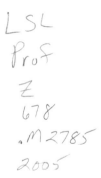

SCARECROW PRESS, INC.

Published in the United States of America
by Scarecrow Press, Inc.
A wholly owned subsidary of
The Rowman & Littlefield Publishing Group, Inc.
4501 Forbes Boulevard, Suite 200, Lanham, Maryland 20706
www.scarecrowpress.com

PO Box 317
Oxford
OX2 9RU, UK

British Library Cataloguing in Publication Information Available

Library of Congress Cataloging-in-Publication Data

Prentice, Ann E.
  Managing in the information age / Ann E. Prentice.
     p.   cm.
  Includes bibliographical references and index.
  ISBN 0-8108-5206-3 (pbk. : alk. paper)
  1. Library administration.   2. Library administration—United States.   I. Title.
Z678.M2785   2005
025.1—dc22   2004026808

Contents

Acknowledgments

Although one individual may have developed the concept for a book and may have prepared the manuscript, that individual relies on others for testing ideas, for tracking down the elusive fact or bibliographic citation, for technical support in dealing with software and hardware, and for moral support when writing becomes difficult or when sheer exhaustion looms.

This author has had support in each of these areas and each of the individuals noted has had a role in arriving at a completed manuscript. Karen Patterson, director of the library at the College of Information Studies, University of Maryland, and her able staff members Chris Eddie and Patricia Verdines spent hours checking facts and completing often nearly impossible-to-find citations. Their professionalism and willingness to dig and dig until the information was found is most appreciated. Christine McDonald, director of the Crandall Library, Glens Falls, New York, located additional material for the chapter on diversity. Eileen Abels, associate professor in the College of Information Studies, provided citations and suggestions regarding special libraries and information centers. Technical support was provided by Gary Videlock and Sandy Kempsell. Continuous technical and moral support was provided by my husband, M. Don Surratt. Thanks to all of you, and especially to Don for supporting me in this three-year project.

Introduction

Management is an *art*, the art of bringing people and resources together to achieve objectives. It is the art of working with a wide range of individuals with different skill, interest, and ability levels, bringing them together to share in a common enterprise and to enjoy that activity. Management is a *skill* in which one utilizes methods taken from psychology, sociology, management, and other disciplines to practice the art. It is a *science* in that one can put forth hypotheses, test them, and measure findings. Technology provides many new tools to assist in managing, particularly in the management of resources.

Numerous studies have been done to determine the most important things a manager does. A manager must have a vision for the organization, must be able to communicate that vision, and must see that the vision is carried into practice. Each of these activities involves bringing people together to achieve objectives. Managers spend from 70 percent to 80 percent of their time interacting in one way or another with individuals. The success of the organization and their success as managers are dependent on how well they do this.

A management text, while it discusses organizations, organizational structure, financial practices, and related activities, is focused on the role of people in organizations and how they contribute to the organization. A management text needs to be forward-looking and not merely descriptive of past practice: "to dispense advice and wisdom accumulated from decades of managing library and information services in a relatively stable and predictable environment that no longer exists is useless to those who must grapple with today's challenges."[1] Writing a management text that describes past practice has little value; looking at past practice and using it as a structure

1

for discussing change, innovation, and the ways in which past practices must change and how that change can occur would be more useful.

What has worked in the past will not necessarily work in the future. The rigid hierarchical management structure often typical of library organizations is poorly designed to respond to our rapidly changing environment. As we move, and we must move, from the slow-to-respond bureaucratic hierarchical structures to a more flexible structure, today's rules may not apply, boundaries for what we do may disappear, and ambiguity best describes the environment. The divisions between public and technical services, between libraries and computing centers, between the library and the classroom, between the user and the reference specialist have become fluid. We need to decentralize the ways in which we provide services in this new and ever-moving environment while at the same time centralizing the ways in which those services are coordinated. "We shall have to make judicious decisions that blend the strengths of the past, the demands of the present, and the uncertainties of the future, and we shall have to balance them continually from both local and institutional perspectives within an organizational structure designed to support the past."[2] New funding patterns, new organizational patterns, and new collection patterns will be developed. The focus on service to users will be even more heavy, with that mission paramount. The organization, its staff, and management will be secondary to user services.

Many organizations are still managed by individuals who predate the information age and who may be uncomfortable with the social, political, and technological changes in the environment in which we live. Most probably, their early work experience was in a highly structured hierarchical environment where each individual had a defined role and a defined place in the organization. The individual who followed the rules advanced in the organization and gradually gained power. This individual might well have expected to manage the same type of organization in which he or she had spent his or her career.

Today's new information professionals have been educated in a world quite different from that of their parents or many of their potential employers. It is a world where information and communication technologies heavily influence education, government, business, not-for-profit organizations, and one's personal activities. The workplace is more diverse and most likely multicultural. Individuals in the organization may have similar educational and professional preparation, but their ethnic and cultural backgrounds may differ, as may their work ethics and attitudes toward the organization. New employees find themselves caught between what they have learned and experienced and the attitudes of management in the structure of the organization they have joined. How does one become part of the organizational culture and still stay true to the attitudes, knowledge, skills, and abilities he or she brings to that organization? Many managers understand working in the new environment. They see the organization as a flexible tool for achieving objectives. However, the new employee should expect to find some discontinuity in any new position between personal attitudes and experiences and those of the new workplace. The new employee has a responsibility to learn the organizational culture, to discover how things are done, and to adapt to the extent possible. The manager or supervisor has a responsibility to learn from the new employee what different and useful knowledge and skills that person brings. During the hiring process, both potential employer and employee have had the opportunity to test their compatibility so that there is some assurance of common approaches in the workplace.

SOCIAL CAPITAL

"We experience work as a human, social activity that engages the same social needs and responses in our lives; the need for connection and co-operation, support and trust, a sense of belonging, fairness, and recognition."[3] Cohen and Prusak define social capital as "the stock of active connections among people; the trust, mutual understanding, and shared values and behaviors that bind the members of human networks and communities and make co-operation possible."[4] We live and work in a world of interdependence and it is essential to be part of the social networks that help further one's personal goals and the goals of one's employer. In a service-based, knowledge-intensive organization, this is particularly useful.

Social capital provides the building blocks of an organization in which all employees at all levels feel a part of the organization and are willing to contribute their best to that organization. Not all workplaces support the individual as she or he works toward achieving personal and organizational goals. How does one function in such a context? How can one meet both personal and workplace expectations? What does one need to know to survive and prosper?

DEALING WITH TODAY AND TOMORROW

In order to deal with today's challenges, we may need to break or avoid a number of habits or assumptions that may have become part of our way of approaching issues. These can serve as guides for both employer and employee.

1. There is an assumption that doing something, anything, is better than doing nothing. If that *something* one does has no relevance to the problem or if it does not strengthen the mission, it is as useful as rearranging the deck chairs on the Titanic. It may actually be negative if the action is a waste of valuable time and resources.

2. There is an assumption that if you discuss an issue and develop plans leading to a possible solution, you have done much to solve a problem. Unless you have communicated the plans to others, unless they have bought into the plans, and unless something actually happens, all the discussion and planning is useless. Indeed, it may be negative if time and resources have been spent to little or no effect. There is little relationship between the quantity and quality of planning and how well the individual or the organization performs. Planning is no substitute for action.

3. Having a philosophy of service and an accompanying mission statement is not in itself useful. Shapiro likens the mission statement in some organizations to a "talisman to ward off evil."[5] It is not enough to support something that is good. One must practice it.

4. What was done in the past is no longer a good guide to the future. Outmoded practices are often a security blanket for the insecure and are hard to remove. Conventional wisdom may, for some, be a substitute for thinking and analysis. Just because we have always done it that way is no reason to make the same mistake again.

5. Consistency is not always the right route to take. The same decision may not work in a different context.

6. Teamwork has replaced individual competition in the organization. Teams working together are usually more productive than the "go it alone" individual approach. In teams, individuals support one another toward common goals.

Pfeiffer and Sutton provide a set of steps that will move the individual or organization forward.[6]

- Know why you are doing something.
- Understand what you are doing.
- Actions count for more than plans, concepts, or elegant charts.
- There is no doing without mistakes.
- Don't let fearfulness interfere with action.
- Evaluate what matters.

In writing this text, I have described current management concepts and structures and then shown how one can go from there to deal with today's problems. A text that urges one to maintain the status quo helps no one. I hope that the reader will find new ideas, challenges, and a call to action along with the descriptions and discussions of management practice.

NOTES

1. Patricia Battin, "Leadership in a transformational age," in *The Mirage of Continuity: Reconfiguring Academic Information Resources for the 21st Century* (Washington, D.C.: Council on Library and Information Resources and the Association of American Universities, 1998), 271.

2. Battin, "Leadership in a transformational age," 271.

3. Don Cohen and Laurence Prusak, *In Good Company: How Social Capital Makes Organizations Work* (Boston: Harvard Business School Press, 2001), x.

4. Cohen and Prusak, *In Good Company*, 3.

5. Ellen Shapiro, *Fad Surfing in the Boardroom* (Reading, Mass.: Addison-Wesley, 1995), 15.

6. Jeffrey Pfeiffer and Robert I. Sutton, *The Knowing-Doing Gap: How Smart Companies Turn Knowledge into Action* (Boston: Harvard Business School Press, 2000).

ADDITIONAL READINGS

Gelerntner, David. *The Muse in the Machine: Computerizing the Poetry of Human Thought.* New York: The Free Press, 1994.

Kanter, Rosabeth Moss. *Evolve! Succeeding in the Digital Culture of Tomorrow.* Boston: Harvard Business School Press, 2001.

Quinn, Brian. "The McDonaldization of academic libraries?" *College and Research Libraries* 61, no. 3 (May 2000): 248–62.

Wallace, Patricia. *The Psychology of the Internet.* New York: Cambridge University Press, 1999.

Part I

LIVING AND WORKING IN THE INFORMATION AGE

Chapter One

The Changing Environment in Which We Live and Work

Change is a process both external and internal to the organization. Changes in the external world place pressure on the organization as it seeks to accommodate new ideas and new directions. Changes internal to the organization are the response; how does the organization implement a process of change that will respond to external forces and will keep the organization attuned to changing needs? Many of the early discussions of change in organizations tended to focus on interpersonal factors and on behavioral change rather than on the external forces. In this chapter, we focus on external forces that trigger internal change. (Discussion of internal change will be found throughout the text.)

   The enormity of the impact of communication and information technology on the way we do business was just beginning to be comprehended by the start of the twenty-first century. Building on scientific advances in the late nineteenth century and into the twentieth century with innovation in travel (e.g., the automobile and the airplane); in communication (e.g., the telephone, telegraph, radio, and computers); and advances in agricultural production that freed portions of the workforce to work in newly designed, mechanically efficient factories, the information age arrived in the latter part of the twentieth century. The development of a worldwide network based on the building of a shared infrastructure made up of information tools and services has been called the key to the growth of the information age.[1] While many organizations began their information technology efforts by developing their own online systems, there was an early recognition that a network based on generally accepted principles would provide broad access and would serve as a foundation for future growth. Dertouzos goes on to say that the company (or, I would add, the organization) that ignores the networked information world and the growing information marketplace will not be connected to the wide array of information and products necessary for success.[2] Ignoring the bigger picture of information beyond one's own organization will limit and even stunt its own organizational growth.

As the worldwide information network grows, international issues emerge, including copyright and intellectual property issues. The tension between for-profit companies who intend to charge for any level of access to their information products and the research and other user communities who believe in fair-use doctrines is ongoing. Efforts to resolve issues of use are ongoing and information professionals are active participants in the dialog. Additional issues have emerged and "many leaders are not yet ready to take on [these] issues in a meaningful way. Even though most readily acknowledge that computers and networks have dramatically transformed the way organizations function as compared to just a few years ago, too few have become actively engaged in the public policy concerns that technological progress has brought to the fore."[3] Leadership in policy directions is essential to ensure service effectiveness and efficiency of the network. The privacy of individuals and security of information—identifying who can be authorized to do what on the network—is of primary importance to its operation. "We must make the technology fit the rights, not the rights fit the technology."[4] Different societies and governments hold differing views on access to information, with some advocating free and open access while others intend to limit what their citizens can access. The overpowering influence of Western culture may have an adverse effect on the cultural content of smaller cultures and may skew that content. As networks become truly worldwide, the effects of many cultures on our global information resource will be felt.

New communities will grow based on common ideas, common cultural interests, common economic interests, or other similarities. A new set of virtual communities has emerged and its impact is felt in many areas of our lives: in political action groups on the web, in networks of young adults exploring areas of interest, in national and international informal information groups that parallel or subvert existing organizations and may strengthen or subvert those structures. At the same time, existing local non-virtual communities such as social organizations and groups at school or in the larger community may have become weakened as the newer virtual communities are explored. Or the new virtual communities may be an addition to and strengthen existing ones. There are risks in developing virtual communities and assumptions are made about their viability.[5] Brock and Boal warn that "an electronic emulation of community is not community."[6] They further warn of government control of the networks, which may eventually both limit and control what one can access. The networked world is too new for us to really know what the risks and benefits are and government interests are still in the formative stage in many areas.

Dizard warns that Americans tend to believe in the myth that any problem can be solved with the appropriate technology and that it is just a matter of time before the right idea will become the right solution.[7] The Wizard of Oz stories so popular in the past century are recognized as authentic American fairy tales in which mechanical know-how can be used to solve problems and make this a better world. Were one to write a new fairy tale bringing Dorothy and her friends into the twenty-first century with her hand-held electronic device at the ready, what wonderful networked adventures could be contemplated.

Although technology has been highly visible as an agent of change, it is but one of a number of changes that are occurring in our modern culture. There are different views as to when the pace of change accelerated from one that was fairly easy for individuals and organizations to deal with to one in which it is difficult to process all the events that are happening and seemingly happening all at once. There is general agreement that since the onset of World War II (1939), technological advances came rapidly and continued to accelerate as one advance builds upon another. In the 1970s and 1980s, our business outlook became more global and the extent to which interconnection of economic systems has come about became more apparent as we saw financial difficulties in one country affecting world markets.

So much is happening in many areas at the same time that it is almost impossible for the individual to process it. The psychologists and sociologists say that this inability to process information as fast as it is being produced creates a disconnect between the human mind and the world people inhabit. Paraphrasing Shakespeare, we are out of joint with our times. This creates stress: the stress of not being comfortable in a world changing too fast, the stress of losing the comfort of knowing that some things one relies on have not changed, and the stress of having to make decisions before all relevant information has been collected. This need to make decisions at what may appear to be warp speed tends to force the individual to focus on the immediate situation rather than on root causes. For example, we may focus on the loss of beaches near our homes and suggest local solutions such as building barriers rather than looking for a root cause—global warming—an issue too complex and too large for any one group or individual to solve. The sociologists and psychologists say that we are no longer comfortable in our world; it is too complex, moves too fast, and never allows individuals to stop and catch their breath.

O. B. Hardison, a well-known humanist commenting on the pace of change, suggested that our language is barely capable of expressing the new thoughts that emerge from the changes that are occurring. He says that we cannot compare the new to the old, as the two are too different. As we move into the unknown, we move further from the Greek view of a world that is orderly and beautiful into a world whose patterns of orderliness are yet to be discovered. He goes on to say that observations reveal truth; once revealed, truth can be generalized. As we generalize to this new world, we move away from tradition and build simple, spare constructs that appear to bear the weight of these new facts.[8] Hardison then says that this is the reason, for example, that modern architecture is spare and functional and that modern poetry has destabilized language and meaning in order to give it a new dimension. He places computer art, computer-generated music, and computer-generated poetry in this same category—the taking of emotional meaning from our world and trying to build a new world from what may appear to be randomness.[9] Florman argues that humanists disdain science and that any change for which science is responsible is suspect.[10] Nevertheless, the humanist viewpoint describes the way in which many individuals cope with the changing world.

Social institutions such as education, religion, and other cultural organizations were built over many centuries and were based on authority of individuals, texts, and the evolving institution. With the information explosion, this framework has become overloaded and falls apart easily, and those who believe that their institutions hold the only true way have difficulty maintaining that attitude. Many people know a great deal about many things and if they don't know, they know how to find out. They can become instant authorities and no longer assume that they need to rely on some individual or institution to tell them what is right.

Manuel Castells, professor of sociology and planning and chair of the Center for Western European Studies at the University of California, Berkeley, describes our world as being in the midst of a "technological evolution centered around information technologies [that] is reshaping at an accelerated rate the material basis of society."[11] He goes on to cite the following major sociological shifts: the fall of the Soviet Union, which has changed global politics; a restructuring of capitalism, which is providing greater flexibility in management, decentralization and networking of firms; the decline of labor movements; the individualization and diversification of working relationships; the massive incorporation of women into the paid labor force; and the undoing of the welfare state.

A massive overhauling of the capitalist society is underway with the global integration of financial markets and the emergence of world regional economies. The Asian-Pacific economy with its cheap labor has become a dominant force in manufacturing worldwide. The economic unification of much of Europe into the European Union has strengthened their collective power. There has been the emergence of a North American regional economy. Russia is moving from its communist approaches to a market economy model. There is now an interdependence of global economies in real time and what affects one will almost immediately have an impact on others. These groups are the economic haves while many countries in Africa, in Latin America and elsewhere that are not part of a regional economy are the have-nots. This split between the economic haves and have-nots will continue to grow and to have serious consequences if some means of bringing the two together is not developed.

Since the end of World War II, the rate of change has doubled and redoubled numerous times. New technologies initially developed to fight a war found peacetime purposes. New energy sources, new machines to organize and manage data, and speedier forms of communication and travel have made the world appear to be smaller and more connected. At the same time, generally accepted rules for interaction among individuals and countries weakened. Over the decades, there was an increasing inequity of participation of nations in their ability to benefit from new technologies and the new wealth. Those countries unable or unwilling to give up their policies of information control were unable to make the change from a centrally controlled industrial economy to the more widely based information economy. Those countries lacking the ability to benefit from technological change fell further behind. Many poorer countries, lacking the infrastructure on which to build economic growth, became the victims of dictators who used the resources of the state to reward their friends or for personal gain, thus building an even greater economic gap between poor countries and their richer neighbors.

Within the United States there is a widening gap between haves and have-nots. The new information-based economy requires a level of education not present in many immigrants or in citizens who, for one reason or another, have not taken advantage of the education necessary to fit them for the kind of jobs available in an information economy. At the same time, many of the unskilled jobs and some skilled jobs have been exported to other countries where labor is cheaper. Publishing companies (e.g., the H. W. Wilson Company) have exported positions formerly held by American workers to other countries, including Ireland. Many data processing positions have moved to India where skilled labor is available at lower cost than in the United States. Some of the more sophisticated positions in software design and related activities are leaving the country as U.S. businesses seek cheaper ways of producing products and services. The outsourcing of an increasing number of low-skilled positions at the same time as an increasing number of immigrants is arriving in the United States to compete for existing positions creates resentment on the part of Americans trying to improve their own economic situations.

Castells groups those excluded from the information/capital society under the heading of the Fourth World and warns that the social exclusion of the discarded creates internal fragmentation within a country as well as new stresses among the have and have-not countries.[12] He goes on to suggest that the twenty-first century is one of general bewilderment resulting from the uncertainty of how to apply the new tools of the information age in a world with such great social and economic diversity. How does a country, a society, bridge the gap between technological overdevelopment in some areas and social underdevelopment in others? And how do existing social structures deal with the increasing anger of the have-nots who want the benefits of the new era but either lack or reject the skills and attitudes needed to participate?

New social movements have grown and continue to grow and attract adherents. There is a useful analogy between these social movements, many of which use the Internet as their means of building community, and the informal communication network in an organization in that each exists to challenge the existing order, be it a national government or a corporation. The informal organization also provides identity and community for those not at the top levels of power. These social movements range from religion-based communities, to groups fighting for social equality, to those fighting to save the environment, to those trying to hold back change in hopes of returning to a safer (for them) patriarchal world where rules applied and everyone knew her or his place. Each has found the Internet to be a means of globalizing his or her community and movements. Castells suggests that these movements and the networks that support them are building new cultural codes that may form the basis for new social structures.[13]

CHANGE AND AMERICAN SOCIETY

The change from an industrial society in which many entry-level jobs were available to unskilled workers to an information society in which education and skills are the requirements for participation has closed off a recognized route to economic independence for many Americans. The outsourcing of many routine positions to other countries has narrowed this route further. The hierarchical structure of the industrial economy is giving way to one in which power within a group of those who have special knowledge or authority is less apt to be centralized. "As we leave the industrial era behind, we are becoming a more diverse society. The old smokestack economy served a mass society. Everything from lifestyles and products to technologies and the media is growing more heterogeneous."[14] This move toward diversity and the free flow of information creates a threat to existing power structures; entrenched power groups will do whatever they can to obstruct changes that may limit their power.

The impact of the Internet on change has yet to be appreciated. Anyone with a computer can communicate with everyone else who is online and can share information of varying accuracy at any time. Mass media, including the Internet, has a major role in forging global opinion. It holds several keys to how change is seen. It has interactivity, mobility, convertibility, ubiquity, and is global. A single government or special interest group cannot manage or control all of the information and information is thus not held hostage to a particular view or set of views. Beyond the sharing of specific information, the Internet and other mass media such as television inform individuals about the social norms of the world around them and give them social cues and skills needed to be successful in mainstream society.[15]

Toffler said that the three main issues that will determine how well society accepts life in the information age are how it deals with education, how it deals with information technology including media, and how it protects freedom of expression.[16] Education has been a focus in the United States since 1645; in recent years, increased emphasis has been placed on basic skills and basic levels of education. The emphasis on reading comprehension and mathematical skills raises concern among those who also wish their children to be versed in history, government, and the arts and who fear that a balance between basic skills and a well-rounded education may be at risk. There is a general recognition than an educated, or at least a skilled, workforce is essential to progress in an information society. Recognizing the massive impact of media, and setting guidelines to regulate it, are ongoing activities that will never end as the technology continues to change and open new opportunities for communicating. Protecting individual rights and the freedom of expression from limitations that different governments, interest groups, corporations, and agencies wish to impose is a continuing struggle requiring participation by all.

In the business and not-for-profit world, new forces that impact organizational success and profitability have been at play since the 1980s. Restructuring of organizations to streamline them, reduce the workforce, and increase productivity often did not work; manipulation of the existing organization— without taking into consideration external factors that impact success— provided insufficient information. New businesses, new technologies, and new customer expectations challenged existing methods of operation. Streamlining of existing activities did not answer the basic question of "Is what we have been doing and are doing what we should be doing?" When the age of steam replaced the age of sail, no amount of refinement of the sailing ship could make it competitive in a new era. The same applies when an industrial-era business or nonprofit organization continues to be structured to meet industrial age challenges in an information economy. New structures and new approaches are needed to meet the demands of customers and other stakeholders. Old processes may interfere with new ways of thinking and acting. Existing organizational culture may interfere with the need to change. What must not change is the attention given to organizational values. New ways of organizing, the development of new products and services, and attention to new customer demands require that each activity be true to the values of the organization and that decisions support that value system.

Parallel to the changes in the economy, the information revolution has provided the tools to accelerate scientific development. The extent to which a country, or an organization, has been able to combine the information revolution with its technological growth is a key factor in its current and future development.

[T]he ability or inability of societies to master technology and particularly technologies that are strategically decisive in each historical period, largely shape their destiny, to the point where we could say that while technology per se does not determine historical evolution and social change, technology (or the lack of it) embodies the capacity of societies to transform themselves, as well as the uses to which societies, always in a conflictive process, decide to put their technological potential.[17]

Examples of this include the inability of the Soviet Union to deal with information technology and its effects on an already turgid economy. The difficulty that have-not countries experience in joining the global economy in a positive way is exacerbated by their limited ability to enter the information age. This coming together of the information age and the restructuring of capitalism, while there are core similarities, differs from country to country depending on history and culture. Just as management theories differ in different countries depending on their approach to human values and the growth of institutions, so do the ways in which countries develop, adopt, and integrate information technologies.

Changes in world economic development and in information technology are related to, and perhaps even a cause of, social change. Issues of gender and gender relationships are under discussion everywhere. As paternalistic authoritarian systems break down, so do their patterns of communication. Groups and individuals who interacted in a particular fashion under those structures have become alienated from each other and may even see others as no longer members of the group but perhaps as strangers and enemies.

In such a world of uncontrolled, confusing change, people tend to group around primary identities; religious, ethnic, territorial, national . . . religious fundamentalism . . . is probably the most formidable force of personal security and collective mobilization in these troubled years. . . . In a world of global flows of wealth, power, and images, the search for identity, collective or individual, ascribed or constructed, becomes the fundamental source of social meaning.[18]

Friedman calls this split between global and local the conflict between the Lexus and the olive tree, with the Lexus representing what it takes to thrive economically in a global economy and the olive tree representing the sense of identity with home and community.[19] While the growth of a global economy was a twentieth-century phenomenon, the power politics that are closely related to it are as old as civilization. We no longer live in a First, Second, and Third World but have moved to living in a fast and a slow world. There has been a democratization of technology, of finance, and of information.[20] Now it is possible for one country to develop a technology, test it, and implement it, and when it has become cheap enough, another poorer country can buy it and install it. Who can borrow from whom has become a worldwide phenomenon and anyone can invest in the global economy. With the advent of satellite communication and the ubiquity of television, information is available to everyone everywhere. Now governments are less in control of what their citizens know about the world and less able to control their citizens' expectations.

A new social structure has come about as a result of the restructuring of capitalism on a global scale and the wide availability of information. Castells calls the resulting development *informationalism.* The "theoretical perspective underlying this approach postulates that societies are organized around human processes structured by historically determined relationships of *production, experience, and power.*"[21] Technology—which gives us tools to do more, better, and faster—has changed where we work, where we live, how we are educated, and how and where we play. It has also had a profound effect on the way we are governed. Individuals have changed as well. Prior to the 1960s, there tended to be a willingness to go along with decisions made by governments, business, and education. Since then, the workforce has become less and less willing to be directed by others and more demanding that they participate in decision making. This is the result of an increasingly educated workforce and increased professionalism in technical areas; for example, engineering has become less a trade and more a profession requiring extended education. Part of this increasing independence has resulted in the loss of power by trade unions, which no longer dominate decision making in the workplace but have to share that decision making with the workforce.

A new elite is growing, that of the technological elite who have developed the expertise to use technology, particularly information technology, and thus gain power through the ability to manipulate that technology and to find and use information previously not widely available. There is the ability to join virtual communities and interact electronically and this has partially replaced the earlier learning communities. Technology as the glue that builds communities is replacing the face-to-face interaction of individuals. Strong communities are built but they are faceless and not always what they seem.

There is the ability to build virtual political movements in opposition to the existing government and then for these movements to burst full grown onto the scene. How does the government equate the right to free speech with the ability of that government to function? Over the decades, in a print-on-paper world and in interaction among groups, the balance has been kept, albeit with difficulty. In a worldwide virtual environment, maintaining this balance is much more difficult. In some countries, e-mail could be received only at a public terminal where anyone could see all messages, thus limiting that medium to nonpersonal, nonthreatening issues. Elsewhere, access to e-mail was limited in other ways. Governments rightly saw the Internet as a destabilizing influence and an influence almost impossible to control.

The information society in which we now live emphasizes the role of information in society. "The information society is a specific form of social organization under which generation, processing, and transmission become the fundamental sources of productivity and power because of new technological conditions emerging in this historical period."(22) All societies vary and the way in which their information society develops differs depending upon the local culture.

THE INFORMATION REVOLUTION

The information revolution is generally recognized as a historical event as important as the industrial revolution. As new sources of energy were the drivers of the industrial revolution, information technology drives the information revolution. Like the industrial revolution, the information revolution has brought about patterns of discontinuity in the economy, culture, and society. The current revolution is not "the centrality of knowledge and information but the application of such knowledge and information to knowledge generation and information/processing communication devices."[23] These new information technologies are not specific tools to apply but processes to develop, and each process extends the capabilities of the individual. While the industrial revolution expanded slowly and unevenly around the world, the information revolution became global within a very short time frame. Despite its global reach, many individuals and countries are not yet part of the information revolution, such as those politically isolated and unable to gain access to communications, those too poor to gain access, and those lacking the education to gain access.

Lessons can be learned from the industrial revolution and applied to the information revolution. The effect of new technologies on our social fabric is often underestimated. The industrial revolution resulted in major shifts in population from agricultural to urban environments. The resulting growth of cities brought with it slums, disease, and related social issues. It also brought new wealth, new ideas, and cultural expansion. New social classes emerged and challenged the landed aristocracy. Those countries such as Great Britain that developed an innovative climate to foster the exchange of ideas in which ideas were posed and problems solved were those most successful in moving the industrial revolution forward and gaining maximum benefit from it. While the length of time between innovation and implementation differed widely, "the historical record seems to indicate . . . that, in general terms, the closer the relationship between the sites of innovation, production, and use of new technologies, the faster the transformation of societies, and the greater the positive feedback from social conditions on the general condition for further innovation."[24]

The information technology revolution began in a number of labs in the United States during World War II. Early work was done at Massachusetts Institute of Technology (MIT) and at the University of Pennsylvania. IBM was an early entrant into the field and by 1964 dominated the mainframe computer industry. Numerous companies sprang up, grew, and died as other companies developed new technologies that replaced existing technologies and products. The real revolution began in 1975 with the Apple microcomputer, which changed everything as it made it possible for anyone to join the information age. Slow to see that microcomputers were not a toy or a passing fad, IBM belatedly moved into the market with the PC in 1981 and regained a dominant role in the computing industry. Bill Gates and others built the software in the 1980s that made the networked computer possible. Then came the interaction between computer technology and telecommunications technology, the information superhighway, and the Internet.

The United States led this development in California's Silicon Valley with the support of Stanford University and the federal government. Silicon Valley became a synonym for innovation and development. Its many companies were born, tried new ideas, kept some, tried others, merged, grew, or died and were replaced by other new companies. The synergy of creative people, university support, and technical skills provided the energy to move ahead. The Route 128 corridor around Boston, Massachusetts, provided a similar environment. Labs in the telecommunications industry, numerous leading universities, and funding from the U.S. Department of Defense supported both of these areas. The first networks (ARPA and DARPA) were developed by the Department of Defense for its own uses. Other smaller confluences of ideas and support grew in other parts of the United States, the United Kingdom, and in other parts of Europe, each one generating new ideas and learning from the others.

THE INFORMATION REVOLUTION AND THE GLOBAL ECONOMY

The coming together of the information revolution and the building of a global economy has resulted in a new economic system. Information technology increases productivity, and technology builds on that increase to build even more and better systems. In the 1980s, there was a huge investment in technology/telecommunications infrastructures both by governments and by private industry. This new environment required cooperation by and among governments and corporations. "By integrating countries in a global economy, the specific interests of the state in each nation became directly linked with the fate of economic competition for firms that are either national or located in the country's territory."[24] Politics and productivity became so linked that it is no longer possible to manage economies differently in each country without considering its neighbors near and far. The global economy works in real time worldwide and does this using the tools of information technology.

While the money supply is managed globally, labor markets tend to be managed locally, although the products they produce may be produced for a country or market not their own. A company may locate a labor force in another country and set up production there, or it may import individuals with specific skills to its own country. While some workers still support the national aspects of their economy (e.g., government workers and retail sales), the strategic cores of the workforce are global. In this new economy, the interaction between historically rooted political institutions and worldwide economic elements is complex. It is also key to the success of the economy of each individual country.

In the past two decades, organizations have had to reorganize their way of doing business, whether that business was a for-profit or not-for-profit activity. The need to cope with the fast pace of change, the integration of information technology into their organizations, and the rapidly changing needs and demands of consumers required that organizations become flexible and able to respond rapidly to market changes. New management methods such as just-in-time production in which products are produced on demand rather than being produced and stored as inventory, total quality management, and team organization rather than hierarchical structures are increasingly present. Networking with and among organizations has become common. The new corporation is organized around processes and its success is measured by consumer satisfaction. Members of the organization are in regular contact with both suppliers and customers to ensure that good relationships are maintained. To ensure a workforce able to function in this flexible environment, information training and retraining is essential for all employees. While cutting the workforce was common in the 1980s and 1990s and was a standard means of reducing costs, it became evident that what was needed was a more efficient labor force, not necessarily a smaller labor force.

In this new world, there is a new theory, that of postindustrialism, in which:

- the source of productivity lies in the generation of knowledge,
- economic activity moves from goods to services, and
- occupations high in information and knowledge content become increasingly important.

The change in occupational needs has changed educational requirements. Automation has radically changed the number of routine jobs that at one time dominated the factory floor and the office. Lower-level jobs no longer exist in the numbers that they once did. Many routine office jobs were held by women and many routine factory jobs served as an entry into factory work for minorities. Are they unduly harmed by the changes in the labor force caused by automation and other technologies? What happens to the large labor force that lacks, for one reason or another, the opportunity, ability, or desire to continue their education? How will they be absorbed into the labor market? Will they be absorbed? If not, what will they do? New jobs require more than a secondary school education, and those in the workforce require regular upgrading of their skills. For those who add to their skill sets, the opportunity for greater participation in the organization and greater opportunity to do satisfying work is available. For those without education or skills, the future is bleak. Given the increasing trend toward outsourcing jobs, the future is even bleaker.

In this new interconnected world where millions are connected to sources of information and to one another and where time and distance are less relevant, how has the traditional role of information services provided by libraries and other information centers changed? What is the relationship of the small, interconnected electronic communities with one another, with the workplace, and with institutions? With the workplace and the home space more and more often interconnected, with working colleagues often on different continents but directly connected via the Internet, what are tomorrow's roles in providing information to the workplace and the individual? What role does the library have in working with those who have been displaced from the workforce or were never part of it? Is the library becoming not a form but a process, a process that brings to individuals and organizations the information they need in the form and at the time they need it? One researcher looking at this issue said that we are globally connected but locally disconnected both physically and socially. Do we put together physical centers of real innovation or do we rely on virtual centers of cultural and political innovation? Libraries, public libraries in particular, take great pride in the library as an institution, a place. How does this sense of institution and place play out in a virtual world?

Age, gender, ethnic background, education, and other definers of individuals are less apparent in a virtual environment, but does this mean that we should ignore the unique gifts each of these attributes brings to the discussion of ideas? How does higher education fit into this environment? Will there be greater and greater emphasis on distance learning, a kind of just-in-time education for the workforce? Will primary and secondary schools join the distance education model and mesh classroom teaching with enrichment from other sources? The application of information and information technology is making a difference in many and the role the library/media center plays in this shift is increasingly important. In 1995, Negroponte said that the digital age had yet to invade the classroom. A decade later, this statement no longer holds true.[26] Many classrooms have incorporated information technology into their daily activities and this is a continuing process.

One can work at home electronically, can take courses via the Internet, and can tune into a wide range of entertainment. What implication does this have for the social relationships it replaces? Those who work and study at home have greater control over their time and can participate in community

activities to a greater extent than when commuting long distances and working a ten-hour day. But do they? In this changing world, what is the role of
the local library, the company information center, the academic library?
While our goal of service has not changed, the ways in which the service is
provided has changed radically and will continue to change as we find new
ways of working in this globally connected world.

One option not available to us is to do nothing; we cannot sit back and
wait for things to change. Our lives and our institutions are changing and
will do so with or without our input. The challenge is to know when to move,
and to balance the risks and rewards of an action at a particular time. Morrison suggests that organizations operate on two curves; the first curve is the
organization's traditional method of operation, which will no longer work at
some point, and the second curve is based on changes in technology, consumer behavior, and geography, which will point the way to needed organizational change.[27] The new technology that is faster, cheaper, and better than
the old ways of doing thing changes the ways the organization does business
and can transform it into a new organization, or it can kill the organization
and create new structures in its place. Consumers are better educated than
ever before and many have more money. They have access to more products
and services and can select what they want from the range of possibilities.
They then want it cheaper, faster, and with more service than ever before.
In order to respond to second-curve opportunities, organizations face major
changes. Hierarchical organizations often don't work well, as they are too
rigid for the new environment. The key is to develop a highly flexible organizational structure that can respond rapidly to current and anticipated consumer needs and to do so in response to local differences. Operational terms
include building alliances, supporting networks, and being able to respond
rapidly to demands. While the organizational structure undergoes changes,
often radical changes, the core values of the organization do not change.
They and the core competencies of the organization are what hold the organization together. The organization, in order to move ahead in this much
more flexible environment, must review and reassess its values and goals so
that there is no question as to what it stands for and what its purpose is.
Morrison suggests the analogy of a fishnet organization, "a web of constantly changing hierarchies linked and managed by information technology."[28] This allows for multiple centers of activity and flexibility in
responding to local needs and overall change.

Not only must the organization reinvent itself, the individual who is part of the organization must do so as well. This may require additional education and training to fit into the new positions that result from organizational revision. It will require a willingness to live and work in a constantly changing environment with an uncertain future. There is a general expectation that those working in an information and information technology-enriched environment will use new tools and thus be more productive. The workforce may become part time, more dispersed, less socially cohesive. Rather than predicting a future based on past experience and observation, the worker can now envision a future that provides flexibility in how to work, where to work, and even when to work. Technology has freed many from the forty-hour week and the long commute. The individual worker as personal entrepreneur frees both the individual and the organization to seek new mutually satisfactory working arrangements. Organizations may provide fewer benefits to the worker who may become an independent contractor and work for more than one organization. This moves even further from an earlier view of employment as a lifetime commitment on the part of both organization and employee. For some, this breaking of the paternalistic bonds is very liberating; for others, it is highly stressful. For those who had a lifetime of loyalty to an organization, it is difficult to see this loyalty no longer returned by the organization. What does this do to morale? How does an organization retain the positive feelings of more loosely connected employees? The emphasis on values, goals, and direction is the glue that holds the organization and workers together. The organization's strategic planning of the future "[will be] an amalgamation of the collective intelligence and imagination of managers and employees throughout the company who must possess an enlarged view of what it means to be *strategic*."[29]

None of these changes will happen at once. There will be different timetables in different organizations, depending on their histories and cultures. Individuals adapt to their new workplace at different rates. It is necessary to take the long view, to anticipate that some organizations and parts of organizations will move ahead faster than others. Not all steps will be taken smoothly.

CHANGE AND LIBRARIES
AND INFORMATION CENTERS

As the industrial economy began to change into the information economy, numerous shifts occurred. One of these was the value placed on information and on the skills necessary to acquire, organize, manipulate, store, and disseminate information. Those involved with computing who created structures to manage data developed new areas of expertise. Existing areas of expertise practiced by librarians and other information professionals were at first ignored and then gradually recognized as valuable, even cutting-edge, contributions to the activities necessary to exploit the information. Librarians and related information professionals with half a millennium of experience in dealing with information had built a base from which today's information theory and practice could grow.

The changing nature of the information professions—due in large part to technologies developed to capture, store, and manipulate large amounts of information—was first recognized outside the library professions by scientists toward the end of World War II. A new group of researchers, *information scientists*, looked at new technologies for storing information, such as microfilm and microfiche, and looked at the possibilities of computing machines to code and store data. Concurrent with these activities, librarians in research libraries saw the benefits of applying these new technologies to managing the explosion of information that was becoming increasingly costly to store and retrieve. Deans and faculty in programs preparing librarians began introducing courses in data processing and related topics into the curriculum in the 1960s. Since that time, the trend has increased so that today's librarian/information professional (regardless of area of specialization) is solidly grounded in the skills needed to use appropriate information technologies to deal with today's information needs. Programs in library information science (LIS) have become centers of research investigating these areas and testing new theories. They have continued to work closely with other disciplines concerned with information, including computer science, psychology, engineering, and linguistics. Today's new graduate from an accredited LIS program combines technical skills with skills needed to interact with users and potential users of information. Today's graduates combine the traditional values of librarianship with cutting-edge technical skills.

What does this mean in the workplace? How will the workplace change? Hawkins and Battin in 1998 asserted that we don't really know the implications of the changes underway.[30] Change is not just doing what we now do but doing it better. It is also exploring new avenues that may not fit within the existing organizational structures. They went on to say, "Information technologies have consistently enabled the continuation of traditional values and missions at the same time as their use actively encourages the unrestrained exploration of new frontiers in the creation of knowledge, application of this new knowledge in their turn radically influence individual and organizational capabilities, thoughts, and behaviors."[31] Because most current management systems are geared to a hierarchical system within the unit (be it a department, a division, a library), it is difficult to use technology at its best as the technology has the power to decentralize access and control. "In the digital library this welcome and beneficent capacity must be balanced with a new concept of central co-ordination mechanisms to achieve maximum connectivity, technical platform interoperability, equitable access to information resources, and reasonable cost control."[32]

Despite more than a quarter-century of predictions for change in organizational structures and the building of new structures that focus on information and communication rather than the traditional hierarchy, change has been very slow to occur. Perhaps this is due to a strong desire for the status quo or perhaps it is the insularity of individuals within their own areas of expertise. External forces, including the emergence of electronic publishing and the changing view of intellectual property, have changed the ways libraries do business. Competition from for-profit agencies offering academic degrees through online courses removed the traditional university monopoly on higher education. Concurrently, academic institutions began to offer online courses and online degrees, thus making higher education available to many more students. The cost of doing business in traditional ways has often exceeded the benefits; new ways of organizing libraries and of organizing universities are emerging. A number of attempts are being made to reconfigure libraries but there is as yet no clear path to the next steps. Those who urge movement to a digital world emphasize the potential and not the actual and are projecting a degree of wishful thinking. Battin stressed that:

> [b]ooks and paper will not disappear. Digital capabilities continue to be add ons rather than simple replacements. But what must change are our human systems for organizing, managing, and financing continuing access to knowledge, be it through books, electronic data bases, or lectures in the classroom. . . . [T]he greatest psychic distance in the world may well be the gap between envisioning the future and realizing the vision.[33]

Similar statements can be made about other types of libraries and information centers; the need to reach beyond current organizational structures, the need to adapt and adopt technologies, and above all, the need to find a path that preserves the integrity of information to create a structure to provide service, and serves the individual who seeks information.

MEETING THE FUTURE

We don't predict a future, we imagine it. Too many variables change too rapidly for us to find a stable platform from which to make predictions. We can and should ask questions that will help us imagine our future.

- Who are we serving today and how will that client base change in the next five or more years?
- How do we interact with our clients today and how will the technology or social changes affect how we may or can interact with them in future?
- With what organizations or groups or individuals do we compete today to serve our clients and how may that list change?
- What new skills and abilities will we need to acquire to serve our clients in the future?
- Are there new and different things we will want to do for our clients or they will want us to do in the future?

In the scenarios we construct for the future, what kinds of resources will we need, what kinds of skills, what new structures? Many libraries and information centers are part of a larger organization—a college or university, a school system, a local government, a business organization—and are tied closely to the structure of the larger organization. They therefore lack the flexibility to determine their future that a stand-alone organization has. Nevertheless, they need to ask questions concerning the direction the parent organization is planning and be a part of that direction.

The organization does not change for the sake of change. There has to be a reason—to provide new services, for example, or to improve existing service. Sometimes this can be done by reconfiguring existing activities, restructuring the organization, or reinventing some aspect of the organization. Most likely, the organization needs to review its goals and reorient those goals, redesign the process by which those goals are implemented, and reskill the members of the workforce so that they can operate in this new environment. Following someone else's road map to do this will get you where they are; what you want to do is create your own road map. Ask the questions: "What can my library be?" "What new approaches will provide better service?" "What new expertise do I need to envision and then carry out that vision?" One does not create a path to lead clients in directions they don't want to go but one can chart a new path to places they didn't know were possible.

SUMMARY

For some organizations, these activities are relatively easy while for others, they are nearly impossible. Unlearning past activities and learning new skills is difficult for some while energizing for others. If, at the same time, workers are expected to be more entrepreneurial and participate in determining their organizational future, this will for some be an exciting time and for others a fearful experience. Maintaining morale is an essential role of senior management. An organization can be held back by its history, its culture, and its cultural biases. Those who hire like-minded new employees have strengthened past experience rather than having sought out individuals with new ideas. It is difficult for some managers to let go of some of their decision-making powers and entrenched ideas and delegate to others. When a small number of individuals makes decisions, there is a tendency for the organization to lose flexibility. Current success in present activities can breed arrogance, the certainty that "we are doing the right thing and there is no reason to question it or change." But the question to be asked is, "Will this be the right thing in the future?"

NOTES

1. Michel L. Dertouzos, *What Will Be: How the New World of Information Will Change Our Lives* (New York: Harper, 1997), 7–16.

2. Dertouzos, *What Will Be*, 287.

3. The Harvard Policy Group on Networking-Enabled Services and Government, John F. Kennedy School of Government, *Eight Imperatives for Leaders in a Networked World: Guidelines for the 2000 Election and Beyond* (Cambridge, Mass.: Policy Group, 2000), 1.

4. Harvard Policy Group, *Eight Imperatives for Leaders in a Networked World*, 3.

5. James Brock and Iain Boal, eds., *Resisting the Virtual Life: The Culture and Politics of Information* (San Francisco: City Lights Books, 1995).

6. Brock and Boal, *Resisting the Virtual Life*, x.

7. Wilson P. Dizard Jr., *The Coming Information Age*, 3rd ed. (New York: Longmans, 1989).

8. O. B. Hardison Jr., *Disappearing through the Skylight: Culture and Technology in the Twentieth Century* (New York: Viking, 1989), 12.

9. Hardison, *Disappearing through the Skylight*, 12.

10. Samuel C. Florman, *Blaming Technology* (New York: St. Martin's Press, 1981), 70.

11. Manuel Castells, *The Rise of the Networked Society*, vol. 1 of *The Information Age: Economy, Society and Culture* (Malden, Mass.: Blackwell, 1996), 1.

12. Manuel Castells, *End of the Millennium*, vol. 3 of *The Information Age: Economy, Society and Culture*, 2nd ed. (Oxford: Blackwell, 2000), 172.

13. Castells, *End of the Millennium*, 172.

14. Alvin Toffler, *Power Shift: Knowledge, Wealth and Violence at the Edge of the 21st Century* (New York: Bantam, 1990), 167.

15. Toffler, *Power Shift*, 343.

16. Toffler, *Power Shift*, 368.

17. Castells, *Rise of the Networked Society*, 7.

18. Castells, *Rise of the Networked Society*, 7.

19. Thomas L. Friedman, *The Lexus and the Olive Tree* (New York: Anchor Books, 2000).

20. Friedman, *The Lexus and the Olive Tree*, 46.

21. Castells, *Rise of the Networked Society*, 21.

22. Castells, *Rise of the Networked Society*, 25.

23. Castells, *Rise of the Networked Society*, 32.

24. Castells, *Rise of the Networked Society*, 37.

25. Castells, *Rise of the Networked Society*, 88.

26. Nicholas Negroponte, *Being Digital* (New York: Knopf, 1995), 225.

27. J. Ian Morrison, *The Second Curve: Managing the Velocity of Change* (New York: Ballantine Books, 1996),

28. Morrison, *The Second Curve*, 27.

29. Gary Hamel and C. K. Prahalad, *Competing for the Future* (Boston: Harvard Business School Press, 1994), 26.

30. Brian Hawkins and Patricia Battin, eds., *The Mirage of Continuity: Reconfiguring Academic Resources for the Twenty-First Century* (Washington, D.C.: Council on Library and Information Resources and the American Association of Universities, 1998).

31. Hawkins and Battin, *The Mirage of Continuity*, 6.

32. Hawkins and Battin, *The Mirage of Continuity*, 9.

33. Hawkins and Battin, *The Mirage of Continuity*, 273–74.

ADDITIONAL READINGS

Black, Ron. "A hybrid campus for the new millennium." *Educause Review* 36, no. 1 (January–February 2001), 16–24.

Brockman, John. *Digerati: Encounters with the Cyber Elite*. San Francisco: Hard Wired, 1996.

Bucholtz, Thomas J. *Information Proficiency: Your Key to the Information Age*. New York: Van Nostrand Reinhold, 1995.

Carr. Nicholas G. ed. *The Digital Enterprise: How to Reshape Your Business for a Connected World*. Boston: Harvard Business School Press, 2001.

Castells, Manuel. *The Power of Identity*. Vol. 2 of *The Information Age: Economy, Society and Culture*. Oxford: Blackwell, 1997.

Dalziel, Murray M., and Stephen C. Schoonover. *Changing Ways: A Practical Tool for Implementing Change within Organizations*. New York: American Management Association, 1988.

Davis, Stan, and Jim Botkin. *The Monster under the Bed: How Business Is Mastering the Opportunity of Knowledge for Profit*. New York: Simon and Schuster, 1994.

Duderstadt, James J. "Technology." *Educause Review* 36, no. 1 (January–February 2001): 48–56.

Dyson, Esther. *Release 2.0: A Design for Living in the Digital Age*. New York: Broadway Books, 1997.

Gelerntner, David. *The Lost World of the Fair*. New York: Free Press, 1995.

———. *Mirror Worlds or the Day Software Puts the Universe in a Shoebox . . . How It Will Happen and What It Will Mean*. New York: Oxford University Press, 1991.

Graves, William. "Virtual operations: Challenges for traditional higher education." *Educause Review* 36, no. 2 (March–April 2001): 46–56.

Hambrick, Donald C., David A. Nadler, and Michael L. Tushman, eds. *Navigating Change: How CEOs, Top Teams, and Boards Steer Transformation*. Boston: Harvard Business School Press, 1998.

Kelly, Kevin. *Out of Control: The New Biology of Machines, Social Systems, and the Economic World*. Reading, Mass.: Addison-Wesley, 1994.

Lanham, Richard A. *The Electronic World: Democracy, Technology and the Arts*. Chicago: University of Chicago Press, 1993.

McRae, Hamish. *The World in 2020: Power, Culture and Prosperity*. Boston: Harvard Business School Press, 1994.

Nardi, Bonnie A., and Vicky L. O'Day. *Information Ecologies: Using Technology with Heart*. Cambridge, Mass.: MIT Press, 1999.

Postman, Neil. *Technopoly: The Surrender of Culture to Technology*. New York: Knopf, 1992.

Talbott, Stephen L. *The Future Does Not Compute: Transcending the Machine in Our Midst*. Sebastapol, Calif.: O'Reilly, 1995.

Chapter Two

The Sociopolitical and Organizational Contexts

"Libraries in America are situated on the boundary between the market and the polity, in a limited space that provides free access to knowledge in order to fulfill the public interest in education and democratic participation. The public quality of libraries derives from a non-market principle of free and equal access to knowledge."[1] The library is part of the social strategy "to create progress in the sciences and useful arts" as called for in the U.S. Constitution. Libraries today are an important part of our social fabric and their role is well established. The information revolution has provided new tools with which to pursue this strategy and, with their rich heritage in working with information and with their communities, librarians/information specialists are ideally positioned to take advantage of the new digital, web-based world.

Libraries have been in existence for thousands of years. Some of the first indications of systematic collection and storage of information comes from archaeological finds from the Sumerians who flourished more than 3,500 years ago. As archaeologists continue to explore the early civilizations of the Fertile Crescent and early sites in China, more and more examples of library-like collections have emerged. The Library of Alexandria, the first widely recognized international effort to bring all knowledge into one location, was founded in the third century B.C.E. Greek and Roman citizens during their periods of domination of ideas and politics in the ancient world often built personal collections as a sign of their knowledge and sophistication. In the centuries after the fall of the Roman Empire, the Church sponsored scriptoria in which monks copied ancient manuscripts and church writings so that they would be available in monastery libraries. The Arabic culture that flowered in the Mediterranean area in the early years of the last millennium esteemed learning and collected and preserved works of the Greeks and Romans as well as producing many noteworthy studies of their own, particularly in the sciences. On the other side of the world, Chinese culture flourished and collections of Chinese works of art and literature were developed and preserved by the emperors and noble families.

The great European libraries began to emerge with the development of universities in the twelfth and thirteenth centuries. Scholars would travel from library to library to study and to write. The libraries of this period were for the elite, for scholars, and for the church. National libraries grew rapidly after the introduction of the printing press in 1436 when a number of governments required that one copy of each book printed be given to the state. While the initial motivation was to control what was being published and impose a level of censorship, an unanticipated result was that this activity served to build great collections throughout Europe based on these royal collections initially established to control the flow of ideas.

In the eighteenth century, with the growth of a middle class that was increasingly literate and had time and money to spend on activities other than the bare necessities, access to books and the building of personal collections expanded well beyond earlier times when the elite (nobility and church) were the primary book readers and collectors. This was also the century of the awakening of political consciousness, with the French Revolution and the American Revolution breaking down traditional structures. There was a growing awareness by citizens that if they were to govern themselves, they needed to be informed. While efforts to bring libraries to the people were taking place in England from the early 1700s, the great move forward in making books and libraries widely available occurred in the American colonies. Ben Franklin's Library Company of Philadelphia, established in 1731, was one of the early organized efforts to make books available to the working man. The Boston Athenaeum established in the same period had a similar purpose. Universal education, the concerns of a new country working toward a democratic society, and the absence (in most parts of the colonies) of a strong social elite all supported the movement toward wider access to books and learning. By 1837, the first public library in the United States had been established in Peterborough, New Hampshire, and not long thereafter, the Boston Public Library was founded. By the end of the century, hundreds of libraries of all sizes had been established. Andrew Carnegie, a self-made steel tycoon, saw the need for and benefits of public libraries and funded no fewer than 2,500 libraries in the United States, the United Kingdom, and its colonies between 1881 and 1920. The public library in the nineteenth century had a single mission, which was to house books that would serve "to educate and nourish the intellectual and civic life of the community."[2] It was an institution devoted to the diffusion of knowledge. For many immigrants coming to America, the public library was their introduction to American culture and provided a free means of self-education. The public library continues this role and has supported many of those who were part of the substantial immigration to the United States during the last quarter of the twentieth century.

Universities and colleges in America emerged soon after the colonists arrived. Harvard College was established in 1636 and, by the end of the century, the College of William and Mary had been founded (1694). Other colleges were established during the next century, mostly along the Atlantic seaboard and included Columbia College in New York City, and Princeton University in Princeton, New Jersey. Their major purpose was to train young men for the clergy or for public service. They tended to be small institutions and had small libraries. During the latter half of the nineteenth century, the recently developed German model of the research university was introduced into the United States and resulted in a revolution in higher education, changing the university from a teaching institution for the elite to embracing a broader mission—the discovery and dissemination of new knowledge. Legislation establishing land grant institutions in each state provided publicly supported higher education for many more Americans. Higher education was no longer just for a select few. Libraries were needed to support these new initiatives and it was during this period that many of our great university libraries were begin.

The last twenty-five years of the nineteenth century were years of growth for libraries in many areas. The American Library Association was established in 1876 by a group of library leaders. Melville Dewey introduced the Dewey decimal system and established the first professional school to prepare librarians for service (Columbia University, 1888). Book publishers began to develop what later became core tools in organizing and selecting books.

Libraries in schools (K–12) grew slowly for many years. After World War II, they grew rapidly in response to the building of new schools to accommodate the baby boom generation and to respond to the 1957 entry of the Russians into space with the launching of the Sputnik satellite. The race for space required a stronger emphasis on science in the schools and this required investment in teaching/learning resources. At this time, the federal government, through a series of legislative actions such as the National Defense Education Act (1958), began to pour funds into school libraries. Many school libraries grew and became integral parts of the teaching program while others in poorer areas continued to struggle with inadequate resources. With the advent of the Internet, school libraries (now school library media centers) have become central to the information and information technology activities of the school's programs. The level of participation and the ability to participate is often determined by the economic resources available to a school system.

Other types of libraries/information centers were established in medical centers to support the information needs of health care professionals. Their information, backed up by the resources of the National Library of Medicine (NLM), a leader in organizing and accessing information for use, provides world-class resources and world-class access. NLM has been a leader for decades in bringing information access into the information age. Special libraries in business and industry, in research operations, and in other for-profit areas were established to meet the specific information needs of specific clienteles. As they are part of for-profit organizations, they are by definition flexible, forward-looking, and attentive to the bottom line. Many special libraries are found in museums, associations, private agencies, and other nonprofit entities. Each has a specific purpose and a particular clientele. Each varies in size and wealth, depending upon their sponsorship.

This wide range of libraries and information centers is interconnected. Individual types of libraries tend to have their individual professional associations (e.g., the American Library Association, the Medical Library Association, the Special Libraries Association) and tend to collaborate on issues of common concern. Beyond this, libraries/information centers use similar organizational schemes for materials, access the same databases, purchase from the same publishers and vendors, have common concerns about intellectual property rights and fair use, and require the skills of librarians and information specialists to manage them. And all are concerned with the ways in which the challenges of the information age provide opportunities for growth and service.

Note: Library history—by type of library, by overarching ideas, biographies of library leaders, the history of publishing, and related areas—is richly rewarding reading. For additional information, it is recommended that the reader check standard bibliographies to locate books, dissertations, and journal articles. And, of course, ask the librarian.

LIBRARIES IN THE INFORMATION AGE

Librarians were ideally positioned to enter the information age, as they have the skills to acquire, organize, store, retrieve, and use information and are accustomed to dealing with large amounts of information. Those coming to information from the engineering and computing perspectives understood the technology they had designed but lacked the skills needed to deal with information content. It took some time before they recognized the complexity of information issues and even longer to recognize that librarians were skilled in working with information content. Once the computing professionals and the library/information professionals found common ground, their joint efforts have contributed substantially to the development of methodologies and tools.

The roles of libraries in support of education and in providing information to support an informed electorate are traditional roles. In today's information world, our economy and our personal welfare are dependent upon information. How we use information, who has access to information, and who controls this access are all issues that speak to our economic health, our independence, and our survival as a free nation. Information policy, once an esoteric topic of little interest to legislators and the public, has found center stage and is debated in many arenas.

The Public Library in the Information Age

There are approximately 9,000 public libraries in the United States, over 16 percent of which have branches, which adds approximately 7,000 additional outlets.[3] Today's public library uses technology to augment its services to the community by providing access to information via databases, by setting up computer labs as learning centers for the community, and by using specialized programs to reach those with language differences or with specialized learning needs. The technology allows for a more individualized and richer information relationship with the community. It extends what public librarians have long done so well—providing personal service to each individual. Most libraries have home pages, most provide instruction and guidance in the use of the Internet, and most have access to a wide range of databases. Many have included e-books, DVDs, and other media in their collections. Technology in support of public services is a means of enhancing services. The library is also a social symbol in the community, a social place, and an information place that is enhanced by the availability and use of information technology.

In its administration and technical services, the public library has, over time, adopted online acquisition services and online cataloging. It collects and maintains circulation statistics electronically, and uses numerous management information systems in its financial activities and to analyze a variety of use and user statistics. It systems are compatible with those of other public libraries in the state and region. Many public libraries are excellent examples of the well-managed organization that uses information technology wisely.

Of concern to public librarians is an idea held by some that libraries are museums, that they can be easily bypassed from one's home computer, and that everything worth knowing is available online. In some communities, the public library is truly the information place while in others it continues to struggle with a misperception that books are dead, computers are the future, and all one needs to do is log on.

The Academic Library in the Information Age

The academic library, as part of the larger institution, reflects and responds to changes in higher education. Radical changes in how higher education is organized and delivered have required radical changes in how the library responds. The growth of online delivery of courses by the university requires a shift in the way libraries support the student and the faculty member. The lecture method of teaching has been joined by group research and other hands-on learning activities that require much more proactive information support than was needed to help prepare the traditional reserve reading list. Many academic libraries support an *information commons*, an area in which students and faculty work with librarians on areas of research. The commons is often open seven days a week, twenty-four hours a day, to accommodate the interaction among students, faculty, librarians, and information with the focus on student learning. Online components of many lecture courses require innovative responses by librarians. The entry into higher education by for-profit online universities continues to grow. Today's anytime/anywhere accessibility to course work requires new models. Those for-profit organizations providing education online may or may not provide information resources to support their courses. What is the responsibility of libraries to assist students enrolled in these courses?

The academic library must not only respond to and support innovative teaching methods, it must also provide access to publications worldwide and serve as portals for the use of resources.[4] Neal says that "academic libraries are now . . . serving as both providers of global publications and portals for users to resources that are increasingly created, stored, and delivered online. The library is both a historical archive and a learning and research collaboratory." It has been recognized that scholarly communication is unwieldy and that new ways to bring new ideas to the scholarly community are needed. Making scholarly papers available electronically for review and comment and expanding electronic publishing activities are ways of making scholarly information more readily available than is possible through the traditional publications processes. The relationship between faculty member, library, and publishing must be rethought. A focus on "electronic pedagogy, electronic publishing, emerging technologies, usability/human factors, and knowledge management" by involved parties can lead to positive new directions.[5]

Neal summarizes the task before the academic library:

> [T]he library must pursue strategic thinking and action, fiscal agility, and creative approaches to the development of collections and services and to the expansion of markets. Libraries affiliated with higher education are advancing away from the traditional or industrial age library, a model that is no longer viable. The combined impact of digital and network technologies, the globalization of education and scholarship, and increased competition for resources will produce a very different library in the academy over the next decade.[6]

The School Library Media Center in the Information Age

Today's ideal school media center is central to the instructional program of the school. Media of all types is available to the student who receives instruction in its use as needed. Even the youngest student works with computer-based instructional programs to learn reading, writing, language, math, and other skills at an individualized pace. Students supplement classroom activities through their access to computing technology and access to information, and can develop independent lines of inquiry. Books and journals continue to provide information not available online or not available in a particular format or configuration online. The challenges in the school library media center are often those of working with classroom teachers and administrators to ensure that the student has the best experiences and that resources are available to provide adequate computing access. In addition, many of the issues of supporting anytime/anywhere instruction that are under discussion in the higher education setting are present in the K–12 arena. The need to develop new means of meshing the information component and the instructional component is not limited to a grade level or type of instruction. As the emphasis on testing in math and reading has become a national priority, and as funds for K–12 education have not been provided to meet the need for this activity, resources to support the school library media center have suffered.

The Special Library in the Information Age

The special library in business and industry has moved from being a traditional print-based resource located in one place to becoming an information service that connects on demand to any research project, marketing venture, or any other activity needing specific information. The librarian/information specialist serves as the link to a broad range of information sources (electronic, print, individual experts). The librarian/information specialist is an active participant in detecting marketplace cues, searching for information, collecting and synthesizing data, and making it available in a timely fashion. In the for-profit sector, all costs must be justified and the costs of information services must add value to the organization. In this most flexible of environments, speed, accuracy, and efficiency rule. Special libraries in other environments (e.g., law firms and museums) support the objectives of their overall organization and the services to be provided. Many special libraries have joined networks and work closely with colleagues having similar interests. Others are contemplating this new world of computing, networking, and worldwide access and deciding how to participate.

SUMMARY

Regardless of the type of library or the organization of which it is a part, the trend is toward collaboration, interconnectedness, and interoperability. "We are . . . watching the continuing demise of traditional, hierarchical computing systems in favor of a flexible, desktop oriented, multi-vendor networked information ecology in offices everywhere—and certainly around the world."[7] This development leads to statewide, regional, type of institution, and other kinds of networks including all types of libraries/information centers. This expands the individual's ability to access information to a level previously unimagined. Added to this are the many technical and administrative networks that are interlinked. With this vastly expanded information world, the role of the librarian/information specialist is expanded in terms of the volume of materials available to acquire, organize, store, and retrieve information, and technology continues to be developed to support the effort. The primary role of the librarian/information professional continues to be that of bringing user and information together in a manner that is satisfying to the user.

Note: Studies are available that describe and discuss types of libraries and information centers. It is suggested that the reader select from these to obtain a deeper understanding of a particular library, its organization, and service patterns.

NOTES

1. Peter Lyman, "What is a digital library? Technology, intellectual property, and the public interest," *Daedalus* 125, no. 4 (Fall 1996): 2.

2. R. Kathleen Molz and Phyllis Dain, *Civic Space and Cyberspace: The American Public Library in the Information Age* (Cambridge, Mass.: MIT Press, 1999), 11.

3. Molz and Dain, *Civic Space and Cyberspace*, 46–47.

4. James G. Neal, "The entrepreneurial imperative: Advancing from incremental to radical change in the academic library," *Portal* 1, no. 1 (January 2002): 1.

5. Neal, "The entrepreneurial imperative," 7.

6. Neal, "The entrepreneurial imperative," 1.

7. Joan Blau, "The library in the information revolution," *Library Administration and Management* 6, no. 2 (Spring 1992): 71.

ADDITIONAL READINGS

General

Branscomb, Anne W. *Who Owns Information? From Privacy to Public Access.* New York: Basic Books, 1994.

Kohl, David F. *Administration, Personnel, Buildings, and Equipment: A Handbook for Library Management*. Santa Barbara, Calif.: ABC Clio, 1985.

Meadow, Charles. *Ink into Bits: A Web of Converging Media*. Lanham, Md.: Scarecrow Press, 1998.

Sonnenfeld, Jeffrey A. "What makes great boards great." *Harvard Business Review* 80, no. 9 (September 2002): 106–13.

Stueart, Robert D., and Barbara B. Moran. *Library and Information Center Management*. 6th ed. Greenwood Village, Co.: Libraries Unlimited, 2002.

Academic Libraries

Basic academic library texts were written in the 1960s and 1970s with some written as late as the 1980s. Since that time, one rarely finds texts dealing with the entire institutions. In their place, texts that discuss specific activities and/or functions have been written. While dated in many ways, the classic texts continue to be useful sources of information on basic organization and structure.

Brown, William L., *Academic Politics*. Tuscaloosa: University of Alabama Press, 1982.

Lyle, Guy R. *The Administration of the College Library*. 3rd ed. New York: H. W. Wilson, 1961.

McCabe, Gerald B., ed. *Operations Handbook for the Small Academic Library*. New York: Greenwood Press, 1956.

Rogers, Rutherford, and David C. Weber. *University Library Administration*. New York: Columbia University Press, 1971.

Tauber, Maurice, and Louis Rounds Wilson. *The University Library*. 2nd ed. New York: Columbia University Press, 1956.

Tsichritzis, Dennis. "Re-engineering the university." *Communications of the ACM* 42, no. 6 (June 1999): 93–100.

Public Libraries

Altman, Ellen, ed. *Local Public Library Administration*. Chicago: American Library Association, 1980.

Sager, Donald J. *Managing the Public Library*. 2nd ed. Boston: G. K. Hall, 1989.

Wheeler, Joseph, and Herbert Goldhor. *Practical Administration of Public Libraries*. Revised by Carleton Rochell. New York: Harper and Row, 1981. (A longtime classic useful for background information.)

School Library Media Centers

Woolls, Blanche. *The School Library Media Manager*. 2nd ed. Englewood, Colo.: Libraries Unlimited, 1999.

Yesner, Bernice L., and Hilda J. Lay. *Operating and Evaluating School Library Media Programs*. New York: Neal Schuman, 1998.

Special Libraries and Information Centers

Mount, Ellis. *Special Libraries and Information Centers.* 3rd. ed. Washington, D.C.: Special Libraries Assn., 1999.

Porter, Cathy A. et al. *Special Libraries: A Guide to Management.* Washington, D.C.: Special Libraries Assn., 1997.

Scammell, Alison. *Handbook of Special Librarianship and Information Work.* 7th ed. London: ASLIB, 1997.

Chapter Three

Diversity in the Workforce

While the application of diversity in the workplace has received much attention in recent decades, diversity has been a fact of our culture since its beginnings. Europeans were not the first inhabitants of this part of the world and, from their first days, had to interact with individuals from different cultural backgrounds. We are a nation of immigrants who came to the new world from many places and for numerous reasons and who found native peoples with their own culture already here. A combination of the effects of disease, military activity, and mutual mayhem reduced the original inhabitants to a small percentage of their numbers. As European culture was transported to the new world, cultural differences among British, French, Dutch, and Spanish colonists was a constant source of irritation as the cultural differences they experienced and warred over in the old world followed them to the new.

During the colonial period, British culture predominated in the north as the British steadily reduced the influence of the French and Dutch. Even here, there was a diversity of outlook between the northern colonies with their middle class, people's religion outlook and the colonies in the south that saw themselves as more aristocratic and better representatives of the truly cultured. Further south, Spanish culture predominated and would become an increasingly important element of American politics as the two cultures expanded and competed for the same space. Vestiges of French culture are still found in Louisiana and areas of New England south of Quebec, and although direct French influence ended with the Louisiana Purchase in 1803, the culture they built continues to add flavor to the American scene. The effects of the slave trade and the addition to American culture of many thousands of Africans has had and continues to have immense implications for our culture. Fewer in number but of great importance is the continuing influence of Native Americans on the American culture and its diversity.

The influence of Britain was the determining factor in the development of American culture from the earliest colonists to the present day. Our language, legal systems, many of our religious affiliations, educational systems, and social attitudes are British imports. As is true of all colonies, colonists adapted the customs of the mother country to their own local needs and interests. The result was a new nation that took its early steps in the late eighteenth and early nineteenth century. The cultural and political differences between North and South came to a head in midcentury and were brutally dealt with in the War between the States (1861–1865). A steady flow of immigrants to the northern states, many from the German states, arrived during the wartime period and many were assimilated into American culture through their experiences in the Union Army. The aftereffects of the war on both North and South lasted nearly another century and some cultural differences between the two regions continue.

As the United States expanded its control of the western territories after the war, it continued to come in conflict with the Spanish-speaking cultures of Mexico; border wars that had begun in earlier decades continued. Several new states in the Southwest and West that were added to the country had strong Hispanic cultural roots. Conflicts with a culture having a different language, different legal system, different religious background, and different views of the individual were present at the beginning of these interactions and continue to be present.

Concurrent with the expansion westward was the increase in the speed of growth of the industrial North. This required a workforce greater than that available locally and the great immigration of Europeans to America was the solution. Political upheaval in Europe and the need for labor by the United States worked together to build a steady stream of immigrants to America. The stream of immigrants grew; in the first decade of the twentieth century, 8,795,386 individuals entered the country. This phase of immigration slowed with World War I and it wasn't until about 1965 that immigration again was a major source of population growth. In the period to 1950, 90 percent of those coming into the country were from Europe or Canada.[1] Since 1950, country of origin has shifted and more than half of the immigrants are from Latin America and more than a quarter from Asia. Since 1965, it has been estimated that up to a million individuals have immigrated to the United States each year. Immigrant children are the fastest growing segment of the

U.S. child population.² This influx into the United States of millions of individuals from cultures other than the dominant culture is causing profound effects on the social and economic fabric of the country. This is true of the many other countries that are experiencing a similar immigrant infusion as well: Turks to Germany, North Africans to France, large numbers of immigrants to Canada and Australia. It has been estimated that for some time we have been in a period of massive worldwide immigration with a hundred million or more people on the move, 20 to 30 percent of them refugees from wars or persecution on religious or ethnic grounds in their native land. The sociological and economic consequences of this movement and the changes that occur in the countries to which they go are profound both for the new immigrant and for the host country.

ASSIMILATION OR ACCULTURATION

For most of our history, the dominant culture was the environment into which the new immigrant melted. There was one American culture and one left behind one's language, one's culture, and one's ways of socializing. There was no looking back; once an individual or family disembarked at whatever port of entry, they were here. There was nothing left for them where they had come from and they were forced to make a new life. It was estimated that within two or three generations they would be mainstreamed into the white Protestant culture. The longer they were in America, the better life would be for them. Through hard work and assimilation, they would amass economic wealth, gain education, and achieve the American dream.

With today's ease of travel, immigrants no longer need to leave family and culture behind but can come to the United States and can also return to visit their families as often as they can afford. Rather than leaving their culture behind, they bring it with them and every time they return for a visit, that culture is reinforced. Members of a family may immigrate and then send money to others still in the home country. Dual identities (and, in some cases, dual citizenship) are no longer rare. Immigrants of color tend to congregate in neighborhoods and are segregated or segregate themselves from the middle-class populations of European origin. Eighty-five percent of Mexicans in the United States live in three states (California, Texas, and Illinois) and there are communities of Mexicans throughout the United States in areas that have employment possibilities for them. This segregation further alienates them from the mainstream. "These immigrants have, by and large, no meaningful contact with the middle-class, white European culture. Rather, their point of reference is more likely to be co-nationals, [or] co-ethnics."[3]

Well-educated immigrants are welcomed in the United States and are given opportunities to enter the workforce. While some have skills that are easily integrated into the workforce, others may not be able to have their credentials from another country recognized and find themselves in jobs well below their education and abilities. Those with few skills can get jobs but these are jobs with little upward mobility. Rather than having things get progressively better for them and their families, things may get worse. Many families end up in poor urban settings without hope of moving up. The youth culture in the inner city may influence immigrant children to reject the family mores and their culture. This is not to say that there is no upward mobility or that immigrants cannot take advantage of education to move ahead. Each country's immigrants are different from those of other origins and they respond to the American culture differently.

Each immigrant and immigrant culture changes upon coming to America and America changes because of them. The melting pot concept so popular a century ago no longer works, as immigrants are not always willing to give up their culture in order to belong. They want to bring the best of who they are and what they represent to what they see here. This requires a recognition by the dominant culture that their contribution is valuable. New ideas, new ways of doing things, are changing our culture and how we respond to differences.

THE DIVERSITY WITHIN

Minority Groups

At the beginning of the twenty-first century, nearly 13 percent of Americans, or approximately 35,000,000 people, were African American. Eighty-two percent of them were high school graduates and 12 percent had college degrees. They form a substantial part of the workforce at every level.[4] The Hispanic population has increased dramatically in recent decades and it is estimated that by 2050 the Hispanic population will have nearly doubled from its current 15.6 percent. Asians, although fewer in number, are expected to nearly double their numbers from 4.1 percent to 7.6 percent during this period.[5] The Native American population of approximately two million is fairly evenly divided between those who live on reservations and those who live elsewhere.[6] Each group of Americans has ties both to its own culture and to the mainstream culture. For some, the different cultural background, value system, and means of communication may be a barrier to full participation in the mainstream culture. Others see these differences as an asset in bringing new ideas to the mainstream culture, thus enriching it.

In assigning tasks to minority staff members, managers may look at ethnic background and assign tasks they assume to be appropriate to the individual's culture, such as providing outreach services to members of the individual's cultural group or developing specific collections and programs geared to promoting greater understanding of that group. While these are necessary activities, they should not be the only tasks assigned to members of minority groups. Such tasks also may place the minority staff member outside the mainstream activities of the library and prevent the individual from participating in daily activities that provide opportunities for growth. In all instances, it is the responsibility of the manager to create and maintain a climate of inclusion and to acknowledge and promote the contribution of all staff members, not only for what they currently do but for what they have the ability to do.

Women

Women comprise more than half the population and their numbers are heavily represented in the paid workforce. By 1984, more than fifty million women were in the labor force. This was 43 percent of the workforce. In recent decades, the percentage of women in the workforce has increased and the percentage of men has decreased. What has not changed is that women continue to be paid less than men. "For as long as data have been available for the U.S., women's average earnings has been about 60% of men's for full time, year round workers."[7] The majority of women work in a small number of occupations, most men work in predominantly male occupations. Despite major changes in the economy, a narrowing of educational differences, and growing similarities in male and female work-life patterns, little change was seen until the past decade when more and more occupations began to be easier for women to enter. "To some extent, the differences in women's and men's earnings and in the occupations they hold reflect . . . past discrimination; to some extent they reflect current discrimination; and to some extent they reflect a host of other factors, such as differences between women and men in their preferences, attitudes, values, experiences, education, training, and so on."[8] These factors are probably interrelated.

A study by the Committee on Women's Employment and Related Social Issues of the National Research Council focused on job segregation by sex. Although the study was published in 1986, its findings accurately describe the barriers to choice that have been erected to limit women's job opportunities. Different cultures have different sex-related occupations; for example, physicians in Russia are more likely to be women and in the United States more likely to be male. Changes may occur over time in an occupation; for example, bank tellers and realtors were at one time almost wholly male occupations and have become occupations almost equally held by women and men. Some occupations are segregated by organization or industry; for example, some restaurants have only male waiters.

Cultural attitudes may influence what is appropriate work for women and for men. There are those who say that woman's role is in the home and that other wishes and choices are inappropriate. If the job extends the domestic role such as child care, teaching small children, nursing, waitressing, or other care-giving activities, that is acceptable. In numerous commercials and entertainment films, the woman can also be represented as creative. She can be a sculptor, run an antique store or a book store, or can dabble in the arts—so long as she doesn't take it seriously and is home in time to get dinner. This attitude also conveniently ignores the one-parent family and any other deviation from the assumed norm of the nuclear family. Some say that women are emotional and don't have the brainpower to have responsible positions. And, of course, they should never supervise men. There is also the myth that women are moral, weak, nonaggressive, and incapable of abstract thought. And they don't mind tedious, repetitive tasks. If a woman didn't fit into certain categories, she was at fault and it was not that the stereotyped category was in error. Labels such as these can influence student advisors in schools and job placement advisors. How many young women were told that being a nurse was what girls do, that doctors were men?

If a woman could get past the cultural barriers and gained the appropriate education for a position, another set of hurdles appeared. A number of laws still in place prohibit women from doing certain jobs as they are seen as harmful to the health. Some jobs required that a person be able to lift up to forty pounds, or be near toxic chemicals, and so forth. Women were labeled as weak or there was concern that toxic chemicals could harm childbearing potential. Seniority systems can keep women from advancement. You can't progress unless you have held certain positions and you can't get that position unless you have worked in another position earlier. And you can't get the first job as they haven't been hiring. Other discriminatory ploys include the excuse that customers want to interact with white males (e.g., a white male lawyer) as they are perceived as more reliable. Or that women disrupt the workplace with their differences. Or that a firm with too many women loses prestige. At one time, a woman lawyer applying to a law firm was often offered the job of legal secretary. In labs, female scientists were offered jobs as technicians. These attitudes are breaking down but the assumption that women will work for less pay and at less desirable jobs still exists.

Institutional barriers form another set of hurdles for women. The job description, organization of tasks, and upward mobility ladders may be constructed so as to limit women from applying. These can no longer be formal efforts, but the informal efforts to have and maintain a workforce "like us" continues. If hired, women can face a work environment that is inhospitable and that says "no women wanted here." The workplace may see itself as family with the woman being the mom or the kid sister and the man being the patriarch or big brother. Those who fit into the work social group are accepted and those who do not have a difficult time. Almost assuredly, women in this environment are excluded from the informal information networks where much information sharing is conducted. While these behaviors are dying out, they continue to be present in many environments.

Women who are looking to work in occupations not seen as sex specific to women may find that they are counseled to look for places they are more apt to fit in. They may be told that certain jobs are unavailable to women or that the job will not mesh with their family obligations. At one time, women were not hired in responsible positions because it was assumed that when the husband was transferred to another area, the woman would resign her job and follow him. In any case, a woman's work was considered less important to the family economy than a man's. Women worked for the little extras and not for rent and food. Single, female parents were treated in a similar manner despite the fact that they were the sole breadwinners.

Since this study, there has been a gradual lessening of overt segregation of occupations due in part to legislation, to higher levels of education of women that have opened positions to them, and to the fact that the white male workforce is constricting and there is a need for workers. But where these attitudes and behaviors still exist, they corrode the workplace and make it unpleasant for all.

WHERE DO WE GO FROM HERE?

The workplace has traditionally been segregated by sex, by race, by education, and by cultural attitudes and a desire to keep things the way they are. Those who have been in charge do not want changes, as these changes would threaten their power. But the industrial business world of past decades is crumbling. We are moving to a global society where the power structure is different. The workforce is increasingly diverse and it is impossible to continue business as usual. There are those who say that the old ways are best and that any changes are for the worse. They want to support the world as it was in their good old days.

While there is still a lack of diversity in the workplace, our society is becoming more diverse daily and that diversity *will* become evident in the workplace. The organization that does not hire and manage a diverse workforce will not be able to compete in our diverse society or in our global economy. Hamel and Prahalad liken a company to a biological organism and say that its health is dependent upon genetic variety.[9] They found that too many individuals spent all of their careers in one company and very few had worked outside the United States. Further, they noted that many companies in the same area of business (e.g., the airline industry) had very similar ways of doing things and few new ideas percolated to the top. They found that

> the tighter the criteria on what kind of people get hired, the more similar their educational background, the more comprehensive the employee induction process, the more widespread and inescapable corporate training programs, the more formal the mentoring of juniors by seniors, the longer the tenure of executives with the firm and within the industry, the fewer outsiders hired near the top, and the more successful the company has been in the past, the more uniform will be managerial frames across the company.[10]

In this environment, employees believe they have found the right way and there is no other. They become increasingly immune to outside influence; they have difficulty adapting and can no longer compete.

The workforce is changing and the kinds of available jobs are changing.

The workforce is increasingly populated by women and minorities. The level of education needed for jobs is changing and our customers are changing both in their diversity and in their demands. We are entering a global economy with a global workforce and a global customer base. There is also an increasing gap between the haves and have-nots—those who have the ability, desire, opportunity, and education to be part of a more highly skilled workforce and those who do not. The concerns of those individuals and groups who are excluded for any reason will need to be considered as they have the potential to wreak havoc. Doing things as we have always done them is a formula for extinction. A solution to at least some of these issues is to look at diversity as a national asset and to incorporate that diversity into the workforce so that it is as strong, flexible, and productive as is possible.

DEFINITIONS

Numerous terms are used to define a diverse work environment: diversity, equity, organizational culture. They are implemented through multicultural education and diversity education. All have the same objectives, which are to:

- hire and keep the best of the new labor pool
- gain access to greater innovation
- achieve better performance among female and minority workers
- gain the ability to make the most of ethnic or international markets.[11]

The Association of Research Libraries (ARL) definition begins by saying that each individual contributes to the overall diversity of the organization through a unique combination of characteristics. They may be biologically determined (age, race, gender, ability), they may be learned (economic status, education, occupation, etc.), or they may be a combination, such as learning style. Further differences include geographical background, marital/partner status, and lifestyle. These diverse characteristics can be brought together and serve as the basis for learning and building an organization. Through this process, similarities among individuals may be discovered.[12]

Equity is the core component of diversity. Equity is "understanding and working affirmatively to amend historical and present misrepresentation."[13] Activities here include working to eliminate "de facto and de jure laws prohibiting entire groups access to educational, social, and career opportunities; economic disparity amplified by sexism, ableism, and racism . . . [also] institutionalized racism which is believed by many to be woven into the very fabric of U.S. culture."[14] Among the mechanisms created for reaching parity is affirmative action legislation, the purpose of which is "to promote equitable access and ensure due process." The combination of a commitment to diversity plus a strong and measurable equity program are essential elements in managing today's workforce.

Each organization has its organizational culture that has developed over the life of the organization. It is a combination of shared values, attitudes, beliefs, and ways of approaching issues. It includes behaviors, appropriate responses to situations, and standards to which individuals are expected to aspire; it determines the accepted forms of communication within the organization. These rules have been created over time by members of the organization and are usually passed on through informal channels. All new employees are expected to learn them and abide by them. In some organizations there is a strong desire for conformity. The melting pot theory still exists. In such an environment, "the rewards and promotion system is driven by making a positive impression on one's immediate supervisor and assimilating into the culture of the firm or the library in terms of work ethic, interaction with colleagues, values, professional activities, personal style, and other factors."[15] Such a cultural environment is not one in which creative individuals or individuals who do not wish to lose their cultural identity will thrive.

Libraries and information centers have a unique culture and each organization within this overall category has its own culture. It may derive from the larger organization of which it is a part or may be a combination of that larger organization's culture and its own unique additions. Some of the variables that go to make up these cultures include the organization of which it is a part; when it was organized; who it serves; and what its goals, objectives, and values are.[16]

To appreciate the value of each contribution to the organization, it is often useful to invest in multicultural education. This activity looks at different cultures as sources of learning, builds awareness of one's own culture, and demonstrates that no one culture is best. One can acquire the skills and analysis needed to function in multicultural environments, examine differences, and see the significance of similarities and differences among culture groups and among individuals within groups.[17] Diversity education asks what characteristics each person brings to the organization and how those skills, talents, and energies can be used to improve the organization. If the organization acknowledges and encourages diverse contributions (as part of its history and values), it has made the decision to leave behind the outdated melting pot and assimilation approach. "Ideally, members of a pluralistic society recognize the contributions of each individual and each group to the common civilization or macro-culture, and encourage the maintenance and development of different yet compatible lifestyles, languages, and convictions."[18] While diverse in its makeup, the organization has a commitment to deal with common concerns in an environment of mutual respect.

AFFIRMATIVE ACTION AND
EQUAL OPPORTUNITY

Because of a history of discrimination in the workplace, legislation was enacted by Congress in the 1960s to require a more open process in employment. The Equal Pay Act of 1963 prohibits employees from paying a person of one sex less than a person of the other sex for essentially the same job. The Civil Rights Act of 1964 (Title VI), enforced by the U.S. Department of Education, prohibits discrimination on the basis of race, color, or national origin in all federally funded programs. Title VII of the Civil Rights Act prohibits discrimination in employment and is enforced by the U.S. Equal Employment Opportunity Commission (EEOC). Additional legislation prohibits discrimination against the disabled (Rehabilitation Act of 1973), against disabled veterans and veterans of the Vietnam War (Vietnam Era Veterans Readjustment Act of 1974) , against age discrimination (Age Discrimination Act of 1974), against Americans with disabilities (Americans with Disabilities Act of 1990) and the Civil Rights Act of 1991, which prohibits intentional employment discrimination. The focus of the legislation is on organizations that receive federal funds or government contracts and is enforced by a number of agencies, primarily the U.S. Department of Education and the EEOC.

Affirmative action legislation is an aggressive approach and requires that individuals from protected groups be included as candidates in search processes. Prospective employers are required to look as broadly as possible to identify possible candidates in order to obtain equitable workplace representation. An institutional formula "that considers the availability of individuals prepared to contribute professionally in a particular category" is created.[19] The institution is required to maintain data on how one advertises a position, conducts a search, if the candidate pool is sufficiently diverse, and the rationale for a hire from the pool if that occurs. While the focus is on the external search process, it applies also to internal promotions, promotion policies, and internal staff training to ensure that opportunities for advancement are open to all and efforts are made to ensure that all members of the staff are involved. For an organization such as a library whose role is to work with a diverse clientele, and this clientele is changing in many of the same ways as the workforce, it is particularly important that it have a strong multicultural approach. Interpersonal communication within the organization is critical and it is also critical to the service provided. Good cross-cultural interpersonal communication skills are key to successful service provision.

MANAGING DIVERSITY

Why should an organization become involved in managing diversity? Some would say that it just happens and we don't need to take steps overtly for it to happen. Others say that it is the right thing to do, given a history of discrimination in the workplace; still others say "let the new and perhaps different worker join our company and learn to blend in." Roosevelt Thomas Jr., a leading expert in diversity management, asks the question, "As a manager goes about enabling/influencing/empowering his/her workforce, and as that workforce becomes increasingly diverse, are [there] things that have to be done differently (managerially speaking) with a diverse workforce than would be the case with a homogeneous workforce?"[20]

The global economy has resulted in a new and diverse marketplace where those to whom we sell products or provide service differ greatly, and a knowledge of their cultural and economic differences is an important factor in meeting their needs. Further, the demographics of the workforce have changed, with women, minorities, and immigrants equaling approximately 85 percent of the new entrants to the workforce. Members of this newly defined workforce are less apt to want to fit into the organization; while they are willing to accept basic rules of the organization, they want their ideas and ways of doing things respected and included. Managing race and gender in this more complex and ever-changing environment is an important part of

managing well. Questions and concerns arise that are new to the manager and need a new approach. For example,

- Two organizations are merged. Organization A has a fairly conservative workforce that has been in place for some time with minor changes. It places a priority on dressing well on the job and following rules and regulations set forth by their superiors. Organization B is a young organization, very creative and ambitious, and places little emphasis on how to dress and what the rules are. How do they interact? How does one respond to diverse work styles?
- An organization has a history of hiring bright young professionals, assimilating them into the organization, and promoting from within. What happens to this like-minded workforce when the market changes or when the organization of which they are a part reorganizes and requires that they reorganize their activities and take on new and challenging tasks?
- This one-right-way organization is very good at the one right way it follows to do its tasks. What happens when a manager with new and different ideas is hired?
- In order to conform to affirmative action goals, an organization hires a number of minorities and women, but few stay. Turnover is high. How can turnover be reduced?

In each case, individual and organizational differences get in the way of progress. How do you take individuals who differ in age, gender, ethnic background, education, lifestyle, sexual orientation, personal values, response to authority and to the goals of the organization, who differ in their levels of creativity, ways of thinking, parent culture, and attitude toward change, and help them become a cohesive work group? You can try to assimilate them into the organization as has been the policy for many years or you can manage the differences and use the unique contributions each person brings to the organization. Assimilation doesn't work very well any more as new hires may not want to lose their identity to the organizational identity. Some have said that when fitting in means that one does things the way white males have said is the only way, they are unwilling to accept it. New professionals are well educated and have good ideas about how things can be done. They want the opportunity to contribute and to test their ideas. When an organization forces individuals to give up their different ideas and approaches, it loses creativity, which is the spark that gives the organization life.

"Managing diversity is a comprehensive managerial process for developing an environment that works for all employees."[21] Thomas goes on to say that managing diversity includes the following:

- Managing diversity means approaching diversity at three levels simultaneously: individual, interpersonal, and organizational. While the traditional focus has been on the individual and interpersonal, it is essential to see diversity as an issue for the entire organization, involving the very way organizations are structured.
- Managing diversity approaches diversity from a management perspective. It deals with the way organizations are managed, how managers do their jobs and is grounded in a very specific definition of managing—creating an environment that allows the people being managed to reach their full potential, getting from employees not only everything you have a right to expect but everything they have to offer.
- Managing diversity requires that line managers learn a new way, spending less time doing the work and more time enabling employees to do the work.
- Managing diversity defines diversity broadly by addressing the many ways employees are different and the many ways they are alike. It goes beyond race and gender and includes many other dimensions.
- Managing diversity assumes that adaptation is a two-way street, a mutual process between the individual and the organization.
- Managing diversity is not a program or an orchestrated set of actions. It calls for more than changing individual behaviors. It requires a fundamental change in the organization's way of life. Implementing it takes many years.[22]

CHANGING THE ORGANIZATIONAL CULTURE

Looking at the organizational culture, the usually unexamined basic assumptions that drive the organization, is the first step in the process of managing diversity. Identify those elements of the culture that are basic, the roots from which corporate behaviors come. Many of our organizations were established in a time when the white male culture was the dominant work culture and the beliefs and values were those of an earlier time. Do they fit today's organization or are they a hindrance? Is this a paternalistic work environment that values centralized authority and rewards it or does it value new ideas from new hires? Does it see women and minorities as equal members of the workforce with white males or does it make special allowances for them? Thomas recommends that the diversity manager sponsor a review of organizational documents, interview employees at every level, and observe behaviors. Often one must infer behaviors from current attitudes. Once identified, these roots are to be assessed to determine if they support healthy behavior in the organization. For example, using teams as they appear in a rough-and-tumble sports environment as a model for organizational behavior may appeal to some individuals but may prevent others from participating. Another less-male-oriented approach to managing could be more inclusive.

James Williams recommends that interviews with library management be conducted to determine their perceptions of and goals for diversity. It is also important to conduct a work history analysis, and interview library staff to focus on perceptions of organizational culture related to socialization, perceptions of hiring and retention efforts, "personal growth and development efforts, evaluation methods, promotion practices, and the extent to which the climate is one that welcomes, values and respects differences."[23]

THE DIVERSITY PLAN

The diversity plan is a product of the organization as a whole. If the library/ information center is part of a larger organization (e.g., an academic library or school library media center), the library's plan follows from the university or school district plan. Although the context of the public, special, industry, or other library/information center differs, the approach to development of the diversity plan is essentially the same. The plan should address

- the strategic framework of the plan including beliefs, values, mission, goals, strategies and results
- the institutional vision of diversity
- a diversity assessment including efforts to build and sustain a diverse student body, staff, and faculty

- benchmarking and establishing operational procedures related to best practice
- description of the diversity planning process
- proposed diversity initiatives
- appendices including definitions, activities, data, budgets, and so forth

The library's plan is derived from the campus plan or other plan of the larger organization of which the library/information center is a part. It includes its own library organizational climate assessment, which involves all staff as well as a sampling of library clientele. The purpose of this is twofold: to determine the environment and to have a forum in which to discuss what diversity is and what it means.[24]

With the plan of the parent organization as a model and with the climate assessment in hand, the library is ready to prepare a diversity plan based on the data gathered and to construct a timeline. Under the leadership of the director/dean, the plan is implemented. The climate in which this plan is then implemented requires constant attention on the part of everyone, not just administration. Opportunities to discover and to take advantage of special approaches and skills should be encouraged. Some organizations invite informal groups to discuss differences in culture, religion, or perhaps learning style with a view to mutual understanding and discovery.

ASSESSMENT

A comprehensive assessment process should be built into the plan in order to get feedback on successes and to identify areas that need attention. Data on specific areas should be identified and collected consistently. To the extent possible, assessment should be data-driven with anecdotal and perceptual information as a secondary input. The evaluation process should be designed to

- establish baseline data
- measure the effects of change
- identify situations needing immediate attention
- uncover latent conflict
- provide bottom-up feedback
- improve management-employer-user relations

- decentralize problem solving
- establish a bias for action by focusing on issues[25]

Williams aptly sums up the reasons for diversity management in the academic setting by saying the following:

> Changes in the scholarly record, the process of scholarly communication (including the use of information technology) and changes in the demography of society are placing a new set of dynamic demands on the library organization—demands that can be addressed only through staffs with new capacities, through the extension and exploitation of the knowledge of existing personnel, and through changes in the composition and structure of library staffs. The diversity management focus in academic libraries thus becomes effective preparation, recruitment, development and deployment of personnel in the changing environment in order for the library to have the best possible staff, composed of individuals who represent and can serve a diverse community—a community that has been variously described as the emergent knowledge society with a technology rich future.[26]

A similar statement can be made to support diversity planning in other types of library/information centers.

FUTURE ISSUES

Affirmative action is the focus of a number of legal actions in which those not in a protected group say that they are being treated unfairly. In some cases, the courts have rolled back affirmative action gains. Some object to the idea of inclusiveness and call it liberal hogwash while others want to go back to the way things were. The issues of diversity and affirmative action have been political issues from the outset, with groups and individuals supporting differing views. Wallis says that civility—an acknowledgment of equality between citizens and the responsibility of individuals to the common good—is being replaced by an uncivil society in which the positions of others are derided and are called evil.[27] Wallis calls this the *new meanness* that results in violence such as bombings of personal property and threats to safety.

SUMMARY

Diversity is here to stay. It is in the makeup of the workforce, of our population, and of the global economy in which we work. We have always been a diverse society and have been proud of that fact. Making diversity more than a social good to be applauded and implementing it in our work world, in education, and in our social interaction requires care and understanding. In the long run, we have no choice.

NOTES

1. Marcelo M. Suarex-Orozo, "Everything you wanted to know about assimilation but were afraid to ask," *Daedalus* 129, no. 4 (Fall 2000): 1.

2. Suarex-Orozo, "Everything you wanted to know about assimilation," 2.

3. Suarex-Orozo, "Everything you wanted to know about assimilation," 3.

4. Alma Dawson, "Celebrating African-American librarians and librarianship," *Library Trends* 49, no. 1 (Summer 2000): 49–87.

5. Alice Robbin, "We the people: One nation, a multicultural society," *Library Trends* 49, no. 1 (Summer 2000): 6–48.

6. Lotsee Patterson, "History and status of Native Americans in librarianship," *Library Trends* 49, no. 1 (Summer 2000): 182–93.

7. Barbara F. Reskin and Heidi I. Hartmann, eds., *Women's Work, Men's Work: Sex Segregation on the Job* (Washington, D.C.: National Academy Press, 1986), 1.

8. Reskin and Hartmann, *Women's Work*, 2.

9. Gary Hamel and C. K Prahalad, *Competing for the Future* (Boston: Harvard Business School Press, 1994), 56–57.

10. Reskin and Hartmann, *Women's Work*, 54.

11. Sharon Nelton, "Meet your new workforce," *Nation's Business* 76, no. 7 (July 1988): 14–21.

12. DeEtta Jones, "The definition of diversity: Two views, a more inclusive definition," in *Managing Multiculturalism and Diversity in the Library: Principles and Issues for Administration*, edited by Mark Winston (New York: Haworth Press, 1999), 7.

13. Jones, "The definition of diversity," 8.

14. Jones, "The definition of diversity," 8.

15. Joan Howland, "Beyond recruitment: Retention and promotion strategies to ensure diversity and success," *Library Administration and Management* 13, no. 1 (Winter 1999): 5.

16. Jones, "The definition of diversity," 10.

17. Margaret D. Pusch and David Hoopes, eds., *Multicultural Education: A Cross Cultural Training Approach* (LaGrange Park, Ill.: Intercultural Network, 1979).

18. Jones, "The definition of diversity," 10.

19. Jones, "The definition of diversity," 12.

20. Roosevelt Thomas Jr., *Beyond Gender and Race: Unleashing the Power of Your Total Workforce by Managing Diversity* (New York: AMACOM, 1991), xv.

21. Thomas, *Beyond Gender and Race*, 10.

22. Thomas, *Beyond Gender and Race*, 12.

23. James F. Williams II, "Managing diversity: Library management in light of the dismantling of affirmative action," in *Managing Multiculturalism and Diversity in the Library: Principles and Issues for Administration*, edited by Mark Winston (New York: Haworth Press, 1999), 40.

24. Williams, "Managing diversity," 38.

25. Williams, "Managing diversity," 41.

26. Williams, "Managing diversity," 29.

27. Jim Wallis, *Who Speaks for God?* (New York: Delacorte Press, 1996), 145.

ADDITIONAL READINGS

Bellah, Robert M., Richard Madsen, William M. Sullivan, Ann Swindler, and Stephen M. Tipton. *Habits of the Heart*. Berkeley: University of California Press, 1985.

Chapter Four

Ethical Issues

Until recently, discussion of ethics and ethical behavior was rarely found in management texts. There may have been a paragraph or two on the need to deal fairly with staff or ways to avoid conflict of interest. It appeared to be assumed that most individuals have a personal standard of behavior and that that standard is all they would need. In some texts, the individual is advised to act ethically, but no guidelines are given to define the limits of ethical behavior. While some ethical standards such as confidentiality and fairness toward others are common to all interactions, different professions focus on particular areas. For example, in the information professions, particular attention is paid to individual rights to privacy and to intellectual property rights. Ethical issues arise regularly in the workplace and a blanket statement that one should act ethically may not provide sufficient guidance.

While ethics as an area of human concern has a long and rich history, professional ethics as a particular area of attention tends to emerge during periods in which unethical activities in business, in government, in a professional area, or in other circumstances become particularly noticeable. In the 1920s during the Harding administration, government scandals engendered fear that America's moral foundations were at risk. The Watergate scandal of the 1970s again raised major concerns about the ways in which public trust was subverted for political gain. And at the turn of the new century, Enron and other major business enterprises provided examples of the damage that is done when the greed of some wipes out the savings of many. In each of these instances, there was a call for professional societies to practice the ethical codes they had developed and for government to impose rules on those who have violated the public trust.

Ethics is a system of values and rules that spells out what is right and what is good. "Ethics directly asks what kinds of acts are right or wrong, good or bad, or ought or ought not to be done, and what the terms involved mean."[1] Emile Durkheim defined ethics as "the rules which determine the duties that men owe to their fellows, solely as other men [and] form the highest point of ethics."[2] He went on to say that a system of morals is always a group affair and can operate only if the group protects that system with its authority. A profession needs to have its own core ethics as a means of self-regulation.

"Broadly construed, professional ethics encompasses all issues involving ethics and values in the roles of the professions and the conduct of professionals in society."[3] Professional conduct consists of making professional services equally available to all, of governing the relationships between the professional and the client, and in being aware of the effects on others beyond the primary client of one's actions. Peter Drucker equates professional ethics with everyday honesty.[4] While clients may assume that professionals conduct themselves honestly and ethically, and most do, sufficient examples of misconduct exist to make the client wary.

The study of the effect of organizations and their structure on ethical conduct has been labeled organizational ethics. Social values within the community and within the organization affect its ethical climate. Community standards in one area may differ from those in another. While right is right and wrong is wrong, different communities and individuals may develop their own interpretations based on local and personal social values. Organizations themselves tend to see issues as legal issues rather than as ethical issues For example, the question of what makes an appraisal system fair or what constitutes misconduct is seen by the organization as a legal issue while to the individual it may be more of an ethical issue. Some organizations, through their organizational culture, may pressure their employees to think or act in certain ways that may either support or produce conflict with personal ethical values.[5] In all instances, community or organizational pressure has a strong influence on what is considered ethical.

As social interactions become more complex, and as technology further complicates human interaction, and as customers expect ever more information and services from the professionals who serve them, the need for a means of managing the professional/client interaction is apparent. In the past two hundred years, codes of ethics have been developed from earlier rules of conduct to provide guidance in the interaction between professional and client. The earliest modern code was developed for the medical profession over the first half of the nineteenth century and was based on ancient laws, current practice, and the Oath of Hippocrates, which emphasized that above all, the physician would *do no harm*. During the twentieth century, nearly every profession and many occupations developed their own codes of ethics, each focusing on the areas most central to its practice.

In 1908, the legal profession adopted a code whose purpose was to control the conduct of attorneys and to instill a social conscience. This code has been revised regularly to respond to changing social and cultural concerns. By 1924, more than two hundred business and professional groups had adopted codes that ranged from perfunctory statements of the "thou shalt be ethical" variety to well-developed statements that defined ethics as seen by the particular group. In 1929, the National Teacher's Association adopted a code which focused on teacher/student relationships, relationship to the community, and to the teaching profession. It appeared to be more of a control mechanism over teachers than a means of supporting the teaching professional. Many of the codes developed during this period focused on conditions of work and labor practices and to a lesser degree with relations with the client or consumer. Many were written by management as rules for employee behavior. As labor unions grew in power, they were more likely to assume responsibility for employee behavior; interest in other elements of the code tended to get lost.

With the concern in the 1960s for social responsibility, ethics assumed a renewed importance. In this iteration, emphasis was placed on the individual and individual responsibility to perform in an ethically responsible manner. The 1966 American Association of University Professor's code emphasized intellectual honesty, responsibility to students, to the community of scholars, the employing institution, and to society at large. The International City Manager's Association code of ethics, first adopted in 1924 and revised regularly since then, has moved toward statements addressing responsibilities of elected officials to provide fair, high-quality services within the context of democratic government. These two codes are representative of the codes developed or revised during the 1960s. They focus on the individual and individual responsibility to perform in an ethical manner. Codes developed during this period tended to be shorter and to stress principle over directives. While some progress has been made, a 1979 survey by the American Association for the Advancement of Science (AAAS) of its member societies showed that more than half had codes of ethics, but most were vague statements rather than action documents; many associations and professions revised their codes regularly in response to the changing demands of society, such as the increased public demand for accountability. Little has changed since that survey. In many instances, it still appears that a code of ethics is seen as necessary window dressing rather than as a guide to action that is taken seriously.

Information technology needs to be singled out for special attention because it was recognized early on that technology is not ethically neutral. Clifford Christians points out that while hardware and software are neutral, the way in which one uses them to organize and manage information is not. "These products are particular. They combine specific resources into distinct entities with unique properties and capabilities. Technical objects embody decisions to develop one kind of knowledge and not another, to use certain resources and not others, to use energy of a specific form and quantity and not some other."[6] These decisions are not made in a purely neutral way. They do tell users how these products can be used. Human actions are fitted into mechanical molds determined by others. How clients can use these systems to search for information or to manage their resources is to a large extent determined by the ways in which others have designed the system according to their interests and not necessarily in accord with the needs and interests of the user.

Computer scientists and others have proposed principles and guidelines to protect the integrity of information content. They include:

- respect for intellectual property
- respect for privacy
- fair representation
- do no harm[7]

In this era of digitized information, violation of intellectual property rights has become a major issue as publishers and producers look for ways to protect their resources. At the same time, researchers are looking for ways to guarantee the principle of fair use so that those resources can be used for teaching and research. Privacy issues affect each one of us. One has only to check various databases on the Internet to find that our driver's license numbers, credit information, and other information is available. We know that our buying habits have been identified and are part of the marketing activities of those stores at which we shop. We have no way of knowing who is profiling us and for what purpose. Information that is only partially presented and therefore not fairly represented can mislead the reader. All of these issues contain major ethical components, and each has the potential of doing harm.

Alfino and Pierce ask the question, "[Are librarians in their practice of ethics] passive captives of larger forces—the demands of patrons, the changing values of the community, the needs and authority of 'knowledge workers' in the various disciplines—that limit their sphere of activity?"[8] Or do they take a leadership role in applying ethical standards to the information issues that confront them daily? In the workplace, librarians have "self-consciously faced a number of specific questions about the nature and extent of their professional life and autonomy, e.g., do they see others as generally self-organizing or in need of guidance?"[9]

Zipkowitz advocated a covenant between librarians and clients, peers and society "that we act in good faith as advocates for our users, and render service to them that is good, just, honorable, decent, proper, scrupulous, complete, and conscientious."[10] Alfino and Pierce operationalize this by saying that "minimally, librarians should be invited to gather, present, and discuss resources which help people think through contemporary and political issues. Librarians are well suited to be curators of the community's cultural experience and identity, providing a kind of 'applied ethology' for the library's service area. . . . In the information age, the library is a point of departure for information and culture that lies beyond its walls."[11] The librarian serves as guide to information both inside the library and what is outside the library. Information is not neutral and neither are librarians. It is the responsibility of the librarian to stay focused on core values and to practice them in all interactions.

Expectations by users of information services are that the professional providing the service conforms to certain principles of service. These are the principles that are set forth in the profession's code of ethics. The elements of the code relate directly to the areas of primary concern to the specific profession. The American Library Association (ALA) code of ethics is an excellent example of a professional code designed to provide guidelines for action. The history of the development of ALA's code of ethics follows a pattern similar to that of other professional associations. After a period of little action during the early twentieth century, a flurry of activity in the late 1920s resulted in a long, prescriptive code. After some activity in the 1930s, little happened until the 1970s when the development of a code of ethics became an important agenda item. The present code was adopted in 1981 and has been revised regularly since then.

THE ALA CODE OF ETHICS

I. We provide the highest level of service to all library users through appropriate and usefully organized resources, equitable service policies; equitable access; and accurate, unbiased, and courteous responses to all requests.

II. We uphold the principles of intellectual freedom and resist all efforts to censor library resources.

III. We protect each library user's right to privacy and confidentiality with respect to information sought or received and resources consulted, borrowed, acquired, or transmitted.

IV. We recognize and respect intellectual property rights.

V. We treat co-workers and other colleagues with respect, fairness, and good faith, and advocate conditions of employment that safeguard the rights and welfare of all employees in our institutions.

VI. We do not advance private interests at the expense of library users, colleagues, or our employing institutions

VII. We distinguish between our personal convictions and professional duties and do not allow our personal beliefs to interfere with fair representation of the aims of our institutions or the provision of access to their information resources.

VIII. We strive for excellence in the profession by maintaining and enhancing our own knowledge and skills, by encouraging the professional development of co-workers, and by fostering the aspirations of potential members of the profession.

The code, as with most such codes, is a system of norms. It deals with integrity, social responsibility, accountability, and the protection of privacy. It addresses the issues of conflict of interest and personal conduct. The code is an expression of the ethical stance of its professional association, which reviews and revises it regularly.

A profession is by definition self-regulating. Its members set the standard of behavior. Members of the association learn of these standards and their relation to practice during their period of professional education and later through interaction with professional colleagues in both formal workshops and informal activities. Professionals are expected to adhere to the standards. In most professions, there is no effective means of disciplining nonadherents to the code. Social pressure, which may or may not be effective, is the primary recourse of the profession. The lack of an effective means to enforce standards of performance and behavior has given rise to numerous accountability measures, particularly in education. Accountability measures are being used as legislative tools to require educational standards of achievement through the testing of teachers and students. (See chapter 15 for discussion of program assessment.) While its usefulness is often questioned, it is an example of an outside agency placing pressure on a profession to perform. Other mechanisms that are active in the market also serve to discipline those who do not adhere to ethical behavior. Examples include the federal legislative response to numerous business failures in the first years of the twenty-first century brought about in part by unethical business practices. The message is clear, although not heard by all professions and professionals: if one does not adhere to an acceptable standard of ethical behavior, some other group or agency will do it for you and your independence of action is lost.

SUMMARY

Social and technological change keep the workplace continuously transforming. New issues arise, new possibilities are presented. What does not change are the principles we use to evaluate our interactions with colleagues and the public. They expect and must receive ethically responsible treatment.

NOTES

1. Thomas E. Hill, *Ethics in Theory and Practice* (New York: Thomas Y. Crowell, 1956), 2.

2. Emile Durkheim, *Professional Ethics and Civic Morals* (Glencoe, Ill.: Free Press, 1958), 3.

3. Michael D. Bayles, *Professional Ethics* (Belmont, Calif.: Wadsworth, 1981), 3.

4. Peter Drucker, *Management: Tasks, Responsibilities, and Practices* (New York: Harper and Row, 1974), 366–75.

5. Mark Alfino and Linda Pierce, *Information Ethics for Librarians* (Jefferson, N.C.: McFarland, 1997), 58.

6. Clifford G. Christians, "Information ethics in a complicated age," in *Ethics and the Librarian*, edited by F. W. Lancaster (Urbana: University of Illinois Graduate School of Library and Information Science, 1989), 8.

7. Richard J. Severson, *The Principles of Information Ethics* (Armonk, N.Y.: M. E. Sharpe, 1997), 17.

8. Alfino and Pierce, *Information Ethics*, 15.

9. Alfino and Pierce, *Information Ethics*, 58.

10. Fay Zipkowitz, *Professional Ethics in Librarianship: A Real-Life Casebook* (Jefferson, N.C.: McFarland, 1996), 2.

11. Alfino and Pierce, *Information Ethics*, 133.

ADDITIONAL READINGS

Bayles, Michael D. *Professional Ethics.* Belmont, Calif.: Wadsworth, 1981.

Bowie, Norman E. *Ethical Issues in Government.* Philadelphia: Temple University Press, 1981.

Carbo, Toni. "Challenges for libraries, creating one world: Information ethics and policy issues for medical librarians." *Journal of the Medical Library Association* 91, no. 3 (July 2003): 281–85.

Carbo, Toni, and Stephen Almagno. "Information ethics: The duty, privilege and challenge of educating information professionals." *Library Trends* 49, no. 3 (Winter 2001): 510–19.

Carlin, Andrew P. "Disciplinary debates and bases of interdisciplinary studies: The place of research ethics in library and information science." *Library and Information Science Research* 25, no. 1 (Spring 2003): 3–19.

Johnson, Doug. "Proactively teaching technology ethics." *Library Media Connection* 22, no. 4 (January 2004): 24–26.

Lancaster, F. W., ed. *Ethics and the Librarian.* Allerton Park Institute #31, University of Illinois, Graduate School of Library and Information Science, 1991.

Lindsey, Jonathan A., and Ann E. Prentice. *Professional Ethics and Librarians.* Phoenix, Ariz.: Oryx Press, 1985.

Part II

MANAGEMENT: PUTTING THEORY INTO PRACTICE

Chapter Five

The Organization and Its Function

An organization "may be defined as [a] large, fairly permanent social system designed to achieve limited objectives through co-ordinated activities of [its] members. . . . Membership and responsibility can be assigned and 'organizational' activities, values, and expectations can be differentiated from those that are extra-organization."[1] An organization is a small social system that inculcates approved ideas, culture, attitudes, and behaviors. An organization is a multipurpose tool for shaping the world as one wishes it to be. An organization is the key structure that brings together resources, including individuals, to achieve goals. It is the structure along which formal communication moves. It is also a tool for controlling the actions of individuals in order to achieve specific purposes and is an important means of gaining and maintaining power. While the organization can be managed by those who are part of it, it has been known to become a driving force in its own right. Presthus suggests that bureaucratic organizations seem less concerned with the individual than with the promotion of organizational goals.[2]

FORMAL ORGANIZATIONS

The formal organization is a clearly defined structure that can be presented on an organization chart that shows positions and their relationship to one another. There are descriptions for each position on the chart. Each level of position reports to the level above it. Communication flows upward and downward through the lines of the organization chart. As the organization grows, the chart becomes more complex. More specialized positions emerge and new units are added. The formal organization represents an ideal situation and is rarely an exact representation of practice, as it is difficult to fit exactly individuals and positions into such structures. While the formal organization works well in a stable environment, it tends to become rigid and therefore does not work well in an environment in which changing conditions, both internal and external, are the norm.

INFORMAL ORGANIZATIONS

Wherever there is a formal organization, there is also an informal organization: "the unofficial and unauthorized relationships that inevitably occur between individuals and groups within the formal organization."[3] These relationships are not subject to management control but operate outside the lines of authority of the formal organization chart. The informal organization meets those individual needs not addressed by the formal organization: social needs, the need for affiliation, and the need for belonging. The informal organization may have its expected standards of behavior—which may or may not conform to the expectations of the formal organization or of management. Its members may, for example, have attitudes toward a diverse workforce that are in conflict with those of management. A woman entering a formerly all-male field such as sports broadcasting may be welcomed by management represented by the formal organization but most unwelcome to an all-male informal organization.

The informal organization can serve as a liaison between the supervisor and staff. When a supervisor assigns tasks in support of organizational objectives, members of the informal organization may discuss appropriate assignments and determine within the group the best way to accomplish the task. When the objectives of the informal organization and those of the formal organization are in agreement, this is a strong positive reinforcement of both elements of the organization. When they are in conflict, it is a signal that serious problems exist that can undermine the formal authority of the manager. In a pre-information-saturated world, the most valuable role of the informal organization was to serve as a communication network, often called the grapevine. In today's information-rich environment, the need to move information up and down the formal organization continues to be most important and is greatly enhanced through the use of e-mail and related activities. It is critical that the informal organization support the objectives of the organization and that the manager work well with it. While management can influence the informal organization, it cannot control it.

ORGANIZATIONAL THEORY

Organization in the twentieth century has, to a large degree, become synonymous with bureaucracy, a hierarchical structure of authority with well-defined rules and roles. The most well-known proponent of the bureaucratic model of organization was Max Weber, who developed it based on his background and experiences in early twentieth-century Germany, and it reflects the culture of that place and time. Weber was concerned by the nepotism he saw in the organizations he managed and looked for a more efficient means of managing. His work did not reach the United States until the 1940s, when it was translated into English by Henderson and Parsons.[4]

Weber's model has three major characteristics, each of which has a number of subcategories. The first of these characteristics is the structure and functioning of the organization. It is assumed that the bureaucratic organization functions on a continuous basis and is a permanent means of maintaining control. The bureaucracy consists of a hierarchy of offices, with each office controlled by the next higher level and, conversely, each office controls the office(s) directly below it. There is a systematic division of labor that is based on the expertise of individuals and on systematic training. In this division of labor, areas of action in which the individual is expected to be competent are specified, as are responsibilities and the power to carry out the responsibilities. Written rules and records of prior actions serve as a means of governing performance and providing control over actions.

The second characteristic of this model is that of rewards. The position in the hierarchy is the individual's primary responsibility and the individual owes it complete loyalty. The individual is accountable for use of the organization's property and the conduct of its affairs. He or she does not own the means of production or administration and cannot appropriate them for personal gain. There is a separation of work life from private life and it is implied that work life takes precedence. For this loyalty and responsibility, there are fixed salaries graded by rank.

The third characteristic of the model refers to the protection of individual rights. The individual holding an office in the bureaucracy serves voluntarily upon appointment by those at a higher level. Promotion is determined by seniority or achievement. Obedience of the employee is to the office and not to the individual who holds that office. The individual is subject to authority only on official obligations and compulsion is exercised only under certain conditions. The individual has the right of appeal.

Perrow describes this rational/legal bureaucratic model in the following manner:

1. Equal treatment of all employees
2. Reliance on expertise, skill, and experience in the position
3. No extraordinary benefits to any individual
4. Introduction of specific work and output standards
5. Maintaining of complete records on work and output
6. Rules and regulations that affect all members of the bureaucracy are set up.[5]

This structure, which evolved over time and came into being as we now know it in the twentieth century, was codified with the work of Weber. The bureaucratic model was designed for situations that do not change or change slowly. It is rigid and adapts slowly to any new priorities or procedures. In a bureaucracy, one can always find a rule or regulation to avoid dealing with problems that do not fit neatly into the structure. Bureaucracy is impersonal; the slot on the organization chart is more important than the individual. If an individual leaves the organization, someone with similar credentials can be slotted in and the bureaucracy continues to function. Over time, individuals holding a particular position in the bureaucracy can become experts in their area and may take ownership of the position, designing and/or manipulating it as they see fit. Changing the position or position description becomes impossible until that person leaves.

Objectives in the bureaucratic organization are broken down into smaller and smaller pieces as tasks are assigned to each level of the organization. What may be a clear objective to the manager at a higher level may become fragmented. Each department may then further fragment the objective until it is difficult for those further down the hierarchy to relate their specific tasks to the objective or, indeed, to know what the objective is.

Although the structure promotes stability in a world of change, critics believe that by its very nature it holds back change. It is also charged that, over time, bureaucracy becomes rule-bound and thus more complex. This complexity leads to a structure that is covered with special rules and, like a boat with barnacles, it becomes unresponsive to changes in direction and slow to move ahead. There is also a history of promoting individuals in the organization based on criteria other than those related to ability to do the work, such as similar political attitudes or similar social or cultural status. Perrow says that the charge of incompetence of a bureaucratic organization may instead be that it is following a different set of objectives.[6] If, for example, a customer wants to get information on a particular product or service and is not given the information, that customer says the bureaucracy is incompetent. From the bureaucracy's point of view, it may wish to discourage queries about that particular product or service.

Organizations may be co-opted by individuals or groups and made to serve personal agendas. Too many rules, perhaps conflicting, may grow up in an organization and cause it to become lethargic. There is an assumption by some that if you make a rule, you have solved a problem. Rules within the organization are made to regulate relations between and among units of the organization. These tend to be made to protect turf or to protect those who held power when the rules were made. Rules become the organizational memory of the ways in which the bureaucracy changes or does not change. Rules tend to remove individual judgment in a situation, to make the organization more inflexible and more standardized. Organizations may change faster than the rules that are made. Rules can be made or repealed to make change easier.[7]

During the late nineteenth and early twentieth century in the United States, the popular assumption was that workers were lazy, dumb, and needed to be controlled in order to make them work. And those who were the elite by virtue of education, birth, money, or some other self-proclaimed value, were those who were meant to control and lead. This was also the period of major migration from Europe and thousands of new workers were entering the labor force. A bureaucratic organization was one means of organizing these workers and getting them into the labor force. These were the days of the melting pot attitude toward diversity and the bureaucratic structure was a way to fit any man into a slot.

During this same period, Frederick Taylor developed his theory of scientific management. He analyzed work being done and broke jobs into tasks, applied time and motion studies to each task, and mandated the one best way in which tasks were to be done and the order in which they were to be done. He graded tasks and workers were then trained to do specific tasks. In doing so, he de-skilled a large component of the labor force. A result of this was that the pleasure in doing a job or seeing it to completion, looking at a better way to do it, or working with someone else on a task were all removed. The worker was just another cog in the machinery and, given the low level of most tasks to be done, was easily replaced should he become injured or object to the working conditions.

The idea that people wanted to be led continued to be central to organizational theory well into the 1930s. Elton Mayo and Chester Barnard said that people want to be led, to be part of something, that they needed to belong. They further said that it was management's responsibility to lead. Mayo described society as consisting of unorganized individuals, not social groups. The individual is capable of logical thought, operates on self-interest, and is not influenced by group norms. It is the responsibility of the elite to show the average worker his place in society. This movement from worker as stupid, unworthy, unwilling, and noncooperative to seeing the worker as perhaps competent but still in need of being supervised correctly was an underlying theme of the first half of the twentieth century. In the 1930s, it became fashionable for psychologists and sociologists to study the worker; numerous studies, many based on assumptions rather than fact, describing who the worker was, did, and might be, were published. Some of these studies tended to ignore data that did not agree with their views that management was rational and the worker irrational.[8]

In 1938, Barnard outlined three distinct trends in organizational theory that informed the next several decades. Prior to this there was no real theoretical base for the study of organizations.[9] These theories were the institutional school, the decision-making school, and the human relations school. Soon after this, Weber's bureaucratic model became widely available and most organizational theory since then has been a contrast between the bureaucratic (which places the structure in the primary slot) and the human relations and related schools (which place the worker in a more important slot). Neither of these solved the problem of defining individual behavior in relation to the organization. Barnard championed the group and saw the individual as subservient to it; people working in a group to achieve common goals was more important than the individual. Inducements were to be present in the workplace to convince the worker to defer to the wishes of the group. Barnard recognized that informal organizational elements were present in the workplace but said that they were of little or no value. His writings glorified the organization and minimized the value of the individual.

Human Relations Model

This approach to organization grew from research, much of it begun in the 1930s by psychologists and sociologists. Their main theme was that workers, if well treated, would work. Fitting this simple statement into a complex organizational structure was a difficult task. One approach, that by Douglas McGregor, was the formulation of Theory X and Theory Y. Theory X stated that the worker is lazy, will not work, and cannot be trusted to do the job. He must be forced to work. Theory Y, on the other hand, stated that the worker wants to work and, given the opportunity, will do a good job. Human relations advocates believed that if one treated the worker better, productivity would increase. This would satisfy the employer because of increased productivity and the worker because of the satisfaction of a job well done.

Rensis Likert's model, published in 1961, was based on the contrast between the exploitative/authoritative model and the participation management model and focused on the interaction of groups. He laid out four systems of organization:

1. The exploitative authoritarian system, which corresponds to Theory X
2. The benevolent authoritative model, which is paternalistic with Theory X as a base
3. The consultative model
4. The participative model

He listed forty-two aspects of organization (increased to fifty-one in his 1967 model) and the values of each aspect were listed under each system. They dealt with such issues as leadership, the nature of motivational forces, interaction, communication, decision making, the setting and ordering of goals, performance goals, and training.[10] Most of the items are generic and difficult to disagree with. After setting up his complex model, he continued to advocate *the one best way*, using the model as a justification of this. Like most advocates of the human relations model, he saw all organizations as basically similar and said that differences such as size, technology, objectives, and goals were irrelevant to the essential organizational structure.

Tannenbaum in 1968 said that neither the bureaucratic nor the participative organization was necessarily the one best way.[11] He conducted a study of hierarchy in organizations in five countries representing five different cultures and concluded that social structure rather than interpersonal relations is a more substantial base for understanding an organization. Perrow argues that the sociological and psychological models on which the human relations models are based assume a rational individual.[12] The sociologists and psychologists then try to fit the rational individual they have defined into behaviors and then into an organization. Taylor, conversely, took the job apart and designed jobs to fit people into slots to complete the job. The human relations school analyzed individual behaviors and then slotted them into the organization. These approaches ignored the whole job and the whole person in favor of the organizational structure in which they were to fit.

The Decision-Making Model

Herbert Simon and James March put forth the concept of organization as a problem of social psychology.[13] They then looked at organizational decision making, saying that organizations are made up of individuals whose individual social characteristics influence their decisions. They assume that the individual is not completely rational and his behavior within the organization can be controlled by the organization.

In Simon's organization, goals are set by the leader and are broken into subgoals for each level of the organization. The goals tend to be stable and rarely change much over time. Routines are set up; there are standard operating procedures that do not change unless objectives are not met under these procedures, and if that is the case then the smallest amount of adjustment is made. Change is slow and reactive. This model drives out planning, as routine is stressed. It adapts information that comes into the organization to the established routine. Information in this model can be seen as a disruptive force, as it may bring into question the objectives or even the routine. The focus is on organizational structure with authority coming from the top. Although Simon said that the organizational structure points to the right way to do things, workers see the leader as giving orders. The leader has the responsibility to mediate among organizational goals and does so by allocating resources. If there is the perceived need to change individual behavior, one does not change the individual but one changes the premise of their decisions. "These premises are to be found in the vocabulary of the organization, the structure of communication, rules and regulations, standard programs, selection criteria for personnel, and so on—in short the structural aspects"[14] Behavior is also shaped through internal communication and the culture of the organization. For those involved in nonroutine work in the organization, usually those with professional responsibilities, premise indoctrination is done through their schooling that is specific to the profession and through the professional organization that reinforces these premises. Community norms outside the specifically professional groups also enforce the premises. The worker at any level in the organization thus knows what is expected and how to behave. High morale is often defined by researchers as how happy one is in working for the organization rather than by salary or working conditions. What is described here is a bureaucratic organization in the Weberian definition plus a paternalistic overlay. One conforms to the organization as it is the approved thing to do and one is expected to be happy in doing so.

THE EVOLVING ORGANIZATION

In the 1960s, other discussions of types of organizations and their differences took place. Perhaps there was no one best way. In the 1950s and 1960s, the sociological view of the organization was that structure is defined by function and function is defined by structure. Perhaps a typology could be based on organizational characteristics independent of structure and independent of goals. Could an organization be described by tasks performed and might a hierarchy of tasks be devised? If there are many nonroutine tasks such as those requiring professional knowledge, a looser organization with less hierarchy could be set. Even when one defines the organization by task, much of what is done will be routine and thus fit into the bureaucratic mode.[15] Looking at the organization from different perspectives and looking it as a whole shows that there are some elements common to all organizations. These include goals, resources, and objectives. Some organizational structures, through their culture and rules and regulations, can become more powerful than those who hold administrative positions of control over the organization. The level of control by individuals or by culture and rules is a defining element of the organization.

There has been an ongoing conflict between bureaucracy and the democratic ideals of "free expression, individual worth, and spontaneity."[16] The bureaucratic organization forces one to choose between what is good for the organization and what is good for one's personal goals. The forced standardization of the individual to fit into the organization has been a common theme throughout the twentieth century and continues. Recall Charlie Chaplin movies in which the hero was constantly running afoul of the machine but by the glint in his eye and the smile on his face, one knew that he was doing it on purpose. Or recall the organization man of the 1950s who, in his gray flannel suit, sublimated home, family, and happiness to the demands of the organization.[17] While these responses were very different, each is representative of the individual's response to functioning in a bureaucracy.

Another thread running through this same period is that systems of organization are rational; when they don't work, it is because the worker is not conforming. There was continuing concern about specialists with special skills and/or knowledge, as they were even more difficult to fit into the organization than the unskilled worker. And they refused to do as they were told. Their knowledge challenged hierarchical control, as they knew the issues and problems in their field and could or would not be told arbitrarily by management how to deal with them. This conflict between management and the specially skilled continues and is prevalent in all organizational structures.

And then came Peter Drucker, who is seen by many as the management guru of the last third of the twentieth century.[18] A supporter of the hierarchical organization, he said that organizational structure follows strategy and that that strategy must be planned. In building the organization, he asked the following questions:

- What should the results of the organization be?
- What components should be connected and which separate?
- What size and shape should each component have?
- What is the placement and relationship of the parts?[19]

He went on to say that management is people and it is their activity that energizes the organization and that its survival depends on good management.[20] While he focused on managing the organization, he was also very clear in wanting a hierarchical structure to manage.[21] His views were very much tied to their decade both in terms of organization and management, his views of the social environment, and his attitude toward technology, although his later books show an evolving view of technology.

Tom Peters, who first came to public notice along with Robert Waterman with the publication of *In Search of Excellence*, approaches organization and management by emphasizing the need to manage ambiguity and paradox.[22] To do this, all organizations must have a capacity for irrationality and creativity. He said that the organization chart is not the organization but is the point at which one begins to change.[23] He warned that it is difficult to take the organization apart, as old habits are present in many individuals who fear change. He also cautions that moving boxes around on the organization chart is not change.[24] Any organizational culture includes deeply ingrained ways of doing things, some of which may no longer serve a useful purpose. There may be structures, rules, attitudes toward workers, or other elements that get in the way of doing the job. There are organizations in which asking questions or suggesting changes are seen as disloyal behaviors.

For Peters and Waterman, the purpose of an organization is not primarily to structure the workforce or the work. Its role is to serve the customer. An organization cannot organize the customer; it can only identify the customer. The customer must want what the organization provides and this is the role of marketing. Peters and Waterman emphasize that the organization, any organization, must be customer-driven and not profit- or quantity-driven. It must have an obsession for quality and a reputation for reliability. It also requires paying close attention to the customer. This holds true in the not-for-profit sector as well as in the for-profit sector.

In their research, Peters and Waterman were not looking for a new theory or plan for an organizational structure. Instead, they identified seven variables that constitute an organization—structure, strategy, management style, systems, shared values (organizational culture), skills present or desired, and people—and then identified forty-three companies with excellent reputations to see what made them excellent.[25] They found that while a rational organizational model is important, one must allow for the human and the irrational. They found that strict adherence to the rational model often killed new ideas and discouraged experimentation and the possibility of making mistakes while moving toward new ideas. The rationalist is not comfortable with informality and is more interested in numbers than in values. Philip Selznik pursues this further to say that "where institutionalization [of the organization] is well advanced, distinctive outlooks, habits and other commitments are unified, coloring all aspects of organizational life, and lending it a social integration that goes well beyond formal coordination and command."[26] Such a situation has advantages but it also tends to limit the ability to see the new and to adapt.

As a result of their research, Peters and Waterman identified four basic human needs in an organization:

1. Need for meaning. "The culture of the organization regulates vigorously the few variables that do count and it provides meaning."[27] They

give IBM's dedication to service to the customer as an example of an organization having meaning.

2. Need for some control
3. Need for positive reinforcement
4. The degree to which actions and behavior shape attitudes and not vice versa.[28]

They go on to list additional important attributes of a successful organization. An organization has a life cycle. As it matures, it may become less nimble and become overly concerned with rules. It is important to keep the organization always moving and always changing to meet its goals. This activity is often referred to as the adapting organization or the learning organization.[29] Decentralization of the organization allows for nimbleness and the ability to respond quickly to local concerns. Setting up small experimental groups to test new ideas or appointing ad hoc groups to study environmental issues provide information for possible new directions. Experimental organizations can be set up to *do it, try it, fix it*.[30] Waiting to go through traditional organizational decision-making steps is long, costly, and by the time a decision is made, it is often too late for the new activity to make any difference. The adaptive organization can move, change, and keep current with and perhaps even ahead of the issue. As an organization grows, communication and coordination become more difficult. New ways of doing things are in order. The authors stress the need for continuous internal communication and the need to set up opportunities for doing so. The extensive use of information technology greatly enhances the opportunities. It can also change relationships in the organization as communication flows in new or broader directions. An organization must have a bias for action and not become tied up in rules or structure or by following precedent. How something was done last year may be helpful to know, but today isn't last year. One should expect a certain amount of messiness in the organization, as individuals do not exactly fit into organizational structures and environmental conditions change daily.

Peters, in both *In Search of Excellence* and *Liberation Management*, is representative of the 1990s and early twenty-first-century writers who subscribe to the view that one gains productivity through people.[31] Rather than building a structured organization into which workers are slotted or developing means to ensure that workers conform to the organization and its culture, one should treat them as colleagues and set them free to use their own skills and knowledge. They will perform well if they are truly treated as colleagues and when, through appropriate training and information, they have the know-how to make decisions. Creativity on the part of workers is encouraged and rewarded. In this environment there are no barriers to communication flow. The use of e-mail has been beneficial here as it opens up all areas of the organization to everyone and everyone can know what is going on at any time on any topic. While there are no guarantees of success, chances are that this is a high-productivity environment.

To summarize his views on organizations, Peters described five forms of organization:

1. The functional organization. This form is efficient, is strong on the basic activities required to achieve tasks and meet goals. It is not particularly creative, adapts slowly, and often misses important opportunities.

2. The divisional organization. This series of organizations within a larger unit is much like the functional format in that it is strong on the basic activities but not particularly creative. Because it can be smaller than the functional format, it is more adaptive. Should it get too large, it can be divided. This format can have a mix of centralized and decentralized activities.

3. The matrix organization. This type of organization is a response to a variety of pressures both internal and external. In focusing on pressures (e.g., political and economic), it has difficulty in focusing on the basics or being creative. This type of organization lacks long-term direction and can degenerate in time into anarchy where each individual does his or her own thing or into a bureaucracy where some form of functional structure is imposed. This is a reactive format and without strong direction does not succeed.

4. The ad hocracy format. This format ignores the basic elements of organization and depends on the individuals involved and on whatever internal and external pressures are at play. It can be very creative and responsive in solving problems and achieving goals. A number of high-technology companies began with this format. Unless they moved on to a more structured format, they did not survive beyond the early creativity period.

5. The missionary format. Here a course of action or a person leads the

activity and is the structure on which it rests. It can be creative or can become rigid and narrow minded.[32]

Taking the best from each of these formats, Peters proposed a three-part criterion for the successful organization. The organization requires a consistent underlying form. This form can be built around the product or service to be delivered. It does not have a life of its own; for example, the bureaucratic organization can be used to structure any activity without attention to the tasks to be performed. It also needs to be based on broad, enduring values that everyone in the organization knows. In addition to the stability provided by strong values and a simple and consistent underlying form, the organization needs to be entrepreneurial. It should be structured in sufficiently small units to keep it close to the activities it performs in order to allow for maximum adaptability. A means of measuring progress and the ability to adapt when progress is not sufficient provides direction. And, finally, one must be willing to change the organizational structure if it doesn't work and to replace it with a new structure.[33] The focus of today and tomorrow's organization is on problem solving and on achieving goals through the efforts of people. To do this, build a simple, small organizational structure that meets that expectation. Adapt the organization to the people and the task, and not, as had been the case for a century or more, adapt people and tasks to the organizational structure.

A decade after *In Search of Excellence*, Peters published *Liberation Management: Necessary Disorganization for the Nanosecond Nineties* in which he said that necessary disorganization is the appropriate approach to organization and decision making.[34] Expanding on his earlier statements, he continued to champion the abilities and possibilities of the employee who is expected to perform well, to be creative, and to move the organization ahead. He also stresses that one does not build the appropriate organizational structure by building on past inadequate structures. "Paving the cow paths" does not solve the problem.[35]

INFORMATION TECHNOLOGY
AND THE ORGANIZATION

Information technology has had and continues to have a profound effect on the bureaucratic structure of the organization. While the skeleton of the organization remains as the structure on which jobs are placed and objectives mapped, the ways in which work is organized and communication and information flow have multiplied. Wherever we look, many variations of organizational forms are present. In times of social and technical change, new organizational forms tend to develop. The industrial revolution gave rise to new structures and the information revolution has done and continues to do the same thing today. The perceived need for order in industry resulted in the development of bureaucracy. With the new technologies, a global economy, and a better-educated and more independent workforce, new forms and variations of organizational structure are emerging.

While the worker in a bureaucratic system could become more and more competent in an increasingly narrow area of expertise, today's workers must continuously learn new skills, adapt old ones, and look for innovation in work patterns. "Instead of a role anchored by the organization and codified by a job description, the new forms are offering a role defined by the task of the moment and the location of the worker."[36] While this situation is just what many workers want, others less adaptable to change find it threatening and highly stressful. Within an organization, the manager will find both those workers who thrive in an ever-changing learning environment and those who wish for what they perceive as stability.

Technological change includes not just the need for an organization to accept new ideas. It goes to the core of how one manages problem solving in the organization. It is not a cosmetic addition to the organization but requires reviewing the organizational structure to see new ways in which individuals can work "across organizational and functional boundaries to identify problems and develop solutions."[37] The need to interact with individuals and units outside one's familiar territory is for many workers an opportunity to learn and grow. For others, it is a threat to their sense of security and control in a defined area.

Technological change causes uncertainty and disruption in the organization. There is a point at which it becomes evident to the staff that changes need to be made in the way they organize their work and carry it out. There will be a point at which there is a readiness for change and it is at this point that the manager will be more successful in implementing change. To reduce the disruption that change can create, careful planning is necessary so that employees know what changes will be made and what the implications may be. They need to be informed before, during, and after the implementation of new processes and activities that will in some way affect them. This learning and informing process tends to ease stress and increase the comfort level with the changes once they are in place. Despite this, Tyre and Hauptman discovered that technological changes often have unexpected implications for parts of the organization not directly affected by the initial change.[38] Those who stress that the organization will be improved by the use of information and communications technology to reduce labor costs, speed transactions, and streamline processes tend not to mention that costs may increase and, while labor costs in one area may be reduced, new staff may be needed to manage the technology.

Brown and Duguid call the office/workplace a social system with a collective knowledge that supports the workers.[39] When technological change disrupts the workplace, it is necessary to reach a new balance. How will the worker in a home office connect to colleagues to share collective knowledge? Is it possible to manage people remotely? (Brown and Duguid say no.) How can someone working remotely learn in and from a community of practice? New connections must be forged in order to connect people who work on the same or similar objectives, but are no longer in the same physical location. Managers may have the sense that they have lost supervisory control over employees who communicate electronically and who are no longer in the same place at the same time. While organizational rules and regulations can be built into the software that employees use, this does not replace face-to-face communication. Zhuboff points out that in a traditional environment, job descriptions define the worker's responsibility and evaluating this is important in allocating raises, giving promotions, and working with the individual to improve performance.[40] In the new world of work, managers need new ways to evaluate performance. The next major area of research on organizations will focus on the appropriate balance between the individual and the technology and ways to gain maximum productivity in the new more flexible organization.

Cosmetic change in an organization does not work.

Success requires a more complete make over, namely rethinking the model for how to organize the work of the whole organization. It requires challenging traditional assumptions about relationships with customers, internal and external communication, decision making, operating style, management behavior, employee motivation, and retention, and then defining a new way. That's a human problem, not a technological problem.[41]

The role of technology is to provide new tools to respond to human concerns.

Bringing information technology into an organization is not a process of determining which current activities can be automated. While early computerization was introduced to allow the organization to speed traditional number crunching, data storage, and access, it became evident that information technology could be used to do more than replicate existing tasks. It also became evident that when one speeded up some processes, there were implications for related activities and staffing. In order to introduce information technology innovation into the organization, it is necessary to review existing processes and ask if they are the best means of accomplishing tasks. What innovation, what changes would improve the process? Or, is the process necessary at all? Once we have looked at the organization's objectives, reviewed current means of achieving them, and assessed those current means to ensure that we have the correct processes in place, then we can ask what technology we need to accomplish the task. In this process, we may have reshaped the organization by combining some activities, separating others, eliminating some, and adding some.

Concurrent with technological advances, the workplace is moving toward new views of work. Sometimes these views come from the possibilities for change because of new technological opportunities and sometimes a new organizational structure is developed and then a technology to enhance it is sought. New individual skills are needed as "the new technologies also force adoption of more sophisticated mechanisms in the hierarchy of coordination, e.g., task forces, teams, project coordinators, and entire integrating of departments."[42] In some instances, researchers found that information technology processes were intended to reduce ambiguity and to come up with stable routines in currently unstable environments. "Traditional organizations reduce complexity by dividing the situation into specific aspects; technical, human, economic, etc., and by stabilizing production processes into routines."[43] "In contrast . . . tomorrow's organizations will be designed as explicit collective learning processes in which teams of individuals or even complex social systems will have as a goal the knowledge about unknown social environments."[44]

The need to group people together in specific ways for supervision and coordination or the need to have either a centralized or decentralized structure is less an issue in an information technology environment. Lucas and Baroudi argue that "many of the organizational possibilities enabled by information technology have either been overlooked or not well understood in the academic literature."[45]

In classical organization design writings, a key element is coordination of activities and or supervision. Organizational structures that at one time required physical proximity can now be dispersed. One can scatter a department throughout a building, an organization, or the world and still maintain close contact. Information and telecommunications technology links people electronically and can add or eliminate links and groups as desired. "In some bureaucratic organizations, layers of management exist to look at, edit, and approve messages that flow from the layer below them to the level above."[46] With information technology, these layers can be eliminated thus making communication easier and streamlining the organization.

Information technology "enables a new form of work, which some described 'as the possibility of setting up an office anywhere.'" The organization brings the combined characteristics of the organic, and network organization to the fore and pushes control down to the operational level.[47] Following upon an analogy that the organizational structure is the skeleton of the organization, Travica calls the communication link that supports individuals and teams in the organization the spinal cord of the organization. The exchange of information through the communications link supports both individuals and teams in their work. Redesigning the organization is a difficult task, as it requires major changes in the ways in which individuals work. It is easier in new organizations that do not yet have an entrenched bureaucracy and rigid ways of doing things. It is particularly difficult to make changes in organizations that are part of a government structure, as the overall governmental structure with its many rules and regulations works to prevent change that is more than cosmetic.

Discussions leading to change that are part of the introduction of technology into the organization give involved workers an opportunity to understand the ways in which the organization is structured. They also give the employee a broader view of the business of the organization as well as a deepened understanding of his or her own tasks and his or her role in the wider organization. "When work becomes synonymous with responsiveness to data [as is the case in an information technology rich organization] it engenders inquiry and dialogue, thus opening the way for workers to envision new possibilities and fresh alternatives to the reigning definitions of process, product, and organization."[48] In the new organization, organizational behavior is more transparent, as more workers can observe activities and have more access to information. "Fast open access to information and the ability to communicate directly with nearly everyone anywhere sets e-culture apart from traditional environments."[49] In this new culture, it is wiser and safer to spread information widely than to try to restrict access, as it is no longer really possible to hide information.

We continue to learn about the opportunities that are available through the use of information technology in creating and operating the organization. There is no area of the organization that is not affected. Among the major changes afforded by information technology and telecommunication is the vastly increased availability of information to all members of the organization. No longer can information, once seen as a private source of power and control by leadership, be held by the few. Internal information is organized into databases available to large sections of the organization. External databases that provide information on competition and the external forces that impact decision making are widely available. The Internet has provided many newly available sources of information and has also provided a new environment for marketing goods and services. It also provides those who use or may use the goods and services with the opportunity to gain insights into the organization and its activities and thus make more informed choices as to whether or not they are interested in the product/service. Peters calls this new state of affairs the "*insiderization* of outsiders and the *informating* of all employees."[50]

E-mail has become a major means of communication, both internal and external. It is a rapid means of communicating within the organization. The project leader can in one message and at one time communicate with all team members wherever in the world they may be. No longer is it necessary to call a meeting or make many phone calls every time information needs to be disseminated. Team members can communicate with one another and with the team leader to share progress, problems, documents, and so forth. This formal communication network binds a team regardless of geographic location. Informal communication flows easily as well and serves to build communities of workers. We have moved from a culture of information being passed down a chain of authority to one in which information goes up and down and across the organization at the same time. Networking internally and externally adds to the richness of an organization's knowledge pool as it connects with experts on a subject, provides access to market information, and connects to the customer. As you change the information flow, you change the organization—ways of reporting, locus of power, and so on. The traditional view of the organization as a structure with goals, objectives, and located in a particular area or areas is a limiting one and does not mesh with the electronic possibilities. Here again, don't just build the new organization on the old foundation but review the old and, where appropriate, revise or build new.

Networks change our definition of size. One can have a core organization that is small but linked electronically in many directions. Some of these links are central to the organization's tasks while others may be used for peripheral information or to join with groups having special expertise. One can decentralize the organization and build an internal network of small task-driven teams that are focused on specific activities but connected to peer task groups. This brings each small group close to the action it is responsible for and to its customers. There is less control in the old bureaucratic, hierarchical sense but more individual accountability. One should not assume that information technology in an organization will save money or necessarily reduce complexity, however. "Administrative overhead, far from being curtailed by the introduction of office automation and subsequent information technologies, has increased steadily over a broad range of industries."[51]

Any discussion of the impact of information technology on the organization becomes dated quickly as new technologies are developed and adopted. The potential for change in an organization and in education has just begun to be realized. As new generations of computer literate and information literate workers move into the workforce, changes will accelerate. These entrants into the workforce will understand more of what an informated work environment can be and will doubtless have less and less patience with slow-moving, highly structured organizations.

As information technology and telecommunications have grown and expanded, there has been a tendency to expect too much from it too soon. While we are no longer in the experimental stages in many areas, much has to be developed by the hardware, software, and information professionals and much needs to be learned by those wishing to use these tools. The heavy load placed on the telecommunications infrastructure by a society anxious for interconnection at many levels has stretched its resources. However, as telecommunication is increasingly able to carry the load, as the technology becomes increasingly sophisticated and user friendly, and as users become more comfortable with information technology, changes will be easier to incorporate into the workplace.

The new organization may well be centered on projec̶ a group of experts who approach the whole task and wor̶ teams plete it. The functional aspects of the task will be taken over by made u̶ bers; units such as finance or personnel may no longer exist independ̶ as the team will manage these aspects as they relate to the project. Projec̶ teams may last days or many years depending upon the task. They may include outsiders, particularly customers and suppliers who bring necessary perspectives. In this team environment evaluation will be based on performance as a team member, external relationship management, the ability to apply expertise, a desire to learn and expand one's expertise, and the willingness to teach others. The team will reorganize constantly to be in the best shape to do the task at the time.[52] The team will be fully connected and informed through the use of appropriate information technology. What does not change in this flexible and informed organizational format is the commitment to goals and underlying values of the organization of which the team is a part, nor does the requirement that one trust one's fellow workers to do their best change

Some individuals welcome the opportunity to telecommute so that they can work from home or elsewhere. Others miss the interaction with colleagues and the opportunity to learn from one another. Brown and Duguid say that the office is a social system with collective knowledge and that this is essential to personal satisfaction in the workplace. In order to gain the most from information technology, workers need to work together and to share information technology in order to have the technology work smoothly for them.[53]

One thing that does not change as rapidly as the technology or organizational theory is the attitude of the individual. People have differing attitudes toward structure and how much structure they need in the workplace to feel comfortable. Some learn new technologies rapidly and find their use a positive challenge. Others prefer to do things as they have always done them. Technology has the potential to slot people back into a rigid structure where tasks are outlined and there is no opportunity for independent action. Standardization of policies, procedures, goals, and ways of completing tasks are all possible through the use of information technology. Experience with Taylor's scientific management and with bureaucratic structures has taught us that this does not work and should be avoided.

THE LEARNING ORGANIZATION

...ning is essential for everyone in an organization. For an ...o survive, employees need to learn more, do more, try more, ...re responsible for personal growth. This means not just learning ...chnologies but also learning to work productively with one another. ...o not control the environment but must adapt to it through continuous ...arning in order to build and adapt an organizational structure that works. "Organizations by and large are not capable of more than marginal changes, while the environment is so volatile that marginal changes are frequently insufficient to ensure survival.[54]

Peter Senge asserts that the ability to learn and to learn faster may be the only sustainable competitive advantage for an organization.[55] He then outlines five component technologies for the learning organization. The first of these is to use systems thinking in approaching issues. Look at the whole picture or pattern and not just one piece of it. He then emphasizes the need for personal mastery, the need for "continually clarifying and deepening our personal vision, of focusing our energies, of developing patience, and of seeing in a truly objective manner.[56] Many organizations beat individuals down and into a shape to fit into the existing structure and to conform to the existing culture. Those individuals who are unwilling to submit look elsewhere for employment. The result for the organization is a loss of creativity and a reduction in morale. Senge recommends that each individual build personal mental models of how she or he sees the world working. Sharing these models can be the basis for a shared vision of future activities within the organization that one can support and work toward. This comes together in the final step of learning, which is team learning. Senge sees these five steps as residing in the team environment.

Organizations don't stay on top long unless they understand the environment and are able to adapt to it. Organizations tend to take on a life of their own and its members can exhibit a number of negative attitudes including the following.

- A confusion of self with the job, where the individual identifies too closely with the job.
- Looking outside the organization for reasons for failure when the reasons are internal. The enemy of progress may be ourselves.

- When facts are missing, there may be the desire to act for the sake of doing something. This usually is guaranteed to make things worse.
- Looking at short-term reasons as the cause of a problem rather than at the problem in a larger context. Senge cites the parable of the boiled frog. If a frog is tossed into hot water, it leaps out but if it is put into warm water and the temperature gradually increased, it does not react as strongly to gradually increasing stress until it is too late to ensure survival. It is important to see the slow-growing threat and not just the immediate one.
- We learn from experience but the new situation is never identical to the old one and experience is only part of what we need to apply to the situation.
- If one thinks that the management team is in charge and it is the sole source of good management, one is shirking one's responsibility to participate.[57]

In the learning organization, finding solutions to problems requires systems thinking. Problems have a history and are often the result of earlier poor decisions that didn't fix the problem. A so-so solution may work for a while but not for long. Solutions are rarely simple or easy.

The learning organization is a community of practice with workers sharing what they know with individuals having similar information needs and interests to build the community. These communities can then become networks of practice, one form of which is the professional organization. Members of a professional organization read the same journals, attend the same conferences, and discuss similar issues. These inputs double back into the organization and its learning activities and have a strong effect on the dynamics of the organization. With the opportunities afforded by the Internet, these communities of practice can be more distributed geographically but closer in their interaction. The *invisible college* of individuals with common interests becomes much stronger in a world networked by technology.

For professions, the professional association forms the basis of very strong networks. Its roles include publication of journals on topics of concern. It fosters common practice and common understanding. Within a large association, there are smaller groups organized by area of interest or by geographic area. Each of these groups, publications, and discussions fosters common understandings that lead to common and changing practice. The documents they produce move into the workplace and become part of the organization's learning resources. For the professional, the professional school forms an added community. Here, the individual is introduced to the profession, to a body of knowledge, and to the questions and issues with which it is concerned. Communities are formed among students and faculty that often serve as long-standing networks as these individuals move forward in their careers.

Brown and Duguid stress that learning is best done within social groups, professional organizations, teams, and other groupings within the work environment.[58] Individuals learn best when in the company of those with like interests. Individuals learn skills and concepts from one another. They assimilate the learning and then that learning informs practice. They go on to say that learning precedes knowing and that "learning makes intellectual property, capital, and assets usable."[59]

The tension between the individual and the organization takes on a different guise in the learning organization. For much of the twentieth century, work was a major factor in assimilating the large immigrant population. Organizations were structures into which everyone fit into a slot and was expected to conform. With the diversification of the workforce to include women and minorities, these organizational slots were less useful and as the workforce became better educated, the worker was even less willing to conform. The learning organization, the adaptive organization, provides workers with the opportunity to bring their unique skills to the workplace, to learn new skills, and to use them. In this information-rich, team-based, adaptive/learning environment, the organization can take many shapes and forms depending on its purpose, its goals, its products and services, its customers, and its resources. The role of the manager is to develop and manage the appropriate organization for the appropriate purpose.

LIBRARY/INFORMATION CENTER ORGANIZATION

Most studies of the nature of the organization have been conducted in the business sector using business settings. They therefore carry some of the biases present in the business world. Studies of not-for-profit organizations such as libraries and institutions of higher education have been conducted in large part by librarians and academics and therefore carry their own biases and limitations. Studies of libraries as organizations by librarians have "resulted in a provincial rather than a universal literature."[60] Libraries, like organizations in general, have goals and objectives, as well as structures designed to achieve these goals. Their organization is traditionally hierarchical with job descriptions, assignments, lines of authority, and lines of communication. They differ from the business sector in that they provide services rather than products and their success is measured by the satisfaction of users.

Lowell Martin, long respected as an expert on library/information center management, indicated a number of ways in which the library/information center organizational structure differs from that of other organizations. His comments derive both from long experience in the publishing industry as well as from years of teaching, research, and consulting in the library world. From these varied experiences, he gained insights into both for-profit and not-for-profit environments. He concluded that:

- for all their general acceptance, [libraries] are currently marked by ambiguous goals rather than clear-cut objectives
- in their long history, they have accumulated a set of conception of function and method that make for rigid structure and resistance to change
- they function as auxiliaries to larger enterprises and not as independent entities
- as a consequence of the auxiliary role, they are subject to external pressures from political bodies, faculties, users, and so forth
- they are staffed in the higher levels by personnel with graduate education, making for a highly educated core staff
- they are administered by professionals who move up from the service ranks and not by career managers
- they seek identity and domain within a host of communication and information sources in the community at large and in their parent organization[61]

Their functions include cataloging, reference services, circulation, and administration plus additional service areas, depending on size and complexity of the library. The goals of the library are allocated to these areas depending on their unique ability to contribute to the goal. Tasks are defined and individuals with appropriate education and experience are assigned to them. Martin cautions that while these activities fit into a functional organization chart and provide a means of organizing work, none of these activities is focused on the main purpose of the organization—serving the user.

TYPES OF LIBRARY ORGANIZATION

Libraries and information centers are typically part of a larger organization; a school, a university, municipal government, business, or other organization. The organizational structure of the larger organization determines to a large degree the type of organizational structure present in the library. It also determines the extent to which the library director has the freedom to adapt the structure to accommodate change or champion the unique goals of the library. The growth of information companies in the latter part of the past century are for-profit businesses focused on the provision of information and are an example of the information service independent of a larger organization as well as of a structure relatively uninhibited by the rules and regulations that encumber a long-established organization.

Universities and schools are typically bureaucratic organizations with the roles and responsibilities of each unit carefully specified. The same is true for local and state government. Business organizations vary and can range from highly bureaucratic to the flexible team-based structure. Most libraries tend to have bureaucratic organizational structures and until recently tended to be operated in very traditional ways. The incorporation of information technology into the workplace has had an increasingly important impact on traditional library structures. Libraries were among the first agencies to see the benefits of information technology to organize records, to store and retrieve records, and to tend to daily tasks such as managing circulation records. Librarians as information professionals are experts in information organization and have led the way in many of the larger organizations in adopting information technology.

At the same time as the public library was welcoming automation, other government agencies not accustomed to dealing with information at the same level were much slower to adopt the technology; when they did adopt it, many were unsure how to use it. In numerous instances, it became evident that libraries were often comfortable with the technology and they were pressed into service in new roles that created conflict in units not previously connected to the range of information systems. The newly appointed computer specialist whose job was to install computers in the workplace had experience with computing machinery but did not know the organization and the uses or users of the information to be accessed by those computers. The need to collaborate in order to share skills became apparent and developing ways to work together often took time. The introduction of a new technology has the potential of changing relationships in and among the units of the larger organization. It can be the source of new productive relationships and/or turf wars. The public library is still carving out its future role as information expert for its community. Information technology has disturbed the bureaucracy and new linkages, and new relationships have been made possible.

The school library media center has become more than the book center of the school. Because school library media specialists have the background and education to incorporate information technology into the student's learning program, the media center has become the learning center where students learn to use information technology as a tool to access information, to learn skills (e.g., mathematics study or language drills), and to connect to students with like interests elsewhere in the world. The bureaucratic structure of the school system, except in certain cases, is slow to change, but the role of the librarian/media specialist has been enlarged to include a wider range of activities and that role continues to grow.

In the college/university setting, similar expansion of roles has occurred. In these organizations, computing centers grew in size and responsibility to manage the business systems of the institution. Often, their organization came into conflict with the library as it managed information in support of teaching and research. Also, telephone system managers were now in the telecommunications business and found themselves needing to interact with computing centers and libraries on a regular basis. Universities have responded to the concerns of academic and administrative computing interests in a number of ways. Some have appointed a vice president for information to whom the computer center director, the telecommunications director, and the library director report. In several instances, the library director has assumed this role. The bureaucratic organization in this instance has adapted to technology by expanding roles or by creating new units. In this still-fluid situation, the library director has the opportunity and the responsibility to adapt the library's organizational structure to changing situations, not just in external relationships but internally as well.

The structure of the library in the business organization varies widely. The library/information center in traditional bureaucratic organizations is usually part of the overhead costs of the organization and its responsibilities have often been determined by managers unfamiliar with libraries or the information needs of the company. The successful librarian/information specialist builds a service within that structure that provides the company with its information needs. The successful librarian/information specialist is entrepreneurial, looks for opportunities to serve, develops and markets products to staff, and pushes the boundaries of the slot into which the library may have been placed. Success is measured by the extent to which the librarian/information specialist can show benefit to the bottom line. In businesses where employees have been organized into teams, the librarian/information specialist may be a team member, providing information, suggesting new information directions, and being an integral part of the team's learning activities.

Technology in the era of slashing staffs to improve the bottom line has often hurt internal information centers, as it was wrongly assumed that one could substitute a few databases for the library, and staff would use them to do their own research without the need for a librarian. As information and information access continues to increase in volume and complexity, it is increasingly evident that the information professional is a key employee. Information entrepreneurs who have built independent business organizations have followed a number of business models. These organizations are relatively recent and therefore do not have the history of a long-standing organizational culture to constrict them. They tend to be fairly small, to be staffed almost exclusively by professionals, and to be highly sophisticated technologically. The structure is typically very simple, with information professionals linked by computer rather than located in a central office. They conduct searches, develop reports, and have similar responsibilities according to a set of agreed-upon rules but work independently most of the time. A fairly high percentage of these businesses are owned and operated by women. The focus of their business is the customer and the organization is focused on meeting customer needs. These are excellent examples of the lean, flexible, customer-oriented organization.

Libraries are located in other organizational contexts such as hospitals, museums, law firms, and many more. Each conforms to its (usually bureaucratic) parent structure and fits closely into one of the four environments already noted. To gain further information on the organizational structure of a particular type of library, it is recommended that one read relevant sections of a text specific to that type of library or information center.

SUMMARY

For the past century, organizational structure in both the for-profit and not-for-profit world has been essentially bureaucratic and hierarchical. The role of the worker in such a structure has been to fit into that structure and conform to the organization. More recent research and practice has advocated building organizations around the talents and interests of the employees and fostering growth of a more flexible organizational structure that can respond more fully and more rapidly to changing environmental forces. Information and communication technologies have the ability either to strengthen the existing bureaucratic structure or to serve as the web on which new structures can be built.

NOTES

1. Robert Presthus, *The Organizational Society* (New York: Random, 1962), 4.

2. Presthus, *The Organizational Society*, 2.

3. Herbert A. Hicks and C. Ray Gullet, *Organizational Theory and Behavior* (New York: McGraw-Hill, 1975), 108.

4. Max Weber, *Theory of Social and Economic Organizations*, translated by A. M. Henderson and T. Parsons (New York: Oxford University Press, 1947).

5. Charles Perrow, *Complex Organizations: A Critical Essay*, 2nd ed (Glenview, Ill.: Scott Foresman, 1979), 4.

6. Perrow, *Complex Organizations*, 6.

7. Perrow, *Complex Organizations*, 30.

8. Perrow, *Complex Organizations*, 96.

9. Perrow, *Complex Organizations*, 67.

10. Perrow, *Complex Organizations*, 116.

11. Arnold S. Tannenbaum, Kkaveis Bogdan, Menachem Rosner, Mino Vianello, and Georg Wieser, *Hierarchy in Organizations* (San Francisco: Jossey-Bass, 1974).

12. Perrow, *Complex Organizations*, 137.

13. Herbert A. Simon, *Administrative Behavior*, 2nd ed. (New York: Macmillan, 1957); James G. March and Herbert A. Simon, *Organizations* (New York: John Wiley and Sons, 1958).

14. Perrow, *Complex Organizations*, 149.

15. Richard M. Cyert and James G. March, *Behavioral Theory of the Firm* (Englewood Cliffs, N.J.: Prentice Hall), 1963.

16. Presthus, *The Organizational Society*, 17.

17. William Whyte, *The Organization Man* (Philadelphia: University of Pennsylvania Press, 2002).

18. Peter Drucker, *Management: Tasks, Responsibilities, and Practices* (New York: Harper and Row, 1973).

19. Drucker, *Management*, 528.

20. Drucker, *Management*, 6.

21. Drucker, *Management*, 526.

22. Tom Peters and Robert H. Waterman, *In Search of Excellence* (New York: Harper, 1982).

23. Peters and Waterman, *In Search of Excellence*, 3.

24. Peters and Waterman, *In Search of Excellence*, 3.

25. Peters and Waterman, *In Search of Excellence*, 10–11.

26. Philip Selznik, *Leadership in Administration: A Sociological Interpretation* (New York: Harper and Row, 1957), 135–36.

27. Peters and Waterman, *In Search of Excellence*, 105.

28. Peters and Waterman, *In Search of Excellence*, 102.

29. Peters and Waterman, *In Search of Excellence*, 108.

30. Peters and Waterman, *In Search of Excellence*, 136.

31. Tom Peters, *Liberation Management: Necessary Disorganization for the Nanosecond Nineties* (New York: Knopf, 1992).

32. Peters and Waterman, *In Search of Excellence*, 314.

33. Peters and Waterman, *In Search of Excellence*, 314.

34. Peters, *Liberation Management*, 63.

35. Peters, *Liberation Management*, 63.

36. Bart Victor and Carroll Stephens, "The dark side of the new organizational forms: An editorial essay," *Organizational Science* 5, no. 4 (November 1994): 480.

37. Marcie J. Tyre and Oscar Hauptman, "Effectiveness of organizational response to technological change in the production process," *Organizational Science* 1, no. 3 (August, 1992): 324.

38. Tyre and Hauptman, "Effectiveness of organizational response," 314.

39. John Seeley Brown and Paul Duguid, *The Social Life of Information* (Cambridge, Mass.: Harvard Business School Press, 2000).

40. Shoshanna Zhuboff, *In The Age of the Smart Machine* (New York, Basic Books, 1988), 29.

41. Rosabeth Moss Kanter, *Evolve! Succeeding in the Digital Culture of Tomorrow* (Boston: Harvard Business School Press, 2001), 72.

42. Harvey Kolodny, Michel Liu, Bengt Stymme, and Helene Denis, "New technology and the emerging organizational paradigm," *Human Relations* 49, no. 12 (December 1996): 1462.

43. Kolodny et al., "New technology and the emerging organizational paradigm," 1468.

44. Michel Liu, Helene Denis, Harvey Kolodny, and Bengt Stymme, "Organization design for technological change," *Human Relations* 43, no. 1 (January 1990): 13.

45. Henry C. Lucas Jr. and Jack Baroudi, "The role of information technology in organization design," *Journal of Management Information Systems*, Vol. 10, No. 4, Spring 1994, pp. 9–23.

46. Lucas, et al., "The role of information technology in organization design," 15.

47. Bob Travica, "Information aspects of new organizational designs: Exploring the non-traditional organization," *Journal of the American Society for Information Science* 49, no. 15 (November 1995): 1241.

48. Travica, "Information aspects of new organizational designs," 1236.

49. Kanter, *Evolve!* 27.

50. Peters, *Liberation Management*, 121.

51. Paul T. Attewell, "IT and the productive paradox," in *Organizational Linkages:*

Understanding the Productivity Paradox, edited by D. Harris (Washington, D.C.: National Academy Press, 1994), 36.

52. Peters, *Liberation Management*, 153–55.

53. Brown and Duguid, *The Social Life of Information*, 67.

54. Herbert Kaufman, *Time, Chance and Organizations* (Chatham House, N.J.: Chatham Houses Publishers, 1991), 66–67.

55. Peter Senge, *The Fifth Discipline: The Art and Practice of the Learning Organization* (New York: Doubleday, 1990).

56. Senge, *The Fifth Discipline*, 7.

57. Senge, *The Fifth Discipline*, 18–28.

58. Brown and Duguid, *The Social Life of Information*, 124–27.

59. Brown and Duguid, *The Social Life of Information*, 124.

60. Lowell A. Martin, *Organizational Structure of Libraries* (Metuchen, N.J.: Scarecrow Press, 1984), 11.

61. Martin, *Organizational Structure of Libraries*, 61.

ADDITIONAL READINGS

Carr, Nicholas G., ed. *The Digital Enterprise: How to Reshape Your Business for a Connected World*. Boston: Harvard Business School Publishing Co., 2001.

Choo, Chun Wei. *The Knowing Organization: How Organizations Use Information to Construct Meaning, Create Knowledge, and Make Decisions*. New York: Oxford University Press, 1998.

Goodman, Paul, Lee S. Sproull, and association. *Technology and Organizations*. San Francisco: Jossey-Bass, 1990.

Hoadley, Irene B. "Somewhere over the rainbow: Organizational patterns in academic libraries." In *For the Good of the Order: Essays in Honor of Edward G. Holley*, edited by Delmus E. Williams, John M. Budd, Robert E. Martin, Barbara Moran, and Fred Roper, 73–83. Greenwich, Conn.: JAI Press, 1994.

Lamberton, Donald M. "The economics of information and organization." In *Annual Review of Information Science and Technology*, edited by Martha Williams, 3–30. White Plains, N.Y.: Knowledge Industry, 1984.

Nadler, Donald A., Marc S. Gerstein, Robert B. Shaw, and associates. *Organizational Architecture: Designs for Changing Organizations*. San Francisco: Jossey-Bass, 1992.

Chapter Six

Leadership

Leadership is a defining theme in the art and skill of managing organizations. In one way or another, it affects all aspects of the organization and all tasks conducted by the organization. Leadership has been of great interest to scholars who have conducted studies to identify what leadership is and how it can be applied. It has been of great interest to politicians who wish to be leaders and want to know what one must do to develop leadership skills. It has been of even greater interest to those who are seeking leadership at work, and in the larger social environments. A fairly large body of research has been conducted since the 1970s to determine the components of leadership and to see how it has been applied, and from those studies to project how it might be applied. Most of these studies have looked at individuals who have been called leaders by those around them, or individuals who have the responsibility to manage large organizations and are therefore defined as having leadership responsibilities. Researchers have identified certain characteristics that seem to be present in a large percentage of individuals called leaders and have then said that those characteristics define a leader. It is generally agreed by researchers that the concept of leadership is difficult to define and that observation of individuals called leaders is an imperfect means of study. They have, however, not identified other more useful means of study.

LEADERSHIP THEMES

The modern study of leadership began with Machiavelli's *The Prince*.[1] Although he wrote in a different time and place, his views on leadership and management are as relevant today as they were half a millennium ago. He stressed that leadership can be taught and is not an inherent talent. He further stressed that the leader should be careful to maintain a good self-image others will respect, and to avoid associating with those who might make him appear to be weak or unprincipled. He defined the role of the leader as one who maintains order in whatever ways may be most appropriate at the time. As one moved through the period since *The Prince*, leadership as a topic was not consistently discussed, but biographies of great men identified as leaders in their time appeared regularly. Their actions were most likely to be political, religious, or military and were played out in the competition among European nation-states. One can consider them early case studies in leadership.

Historians have long been fascinated by "great man" themes and numerous studies of leaders exist. The English historian Thomas Carlyle asked if one person could change the course of events. Evil individuals such as Hitler or Stalin saw a power vacuum in the environment and through force dominated a country and period in history. Rather than being leaders, they were controllers. This question continues to be posed, often in relation to an individual who may have had a major impact on events. For the historian, leadership is usually defined or redefined as political leadership.[2] How historians deal with leadership varies by time, place, and culture and the concept of leadership is directly tied to the culture within which it exists.

As the sciences of sociology, anthropology, and psychology emerged during the latter part of the nineteenth and into the twentieth century, questions pertaining to leadership were approached from new directions. Psychologists argued that humans have a primal need to follow and need leaders in order to obtain a level of security. Anthropologists cited other societies and the ways in which they organized around a leader who determined the activities of the tribal group. Those studying primates identified similar needs for leadership among apes. Chester Barnard was one of the first to look at leadership in the context of the corporation, which he described as a social organization.[3] Leaders set the tone of the social organization by giving "common meaning to common purpose." His approach to leadership meshed well with the growing interest in studying workers as individuals rather than as interchangeable parts of the corporate machine.

The scientific study of leadership is a twentieth-century phenomenon and can be divided into three periods. The first of these periods (1910–1939) focused on the idea that leaders were somehow different from their peers. If one could identify the traits that made them different, one could identify leaders. The second period (1940 to the late 1960s) focused on behavior with the idea that if one studied behavior, one could identify leaders. The third period (1970 to date) looked at the situations in which individuals found themselves and looked for common responses as to how they dealt with the situation.

Using the definition of "leadership as a process of innovation and leadership as the recurrent interplay between private personality and public performance," authors from numerous disciplines looked at leadership from their unique perspectives.[4] They approached their study by developing a series of biographical essays of individuals called leaders to see how they performed in situations where leadership was needed and perhaps to identify some commonalities. Men—including Gandhi, de Gaulle, and Bismarck— were studied to determine how they became leaders and how they functioned in those roles. These men were seen as part of a social movement for change, men who became spokesmen for change and who *spoke* to those existing in an unbearable situation. The individual who has "extraordinary powers of vision and the communication of vision, especially when this vision relates to the possibility and ways of overcoming distressful conditions" is said to have charisma.[5] There are continuous questions throughout the study of leadership as to whether leaders are born with special attributes or whether anyone can exhibit these characteristics given a stressful situation in which action is needed.

In addition to study of the charismatic leader, others have studied the leader as manager to determine what characteristics identified individuals have in common. Much of the early framework for this approach to the study of leadership was provided by Emory S. Bogardus, who pursued a multidisciplinary approach to identify characteristics of leaders.[6] He stated that leadership is part of a social process and needs to be discussed in that context. The Leader Behavior Descriptive Questionnaire developed at Ohio State in the 1950s focused on a limited list of dimensions or traits: "initiation, membership, representation, integration, organization, domination, communication, recognition, production."[7] Results of the questionnaire revealed four dimensions central to leadership: consideration, initiating structure, production emphasis, and social awareness. Other researchers looked at how one could develop behaviors that would result in good leadership or how the leader works in and within the group.[8]

Considerable research was conducted in the 1970s and 1980s to define leadership and the role leadership plays in the successful enterprise. Many of the studies drew on field experience; for example, study one hundred individuals with responsibilities in successful enterprises and identify common traits. No generally accepted theory emerged. One of the most important studies during this period was James M. Burns' study of leadership.[9] Burns discussed three types of leaders (moral leaders, transactional leaders, and transformational leaders) and the ways in which these different types of leaders influence the organization. Studies of leadership continue to be multidisciplinary. They are also culture dependent; for example, those characteristics that appear in studies of American leaders may or may not appear in similar studies done elsewhere.

James Cribbin identified a number of changes in the workforce that became apparent in the 1970s.[10] Workers were no longer seen as cogs in a wheel but as thinking, active, self-interested individuals who expected to be heard and to be paid what they were worth. The idea that treating workers with respect appeared to be a new idea, or perhaps just new to management. Within this context, Cribbin defined leadership as "the ability to gain consensus and commitment to common objectives which are attained through the efforts and experiences of others."[11] The leader/manager responds to this new view of workers by being more sensitive to their concerns. Cribbin's approach, while recognizing the changing relationship of the leader to the worker, continues to have strong elements of traditional hierarchical management. It is as though the leader/manager is not really sure that the newer definition of the worker is accurate and that the worker still needs to be led by those more able to lead.

In 1985, Warren Bennis and Burt Nanus conducted a study of leadership that serves as a benchmark for studies of leadership.[12] Leadership was defined "as the pivotal force behind successful organizations and that to create vital and visible organizations, leadership is necessary to help organizations develop a new vision of what they can be, then mobilize the organizational change toward the new vision."[13] Bennis further stated that while leadership competencies remain the same, how they work and how they may be applied have shifted. Despite more than 350 definitions of leadership, there is no basic understanding of what differentiates effective leadership from the ineffective or effective organizations from the ineffective. Furthermore, many of the definitions are in conflict. Bennis described the changing context of leadership, which began in the early 1980s, by saying that there appeared to be an increasing lack of commitment to working, or perhaps to the organization. He talked about the economic shifts and organizational changes underway. Among these shifts are the moves from an industrial society to an information society, from bureaucracy to networking, and toward a high-tech society. The credibility of the organization has been challenged from all directions and the information age has hatched a new public awareness of leaders and leadership. Leaders no longer have privacy but must justify their actions to a wide number of external and internal constituencies. Bennis stressed that in today's rapidly changing times, new leaders are needed to move to the next steps.

Within this context of change, he made the assumption that leadership is the central component of progress and that by studying identified leaders from both the profit and nonprofit sector chosen to reflect the practice of those who break new ground, a new definition of leadership would emerge. A total of ninety leaders were chosen; sixty CEOs from business and thirty leaders from the private sector. With a focus on leaders directing new trends, this two-year study included interviews and observations using unstructured observation except for three questions asked of all participants:

- What are your strengths and weaknesses?
- Was there any particular experience or event in your life that influenced your management philosophy or style?
- What were the major decision points in your career and how do you feel about your choices now?

Nearly all of those interviewed were white males, as at this point there were very few women or minorities in positions of leadership.

From the interviews, four types of leadership skills emerged.

1. Attention through vision: The leader creates a focus and an agenda, and has a vision that leads to an outcome. Employees know that the leader has a vision, where it leads, that it has outcomes—and they buy into that vision. The leader knows the context of the vision and sets direction within that context. If the leader feels she or he can make a difference, energy is expended in support of the activity. Where does one find vision? It may come from many sources including ideas from staff, other leaders, opportunities in the environment, past experience, and current trends.

2. Meaning through communication: Unless one can articulate the vision and make it real through an agenda, no one will be able to understand what is expected. Leaders define what has previously remained implicit or unsaid. They invent images to organize meaning. Those expected to follow require a common interpretation of reality to guide them so that they know how to act in new situations. "Even the best ideas are only as good as their ability to attract attention in the social environment."[14]

3. Trust through positioning: Bennis says that trust implies accountability, predictability, and reliability. A leader needs to indicate the direction if individuals are expected to follow. Further, this course of action should not keep changing but should indicate a steady direction and an effort on the part of the leader to be persistent and to stick with it. The leader needs to position the organization in relation to the vision, communicate the vision, and consistently maintain the vision. This provides an identity others can buy into. An organization can be described in four ways:

   - the organization on the organization chart
   - the assumed organization—what individuals perceive as actual
   - the extant organization—what study of the organization shows
   - the requisite organization—as it would look if in accord with the reality in which it exists.

   When any of these four are in contradiction, there is confusion. The leader's vision must incorporate all four.

4. Deployment of self through positive self-regard: leaders know their worth, their strengths, and their weaknesses. The leader has positive regard for others and treats all with respect. How the individual sees himself or herself often determines the outcome of a situation. If one assumes failure after an initial effort, little has been gained. If failure is seen as an opportunity to analyze a situation and develop new strategies, it is not failure.

Bennis summarized his study by saying that the leader is a catalyst. He also identified five myths of leadership: that leadership is a rare skill; that leaders are born and not made; that leaders are charismatic; that leadership occurs only at the top of the organization; and that the leader controls, directs, prods, and manipulates the organization. None of these is true. Leadership is a skill that can be learned through trial and error, very few leaders are charismatic, leadership can and does occur at all levels of the organization. The leader does not lead by force but by the quality of the vision and the ability to make it work.[15]

In 1991, a replication of Bennis' study using library leaders as the group interviewed was conducted by Brooke Sheldon.[16] The purpose was "to gain an understanding of the qualities held in common by leaders in the library profession."[17] It was hypothesized that the differences between library leaders' responses and those elicited by Bennis would be insignificant. Sixty leaders were interviewed and asked the same three questions as Bennis asked plus two additional questions: "What, if any, has been the influence of mentors on our career?" and "How do you feel about the future of the profession?"

Library leaders have strong visions. One interviewee said that vision is "setting your sights on what would be the best possible thing, not under the naive assumption you'll ever get there, but to make certain that if you do certain things, you go in that direction rather than some other direction."[19] Leaders are also very results oriented, and many have the personal drive and magnetism to capture attention, draw people in, and move forward with them to a common goal.[18] They believe in what they are doing and have a deep commitment to the importance of librarianship and its role in society.

Library leaders are competent communicators of their vision. They are able to see the big picture and the role of their organization within that picture. They have a global view and see the library within that view. They develop coalitions and network with other individuals and organizations as they know that interdependence is crucial to achieving goals. Within the organization, they see the need to reshape the social architecture by involving all the staff in achieving the vision. They place an emphasis on simply stated values and develop one or two themes; for example, the goal is client-centered service, and they look at current structures to determine if the organization supports the goal. They have a talent for listening and working closely with staff to achieve the goal. The library leaders are consistent in their vision and in communicating what they expect from their staff. They have a healthy self-image and respect their staff. They build consensus for innovation and lead the effort. Other than having a stronger service orientation than those interviewed by Bennis, there was little difference between those interviewed in his study and these individuals.

LEADERSHIP AND MANAGEMENT

Throughout the study of leadership, there have been differing views of where leadership ends and management begins. Some have insisted that there are two different sets of abilities and that they do not reside in the same person. Others have argued with equal skill that the capable leader is also a good manager. Kouzes and Pozner studied 780 middle and senior managers in the public and private sectors by administering a brief two-page questionnaire.[20] They had set up an a priori structure of what they assumed leadership meant, using the many definitions of leadership currently available. They then administered a longer questionnaire to a subset of 550 subjects and followed this with forty-two in-depth interviews. Sample questions included: "How did you challenge others to attain high levels of performance, to excel, to do better than ever before?" "How did you build a sense of enthusiasm and excitement for the project?" "How did your team celebrate its accomplishments, its milestones, its achievements?"[21]

The a priori structure was useful as it served to provide a pattern for organizing questions asked and responses. Five practices with accompanying basic strategies were identified and the researchers easily fit 70 percent of the responses into the structure.

Five Practices and Accompanying Strategies

1. Challenging the process
   - search for opportunities
   - experiment and take risks
2. Inspiring a shared vision
   - envision the future
   - enlist others
3. Enabling others to act
   - foster collaboration
   - strengthen others
4. Modeling the way
   - set the example
   - plan small wins
5. Encouraging the heart
   - recognize contributions
   - celebrate accomplishments[22]

The findings supporting these practices were analyzed in numerous ways. It was found that male and female managers' responses were essentially the same except that women were stronger in category five, Encouraging the Heart. No significant differences were found between for-profit and not-for-profit managers. Cross-cultural differences with managers in Australia, Britain, the Netherlands, and Germany were investigated and here, too, there were no significant differences.[23]

A managerial effectiveness scale was developed from the findings. It was noted that managers whose actions were listed in the Leadership Effectiveness Scale were more successful.

"Leaders do exhibit certain distinct practices when they are doing their best and this behavior varies little from industry to industry, profession to profession. Good leadership, it seems, is not only an understandable but also a universal practice."[24] It is a process ordinary managers use when they are bringing forth the best in themselves and others. The authors define leadership as a process and not a place. They define the manager's role as one of maintaining stability, exerting control through systems and procedures, and define the role of the leader as being a change agent, of controlling the vision, and empowering the workers to follow it. Management and leadership are two essential elements in organizational success and one leads from the other.

Leadership and management are found at all levels in the organization and not just at the top. A strong organization has individuals who are responsible for projects, units, and activities exhibiting leadership throughout the organization. Of the various studies of leadership, this is one of the most rigorous and informative. It is therefore appropriate to devote some time to their descriptions of leadership practices.

Challenging the Process

Leadership is an active process and the leader seeks out challenges. He or she is alert to changing technology, changing markets, who the competition may be, and is open to ideas that could make a difference.[25] The leader is willing to take risks, to innovate, and to experiment. The new ideas may come from customers, from vendors, from employees, from reading the literature, and from talking with colleagues. The leader's task is to recognize good ideas, to support them, and to get them into the system, recognizing that some may fail and also recognizing that through that failure, new information is gained.

Inspiring a Shared Vision

The authors say that "a vision is the force that invents the future."[26] A leader wants action, wants things to happen, and inspires others to share that vision. To do this, the leader must be able to communicate that vision in words and deeds that those who are asked to follow understand. Subordinates must be able and willing to buy into the vision. The leader must be enthusiastic about the vision and able to get others to share that enthusiasm.

Enabling Others to Act

The leader enlists the support and assistance of all individuals and groups who would be involved in the project. Collaboration and team building are essential as they provide a structure in which others can act. Anyone who will have to live with the results of the idea should be part of the planning and development.[27] Building a sense of ownership in the idea requires open communication among those involved. There must be a feeling of trust in the leader by the staff and the leader needs to be able to trust the members of the teams that are set up.

Modeling the Way

A vision needs a rationale of why we should develop this program or change this process.[28] It needs detailed plans of how one will achieve the objective and sets of measures that will let one know when the plan is achieved and with what success. Someone needs to develop a process to meet those objectives. Funds and resources must be identified and obtained to go forward. This goes beyond simply managing the process, as the planned activity is new and different and there are no firm guidelines. Decisions are made at every point and are made to reflect the vision of the leader and paying attention, not to how we have done things in the past, but to identifying and pursuing what is important. Tom Peters, author of *In Search of Excellence*, in conversation with the researchers, said that "leaders act in ways that are consistent with their beliefs, they are persistent in pursuit of their visions, and they are always vigilant about the little things that make a big difference."[29]

Encouraging the Heart

Leaders should publically express thanks for work well done. They should celebrate success, recognize milestones, and show that they appreciate the efforts of those who have worked with them.

As a follow-up to this study, the researchers conducted a survey of approximately fifteen hundred managers, asking them what values they looked for and admired in their supervisors. More than 275 values were listed in the responses, with the three following values being those most frequently mentioned:

- Integrity was most often listed. Is the leader truthful and trustworthy? Does he or she practice the values that he or she preaches? Do you know where you stand in relation to the leader and is that relationship consistent?
- Competence focused on whether the leader can do the job, but not just do the job now being done but also do that extra something that is needed to add value to the job.
- Leadership focused on whether the leader provides direction, is decisive, and is forward-looking. Is there a sense that the leader knows where the organization is moving?

When employees believes that management has high credibility and a strong sense of the importance of what the organization doing, they are more likely to be proud of the organization and to support its activities. Conversely, when there is an absence of credibility in the leadership, individuals rarely put out their best efforts.

LEADERSHIP IS . . .

From the studies by Bennis and Nanus, Kouzes and Pozner, and those of numerous other researchers in the 1980s and 1990s, a relatively long list of qualities or characteristics of the leader has been identified. Of primary importance is that the leader is willing to challenge existing processes and to be an agent of change. A leader sees what can be rather than what is and works toward creating a new environment. The leader focuses on those activities that will make a situation better and will result in real improvements. A leader listens to the good ideas of others and runs with them. In many instances, the good idea may be suggested by a superior who gives an individual the leadership responsibility to make that idea real. This may require new skills and new approaches or a new way of looking at issues. Knowing that routine work and the status quo can keep one fully occupied and feeling busy, the leader breaks out of that rut by innovative thinking and by changing those parts of the routine that are counterproductive. Thinking outside the routine boxes in which many activities have sunk and finding new connections is risky but essential to ensuring that the organization is functioning at its best. This requires an understanding of the organization and knowing when to break rules and when to leave them alone.

The leader is an excellent communicator, listening to both internal and external realities. He or she knows the market for the product or service being produced and is in touch with users and vendors. Going to conferences provides opportunity to talk with colleagues and to test ideas as well as to gain new ideas. The leader reads, talks, and listens—and not to the same individuals or groups all the time. New ideas come from cognate areas and from individuals who initially might not seem to be relevant to the leader's organization.

The leader knows how to put information together into an understandable vision of what new product, service, or organizational change will do for the entire organization. In one, two, or five years, how will this idea have changed what is currently being done? How can the leader be sure that those who will work with her or him see the same vision as the leader? One way is to set scenarios of how things will look in the next year with the change or if no change occurs. Another way is to build an agenda based on the innovation so that individuals can see what steps need to be taken and what their role will be in taking those steps. Some researchers have said that the leader needs to teach the vision and this is a means of teaching the vision.

The leader knows how to enlist others to support that vision—internally with employees and externally with the many stakeholders who include users, government officials, business interests, and so forth, depending upon the location of the library or information center within the structure. When these constituencies understand the vision and its purpose, employees have a better sense of where the organization is moving and their role in its future success. As they share the vision of the leader, they will take the next step, which is collaboration in achieving the shared vision. Teamwork builds a feeling of ownership in the activity and demands the personal best of everyone on the team to achieve the objectives. The leader needs to delegate authority to the team and to keep it on track. This requires continuous feedback and measuring decisions against values to ensure that the purpose of the activity continues and is not lost along the way. It also requires sharing of information so that all members of the team and not just the leader know the same information and can make decisions within the same framework. As work progresses, team members need to have their efforts recognized. The leader sets the example, keeps on task, keeps the team on task, and recognizes achievement.

Researchers have spent time identifying personal characteristics of the successful leader and have stated repeatedly that leadership is not something one is endowed with at birth but it is something one can learn by observation, trial and error, experience, and education. They stress that leadership is self-development and the ability to expect the best from one's self. Wess Roberts in *Leadership Secrets of Attila the Hun* identified a number of personal qualities that describe the leader.[30] Among these, he lists loyalty to the best purposes of the organization; the courage to act with confidence; the desire and commitment to influence people, processes, and outcomes; the emotional stamina to maintain perspective and recover quickly from disappointment; and the physical stamina to maintain effort.[31] He goes on to say that to be a successful leader, one must want to be in charge and must bring the above qualities to the position. Leaders are responsible for creating the atmosphere in which they lead: collaborative, with mutual self-respect, and disciplined. The leader exhibits high standards, leads by action, provides direction, and has the moral courage to stick with the right decision even when it is difficult to do. The leader (like Attila) is always on the offensive. He or she negotiates rather than dictates. He or she never trusts to luck or overestimates personal abilities. While the leader over time has a good track record, she or he knows that she or he won't win them all but when defeated, will learn from that defeat and will accept a loss if it furthers the objective. Defeat provides information to reassess, try a new approach based on lessons learned, and move forward. Others stress the importance of courage and confidence in ultimate success. With a take-charge attitude, the leader studies an issue (not for too long), takes risks, makes decisions, and challenges the bureaucracy in support of excellence. The leader believes in what he or she is doing, as the doing is a twenty-four/seven task and only the committed are willing to spend that amount of time.

In discussing the role of the academic leader, Theodore M. Hesberg, then president of the University of Notre Dame, said that clarity of mind and warmth of heart move toward the vision, and that the vision must have constant reiteration for others to buy in. He cautioned that vision has many facets and not all succeed at the same rate.[32] Judith Eaton says that leaders reflect the values of the society in which they exist and are creatures of those they lead.[33] She further says that "leadership is a series of important messages conveyed through decisions and demeanor."

> In the main, leadership has a profound impact through its style. The dimensions of leadership behavior communicate more about a leader than most of the pronouncements or opinions that may be offered. Style is what constituents and peers hear and see. Style is what persists in the perceptions of those who surround a leader. Consider attention: Where does a leader direct it? Language: How does a leader use it? Sanctioning: What is a leader's attitude toward policy, moral issues, law? Personal demeanor: How does a leader carry himself or herself? Is he or she genuine? Distant? Warm? Aloof? Available? What about self-awareness? What sense does a leader have of the values conveyed by his or her behavior? Style is loud, clear, and public. A leader cannot hide it, explain it away, or be free of it. If we lead by constant compromise and negotiation, if we lead by ignoring the obvious decay of our spirit and our strength, then we reflect what is worst in our society. This is not to argue that we will end the world's problems through leadership. But it is to acknowledge the centrality of leadership in ensuring the dignity of individuals, of our institutions, and of society."[34]

The leader is responsible for setting the tone of the organization. An individual who is arrogant, who consistently finds fault with others, and who refuses to look at her or his own behavior creates a toxic environment in which there is a fear of acting beyond one's narrow job description or of seeking new opportunities. Conversely "a leader [is one who] makes sure that he is not only in an optimistic, authentic, high energy mood [but who] through his chosen actions, his followers feel and act that way, too."[35] Goleman and associates found that "people catch feelings from one another," that positive feelings are more contagious than negative, and that there is a direct relationship between positive attitude and increased performance. The need to project a positive attitude, a can-do, "I know what I'm doing" attitude is essential to successful leadership. It must be real and not faked. It must be evident that the leader truly believes in the activities underway and believes that she or he has the ability to achieve.

A relatively recent approach to leadership studies has been to explore the emotional intelligence of the leader. Self-awareness, knowing what you are doing and how those activities affect others, is the basis of emotional intelligence. The ability to control one's emotions and to act with honesty, integrity, self-management, and the ability to sense the emotions of others and to be empathetic are essential components. Finally, the ability to communicate clearly and convincingly, to neutralize conflicts, and to build strong personal bonds with colleagues are powerful leadership tools.[36] Emotional intelligence doesn't just happen. It needs to be cultivated and practiced. Ask yourself "Who do I want to be?" and "Who am I now?" The ability to listen to constructive criticism without being defensive provides insight into the way one is perceived by peers, subordinates, and superiors. Using these inputs, it is possible to identify strengths and weaknesses and to lead to a greater level of success in interacting with others.

Pagonis stresses that leaders must demonstrate empathy and expertise if they expect to be successful.[37] They must respect others and respect the work they are doing. Awareness of cultural differences and of different ways of approaching tasks is essential. The leader who has worked at some time in routine, often boring, jobs has an appreciation of the feelings of those in the organization who hold such jobs. The broader the experience of the leader in different types of work situations, the more opportunity there is to develop an understanding of the positive and not-so-positive elements of different types of work. Leaders need to develop expertise in the areas of their responsibility and to demonstrate that expertise. Again, a range of experiences deepens expertise and the ability to deal with different situations. Those who want to develop the next generation of leaders make particular efforts to expose newly hired individuals to a range of different activities. Internships in organizations recognized for the quality of their performance provide excellent opportunities to identify potential leaders and to provide the mentoring needed for them to take the next step.

To lead, one must have the facts, a steady and accurate flow of information from all sources (internal, external, superiors, subordinates) organized for ready access. Knowing how to apply the available information to the situation at hand is the next key to leadership. And being known as a person who acts on information, not whim or bias, and who follows through to the conclusion of the activity is the best way to ensure that someone out there is following the leader. Throughout the process of collecting facts, applying information, and following through, the leader needs to communicate appropriate information to those affected by the information. Superiors need to know that their expectations are being carried out and how, subordinates need to know why they are expected to perform in a certain way, and those outside the organization who will be affected by those actions need to know the impact. The leader who has the expertise to act and who has the empathy to understand how those actions affect others and communicates that empathy will be successful.

Leaders each have a style of leadership they are most comfortable using, but depending upon the circumstances that style may vary. In a study of nearly four thousand executives, Goleman identified the leadership styles most often used.[38]

- The *coercive* leader demands immediate compliance, drives others to achieve, and works in a crisis mode. This style creates a negative work climate and is harmful when used for longer than a brief crisis period.
- The *authoritative* leader mobilizes staff to accept a vision and sets them on a clear path of action. This leadership style exhibits self-confidence and with a positive attitude toward style will move the vision and the organization forward.
- The *democratic* style forges consensus through participation, collaboration, and communication. This style is most useful when asking others to buy into new directions or new solutions for existing problems.
- When high performance standards are needed to gain quick results, a *pacesetting* style is called for. This works best when one has a highly motivated team and is best used for short-term activities.
- The *coaching* style is used to develop future leaders and to help employees improve their performance.

Each of these styles builds on the foundation of empathy and expertise and each has a place in moving the vision for the organization forward.

TECHNOLOGY AND LEADERSHIP

To date, few researchers and writers have paid much attention to the impact information technology might have on leadership. Some have indicated that there is little or no impact. Garten's research challenged this attitude.[39] He selected forty CEOs whom he identified as those who were changing the world of business for the next decades by building new structures and moving their companies toward globalization. Decisions made in this environment have to be made at warp speed. The information assembled and analyzed to do this is done in large part through the use of the application of technology to large databases. The technology is moving so rapidly that one innovation is often not in place before there is a successor. The learning curve for managers and leaders is impossibly steep. The leaders Garten interviewed knew that the Internet is changing how people do things. Lines among producers, suppliers, and customers are blurring and national boundaries are becoming transparent. This brings together and often causes conflict among differing agendas of nations, businesses, and other for-profit and not-for-profit agencies. Changes caused by the Internet are seen as deep and permanent.

The movement of information and availability of information to many more individuals and groups than before challenges some of the traditional ideas of leadership and the traditional cultural and organizational structure within the organization. No longer is information held only by those in authority. Anyone inside or outside the organization can find out nearly anything about the organization. Leadership is no longer controlled by those who know, as now anyone can know and many will challenge the leader's actions. The vision the leader has and how information meshes with the vision and the organization's commitment to moral good is available to all. Information based solely on personal authority is no longer as powerful as it once was. Authority now rests on ability, integrity, and the power of the ideas pursued. One can ask if technology is destroying the existing order or serving as the midwife of the new. In either case, it is a powerful tool.

One of the 2002 *Harvard Business Review* breakthrough ideas for today's business agenda begins with the statement "The Internet is not about you" and the authors go on to say that the trend is to move away from proprietary systems to the open system that is the Internet.[40] No longer will you or should you build your own system. You will have seamless integration of information within and across organizations. As lines between organizations blur, the role of the leader becomes more complex. In response to the tragedy of September 11, 2001, one leader said that in challenging times one must think globally and act locally. This is also the best advice for the leader when contemplating a world connected by technology where globally indeed means global.

Discussion of differences between managing and leading is ongoing. Kotter said that leadership and management are distinctive and complementary systems of action, both of which are necessary to the health of the organization.[41] Management is defined as coping with complexity. Its components were developed to bring order and consistency to large corporations that developed over the past century or more. Leadership focuses on coming to terms with change. In an era of increasingly rapid change due to elements including technological innovation, globalization, the availability of information, a changing workforce, and a changing customer base, leadership is increasingly essential to the health of the organization. Both management and leadership need to be present in the organization. Both develop networks and relationships to accomplish task, and both need to have ways to ensure that individuals accomplish assigned tasks. While many elements are common to both leadership and management, the ways in which those elements are used often differ. Managers "develop the capacity to achieve a plan" by organizing and staffing a structure.[42] Leaders communicate a vision and align it with the individuals in the organization who are committed to achieving it. Managers use controls and monitor results to ensure that goals have been met while leaders motivate and inspire individuals to move forward to accomplish the goal.

Leaders are committed to producing change. They gather information from many sources, looking for patterns and linkages. They look for new ideas and for new insights into existing ways of doing things. They consider what the organization is now, what it should become, and how to get there. A vision of what the organization should be is created and strategies are developed to move toward that goal. The vision need not be original but it does need to describe the future organization. Long-term planning, once considered an essential component of management, is less useful in an environment in which change is so rapid. It is an expensive and time-consuming activity and plans covering more than the next year or so in advance are unreliable. The manager knows the goals of the organization and allocates resources to achieve those goals. When a new vision is set, the goals and priorities change. The manager devises a set of structures and provides training so that staff have the skills to complete tasks within a supportive work environment. Staff are informed of their responsibilities and a system of review and assessment is set in place. The manager's role is to take the assigned goals and make sure that they happen. The manager sets targets to be met and helps staff achieve them.

The leader focuses on the vision. Communication with all stakeholders to identify new needs and to develop new strategies is essential to crafting the vision and to ensuring that stakeholders are a part of its creation. Individuals are empowered when they have the opportunity to help shape the vision. The leader motivates individuals to achieve by stressing the role each has in the success of the vision. Individuals have the opportunity to grow and to learn new skills. Their role in the success of the vision is recognized and rewarded.

The successful organization combines the management structure with the means to respond to the vision of the leader. Pagonis stressed that a context for leadership needs to be developed.[43] A system that combines centralized control and decentralized action and one that is networked in numerous ways to allow for continuous communication provides the flexibility necessary to respond. Bringing people together to think collaboratively and to anticipate new opportunities or problems can be a regular aspect of a flexible organization in which individuals throughout the organization have responsibility for making decisions in their area of expertise.

The leader/manager is one who focuses on new approaches and ideas and then creates an organization that can respond. He or she establishes new goals, new options, and ways to respond to change rapidly, all of which are adopted by the organization. While the leader works to change the organization to meet new goals, he or she (at the same time as the managers) monitors the change so that it can be implemented with a minimum of stress.

Change occurs most often within existing organizations rather than through building entirely new organizations. Leading an existing organization to adapt to new conditions requires a combination of management and leadership skills. Leadership here is in large part empowering members of the organization to use their collective intelligence to help shape the vision of what the organization should become. While the leader may already have the vision in mind, participation by staff, customers, stakeholders, and with environmental factors in mind will shape the vision and ensure that they buy in to what they have helped to create.

The leader/manager is responsible for the direction of change, for the rate of change, and for making adjustments along the way. She or he must also "get employees to confront tough trade-offs in values, procedure, operating styles, and power."[44] The leader/manager gives the work back to the people. Decisions are made throughout the organization and not just at the top. Everyone has a stake in the vision, and each individual's task is to act to promote that vision. In this environment, individuals can feel that their contribution is important, that it counts. With a unity of purpose around the vision and the work being done, a feeling of community arises. The leader has succeeded as a leader when those he or she leads have the sense that they are doing important work, that they can acquire the needed skills to grow in their job, that they are challenged to grow, and finally, that they have gained personal satisfaction in what they do. The success of the leader is gauged by the attitudes and accomplishments of those who follow.

SUMMARY

Leadership as concept and as practice has been with us always—early on, through the examples of great men in history, and then through the examples of individuals responsible for managing businesses and organizations. Defining leadership has always been difficult and hundreds of different and often conflicting definitions have arisen. Some see leadership and management as totally different skills while others see leadership as an aspect of management and vice versa. E. Grady Bogus says that "leadership is an art form whose effectiveness is improved by the mastery of leadership and management research and the display of personal integrity."[45] He goes on to elaborate that management is an art form because it orchestrates talent. Management can also be a trap if it becomes overly interested in the tools of management rather than its purpose, and leadership can become a trap if the potential leader sees the role as one in which personal power or a personal agenda outweighs responsibility to the organization and its future.

NOTES

1. Niccolò Machiavelli, *The Prince* (London: Penguin, 1999).

2. Bruce Mazlish, "History, psychology, and leadership," in *Leadership: Multidisciplinary Perspectives*, edited by Barbara Kellerman (Englewood Cliffs, N.J.: Prentice-Hall, 1984), 13.

3. Chester Barnard, *The Function of the Executive* (Cambridge, Mass.: Harvard University Press, 1938).

4. Dankwart A. Rustow, "Introduction to the issue 'Philosophers and kings: Studies in leadership.'" *Daedalus* 97, no. 3 (Summer 1968): 683.

5. Robert C. Tucker, "The theory of charismatic leadership," in *Daedalus* 97, no. 3 (Summer 1968), 748.

6. Emory S. Bogardus, *Leaders and Leadership* (New York, Appleton-Century-Crofts, 1934).

7. Bogardus, *Leaders and Leadership*, 6.

8. For development of leaders, see Chris Argyris, *Increasing Leadership Effectiveness* (New York: John Wiley and Sons, 1976); for leaders in a group situation, see B. M. Bass, *Leadership and Performance beyond Expectations* (San Francisco: Jossey-Bass, 1978).

9. James M. Burns, *Leadership* (New York: Harper and Row, 1978).

10. James J. Cribbin, *Leadership Strategies for Organizational Effectiveness* (New York: American Management Association, 1981).

11. James J. Cribbin, *Leadership Strategies*.

12. Warren Bennis and Burt Nanus, *Leaders: The Strategies for Taking Charge* (New York: Harper and Row, 1985).

13. Bennis and Nanus, *Leaders*, 2.

14. Bennis and Nanus, *Leaders*, 42.

15. Bennis and Nanus, *Leaders*, 222–24.

16. Brooke E. Sheldon, *Leaders in Libraries: Styles and Strategies for Success* (Chicago: American Library Association, 1991).

17. Sheldon, *Leaders in Libraries*, 2.

18. Sheldon, *Leaders in Libraries*, 7.

19. Sheldon, *Leaders in Libraries*, 10.

20. James M. Kouzes and Barry Z. Pozner, *The Leadership Challenge: How to Get Extraordinary Things Done in Organizations* (San Francisco: Jossey-Bass, 1989).

21. Kouzes and Pozner, *The Leadership Challenge,* 305–307.

22. Kouzes and Pozner, *The Leadership Challenge*, xxi.

23. Kouzes and Pozner, *The Leadership Challenge*, 8.

24. Kouzes and Pozner, *The Leadership Challenge*, 9.

25. Kouzes and Pozner, *The Leadership Challenge*, 10.

26. Kouzes and Pozner, *The Leadership Challenge*, 11.

27. Kouzes and Pozner, *The Leadership Challenge*, 12.

28. Kouzes and Pozner, *The Leadership Challenge*, 12.

29. Kouzes and Pozner, *The Leadership Challenge*, 13.

30. Wess Roberts, *Leadership Secrets of Attila the Hun* (New York: Warner Books, 1987).

31. Roberts, *Leadership Secrets of Attila the Hun,* 17–19.

32. Theodore M. Hesberg, "Academic leadership," in *Leaders on Leadership: The College Presidency (New Directions for Higher Education)*, edited by James L. Fisher and Martha W. Tack, 5–8 (San Francisco: Jossey-Bass, 1988).

33. Judith Eaton, "Love me, lead me, or leave me alone," in *Leaders on Leadership*, edited by James L. Fisher and Martha W. Tack, 75–79 (San Francisco: Jossey-Bass, 1988).

34. Eaton, "Love me, lead me, or leave me alone," 79.

35. David Goleman, Richard Boystzes, and Annie McKee, "Primal leadership: The hidden driver of great performance, "*Harvard Business Review* 79, no. 11 (December 2001): 44.

36. Goleman et al., "Primal Leadership," 49.

37. William G. Pagonis, "Leadership in a combat zone," *Harvard Business Review* 79, no. 11 (December 2001): 107.

38. David Goleman, "Leadership that gets results," *Harvard Business Review* 78, no. 2 (March–April 2000): 78.

39. Jeffrey E. Garten, *The Mind of the CEO* (New York: Basic Books, 2001).

40. Editors, "The 2002 HBR breakthrough ideas for today's business agenda," *Harvard Business Review* 80, no. 3 (March 2002): 58–66.

41. John P. Kotter, "What leaders really do," *Harvard Business Review* 79, no. 11 (December 2001) 85–96.

42. Kotter, "What leaders really do," 86.

43. Pagonis, "Leadership in a combat zone," 114.

44. Ronald A. Heifitz and Donald L. Laurie, "The work of leadership," *Harvard Business Review* 79, no. 11(December 2001): 131–40.

45. E. Grady Bogus, *The Enemies of Leadership: Lessons for Leaders in Education* (Bloomington, Ind.: Phi Delta Kappa Educational Foundation, 1985), 4.

ADDITIONAL READINGS

Batten, Joe D. *Tough Minded Leadership*. New York: American Management Association, 1989.

Collingwood, Harris. "Leadership's first commandment: Know thyself." *Harvard Business Review* 79, no 11 (December 2001).

Covey, Stephen R. *The Seven Habits of Highly Effective People*. New York: Simon and Schuster, 1989.

Galbraith, John Kenneth. *The Anatomy of Power*. Boston: Houghton Mifflin, 1983.

Hayes, James L. *Memos for Management: Leadership*. New York: American Management Association, 1983.

Helgessen, Sally. *The Female Advantage: Women's Ways of Leadership*. New York: Doubleday Currency, 1990.

Kellerman, Barbara, ed. *Leadership: Multi-Disciplinary Perspectives*. Englewood Cliffs, N.J.: Prentice Hall, 1984.

McClure, Polley Ann. "10 lessons in leadership." *Educause Review* 39, no. 2 (March–April 2004):18–26.

Neuman, William H. *Administrative Action*. New York: Prentice Hall, 1950.

Peters, Thomas J., and Robert H. Waterman. *In Search of Excellence*. New York: Harper and Row, 1983.

Reichheld, Frederick F. "Lead for loyalty." *Harvard Business Review* 79, no. 7 (August 2001): 76–84.

Chapter Seven

Motivation, Management, and the Manager

Motivation and management are intertwined. The manager's role is to ensure that workers are motivated to do their best work, to enjoy their work, and to be productive employees. An understanding of how one motivates individuals to succeed is an essential tool in this process.

MOTIVATION

Motivation studies of work and workers paralleled the rise of industrialism. Employers were anxious to get the greatest productivity from each worker and the early focus was on how to make workers work harder and better. There was little interest in what workers thought about the job. In the late nineteenth and early twentieth century, Frederick W. Taylor's scientific study of work was aimed at making the worker a more efficient part of the machinery. During the early part of the twentieth century, this focus of worker as cog in an industrial machine was an underlying theme for study. Seeing the worker as an individual whose attitudes could have an impact on productivity gradually began to change the direction of research. As a result of this slowly changing attitude, research moved from an emphasis on scientific management in which individuals were seen as part of the machine-driven environment to a human relations perspective in which worker attitude became increasingly important and ways to motivate the worker became central to the study.

Of the numerous studies of worker motivation as it moved toward the human relations approach, those of McGregor, Likert, Herzberg, Argyris, and Maslow are among the best known and represent the progression from scientific management theories to present-day theory and application. McGregor identified two approaches the worker would most likely take to interact with the organization and labeled them Theory X and Theory Y.[1] Theory X assumes that the worker is lazy, unwilling to work, and must be forced to do the job. There must be external control of the worker's behavior and it is the role of management to determine policy and organize the work. The worker is assumed to lack ambition and dislike responsibility. Theory X fits well with the scientific management school of thought and, to an extent, justified the close control scientific management proponents advocated. Theory Y assumes that management is responsible for organizing the means of production and that within that context, the worker has the potential to take responsibility and to be productive. Management's role is to facilitate the activities of workers so that they are productive and that they gain personal satisfaction from their work. This approach embodies the human relations approach to motivation.

Rensis Likert concluded that managers fall into two categories: those who are employee-centered and focus on the worker and the environment necessary to do the job, and those who are production-centered and exert strict control over the workplace and who see employees as tools to get the job done.[2] Likert found that productivity was higher under the employee-centered supervisor. Additional research tended to modify this, finding that for some types of work, such as routine tasks requiring little independent thought, a production-centered approach was more successful. Likert also described a number of motivational management styles or systems that may operate within an organization.

System 1 describes a situation in which the manager has no confidence in subordinates and therefore does not involve them in decision making. The manager retains all control and uses fear, threats, and the occasional reward to motivate workers. To counter this, an informal organization of employees usually emerges to support the worker and to counter the goals of the formal organization in indirect ways.

Likert calls System 2 a master-servant relationship. The manager has some confidence in subordinates but retains most of the control, allowing some subordinates to make decisions. Here, too, fear, threats, and the occasional reward are the major motivating practices. Employees seldom communicate with their supervisors, as they fear punishment or disapproval if the supervisor is displeased with their input. Informal organizations in this context resist the goals of the formal organization and support the worker but are more subtle in that resistance than in System 1.

System 3 involves a greater level of confidence by the manager in the subordinates and some decision making occurs at all levels. Management delegates responsibility throughout the organization. Policymaking and major decisions continue to be centered at the top of the organization. Communication flows easily both downward and upward. The informal organization may or may not support the goals of the formal organization.

System 4 describes a situation in which management has complete confidence in subordinates and decision making is at all levels. Communication is open and moves freely upward, downward, and laterally. Subordinates are motivated to participate in goal setting, improving methods of work, and assessing progress toward agreed-upon goals. The formal and informal organizations are essentially the same or operate in tandem, as the subordinate does not need protection from the supervisor.

In most instances, Likert saw a positive relationship between the organization and the individual growing from a sense of loyalty and worth based on motivation. He suggested objective measures to assess organizational well-being, such as measuring the rates of absenteeism, job turnover, and grievances. When any of these is high, job satisfaction is in question. Conversely, when these numbers are low, one can assume that the level of job satisfaction is high.

Herzberg identified two sets of workplace factors: hygienic factors and motivational factors.[3] Hygienic factors are those conditions of work the employee expects to experience in the workplace, such as a safe and clean work environment, health benefits, and a fair salary. These are expected conditions and while their reduction or absence will cause objections, in and of themselves they are not motivators. He named achievement, recognition of achievement, the work itself, responsibility, and opportunities for growth and advancement as major motivating factors. Motivational satisfiers relate to the job content while dissatisfiers or hygienic factors are part of the job context. Later research by House and Wigdor identified a third motivational factor, that of the job/work situation.[4] It was determined that the immediate work environment and the overall organizational style affected motivation, as did actions and attitudes of peers and supervisors. While the organizational style sets the tone for the supervisors' actions in their units, each supervisor has a managerial style. For some supervisors, it is difficult but necessary to defer to the organization's style and to modify one's own management style.

Writing in 1987, Herzberg stressed that KITA (kick in the ass) practices may be assumed by some to motivate workers but they, in fact, do not.[5] Activities suggested by management and mistakenly determined by them to motivate workers include the following:

- Reduced time at work may be seen by management as a motivator, as they assume individuals want to work less. In fact, the motivated individual wants to work more and can become frustrated by limits imposed on the work time.
- While increased wages motivate workers to earn more, fringe benefits are seen as a right and no longer serve as motivators. In those instances where employers reduce existing benefits, employees tend to become angry and may grieve or leave. Restoring benefits does not motivate, it simply restores an expected right.
- The emphasis on human relations training including communications training, employee counseling, and other management imposed "motivators" rarely work as they contribute little to achievement, recognition of the work done, responsibility for work, or to personal growth.

Herzberg proposed enriching the job by upgrading its scope and challenge and increasing worker responsibility for the job. This emphasizes his earlier statement that it is job content and not context that motivates.

Maslow proposed that all humans have needs.[6] Once one level of need is met, another level of need receives attention. Satisfying these needs is what motivates individuals. He identified the following hierarchy of needs:

1. Physiological needs
2. The need for safety and security
3. Social needs
4. The need for esteem
5. The need for self-actualization

Physiological needs are basic needs required for the maintenance of life including sufficient food and water and the need for warmth. Without these, it is not possible to exist or to move to another level. One can see pictures and descriptions of refugees in war zones to see that their focus is on physical survival, a need that pushes out all others.

The need for safety and security requires a stable environment in which one is safe from bodily harm or psychological damage and is essential to human development. Many individuals have a very strong need for security and safety and hesitate to try new things that might disrupt their feelings of security. They resent change and tend to be very conservative in their actions. They need to know what the rules are and what to expect. Any changes in rules or expectations create stress. Other individuals function well in a less secure environment and are willing to try new things. Each individual, however, needs some level of safety and security to function successfully.

Once the basic physiological needs and the needs for safety are met, the individual reaches out to others, seeking social interaction. In the workplace, social interaction occurs as workers share information, discuss work-related problems, and learn of areas of common interest outside the workplace. Social interaction takes place elsewhere in the worker's world: at home, at church, in social groups, and in the community. There may be conflicting social pressures if and when the social norms of the workplace do not relate well to those outside the workplace or to personal concerns. For example, the individual who is active in environmental groups may find it difficult to work in an industry known for its lack of concern over the pollution it creates.

Individuals strive for the respect of others through such activities as work well done. Esteem from fellow workers is highly important. Self-esteem comes from knowing one has done a good job or knowing that one's job is important and that one is respected for doing it well. Esteem is often measured by external factors such as salary increases and awards. Being elected to office or selected to manage an important task are signs that the individual is held in esteem.

Self-actualization is the feeling that one has reached one's full potential. This requires that the individual know what his or her full potential is. The desire to "be all you can be" is a goal toward which the individual strives, but it is rarely met as there is always a new challenge.

Each individual operates on several levels at the same time. Those in very difficult circumstances spend much of their time fighting for food, shelter, and a level of safety. If they have remaining energy, they look to their social needs. In the workplace, the basic needs are usually met and the individual operates in the social and esteem levels of motivation, and perhaps on the self-actualization level.

Another way of looking at motivation is to assume that individuals learn from experience and what they do today is to an extent based on the outcomes of past actions rather than on need or specific motivation. At work, the manager's behavior and actions serve as the stimulus for the worker's behavior and actions. This reinforcement theory, associated most often with B. F. Skinner, aims at strengthening positive behavior and correcting negative actions.[7] Skinner went as far as to say that "what we need is a technology of behavior."[8] In some ways this goes back to Taylor or to McGregor's Theory X where the worker is seen as not capable or willing to pursue work without external controls.

Kanter suggests new tools for motivating people in an environment in which hierarchical structures are less evident (but still present).[9] A belief in the mission of the organization is a strong motivator, particularly in the not-for-profit sector. Individuals who select a career in the information professions are often motivated to do so as they believe that access to information is a major component of a democratic society. The information organization that actively pursues this mission will maintain the interest and support of those staff members with like interests. The individuals who have a level of control over their own professional life are strongly motivated to contribute their skills to furthering the mission. The opportunity to share in the continuing development of the organization's mission and to learn new skills further strengthen the individual's desire to participate. Recognition of their efforts reinforces their self-esteem. The feelings that one is doing a good job, that the job has value, and that others recognize that value constitute the most powerful motivator.

Livingston stressed that the way in which one treats a person determines in large part how that individual will perform.[10] The manager who is indifferent to a worker, who expects little from that individual, and who rarely admits that the individual is performing well can destroy the self-image of even the most confident worker. If goals are unrealistically high and if there is little or no effort to help the employee reach goals, and when there appears to be a lack of respect for the employee, that individual will most likely move to a different solution or to a different career.

New employees need to be mentored by experienced managers who can help them develop their talents within the organization. At one time it was often heard that the first thing one should do with a new employee was "to knock out all of those funny ideas they learned in school and to introduce them to the real world"—that is, the existing environment in the organization. Today, managers take the approach that the organizational culture benefits from the new insights brought to it by new employees and should ideally be sufficiently flexible to include those new insights. New employees should also be sufficiently flexible to adapt their work style to the organizational culture of which they have become a member. A new employee may not fully understand what is expected in the new work environment and it is the role of the manager as mentor to explain organizational culture and the employee's role in the organization. It is also the mentor's role to identify the skills and insights the new employee brings to the organization and to fit them into the existing culture. Changing another person's behavior does not work, but reframing or recasting a situation may lead to solutions. Often, problems in the new employee's motivation stem from differing perceptions of the work situation or the problem. If the discussion focuses on the problem and not on the individual, and if there is a willingness by each individual to listen to others, problems can usually be clarified and then can be solved. Problems with motivation are often problems of communication rather than problems of unwillingness to work.[11]

Managers may try to tell the employee that they should follow a particular set of steps to meet an objective, but these steps may differ so much from the individual's thought processes that failure or frustration results. One solution is to state the objective and charge the employee with achieving it. Or in discussion with the employee, blocks to performance may be identified, for example, the lack of a particular skill, lack of specific information, or lack of organizational support. Sometimes the manager is unable to communicate with an employee, is judgmental, or treats the employee in ways seen by the employee as disrespectful. The motivation problem may be partially that of the manager's style or the way in which that style is perceived. However, the employee who does not appear to fit into the organization because of different responses to authority or because of a different approach to problem solving may still become a valuable asset.

From the manager's perspective, it is necessary to determine the stimuli that will motivate an individual to work productively. A number of theories have been put forth and each suggests needs and/or activities that will move the employee to higher levels of productivity. The manager needs to be aware of these various theories and the motivational processes they describe. Motivation is personal and each individual responds or does not respond depending on that individual's own situation. Each individual is different and what works for one person will not work for another in exactly the same way. Further, as Maslow pointed out, individuals are motivated by different factors at different times.

Employees need to know what equals successful performance in the organization and should receive assistance in achieving it. Most individuals want to do a good job; to do a good job, they need to understand the objectives, priorities, and values of the organization of which they are a part. They need to be able to assess their own performance objectively and to adjust as needed. In the industrial age, workers were seen as rented labor that could be replaced as easily as a piece of malfunctioning equipment. In the information age, workers have become recognized as the organization's core asset, whose skills and abilities bring strength to the organization.

> In motivation, managers are faced with complex and interrelated problems. Managers must provide for an orderly hierarchy of responsibility and authority, and logical, rationally placed distribution of work in order to meet organizational objectives. From the standpoint of the individual, organizations provide channels through which personal goals can be achieved and a set of boundaries within which actions take place . . . but individual and organizational objectives can be integrated by emphasizing their mutual interdependence. . . . The achievement of positive motivation in organizations depends not only on understanding the concepts of motivation but also on accepting the commitments required and in actually living effective motivation within the organization.[12]

MANAGEMENT

Management is the process of working with people to accomplish objectives. How one does this has been an area of comment and study for many years. Management philosophies and processes have, for the most part, been developed in the for-profit sector and then adapted with more or less success to the not-for-profit sector.[13] Keller says, "Management is to organizations other than the state what statecraft is to the state." He goes on to differentiate management from administration by saying that management emphasizes doing the right things while administration focuses on doing things right. Administration looks at the efficient operation of current activities while management focuses on those things that make a difference in the organization, on the effectiveness of what is done.

In current books, such as Wess Roberts' *Leadership Secrets of Attila the Hun*, the argument is made that our ancestors from the beginnings of social interaction were searching for ways to accomplish their objectives through the organized efforts of individuals.[14] Machiavelli's *The Prince*, a product of Renaissance Italy, is the first management classic whose concepts have stood the test of time and continue to influence today's managers. Management is now defined as a product of the social, economic, and political developments of the past century with inputs from earlier efforts to determine ways to organize work and workers and to exert authority over the process. Each culture has shaped its own approach to management depending upon the social values and the role of organizations and institutions in the culture.[15] Drucker calls management the activity that energizes the institution; that it is the relationship between strategy and structure.[16] He further identifies management as the crucial factor in economic and social development.[17] Management is a practice, not a science, a practice based on knowledge. It is a generic function that

- gives direction to the organization it manages
- sets objectives and organizes resources
- directs vision and resources toward the greater results
- organizes work for productivity
- leads the worker toward productivity and achievement
- is responsible for the social impact of the enterprise
- is responsible for producing results[18]

Foundations of Management

While management as an activity has been part of social interaction from earliest times, modern management has its roots in the nineteenth century and is largely a twentieth-century development with an emphasis on the latter half of the century, particularly the period after World War II when there was a significant growth in the size and number of organizations both in the for-profit and the not-for-profit sectors. The workforce was more sophisticated than it had been prior to World War II and included a large component of returning veterans, many of whom had taken advantage of the G.I. Bill to advance their education. From this combination of massive growth in business and industry plus the presence of a new kind of workforce, management as we now define it emerged.

Although modern management styles emerged during this period, their roots go back to the rise of industrialism and the factory system when factory owners wanted to ensure that maximum productivity was realized in the interaction of workers with their machines. John Stewart Mill in Britain in the nineteenth century studied the factory worker and was noted for his work in analyzing and synthesizing human emotion. Charles Babbage looked at the benefits of work specialization and division of labor. He continued Mill's work by conducting time and motion studies. Additionally, he factored in the cost of each activity.

It was a short step to the development of scientific management studies in the United States in the late nineteenth century. Frederick W. Taylor conducted time and motion studies in the American factory to determine how long a task should take and how many times the worker should complete it in a day. The Galbraiths, Frank and Lillian, added to the time and motion studies by specifying ways in which the worker should move and the order of movements in order to achieve maximum productivity. In effect, man became part of the factory machinery and his role was to enhance the operation of the machine.

Taylor's second effort in scientific management was to recommend that the worker be paid based on what he, Taylor, determined to be a fair number of times the worker's specified activity should be completed in a specified time period. Exceed the number of times the task was done and more pay would result. The worker had no part in deciding the fairness of the number of tasks set, nor did he or she have any control over slowdowns caused by delays such as slow delivery of materials, illness of other workers, or power failures. Harrington Emerson's twelve principles of efficiency were aimed at "eliminat[ing] wanton, wicked waste."[19] He urged management to have clearly defined goals, use common sense in decision making, seek advice when necessary, and apply rules fairly. He supported and furthered the application of scientific management.

The emphasis on man as a cog in the factory's machinery focused on doing the task as efficiently as possible. Treating individual workers as part of the mechanized process and not as people worked only because of the social environment of the period. The 1880s to World War I (1914–1918) was in the United States a period of high immigration with thousands of new workers, many of whom lacked formal education and/or a command of

English entering the workforce. It was also a time in parts of the country when rural areas had a surplus of labor and workers were moving to the city and factory jobs. Being able to step into a job that required a minimum of either education or language proficiency was a quick route to participation in the economy. In other countries, the workforce coming from rural or colonial areas could also blend into the factory environment with a minimum of preparation.

The emphasis on worker productivity and the absence of concern for the worker as an individual came to receive criticism for its one-sided approach. The decades from the end of World War I (1918) to the end of World War II (1945) saw a gradual recognition that workers were individuals and that they responded positively to being treated as individuals. Munsterberg and Scott both studied worker's attitudes and the impact of these attitudes on productivity.[20] They were among the first to approach the worker from a human relations point of view. One of the seminal studies from the early human relations perspective was conducted at Western Electric's Hawthorne, Illinois, plant by a team of researchers from Harvard Business School under the direction of Elton Mayo, a noted proponent of the human relations approach. Begun in 1927, the study's purpose was to determine the validity of a suggestion made earlier by the Galbraiths that brief periods of rest during the day would improve worker production. Their specific interest was in the relationship of worker fatigue to productivity. Mayo's researchers varied the length of rest periods, their timing, and other variables and found that, regardless of the variable they changed, productivity increased. It was illustrated as a result of the study that workers behaved differently when they are being observed. This Hawthorne Effect was interpreted by some to mean that if one pays attention to workers, regardless of the specific actions, productivity will increase; others have questioned this conclusion. Mayo continued his research on the worker and rejected the long-held hypothesis that workers worked only from self-interest and did not interact as a group but were largely disorganized. From his research, Mayo established that group membership was important to the worker and that group norms have a strong effect on the worker's motivation and productivity. That same group membership serves as a support to the worker outside the workplace. Mayo and his associates stressed that workers have personal psychological needs in addition to the group needs and said that managers must be sensitive to both if they are to achieve organizational objectives.

Elements of Management

Fayol outlined a general theory and a set of principles of management that form the basis of most listings of those elements that are part of management.[21] Although first published in 1916, his work continues to be cited regularly. While later research and practice has modified them to a degree, Fayol's listing continues to be at the core of management practice.

1. Division of work specialization. Jobs should be designed to be fairly limited in scope so that the worker can develop a high degree of skill and thus increase personal productivity. It is easier for the supervisor to maintain control if only a small number of activities are assigned to any one person. As the workforce has become better educated and as work is more and more often assigned to teams or other groups, specialization is giving way to some degree to broader work assignments. Still, within the more flexible work situation, individuals are expected to have special skills.

2. Authority and responsibility. These two elements go together. The supervisor who has the authority to supervise is also responsible for seeing that objectives are accomplished. As authority for making decisions is pushed further down in the organization, each worker who is expected to make decisions also carries the responsibility for their outcomes. When teams are formed to accomplish tasks, authority and responsibility rest within the team.

3. Discipline. Rules for conduct exist within each organization. Some are part of the organizational culture, others derive from federal and state law, while others derive from the job itself or from the technology used to accomplish tasks. In all cases, the workplace operates according to a web of rules that is in place and is to be enforced fairly. Should rules conflict or become dated, they are to be reviewed and revised in accordance with the new situation.

4. Unity of command. No individual should report primarily to more than one person. There should be clear lines of authority. In a hierarchical organization, this is fairly easy to chart. In other organizational structures where, for example, a team approach is taken, the authority may be determined within the team by team members. But the total team effort is directed toward an activity determined by someone to whom the team as a whole is responsible. Often, an individual is tem-

porarily assigned to an area or task different from the primary job or may be assigned a task that covers activities in more than one unit. In each instance, there should be a primary report. Some may work half-time in one area and half-time in another. These are actually two separate jobs, each with a primary report. Consider a children's librarian in a branch library who is responsible both to the branch librarian and to the children's/young adult coordinator in the central library. In this case, the two supervisors need to determine the reporting responsibilities and inform the children's librarian of the decision.

5. Unity of direction. There should be only one plan of action and one person responsible for that plan. All activities that have the same objective should be the responsibility of one individual.

6. Subordination of the individual to the general interest. When an individual joins an organization, that individual agrees to follow its rules and support its objectives. If these diverge from personal objectives, those of the organization prevail. If the individual does not or cannot support those objectives, she or he should resign.

7. Remuneration. Payment for work is to be fair and appropriate and acceptable to both employer and employee. Performance reviews, fairly and regularly conducted, are the basis for remuneration. While performance reviews were not common when these elements were initially set forth, they have since become a standard part of determining salary increases.

8. Centralization. For Fayol, centralization of activities was desirable as supervision was easier and lines of authority clearer. With improved telecommunications and information technology advances, and with the many options for organizational structure, physical centralization is less necessary for good management than it once was. So long as there is a centralization of lines of communication, physical decentralization may be a preferred structure.

9. Lines of command or scalar chain. Fayol stressed the need for a hierarchical structure and clear lines of command. Again, as with centralization, the range of organizational structures has multiplied and a strictly hierarchical organization is no longer the one best way of doing things.

10. Order. Units in an organization should be coordinated so that individuals and groups work together in harmony. Responsibilities of each unit should be clearly understood, as should their relationship to other

units. When cross-functional teams or committees are set up, there should be a clear understanding of how they relate to existing units.

11. Equity. Employees are to be treated as individuals in a fair and equitable manner. Managers who play favorites or are perceived as doing so create a dysfunctional environment.

12. Stability of tenure. High turnover of employees is costly in a number of ways. The hiring process and need to train new staff is costly. Work that could be done easily by an experienced employee may not be done, may be done poorly, or may be assigned to others who already have a full set of responsibilities. It takes time for an employee to become a valued employee, and to know how the organization functions and how to work within it to accomplish objectives. A high turnover rate indicates that a motivational or management problem exists. The supervisor may be difficult to work for, the job itself may not be satisfying or may require skills not compatible with the job description, pay may not be competitive, or working conditions may be uncomfortable or unsafe. Whenever turnover is unduly high, the reasons are to be identified and the situation corrected.

13. Initiative. Initiative on the part of employees should be encouraged. While some organizations promote conformity, the creative employee often has greater interest in the work and may suggest new ways of doing it. The employee has greater interest in doing a job if there is an opportunity for input in how it is to be accomplished.

14. Esprit de corps. With a sense of unity in the work group, there is a feeling of working together to achieve common goals and a willingness to support coworkers.

Fayol's listing is as useful today as when it was first published. While some of the elements have been modified through research and practice, and telecommunications and information technology has been incorporated into the workplace, they still apply.

Today in Management

Each school of thought builds on what has gone before, modifying, adapting, rejecting, and introducing new concepts. It has become increasingly apparent that the social, cultural, economic context within which we live exerts considerable pressure on how we manage. Management is not value-free. It is closely tied to the society in which it operates. The workforce changes with each new person hired. Drucker listed seven areas in which he saw innovation in management as important.[22] Although his first listing was in 1973, his later writing has supported its elements. He stressed the following areas for additional study.

- Scientific management of work is the key to productivity. While early work in scientific management focused on labor, it is now recognized that productivity is the balance of land, labor, and capital. The worker wants affluence and a clean environment. Management wants productivity. To achieve both, we must understand the broader principles of production.
- Decentralization has become a basic principle. New models of organizing the workforce and new ways of structuring activities are possible. Advances in information technology and telecommunications allow us to build fluid organizations responsive to today's objectives and workforce, and organizations that can change easily to meet tomorrow's demands.
- Personnel management in today's environment requires a new look at how one organizes work, manages people, and evaluates their productivity. New approaches to leadership in a less obviously hierarchical structure, such as team approaches or participatory management, allow an opportunity to refocus the leadership role. No longer are the roles of manager and controller always appropriate. Leading, directing, and mentoring may be better approaches.
- Develop managers for tomorrow's needs. Managers can no longer just manage their unit or organization but must tie into the larger world. The manager must understand the environment and look for opportunities to be entrepreneurial and innovative. The manager must also be able to work with a more technically sophisticated, better educated, and more diverse workforce and to coordinate their efforts while meeting their needs for satisfying work and the opportunity for growth.
- Managerial accounting and the ways in which the analysis and use of financial information can be used to improve productivity is an increasingly important tool. Information technology systems allow us to develop and maintain up-to-the-minute awareness of the location and growth and increase or decrease of our resources. Early in the study of productivity, cost was considered as a factor. Current technology allows

us to use cost and other financial data in daily decision making and to fully exploit cost data.

- Marketing, once seen narrowly as advertising a product or service, has become much more than that. It is now seen as a means of informing the public of the value of the organization and its contribution to general comfort and welfare.

- Long-range planning has become a cornerstone of all organizational activity as we constantly look to tomorrow to position the organization to meet new challenges. This does not mean that complex plans are devised to be followed rigidly, but that long-range directions are projected based on the wide range of information available and are adapted as appropriate.

Drucker emphasizes the role of the knowledge worker in each of these activities to design and develop systems to aid in management, to help interpret data emerging from these systems, and to use the information derived from these systems to conduct daily activities. Supporting the knowledge worker are the engineer and computer scientist who develop new technologies that the knowledge worker can apply in the work setting. Transformation of the workplace through technology, while already impressive, has only begun. The potential to reengineer how we conduct business and provide services is being realized. How technology interacts with management and management structures is a continuing saga.

The Manager and Information

As organizations continue to build their information systems through increased use of technology to manage many aspects of planning, personnel, financial, evaluative, and other activities, it is increasingly necessary to manage the information in support of the organization. These inputs are in addition to the increasingly recognized need to see each employee as a source of usable unique information, to tap that information, and to bring it to bear on the activities of the organization.

Managers often ask why the information that is available is not used in managing the organization. Consultants are hired to give advice but that advice is often shelved rather than taken. Staff members know what to do but often do not act. Learning that occurs in one department often does not find its way to similar situations in other departments. In a study of management practices, Pfeiffer and Sutton asked managers to rate the importance of twenty-five practices for sharing information and then to indicate if they were carried out in their organization.[23] In every case, managers were doing less of what they knew to be important.[24] They often gave elaborate reasons for this gap between knowledge and action. Researchers found that managers were most likely to implement what is known (e.g., best practices) than to implement something new.[25] They tended to talk about what they and their staff do but in fact did not know if they were actually doing it. Talking about an activity is not the same as doing. Knowing what to do is not the same as knowing how to do it. A difference between technical and professional staff is that while technical workers know what to do and how to do it, they may not know the implications, organization wide, of what they are doing. Professional staff have the broader perspective to understand the context in which they are working but may not know how to implement an activity. Many so-called knowledge management practices in the organization are really a reorganization or redistribution of existing resources rather than the use of new knowledge to set a new direction

Pfeiffer and Sutton further determined that managers often do not know how people use information in their jobs. They equated the use of technology to gather data with a functioning knowledge management system and did not appreciate the value of informal transfer of information among individuals working on the same or similar tasks. While information technology allows us to gather and analyze masses of information to support decision making, the manager must be aware of the value of communication among workers who are doing the job and who know what the problems are and who may have solutions. The manager's role in an information-rich environment continues to evolve as use of information in support of management functions grows in importance and complexity.

THE MANAGER

Management is a social function, conditioned by the culture in which it has developed. Its purpose is to ensure that organizations operate smoothly. The role of the manager is to ensure that the work of the organization or subunit for which she or he is responsible is accomplished at a high level of quality and in a timely manner. The manager is often called the energy that moves the organization forward. The manager may be the CEO of the organization, a department head, or the supervisor of a work team. The authority and responsibilities at each level differ but the range of activities is similar. In all cases, the manager has formal authority over an organizational unit and performs a set of roles.[26] Mintzberg identified ten roles of the job. The extent to which each role is exercised depends on the level in the organization at which the individuals manage. Three of these roles are interpersonal: figurehead, leader, and liaison. As a figurehead, the manager represents the unit to other internal units and to external groups. In a social context, the manager appears at functions that reward efforts and celebrate personal and work achievements. This is the public face of the manager and of the unit represented. How those outside the unit view the unit is in large part dependent on how well this role is performed. Internally, the manager is a leader who motivates staff in their work and assures them that they are working toward agreed-upon goals. The manager has the power and authority to insist that employees' efforts further the organizational goals. The third interpersonal role is as a liaison with other units internally and with external individuals and agencies whose concerns and activities impact the work unit. These include suppliers, government agencies, and most importantly, the users of the service/product produced. Liaison with other units may focus on coordinating existing activities or it may focus on changing relationships. Managers should have the flexibility to think beyond limitations imposed by the organizational structure and to devise more useful interactions when desirable. This may cause difficulties when someone else perceives that their turf is being invaded. Working with other managers to find the best means of cooperative action to work toward common objectives is a central component of the liaison function.[27]

The three information roles of the manager are to monitor the environment, disseminate information, and identify trends and issues that may impact the organization. An organization is closely tied to the environment in which it functions and it is an essential part of the manager's job to know what the environmental conditions are. The manager's second information role is to share information with those within the organizational unit so that they have the information they need to do their job and that they are aware of the environmental factors that may impact their job. The third information role is to serve as spokesperson for the unit. Reports prepared by the unit for internal and/or external consumption, public statements, and concerns voiced by members of the unit that do not respond to internal solutions are all the responsibility of the manager to move to the next level for acceptance, approval, or attention. The competent manager treats each of these very carefully and moves forward for decision making only those that require authority or responsibility not resident in the unit.

The four decisional roles of the manager include entrepreneur, disturbance handler, resource allocator, and negotiator. As an entrepreneur, the manager seeks new and better ways to get the job done. Improvements in process as the result of internal initiatives enhances flexibility of the unit and shows employees that initiative on their part is welcome. As disturbance handler, the manager solves problems that may arise from misunderstandings, breakdown of equipment or processes, or other glitches. As resource allocator, the manager sets priorities for action by giving resources to top-ranked objectives and reducing resources for less urgent objectives. Each of these decisional roles involves negotiation, the final role of the manager.

Each of these roles is interrelated and the manager exercises each of them regularly. While some see the role of manager as that of a thoughtful, systematic planner, in reality the manager responds to the pressures of the moment and is expected to make the right decision quickly and to make several decisions at the same time, often on unrelated topics. The manager's day is a mix of routine activities and crises. In order to be productive as a manager, it is essential that deadlines be met. To do this, the manager must make the best use of time and be vigilant so that time is not frittered away on unimportant activities. Today's manager must be sensitive to the needs and concerns of today's worker, whose expectations for fair treatment in the workplace are much higher than those of an earlier time. As has been stated earlier, workers tend to be better educated than earlier generations of workers and have higher expectations that their work and working situation be satisfying.

Regardless of how decisions are made, the manager is responsible for those decisions he or she makes. How that decision is reached depends on a number of factors. Tannenbaum and Schmidt identify three factors that determine how one reaches decisions: forces in the manager, forces in the subordinate, and forces in the environment.[28] Managerial forces include the manager's personal value system and level of comfort in interacting with others. Their confidence and level of trust in subordinates, their own leadership inclinations, and their feelings of security in an uncertain situation contribute to their comfort level. Subordinate forces include a willingness to assume responsibility, their interest in the problem under discussion, and their level of information about an issue. Can they deal with ambiguity and do they expect to participate in making decisions? Environmental forces include the type of organization, its values, and its culture. The size and effectiveness of work units, the nature of the problem, and the pressures of time all affect the manager's comfort level in sharing activities leading to decisions.

The manager is sensitive not only to the environment in which the organization functions but also to the individuals who are part of the work team. These individuals expect to know what the organizational priorities are, if and when they change, and if the individuals' role or relationship to the organization and to stated priorities has changed. This requires more than communicating information to staff. It also requires discussion, the opportunity for the staff to ask questions, to refute or agree with recommendations, and to be satisfied that their concerns are heard and their views respected.[29] They should also be informed of changes in practices and any changes in their assigned activities or status. While the manager has ultimate responsibility, staff members need to be fully informed in a timely fashion of issues, of decisions made, and of outcomes of those decisions. This allows each member of the organization to contribute unique knowledge to an issue and therefore to be a part of the final decision.

An effective manager works with staff to encourage skills that support participation in decision making. Individuals who think independently are self-starters and risk takers may at times cause the manager stress, but these characteristics make them valuable members of the organization. The individual who has a creative approach rather than always following the standard company approach may be the one who seeks out better ways of accomplishing tasks and meeting objectives. Managers work with staff so that they are comfortable managing themselves and are able to discern their own strengths and weaknesses. They serve as mentors and provide advice and feedback to staff members so that staff takes ownership of the goals of the organization and contribute to meeting them. The successful manager is a coach who motivates workers, gives feedback, and offers suggestions for improvement. Employees expect their manager to give them an honest statement of their responsibilities and honest feedback on their performance. They expect consistency and fairness so that they know what to expect. They want interesting work, a feeling of economic stability, and the opportunity for personal growth. As a manager, one has the personal satisfaction of managing a process that satisfies both the manager and the staff and those to whom the manager reports. The successful manager achieves goals with the participation of a staff that is motivated and productive. "Rank, title or official charter will be less important factors in success at the new managerial work than having knowledge, skills, and sensitivity to mobilize people and motivate them to do their best."[30]

In difficult times, such as those that occur when major changes are imposed on the organization or when financial difficulties require extensive review of priorities, the manager does not revert to a more authoritarian approach but involves staff in the decision-making process by informing them fully of the situation and by involving them in the discussion of ways to approach the difficult issues. Although the decision is that of the manager, openness in sharing information and encouraging discussion ensures greater acceptance of decisions when made.

The manager has a manager. It may be the director of an organization, a government official in a larger unit, a board of trustees, the university provost, or some other higher authority. As the link between the unit and the next higher level of the organization, the manager is part of both structures and has responsibilities and expectations from both directions. The relationship between the manager and the next higher level of authority is one of mutual dependence. It is necessary to recognize the strengths and weaknesses of one's managers and to understand their preferred style of management and to adapt one's style to it to the extent desirable. Know how your manager wants to receive information and manage its upward flow accordingly (the format, not the content). Know what your manager's responsibilities are and how you can assist in supporting them. Managers who understand the power structure of the organization and how to get things done in the larger organization strengthen their unit's ability to perform. Managers are facilitators both within and outside their primary area of responsibility.[31]

The manager as coordinator and organizer is dependent on others to supply resources either through the organization or from outside. The manager is also dependent on others to do much of the actual work of the unit. While the manager has the power to exert authority over staff in the unit, it needs to be exercised carefully, fairly, and should be done to support the unit's objectives. The manager is sensitive to what staff consider the legitimate use of power and understands the various types of power and influence. The manager is comfortable using power and recognizes that the use of power affects the lives and well-being of others.[32]

Kanter sees today's manager involved in fewer hierarchical situations and in charge of more cross-functional teams and joint ventures.[33] She says that managers add value to activities by building connections and by being skilled in negotiations. As they continue to be increasingly involved in cross-boundary negotiations, managers tend to push authority for decisions downward. In this environment, prime requirements are knowledge and skill plus the ability to motivate others. This tendency plus "the absence of day-to-day restraints, the admonition to assume responsibility, the pretense of equality, the elimination of visible status markers, the prevalence of candid dialogs across hierarchical levels—these can give employees a false sense that all hierarchy is a thing of the past."[34] Despite more flexible organizational structures and an increased collegial atmosphere, there is still a reporting structure and a higher authority. It is the responsibility of the manager to maintain focus on organizational objectives and to exert that authority as appropriate.

The New Manager

The new manager, new to a particular management position or new to being a manager, is responsible for the activities of the unit(s) to be managed. The manager at the next level of authority may be an excellent guide to assist in indicating what is expected or may have little knowledge of what needs to be done in a particular unit or may have unreasonable expectations of what the new manager is to do. The new manager should always learn from his or her manager what the job expectations are for the first ninety days, for the first year, and for the long term.[35] The new manager should also learn how people in the organization communicate. What are the communicating and reporting formats and what are the informal channels? Are there particular people or groups (internal and external) who need to be included in discussions? Reviewing personnel files, reviewing the unit's budget history to determine if and how allocations of resources have changed, and reviewing all other resources available to the unit is essential to understanding what resources are available to work with. Meeting separately with each direct report is an important means of opening communication lines as well as assessing the strength of existing staff. It is a two-way activity as it allows staff to get to know the new manager.

The new manager needs to develop a management attitude. The manager is expected to be responsible for the unit and to take charge of activities. Often, the new manager finds a number of unresolved personnel and resource problems not solved by the former manager. The expectation is that the new manager will sort out the problems, make wise decisions, and see that they are implemented. This requires that the manager take an immediate active role by learning how things work and do not work within the unit, by interacting with staff, and by making decisions. One learns on the job and does so from day one. The manager who shows confidence and takes charge immediately gains the confidence of staff and superiors.

Women as Managers

Do women have unique qualifications as leaders? As more and more women become managers and leaders, it is possible to view their activities and identify ways in which they differ from male managers. Studies of leadership and management until fairly recently have focused on white male executives because women and minorities were poorly represented in executive positions. The first women and minorities elevated to management and leadership roles were expected to conform to what men saw as appropriate leadership styles and to work within their designated space in the hierarchy.[36] Helgesen's study of how leading women executives managed provides a well-rounded picture of the woman as manager. Using a diary approach similar to that conducted by Mintzberg in 1973 when he studied what male managers did each day, she identified patterns of managerial activities. As she used Mintzberg's methodology, she was able to compare and contrast her findings with those he had reported earlier.

Mintzberg found that approximately 60 percent of the male manager's day was taken up in formally scheduled meetings. The day was characterized by interruption, discontinuity, and fragmentation. Secretaries were used as shields to protect against this chaotic situation. Lack of external nonwork stimuli led to intellectual isolation. While they had a wide range of connections with individuals outside the organization, the men's contacts were focused on information gathering for the job. Daily demands prevented time for reflection and planning. Mintzberg found that male managers had little time for nonwork-related activities and home was seen as just another place to work. Mail and phone calls were seen as burdens to be relegated to secretaries. Male managers identified themselves closely with their job and the personal prestige the position offered. They had difficulty in sharing information, which they equated with power. They saw employees as a means to an end, that of completing tasks. Sacrificing the family to the job was not seen as a problem. Helgesen found when she began her study that organizations had changed since Mintzberg's study and that the pattern of the manager solely focused on the job to the detriment of all else had eroded.

In looking at women's managerial styles, she found similarities and dissimilarities. Women tended to work at a steady pace but took regular short breaks. They did not see unscheduled tasks and encounters as interruptions but as opportunities to interact with staff. Women managers placed a greater focus on relationships and on ensuring that staff knew she cared about them and about what they are doing. Women managers saw secretaries as information conduits rather than as protective shields. While preferring direct encounters, mail, telephone messages, and so forth were seen as an essential means of maintaining contact. Like men, women maintained a large, complex network of external relationships. Women managers kept a continuous focus on the long range and on the world around them as it impacted their work. They made time for activities not directly related to work and overtly avoided intellectual isolation. Family life was very important.

Helgesen looked for factors that might account for the differences in management style. Women managers looked for metaphors descriptive of cooperation while men touted the sports metaphor in which there are winners and losers and competition is king. Women managers saw themselves in the middle of the organizations as facilitators rather than perched atop a pyramid directing all activities. Women managers are guides, not dictators. They tend to be people centered and see people as the key to accomplishing tasks. Collaboration replaces dictating. A supportive environment in which each individual has a role describes what some call a woman's way of managing.

As hierarchy in the organization has become less the model and as types of organizational structure have proliferated, the variety of management approaches has increased. Many of the approaches once called feminine and too soft to be of use have become part of the toolkit of all managers.

SUMMARY

Employee motivation to work is directly related to the personal need for achievement and the extent to which the work situation meets these needs. The role of the manager is to coordinate the skills and abilities of workers to accomplish the objectives of the organization and to do so with an understanding of what each individual can contribute.

NOTES

1. See chapter 5; also, see Douglas M. McGregor, "The human side of enterprise," *Leadership and Motivation* (Cambridge, Mass.: MIT Press, 1966), 3–20.

2. Rensis Likert, *The Human Organization: Its Management and Value* (New York: McGraw-Hill, 1967).

3. Frederick Herzberg, Bernard Mausner, and Barbara Block Snyderman. *The Motivation to Work* (New York: Wiley, 1959).

4. Robert J. House and Lawrence Wigdor, "Herzberg's dual factor theory of job satisfaction and motivation," *Personnel Psychology* 20, no. 1 (Winter 1967): 369–89.

5. Frederick Herzberg, "One more time: How do you motivate employees?" *Harvard Business Review* 65, no. 5 (September–October): 109–20.

6. Abraham Maslow, *Motivation and Personality* (New York: Harper, 1954).

7. B.F. Skinner, *Beyond Freedom and Dignity* (New York: Knopf, 1972).

8. Skinner, *Beyond Freedom and Dignity,* 5.

9. Rosabeth Moss Kanter, "The new managerial work," in *Managing People and Organizations*, edited by John J. Gabarro, 67 (New York: McGraw-Hill, 1992).

10. J. Sterling Livingston, "Pygmalion in management," *Harvard Business Review* 81, no. 1 (January 2003): 97–106.

11. Nigel Nicholson, "How to motivate your problem people," *Harvard Business Review* 81, no. 8 (January 2003): 57–75.

12. Herbert C. Hicks, *The Management of Organizations: A System and Human Resources Approach.* 2nd ed. (New York: McGraw-Hill, 1972), 320.

13. George Keller, *Academic Strategy: The Management Revolution in Higher Education.* (Baltimore, Md.: Johns Hopkins University Press, 1983), 41.

14. Wess Roberts, *Leadership Secrets of Attila the Hun* (New York: Warner Books, 1987).

15. Herbert A. Hicks and Craig Gullet, *Organizational Theory and Behavior* (New York: McGraw-Hill, 1975), xv.

16. Peter Drucker, *Management: Tasks, Responsibilities, and Practices* (New York: Harper and Row, 1973), x.

17. Drucker, *Management*, 13–14.

18. Drucker, *Management*, 17.

19. Harrington Emerson, *Twelve Principles of Efficiency* (New York: Engineering Magazine, 1912).

20. Hugo Munsterberg, *Psychology and Industrial Efficiency* (New York: Houghton Mifflin, 1913); Walter D. Scott and R. C. Clothier, *Personnel Management Principles, Practices, and Points of View* (Chicago: A. W. Shaw, 1923).

21. Henri Fayol, *Administration Industrielle et General* (Paris: Dunod, 1962).

22. Drucker, *Management*, 37–38.

23. Jeffrey Pfeiffer and Robert I. Sutton, *The Knowing Doing Gap: How Smart Companies Turn Knowledge into Action* (Cambridge, Mass.: Harvard Business School Press, 2000).

24. Pfeiffer and Sutton, *The Knowing Doing Gap*, 10.

25. Pfeiffer and Sutton, *The Knowing Doing Gap*, 14.

26. Henry Mintzberg, *The Nature of Managerial Work* (New York: Harper and Row, 1973).

27. Matthew Bellman and Robert H. Shaffer, "Freeing managers to innovate," *Harvard Business Review* 79, no. 6 (June 2001): 22–32.

28. Robert Tannenbaum and Warren H. Schmidt, "How to choose a leadership pattern,"

in *Managing People and Organizations*, edited by John J. Gabbaro, 32–42 (New York, McGraw-Hill, 1992).

29. W. Chan Kim and Renee Mauborgne, "Fair process, managing in the knowledge economy," *Harvard Business Review* 75, no. 7 (July–August 1997): 65–75.

30. Kanter, "The new managerial work," 69.

31. Gary McClain and Deborah S. Romane, *The Everything Managing People Book* (Avon, Mass.: Adams Media, 2002).

32. John P. Kotter, "Power, dependence, and effective management," in *Managing People and Organizations* edited by John J. Gabbaro, 46 (NewYork: McGraw-Hill, 1992).

33. Rosabeth Moss Kanter, *Evolve! Succeeding in the Digital Culture of Tomorrow* (Cambridge, Mass.: Harvard Business School Press, 2001).

34. Kanter, "The new managerial work," 65.

35. Julie Todaro, "The truth is out there: What's a new manager to do?" *Library Administration and Management* 15, no. 4 (Fall 2001): 249–50.

36. Sally Helgesen, *The Female Advantage: Women's Ways of Leadership* (New York: Doubleday Currency, 1990).

Chapter Eight

Communication

Communication, the sharing of information of any type with individuals in any manner, is a fundamental human social process. Communication is based on relationships and its purpose may be to share knowledge of the environment, socialize individuals to a group, to gain consensus, to persuade, or to control. It may also be used to entertain.[1] Communication is an essential element in the success of the organization. Ideally, it is a two-way process in which a message is transmitted, a listener responds, and dialog occurs until there is mutual understanding of what has been said and what is expected.

Each communication occurs within a context—a work-related context, a social context, or other environment—and is specific to a particular place or time. The context of communication may change daily, as may the attitudes of those in communication. Even the words used may change in their meaning given a different day and a different place. "The communication process is complex. It is holistic; it is two-way. It must be considered in the context of what has been previously communicated. It must be considered in terms of the values and objectives of the organization and in terms of the specific communication transaction."[2] Communication is influenced by a number of factors, including the credibility of the sender and the form of communication. The individuals whose behavior reinforces their words have a higher level of credibility and will receive more attention than those who have a history of saying one thing and doing another.

Most communication is either oral or written. Oral communication includes face-to-face interaction between or among two or more people. It can also include telephone conversations, conferences, and meetings, as well as communication intended for large audiences and delivered via television, computer conferencing, radio, or film. Written communication may be in the form of notes, memos, letters, newsletters, instruction manuals, newspapers, magazines, or reports. E-mail as a means of written communication has supplanted many of the more traditional forms of both oral and written communication due in part to the speed with which it can be sent to one or thousands at the same time.

The form of communication used depends in large part on the objective of the sender. Oral communication, unless it is a formal presentation intended for a large group, is usually less formal and more interactive than written. If its purpose is to discuss an employee's work performance, to inform a group of individuals of an issue in their area of responsibility that needs attention, or to introduce changes in their responsibilities, face-to-face interaction is the best as it provides an opportunity for immediate feedback in order to clarify the message and to be assured that both the sender and receiver agree on what that message is. If the purpose is to introduce new policies or to announce changes in the organization, an oral presentation followed by written communication may be the appropriate means. Formal statements that outline direction and identify expectations are best presented in written form as they can serve as a reference point for future action. Complex reports on a particular topic are best presented in written form as they provide organized factual information that is difficult to present orally. In selecting the form of communication to be used, it is necessary to determine the context of the interaction, the audience for the interaction, and the extent to which feedback is anticipated or desired. Oral communication is the richer form of interaction in that gestures, voice inflection, facial expressions, and other cues can contribute to the interaction and can give each individual discussing the topic a more complete sense of whether there is agreement or disagreement on what is being communicated. In written communication, there is little opportunity for immediate feedback and the sender can only hope that the message has been understood as sent.

Written communication is useful in that it provides formal statements for the record. Policies, goals, official reports, personnel files, and similar documents that provide the basis for action and evaluation should be written. Written communication is also more difficult to prepare than is oral communication, as the written message must be clearly written, specific to the topic, and it must take into account all other communication on the same topic so that there is no internal disagreement. When immediate feedback is not possible, the message must communicate exactly what the sender wishes to say as directly and briefly as possible.

Before the advent of e-mail, many libraries/information centers issued memos for most information to be disseminated, including recent news, directives from supervisors, directives dealing with daily staff rosters and comments on neatness of work spaces, and many, many other routine communications. E-mail messages have replaced the blizzard of paper memos that at one time covered the desks of supervisors and staff. While some fear that e-mail provides the opportunity for information overload when it is used for daily communication, it is much less onerous than the daily stack of memos to which library staff were at one time subjected. E-mail messages provide immediate information and allow for immediate feedback; although they should be crafted carefully, they can be revised based on early feedback. It is important to remember that every written message, e-mail or not, is on file somewhere and may at some time be used to support or criticize an action.

In some organizations, informal oral communication and interaction among staff and with all levels of the organization is the norm; in other organizations, there is a more formal process in which written communication is preferred. Organizational culture can determine to a considerable degree how individuals in the organization communicate about their work.

EFFECTIVE COMMUNICATION

Effective communication is the responsibility of each staff member from the director of the organization to the part-time student worker. Each has the responsibility to understand messages given and to be certain that what one says is received in the manner intended. Lack of communication or misunderstood messages are the most common cause of difficulties within the organization. Most staffs are made up of individuals from differing cultures who have varying attitudes toward authority and toward the ways in which they interact with others. Professional and support staff may see interactions from differing perspectives because of their status in the organization. Staff members of different ages may have difficulty communicating as they may see issues from different perspectives or may think that because they are older they should be treated with more deference than a younger staff member. Words may mean different things to different people and misunderstandings may arise. Different individuals approach their work differently depending upon their work style. Myers-Briggs testing has identified several work styles and ways of interacting with others and it has been found that managers must take into account these work styles as well as their own work style and how it affects those around them.[3] One cannot assume that there is a common set of behaviors or understandings in a multicultural, multiaged work place. To a large degree, the organizational culture of the library/information center provides a common base from which staff members communicate and work. New staff are socialized to the culture but the individual still retains a personal set of filters that affects communication. It is the responsibility of the manager to be aware of the range of differences in how staff communicate and to work toward building a common work culture with common understandings and mutual respect. It is the responsibility of each staff member to see how he or she communicates, to know what is expected within the organizational culture, and to share in shaping and in responding to that norm. This goes well beyond verbal communication to include those nonverbal cues that accompany oral communication.

The real communication leaders in the organization are the supervisors who lead a unit or department. They have day-to-day responsibility for ensuring that communication is effective. They represent the needs and concerns of their unit to the next level of management and are the ones who translate directives from above into action for their unit. When organizational change is taking place or if a crisis occurs, they are the individuals who will be listened to. Their ability and willingness to communicate with staff is determined by the respect their staff have for them and their ability to represent staff concerns. It is also determined by the extent to which they respect and trust their own supervisors.[4]

Listening

Informing is half the communication process. Equally important is the art and act of listening. It has often been said that 80 percent of a manager's time is devoted to listening to others or being listened to. Giving information is important but unless it is received and acted upon as intended, the message sent is not useful. Listening, while the most important component of the communication interaction, is often the weakest component. Individuals are not naturally good listeners. They need to know how to listen and to how to remember what they have heard. Studies have shown that only one-half to one-third of what is said is remembered for more than eight hours. After two months, less than one-quarter of what was said is remembered. Nichols and Stevens suggest that one needs to learn to be a good listener.[5] The good listener focuses on the speaker and is not distracted by other thoughts or ideas or by other activities going on around them. Good listeners think ahead of the person talking to anticipate what will be said. They evaluate what is being said to determine if it is valid. They summarize the speaker's words as they listen and they listen for the ideas and not just the facts. They also listen between the lines to pick up nonverbal cues that will further inform what is being said. Each listener has emotional filters through which what is being said is processed: Do we agree with what is being said? Does it anger us? Does it satisfy our concerns? So as not to let emotional filters interfere with the message, the good listener withholds evaluation until the speaker has finished speaking and then reviews what has been said. Are important facts missing? Has the speaker reached untenable conclusions? Does the message agree with the facts presented? Ideally, the listener has the opportunity to provide feedback and to clarify the message.

Conferences and Meetings

Conferences and meetings are an essential component of oral communication in which listening skills play an important role. It has often been said that conferences are meetings in which individuals with similar or related expertise come together to talk at one another. Speakers are often more interested in telling what they know than in getting feedback or listening to the presentations of others. Teleconferencing, which may be less formal than the traditional conference, may provide an easier means of feedback and thus reduce the amount of talking at one another. The experts who are convinced that they are right and have no intention of listening to other points of view contribute little to discussions.

Meetings are an important means of oral communication and take place in all organizations and groups. Supervisors meet to discuss management issues, department members meet to discuss technical or management issues within the department, work teams meet to discuss actions and progress. To some extent, meetings are the glue that holds the organization together. They build loyalty to the organization and to one another by strengthening social ties and by supporting the common purpose of the organization. The meeting itself defines a team or other organizational unit and gives team members a sense of belonging.[6] The meeting is a place where the group shares knowledge and experiences, where its members review and update activities, and where they collectively plan the next steps. Each member of the team or unit understands the collective aim of the group and her or his individual contribution. The meeting group is a status group in which members discover their standing and the standing of the unit they represent in that group.

Meetings vary in size, frequency, and purpose. Large meetings (100 or more) are those in which the organization's leader will speak and others will listen with little or no opportunity for feedback. The presentation has been crafted carefully to send a particular message. Midsize meetings (forty to fifty in attendance) are leader centered and questions may be asked, allowing for limited feedback. Smaller meetings (fewer than twenty in attendance) are chaired either by a leader selected for the group or by the group; in this context, discussion flows freely while focusing on a specific topic. Larger meetings tend to be less frequent than smaller working meetings and are used to provide periodic updates, to take action when needed, or to respond to crisis. In the event of an ongoing project where individuals are operating under common objectives and need to move ahead rapidly, meetings may occur daily.

The success of any meeting is, to a large extent, dependent on the attitude and skill of the chair. If chairing a meeting is seen as a way to dominate discussion and to dictate direction, little will be accomplished. The chair who focuses on the issue, leads discussion, and ensures that issues are discussed thoroughly, with all present contributing to the discussion while at the same time avoiding repetition and extraneous input and bringing the meeting to a mutually satisfactory conclusion in an acceptable time frame, will strengthen communication within the group as the group will know that they have been part of the decision-making process.

Meetings and other forms of oral communication are influenced by the organizational culture and the attitudes of supervisors toward subordinates. Supervisors can determine the way in which a meeting or dialog is conducted. They can be open and invite discussion or they can dictate what is to be done and allow little or no response. In many instances, when meeting chairs and other team leaders encourage discussion and disagreement on the issue under discussion, the group becomes more productive and cohesive as its members work together toward a solution. High-performing groups feel empowered when their ideas and the experience they bring to the discussion are respected. They will hesitate to contribute if they sense that the supervisor is not comfortable with open discussion

Subordinates wish to have approval and will conduct themselves in a manner to receive approval. They also want respect, and to have their ideas, expertise, and feelings considered. The staff member wants to be able to trust the supervisor, to be assured that the supervisor is competent and honest and will treat the subordinate in a fair manner, and by acknowledging that individual's contribution to the workplace enterprise. When the subordinate loses respect for a supervisor, the supervisor is no longer given information to know what that individual can contribute to solving problems. The body language may change as well. With a loss of trust in the supervisor, communication all but ceases, morale declines, and library patrons may begin to complain about the quality of service or staff attitude.[7] Supervisors should never find themselves in such a situation, nor should their supervisor allow such a situation to occur. Rebuilding trust may require the removal of the supervisor. It could also require changes in organizational cultural to ensure that open and candid communication is viewed as the norm in the organization.

Relationships among Groups

The relationships among individual groups, organizations, and governments change. New linkages are forged and others separate. Analysis of interactions among these groups show the strength of communication linkages and whether they are between equals or between supervisor and subordinates, if there are both business and social linkages, and if the linkages are direct or indirect. The roles each individual plays in this linked environment differ. It may be that of group member, group linker, or isolated individual. Each person in the group has ties to others in the group that differ from person to person and each has different external contacts. Some are more knowledgeable than others and some are more open to discussion to others. In looking at communication in and among groups, it is useful to analyze the interaction, as it helps to understand why some groups work well together and others do not. Here again, culture, age, work style, and other different approaches to working within the group are important to observe. It is also useful to see how information technology has been adopted within the group and how it affects interaction.[8]

COMMUNICATION FLOW

In a hierarchical organization, communication flows from the director down the organization and from the smallest unit up the organization. For communication to be effective, each staff member should feel able to participate and should also feel assured that the messages flowing up and down communication lines are not distorted. In many organizations, supervisors do not really listen to subordinates. This causes subordinates to withdraw from the communication network and to be reluctant to provide information or to raise issues that require discussion. The supervisor who listens, asks questions, and investigates issues raised rather than criticizing, showing displeasure, giving an immediate opinion, or ignoring the issue brought forward accomplishes two things: issues that may require attention are brought forward by staff and because of the supervisor's attitude, the communication chain remains healthy. The supervisor who does not listen and does not value the information put forth in formal communication channels will soon learn that informal communication may become more important to staff, thus potentially weakening formal lines of communication and reducing the supervisor's ability to know what issues concern staff and may need attention.

Formal and Informal Communication Flow

Communication in the workplace is both formal and informal, with the two types of communication existing concurrently. Formal communication follows the structure of the organization chart and "represents an ordered system that regulates authority and communication flows, links decision makers at different levels with defined data-transmission channels and generates an orderly flow of information and decision processes."[9] In this type of structure, communication about policies, procedures, practices, and work assignments moves downward in the organizational hierarchy. Communication moving upward provides feedback on the work assigned and any problems that might arise. This communication flow is primarily vertical. Formal lateral communication between department heads or staff working on common issues provides linkages at similar levels in the organization chart. Charts showing the formal communication in an organization display a well-ordered means of moving information through the organization. In fact, the formal flow can be "rigid, slow, unreliable and of finite carrying capacity."[10]

Information can get lost or misinterpreted as it moves up and down the formal structure. Insufficient information may be provided or directives may be issued that conflict with current activities or may not take into account new information. As information moves up the formal channels, it may be adjusted at one or more level to meet particular interests or objectives. Formal communication structures often do not take into account the need for additional or peripheral information, rapidly changing situations, or sensitive political issues. Depending on the management style prevalent in the organization (e.g., authoritarian environments in which decisions are made from the top and then announced or participatory in which staff at more than one level are involved) and on the level of trust in those who are making decisions, formal communication structures will be more or less useful.[11]

There may be several communication structures within the organization in addition to the formal structure. Technical staff may develop a network that is task based and that may extend beyond one library/information center. They use the network to discuss nonroutine problems, new technology, and related issues. There may be an administrative network that goes beyond one library/information center to include administrators in a system or region who meet to discuss issues of common interest. These networks, which may be formal or not, serve to expand and extend linkages within and among libraries and individuals with shared interests and concerns.

It has long been recognized that individuals in any social structure will communicate with one another in unregulated and unstructured ways. They will form networks based on friendships and common interests, on shared technical expertise, or on their concerns about dealing with the formal structure. The informal communication structure keeps employees informed, particularly when the formal structure is not responsive, does not provide needed information, or when its directives are in conflict with actual work situations. The two communications networks exist in all organizations and are interdependent; each needs the other.

While informal communication networks do not follow a particular structure or set of rules, there are understandings that guide informal interactions. The informal communications network has its own leaders, its own culture, and its own attitudes. Individuals in the organization who may not be part of the administrative hierarchy may—because of their experience in the organization, the level of respect they receive from coworkers, or for other reasons—become leaders in the informal structure. They are not appointed, but emerge from the group. They may serve as central connectors, or they may serve as boundary spanners who bring together information from different to parts of the organization or from relevant external sources. They may be information brokers or peripheral specialists.[12] Central connectors are those who link together most of the individuals in the informal organization. They are the *go to* people who know how the organization works, who have the needed internal information, and who know how to get things done. They are not usually formally designated individuals. These individuals hold power in the organization and should be recognized by it for their contributions. Boundary spanners connect informal networks with one another in the organization and among organizations. They have been called roving ambassadors, as they have wide internal and external contacts. They are the *go to* people when this type of information is needed. When new kinds of information not available in the networks are needed, those with the information share information from the various subgroups in the organization so that information is communicated to those needing it. The peripheral specialist is a source of specialized information and is available to anyone needing that information. Wise managers know what the informal networks are and how they function, and work with them to enrich overall communication. Managers are wise to recognize the usefulness of informal networks and the feedback they can provide on issues not adequately covered in formal communications on issues such as staff satisfaction or dissatisfaction and related work issues. It is also a powerful vehicle for influencing decision making, as new ideas may emerge or current directions be questioned. Decision makers who ignore the information available on informal networks and the extent to which the informal network can support or not support decisions made will be less successful in implementing those decisions. In the organization that is not well managed or is perceived as not being well managed, the informal network can be a powerful tool for expressing dissent or disagreement with policies, decisions, and tasks handed down through the formal chain.

Informal communication paths may develop in response to a new technology, to architectural or other relocation changes in an organization, to an ineffective formal network, or as part of the organizational culture. The introduction of e-mail into the workplace typically increases communication levels among those with like interests; for example, technical specialists might now have enhanced capability to discuss technical issues with experts inside and outside the organization or reference specialists who could discuss with others new search strategies. Architectural changes change the work flow and the communication necessary to carry out their activities. An example of this is a public library that began in a storefront in a mall. As it grew, space became crowded and staff interacted constantly because of the close quarters. They worked well together and each knew that they were active participants in providing quality service. When a new building was completed and the library moved to its new and much larger quarters, the close communication previously experienced no longer existed and it took time for staff to recognize that they needed to rebuild their informal communication network to accommodate a situation in which they were no longer in constant physical proximity.

The informal communication network is often referred to as the grapevine. Managers may see this network as carrying office gossip and that it is insignificant and can be ignored. Studies have shown that the grapevine is quite accurate and that it is usually the fastest means of finding out about decisions made, individual activities, and organizational problems.

INFORMATION TECHNOLOGY
AND COMMUNICATION

Information technology in the workplace changes existing communication patterns. Beginning with the willingness of staff to adopt communication technologies and continuing through decisions of what technologies to adopt, and through their adoption and implementation, all staff continuously change their patterns of interaction. When an information/communication system is selected for adoption, it is most important that the system be culturally consistent with the dominant organizational culture. If the organization is decentralized in its management and activities, select a system that supports this. Installing a system that requires a high level of centralization would require major changes in the structure and interaction within the organization.[13]

"Technical choices are far from neutral in their effects on organizational design and functioning. Choices about implementation of [communication and] information technologies are not simply questions of technical features to be left in the hands of information systems staff."[14] A technology policy for the organization that ties to its goals and objectives and takes into consideration its preferred management style will serve as a guide for the selection of appropriate communications technology and its application and use.

Backing into a technology or relying on technical experts to make decisions is rarely successful. The organization needs to develop a communications plan and to ensure that it supports organizational goals as well as the organizational structure and culture. The technical plan is derived from the communications plan developed by library/information center decision makers and is in accord with the planning activities of the parent organization, government agency, other campus information units, and similar groups. Technical experts show planners how the goals and objectives of the plan can be achieved. It is the role of management and other decision makers to determine what should be achieved and in what order. Once technical experts are given the overall plan, they work under the direction of an oversight group that ensures that the focus is not lost and that the technical decisions follow the plan and do not distort it. The oversight group continues to monitor implementation, is aware of continuous changing technology, and supervises the steps that need to be taken to maintain a technologically current system. The communication plan takes into account the range of users and their needs. Internally, staff have specific requirements for support.

Library/information center users are diverse in their needs and vary in the kinds of information they are seeking and in the extent to which they communicate and collaborate with staff in gaining information. They vary in their level of expertise in using technology. Some may have disabilities that require additional technical support to enhance limited visual, auditory, or other capability. While those who use library/information center service will benefit from enhanced access to information resources and communication with staff who can work with them as they seek specific information, the greatest changes brought about by communication and information technology are in the organization itself.

Drucker speaks of the development of the new organization. He predicted that information technology would change the way we work, the way we interact with others, and the jobs we do. To survive in today's global, ever-changing, service-oriented world, new organizational forms are needed. Information and communication technology allows us to move away from traditional hierarchical formats to flatter and leaner organizations that are more flexible and responsive to change. Information- and communication-enabled organizations have the abilities to gain information faster, to learn from a broader environment, and to act more quickly on what they learn. In this environment, there is less expectation that there will be a permanent organizational structure in which they reside. Project teams, consisting of permanent employees, temporary employees, and consultants, are assigned tasks; as soon as the task is completed, the team is dissolved and relevant members join other teams and other tasks. There is "an enhanced focus on communication links and relationships in organizations as opposed to status and formal roles."[15] While libraries and information centers will continue to need an organizational structure, it will be less rigidly hierarchical and more likely to be based on tasks to be conducted. The final assumption is that an increase in electronic communication links will overcome any barriers to communication and participation. Some agree while others say that electronic communication enables greater use of existing social patterns and thus strengthens existing barriers. Increased communication in itself does little to break down existing inequities in the system. Those who do not have access to information in the current system, such as some maintenance and security staff, will not automatically have access in an enriched system.

Communication technologies in an organization are oriented toward achieving management goals—for example, more effective work groups and faster internal communication. For maximum benefit, technology needs to be designed to fit the organizational culture. However, that culture is expanded by communications technology to overcome barriers of time and space. This in itself will change the organization and its culture. In the new environment, there has been a dramatic increase in the speed of communication. In the early 1990s, the fastest regular communication with other countries was by airmail or telephone—one relatively slow and the other relatively expensive. Today, an e-mail to China takes no longer than an e-mail sent to an officemate. The amount of information moving from place to place has increased dramatically as well. Along with speed of communication has come an increase in bandwidth, allowing for transmission of text, voice, data, and video in a common system as well as greatly increased connectivity. It is now assumed that network connections are a given in the work environment. Because of instant communication, staff members can work from anywhere and do not need to be at their desks in a particular location to do their work. They can team with other staff members in other locations to work on a common project. Fulk and De Santis suggest that the hierarchical structure in the organization still retains a role: that of dealing with policies, procedures, programs, and common goals.[16] The work itself is coordinated electronically so that units or groups can be brought together to complete a task or disperse as needed. In the library/information center, the basic structure will continue to exist and exist in a place convenient to collections and users. But many collections will be electronic; many tasks such as online searching and many interactions with users will no longer necessarily be place bound. A library branch could be virtual, with users in one location contacting the information professional online in another location, who would respond to questions from a range of electronic sources located in still other locations. While many libraries/information centers are traditionally conservative, and many of the opportunities made available through communication technologies for different ways of organizing services, of allocating staff, and of serving patrons will not be of interest, no library/ information center will remain untouched by this new world of communications.

RESEARCH ON COMMUNICATION

Research on the impact of communication technology has paralleled the development of innovation. It has focused on both individual communication and organizational communication. While researchers continue to stress that face-to-face communication is the richest communication medium, with telephone and written messages following, they see benefits in online communication in that it involves personal interaction and there is a record of the communication. E-mail had not come into its own at the time of early studies (1980s) and there was limited awareness of the impact it would later have. At that time, higher-level managers relied on face-to-face communication and lower-level managers, whose tasks were less ambiguous, used the telephone and written communication. It was assumed that there would be variations in the use of communications technology in the organization and that this variation was due to the social environment in the organization. Some work groups and individuals saw e-mail as useful while others did not—but the more e-mail was used by a group, the more useful it was perceived to be.[17]

The choice of communication medium is strongly influenced by organizational culture, policies, and resource constraints. A strong verbal culture would typically prefer face-to-face or telephone interaction while a more formal culture would typically prefer written documents. E-mail—which has the informality of much face-to-face contact and the documentability of written messages—falls somewhere between the two. Research since the 1980s in the use of communication technology focused on the use of communication in decision making and the use of decision support systems, group work, and online meetings. Decision support ware has three levels, the first of which includes use of e-mail within the group, the facility to display ideas, and the ability to compile votes on ideas presented. The second level adds decision support tools such as GANTT charts, budget allocation models, and decision trees. A third level imposes structure on communication patterns and controls timing and content. The first two levels are those most heavily used and research has focused on them.[18] It was found that e-mail allowed for more equal participation than face-to-face interaction in which a few individuals often tend to dominate. For some this was seen as positive while others deplored the loss of the visual and social cues that contribute to face-to-face communication. Early studies during this period in which decision support systems were being introduced varied in their findings. Some studies pointed to higher quality in decisions made while others disagreed. Greater speed in decision making and greater satisfaction with this mode of interaction received both positive and negative comments. As employees became more comfortable with these communication modes and tools, as the technology became more sophisticated and easier to use, and as it became socially more necessary to participate, online communication has increased so that today e-mail and other online communication activities are a standard part of internal and external organizational networks.

Of the several types of electronic communication, e-mail has rapidly become the most ubiquitous and it is now difficult to think of an organization or work group operating without it. For many, the thought of going back to mimeographed memos to staff is not pleasant while others have never seen a mimeograph machine. E-mail has numerous benefits and relatively few drawbacks. E-mail does not require that the person being contacted be immediately available, thus avoiding telephone tag. In one message it is possible to contact one or thousands of individuals. One can record, manipulate, and store important messages thus eliminating paper documents. E-mail is faster and cheaper than other forms of communication and one can get confirmation that the message has been received. E-mail saves time for the sender and the receiver. It is possible to suffer from e-mail overload and some management of messages is needed, but this is an element in all communication systems.[19]

The impact of communication technology on interaction in the workplace has had a major impact on the way in which the organization is structured and on the ways in which individuals work together. The hierarchical organization that sent communications up and down the organization from one level to another is less powerful. Information received is more immediate and less subject to interpretation at each level. Those levels in the hierarchy responsible for moving information downward are no longer needed in an era when the director can communicate with all levels at once.

COMMUNICATION AND THE VIRTUAL ENVIRONMENT

With instant communication available, the organization no longer needs to be located in one place but can geographically separate its activities to meet specific needs, such as providing full branch services in some areas through the use of a virtual branch. Staff whose activities are not needed for daily interaction with clients can work flexible hours from home, while on travel, or in the library/information center. This could include staff doing extended research for patrons, or those developing action plans or writing reports. Communication technology has freed many staff from being place bound and allows much work to be done in various locations. Networked work-stations allow individuals regardless of location to work together, to access shared files, and to communicate regularly. "Socio-technical factors [of these communication systems] play a large role in the design and use of these systems by transforming work through the subtle characteristics of the technology."[20]

When work groups are separated geographically but share common responsibility for an activity, they rely heavily on effective communication. While physical proximity increases interaction, it is possible to maintain a sufficient level of interaction when geographically separated. Success of the activity depends on the expertise, skill, training, and attitude of the group members. If they share expertise or if their expertise is complementary, if they are skilled in group process, and if they are willing to participate in an online mode, the interaction is successful.[21] Some activities such as brainstorming seem to be more successful in an electronic mode. There is greater participation and ideas presented are more creative because they are not immediately shot down by an unbeliever. It also tends to equalize status issues prevalent in face-to-face communication, in which men may dominate women and managers may talk more than subordinates. E-mail breaks down structural boundaries that inhibit open communication. It expands the community of discussion beyond that of a few and can bring in external experts with innovative ideas. It links core decision makers with those on the periphery and enhances the feeling of being well informed. For those managers who are most comfortable in a hierarchical structure, an environment of open communication is worrisome. For those who welcome new ideas and shared responsibility, e-mail and related communication modes provide a rich resource to support innovation and change.

New communications technologies allow for new types of interaction by a wider range of individuals. The elements of human communication remain but are played out in a larger arena. The types of communication, voice, data, and video have greater options for presentation. While research has shown that information technology has as yet not had a major impact on organizational culture in such areas as the chains of command, span of control, and centralization of authority, we are still in a transition period. We will continue to experiment with communication technology and its impact on management and the organizational structure. Cairncross summarizes the communications technology world in which we function by saying that "what matters most about a new technology is not how it works, but how people use it and the changes it brings about in human lives."[22] We will continue to misjudge the technological future as elements change, needs change, and the rate of adoption varies by culture. The level of impact of communications technology usually takes a fairly long time before the full impact is realized.

SUMMARY

Communication is the glue that holds the organization together. Each member of the organization is responsible for contributing information and for listening to others. Formal communication consisting of policies and directives is paralleled by the informal communication network in which tasks and procedures are discussed. Interaction within and external to the organization affects and informs all activities. Communication technology including e-mail has opened the organization to new structural models in which work is no longer place bound.

NOTES

1. Wilbur Schramen and Donald Roberts, ed., *The Process and Effects of Mass Communication* (Chicago: University of Chicago Press, 1977).

2. Robert L. Woodruff Jr. "Communicating," in *AMA Management Handbook.* 2nd ed., edited by William K. Fallon, vol. 7 (New York: American Management Association, 1983), 93.

3. Raymond J. Corsini, "Myers-Briggs type indicator," *Encyclopedia of Psychology*, vol. 2 (New York: John Wiley and Sons, 1984), 414.

4. T. J. Larkin and Sandra Larkin, "Reaching and changing front line employees," in *Harvard Business Review on Effective Communication*, edited by Harvard Business Review Editors (Cambridge, Mass.: Harvard Business School Press, 1999), 145–69.

5. Ralph H. Nichols and Leonard A. Stevens, "Listening to people," in *Harvard Business Review on Effective Communication*, edited by Harvard Business Review Editors (Cambridge, Mass.: Harvard Business School Press, 1999), 1–24.

6. Anthony Jay, "How to run a meeting," in *Harvard Business Review on Effective Communication*, edited by Harvard Business Review Editors (Cambridge, Mass.: Harvard Business School Press, 1999), 25–57.

7. Fernando Bartolome, "Nobody trusts the boss completely, now what?" in *Harvard Business Review on Effective Communication*, edited by Harvard Business Review Editors (Cambridge, Mass.: Harvard Business School Press, 1999), 79–100.

8. Janet Fulk and Brian Boyd, "Emerging theories of communication in organizations," *Journal of Management* 17, no. 2 (March 1991): 407–46.

9. Kerry Grosser, "Human networks in organizational information processing," in *Annual Review of Information Science and Technology*, edited by Martha Williams (Medford, N.J.: Learned Information, 1991), 352.

10. Grosser, "Human networks in organizational information processing," 353.

11. Charles McClure, "The information rich employee and information for decision making: review and comments," *Information Processing and Management* 14, no. 6 (June 1978): 381–94.

12. Rob Cross and Laurence Prusak, "The people who make organizations go or stop," *Harvard Business Review* 80, no. 6 (June 2002): 105–9.

13. John R. Oglive, Michael F. Poblen, Louise H. Jones, "Organizational information processing and productivity improvement." *National Productivity Review* 7 no. 3 (Summer 1998): 229–37.

14. Fulk and Boyd, "Emerging theories," 428–29.

15. Peter Drucker, "The coming of the new organization," *Harvard Business Review* 66, no. 1 (January–February 1988): 45–50.

16. Janet Fulk and Geraldine DeSantis, "Electronic communication and changing organizational forms," *Organizational Science* 6, no. 4 (July–August 1995): 337–49.

17. Fulk and Boyd, "Emerging theories," 407–46.

18. Fulk and Boyd, "Emerging theories," 416.

19. Bor-Sheng Tsai, "The effectiveness measurement of electronic mail communication within a special professional community," *Proceedings of the 55th Annual ASIS Meeting* 59, (Pittsburgh, Penn., 1992), 76–85.

20. Jonathan K. Kies, Robert C. Willigen, and Mary Beth Rosen, "Coordinating computer-supported co-operative work: A review of research issues and strategies," *Journal of the American Society for Information Science* 49 no. 9 (July 1998): 776.

21. Mary Alice Citera, "Distributed teamwork: The impact of communication media on influence and design quality," *Journal of the American Society for Information Science* 49, no. 9 (July 1998): 792–800.

22. Frances Cairncross, *The Death of Distance: How the Communications Revolution Is Changing Our Lives* (Cambridge, Mass.: Harvard Business School Press, 2001), ix.

ADDITIONAL READINGS

Davenport, Thomas K. "Saving IT's soul: Human centered information management." *Harvard Business Review* 72, no. 3 (March–April 1994): 119–31.

Hinds, Pamela, and Sara Kiesler. "Communication across boundaries: Work, structure and the use of communication technologies in a large organization." *Organizational Science* 6, no. 4 (July–August 1995): 373–93.

Perlow, Leslie, and Stephanie Williams. "Is silence killing your company?" *Harvard Business Review* 81, no. 5 (May 2003): 52–68.

Chapter Nine

Marketing

Marketing is "the effective management by an organization of its exchange relations with its various markets and publics."[1] The organization provides a product or service to selected groups or markets in exchange for money or something else of value. Marketing is a management process that encompasses analysis, planning, implementation, and control to identify both product or service and the public willing or desirous of receiving that product/ service in exchange for something of value. Marketing provides a different orientation for the organization in that the focus is on the public or potential market and what the organization can do to attract that market. Marketing assumes that the purpose of the organization is to determine the needs and wants of the customer and to meet those needs rather than to focus on the intrinsic value of the product/service or the efficiency of the organization providing it.

Marketing on a widespread scale is a relatively recent activity developed in the 1950s in the for-profit sector and adopted by the 1970s in the nonprofit sector. Prior to the development of the marketing approach, the tendency, particularly in the not-for-profit sector, was to develop a product/service and wait for customers to find and use it. Little effort was made to identify who those customers might be, how many there might be, or where they were located. Neither was there an effort to determine what their needs and wants were or to develop products/services to satisfy those needs and wants.

Marketing is not selling. Selling focuses on the seller and the product/ service being sold.[2] Marketing is aimed at providing greater customer satisfaction and is customer focused, measuring both customer needs and satisfaction. There is increased customer participation in product/service development both in the development of new product/services and in revising current product/services to meet customer needs and wants more closely. The customer is an integral part of the design and development of products/ services. The marketing approach, to be successful, is pervasive in the organization and influences decision making and activity at every level. It is a combination of attitude that focuses on customer satisfaction and on the technical knowledge needed to provide that satisfaction. The total focus is on the customer; the organization is viewed as a structure existing to meet the customer's needs and wants.

Since the adoption of marketing as a methodology for nonprofit organizations, Philip Kotler has written most extensively on this topic. His work since the 1970s has provided a foundation for much of the publication and practice dealing with marketing in the not-for-profit sector. Much of the following discussion relies heavily on his work, as does much of the writing in this field. Kotler emphasizes that marketing's central concept is that it is an exchange process in which the organization offers or exchanges something of value for something else of value. If the organization's purpose is to serve social needs, then marketing can be seen as a social process. Marketing is a process of selecting market targets with the objective of selecting those market segments most apt to bring results. There is no effort to meet the needs of everyone. Marketing is aimed at "achieving organizational objectives . . . [and] relies on designing the organization's offerings in terms of the target market's needs, not the seller's personal ideas."[3] Marketing is user oriented, not seller oriented.

In the case of libraries and information centers, marketing is a particularly useful tool. In those organizations such as the public library where service to the entire community is required, one cannot decide to serve just a part of the community. Through marketing, however, one can describe the total community and select groups within the community to which it can direct specific *programs* while at the same time providing a level of service to all.

MARKET PUBLICS

Kotler identifies a public as "a distinct group of people and/or organizations that have an actual or potential interest and/or impact on an organization."[4] He says that *internal publics* take the resources of certain *input publics* and convert them into useful products that *agent publics* take to *consumer publics*. Internal publics are professional and nonprofessional staff and others who manage and provide the product/service. They can also include trustees, regulatory groups, suppliers, and professional organizations. Input publics are defined as supporters of the organization who give time, money, and expertise to the organization. The agent publics are those who distribute the product/service and consumer publics are the direct users of the product/service or general consumers whose consumption is less direct. Kotler gives the example of the university in which students and faculty are direct consumers of the teaching and learning process while parents and the general public, while interested, are less directly involved.

Additional publics include:

- Reciprocal publics in which organizations are interested in one another. This would include the interest of a funding agency such as the National Science Foundation in the university and the university's interest in maintaining good relations with the NSF.
- Sought publics are those with which the organization wishes to build with another group. An example of this would be the efforts of a public library to forge good relationships with a community college or university library in order to develop joint services.
- Unwelcome publics are those organizations or groups interested in the library but the library is not interested in them. For example, a political or religious group may wish to donate materials to the collection that express their specific point of view, but these materials do not meet the collection policies of the library.[5]

TYPES OF NONPROFIT ORGANIZATIONS

There are three major types of nonprofit organizations: the service organization, the mutual benefit organization, and the commonweal organization. The service organization includes schools, libraries, social service agencies, museums, and other groups that provide services to clients. They have two markets: clients who receive services and donors who contribute to those services. Clients' needs are identified and services appropriate to those needs are provided. Donors contribute resources to the service organization and the benefit they gain from this is to feel that they are contributing to the social benefits available in the community. The mutual benefit organization consists of members who join the organization, pay a fee, and receive benefits from the organization. This includes labor unions, professional societies, political parties, and clubs. Union dues are used to support the needs and wants of the members in the workplace, professional society dues further the goals of the organization, political parties campaign for a particular set of interests, and clubs provide a social environment for members. Common-weal organizations are created by the public to do tasks for the public. The military, police, and fire departments fall into this category as do philan-thropic groups who serve the public good.[6] Education and libraries fall into this latter category in some cases.

Any of these types of organization may have a tendency to build a bureau-cratic structure and thus become rigid and unresponsive to the changing needs of their publics. The assumption among those who provide services in any of these contexts may be that they are the "professionals" in their area and know best what the public needs. Any criticisms or suggestions for improving the service are ignored. A reorientation to customer needs through marketing is essential to the revitalization of such organizations. Success is then determined by the level of customer satisfaction, not by the number of services provided or the level of satisfaction or self-satisfaction on the part of the service provider.

MARKET IDENTIFICATION

Each organization has markets and potential markets. How does one identify them? Who are they and what do they want and need? The library/informa-tion center has several markets, each with different interests, and each type of library/information center has its own market as well. A first step in iden-tifying the market is to identify the product/service available and then to assess consumer need for the product/service through an analysis of the demographics of the area served. Through demographic analysis, one can determine the age range of those in the service area and group the population in this way. One can also spot trends and determine if the community is a young community, an aging community, or a community that remains rela-tively stable in its age ranges. It is then possible to project future age group-ings that may at some point alter the mix of services desired as the community ages or new residents move in.

Demographic analysis also provides information on ethnic groups within the community and whether any groups are increasing or decreasing. Income levels, education levels, occupation levels, and related information add to the picture of the market. The reading/research interests of current library patrons provide additional input. This does not, however, provide information on the reading/research interests of *potential* users. Services currently used add to the profile but, here again, this applies to current and not potential users. Expectations of the library/information center by its publics can be determined by questioning current users, funding agencies, other stakeholders, and potential users. The range of responses can provide a wide array of needs and wants. Finally, levels of satisfaction with current services identify those services most currently desirable.

Libraries/information centers can also divide their markets by whether they are knowledge markets or leisure markets. Public, school, and academic libraries serve both information needs and recreational needs to a greater or lesser extent, depending upon their charge. Some users avail themselves of both services while others prefer to use one or the other service. Their interests and needs may differ and may suggest different programs be developed or different material expenditure decisions to be made. The many user studies conducted by libraries/information centers provide information on user satisfaction with existing services and the extent to which those services meet the needs and wants of users. User studies, when carefully designed and administered, can be a useful source of information for marketing decisions.[7] Each type of library/information center has a different type of service area and each type of library/information center will have some different demographic, use, and needs/wants questions to answer. The public library is responsible for serving all residents in a defined political area. Determining who those individuals are and what their needs and wants may be is of primary concern. The academic library role is to serve students, faculty, staff, as well as other libraries and selected members of the public. The school library media center has similar categories in its market. Specialized information centers follow the market configuration of the parent organization or company. They may serve the internal needs of the company and hence their market is defined by the employees of the company or they may serve some of the same external markets as their company does. In each of these instances, the total population that the specific library/information center serves is the market. Within this largest area, the specific markets to be served are identified.

The environment in which the service is provided exerts influence on needs and wants. If the school library media center is seen by the teaching staff as central to the educational process in the classroom, or if the research lab uses its library/information center regularly in its work, the environment is much more positive toward the services performed and the introduction of new services than if the library is seen as peripheral to the teaching/learning or research process. The attitude of the service community is important to measure. Are there services highly desired, such as access to the Internet and the teaching of skills to make this possible? Are there services questioned by some in the community, for example, access to the Internet by children? Can the library/information center deliver the programs the community wants and needs? Can it introduce new programs that the community didn't know it wanted or needed because it didn't know certain opportunities existed?

Marketing Information

In locating information to do market surveys, a number of existing databases will be available, including census data, municipal databases, and university databases in areas including students, faculty, and research activities. Environmental scanning, which is used for overall planning, is also an important element in developing the marketing plan. Scanning an identified set of newspapers, periodicals, news broadcasts, selected journals, annual reports, five-year plans of selected organizations, and other media relevant to the library/information center provides a broad view of trends and may identify possible directions. While identifying the market through the above activities, it is important to establish a methodology for collecting data so that all relevant and available databases are scanned. It may be helpful to develop one's own database from these resources or develop a means of sampling identified resources regularly. A continuously updated marketing database provides highly useful planning information as well as specific answers to particular marketing questions. (For additional information on scanning, see chapter 10.)

Internal information on trends of use of the library/information center and on specific programs is collected regularly by most libraries/information centers and is readily available for review. One can see which services receive heaviest use, which services have declining use, and which services are increasingly used. Cost data is also available to determine the cost of each service to the library/information center. Additional data on markets is generated through questionnaires and related investigations of what services people use and why. Market researchers rely heavily on the tools of the social sciences to study consumer attitudes and behavior.[8]

Wood says that the marketing task differs in every organization and the data to be collected differs to some extent as well based on:

- the kinds of purchaser [user] and their behavior
- the product/service involved; is it a basic need, a discretionary item, a consumable?
- the nature of the marketing effort; is the emphasis on providing the most convenient access, on the value of the product/service, or on impulse buying?[9]

Market Demand

There are several levels of demand that can apply to a product/service.[10] Is the current level of demand above, at, or below the desired level (e.g., the level that demographers suggest it should or could be)? Is it possible to regulate demand? Kotler lists eight levels of demand the marketer needs to review:

1. Negative Demand. In this situation, there is the need to change attitudes about a product/service, or to refurbish or revitalize attitudes about a product/service that is viewed negatively.
2. No Demand. Here it is necessary to create demand. While in a negative demand situation it is necessary to deal with aspects that are not productive, one starts with a clean slate in a no-demand situation.
3. Latent Demand. A need exists but there is no product/service to fill it. An opportunity presents itself here for new product/services.
4. Faltering Demand. The marketer revitalizes the product/service by revising it, updating its elements, and making it desirable again. If this is not possible, the product/service may be discontinued.
5. Irregular Demand. This may be seasonal demand or based on some form of irregular availability. It is often not possible to change this.
6. Full Demand. One needs only to maintain the demand at full capacity.
7. Overfull Demand. When demand exceeds the ability to meet it, steps are taken either to increase capacity, discourage use by charging for the product/service, or by limiting access in some way.

8. Unwholesome Demand. This is any demand that is bad for the individual, such as the overuse of alcohol or the use of drugs.

Marketing Audit

Kotler presents a marketing audit process to assess the marketing environment of the organization.[11] The first question is, "What is the market?" The initial step is to identify the major markets and assign them a relative importance. The university library has many markets: students, faculty, administration and staff, research agencies, other universities and their libraries, and community users. Each market has segments and these are to be identified. Students can be divided by graduate, undergraduate, part time, continuing education, resident, or nonresident, and so on, and then within these categories by academic major and by other useful variables. Data is collected on each market as to size and probable growth or decrease. University data is available in university databases and is paired with library data. The decision to develop or reduce an academic major is also part of university records, as are other policies and decisions affecting the market. Using current data and data projections, the market in the next few years is projected.

A second audit question is, "How is the organization viewed by those who use its products and services?" Does the university library have the reputation of providing quality service to all? Is it seen as ignoring undergraduate needs? Is it perceived as having the information resources, both print and electronic, to support the curriculum? Does it foster a pleasant environment for research and study? What other factors motivate consumers to use it and how high is the level of satisfaction? Data to respond to this question is usually collected by the use of questionnaires and some interviews. Kotler raises the issue of image and reality, and cautions that the potential customer or current customer may respond to their perceptions of the organization rather than to its reality. He defines image as "a set of beliefs about an object"; these vary from person to person and differ in clarity and complexity.[12] An individual may not have visited the public library for some time and may be unaware that it has moved aggressively into electronic information access. When that individual wishes to use the Internet, the earlier image of the public library may interfere with current reality and the individual's choice of action.

Marketers often use interviews and focus groups to determine what the image of the organization is within certain groups. They look to see if image is determined by how individuals perceive the object and if it is due to personal bias or lack of information. Researchers find that image is a combination of objective characteristics and subjective perception. Modifying an image is difficult to do. What is a positive image to some is negative to others. A service highly regarded by some does not interest others. A particular product/service may be rejected because it is considered out of date, is too costly, is too hard to use, lacks appeal to the potential user, or is of no value to that person. The goal of the organization is to satisfy its customers. This is a continuing activity. In the process of meeting customer needs, ensuring a positive image requires continuous careful attention.

Market Segmentation

The market is defined as the maximum potential for all sellers and is centered on the demand for a product or service. A market segment is a part of the market defined by region, by type of market, (e.g., educational), or by classification of buyers or by other relevant variables.[13] Market segmentation is conducted to "determine what sets of motivational and behavioral criteria can be applied to delineate different groups within the market."[14] What motivates them to use one product or service over another? How do they process and act on their needs? What is their purchasing power? What communication channels do they use? Do they exhibit any patterns or characteristics that would help an organization serve them? Psychographics provides an additional set of variables to be used to refine placement in a particular market segment. This includes factors such as lifestyle, personality, social and professional status, benefits to the individual for using a service, and level of loyalty of the individual to the product/service or to the sponsoring organization. And, finally, how ready is the individual to try a new product?

Once these criteria have been determined, one then selects particular market segments based on their common characteristics and promotes specific products/services to them. The target market may be a geographic area, an occupational group, an age group, an educational level, or other identifiable segment. This process is designed to achieve improved satisfaction on the part of the target market in that the product/service is tailored to their specific needs and wants. It is also possible to provide for the needs and wants of the target market more efficiently than to a larger market where target market interests can get lost.

What specific market niche does your product/service fill? What niche do you want it to fill? If you want to be seen as the first place for those without home computers to access the Internet, how do you design the service and the environment to achieve this? What do you do, will you do, that is special? What is your competition? What do you do that they don't do? Do you continuously strive to improve the product/service so that you maintain the desired niche?

The Marketing Plan

The organization's marketing plan describes the target audience, discusses problems and opportunities, lists measurable objectives, produces a budget, and includes an evaluation plan.[15] The target audience has been determined through careful analysis of the library/information center's public, including the segmentation of markets resulting in a listing of markets with decisions as to which markets to pursue most vigorously. In most library market situations in the nonprofit area, there is the legal requirement governing primary service responsibilities. Within this requirement (e.g., serving students in the academic library or providing service to the entire community by the public library), there are products/services to be developed that are directed toward a particular segment. Problems and opportunities of serving a particular target market are discussed. Is this a new target audience or an audience that has been dissatisfied with a service that has been identified as one that will be improved? What resource issues are relevant? Is there competition in this market segment? What are the long- and short-term objectives of the product/service? Are they achievable by the library/information center given current resources or added resources? Are they stated clearly and in measurable terms? Are the objectives of the proposed program/service stated in order of importance to the library/information center? Is staff expertise and information access material available? Is the budget sufficient to achieve stated objectives?

It is useful to include a set of assumptions on which the use of the product/ service is based (e.g., anticipated number of people using the product/service, the number of employees needed to provide the service, or the cost of brochures and other advertising). Include both direct (e.g., workstations, online access, staff time) and indirect (e.g., space, maintenance, security) costs in the budget. Project the costs based on past experience with similar products/services. Evaluation of the product/service will determine if the service was worth the effort and resources expended. Was it heavily used?

Were there problem areas? Can those areas be fixed? Of the projected service population, what percentage was served?[16]

When nonprofit agencies spend money on marketing activities, they are liable to be criticized for wasting public money. It is therefore most important that the public understand the reasons for the marketing activity, be it seeking information to define the market and its segments, communicating about services through advertising, or assessing the success of a program in order to make decisions on its continuation. A marketing plan should clearly show that resources are being used wisely and to the benefit of the community.

The Marketing Staff

Every organization has markets and publics and has products/services it wishes to make available. Each organization needs to have a plan to conduct its marketing activities. In the smaller organization, there is usually no position of marketing director; responsibility for these activities is held by the director of the organization, who may from time to time contract with an outside agency for specific services such as a market survey, a user study, or brochure development. Libraries/information centers often have a public relations officer whose expertise is in communicating to the public information about the library/information center and its programs and activities. These individuals rarely have the expertise to conduct market research but can do much of the advertising and publicity needed by the library/information center once products and services are identified for particular attention. Larger organizations may have a marketing department that is responsible for collecting, maintaining, and using data that defines the current customer base and looking for trends that would signal a change in the customer base. The marketing department is also responsible for developing and working with the marketing plan. It produces advertising, develops brochures, and looks for opportunities to showcase the organization.

Regardless of the size of the marketing operation or its structure, the best marketing strategy is to involve each member of the organization in marketing so that in some way the members know that each interaction with the public and with one another has an effect on how the organization is perceived. Staff should be known for their positive and professional attitude, their information skills, and their appreciation that the user's time is a valuable resource. A positive attitude of staff toward customers and toward one another is the best possible marketing tool, as it shows mutual respect and concern for the needs of others.

THE PRODUCT/SERVICE

Libraries are concerned with all of their potential users and are known for seeking out ways to provide innovative or extended services. This is both a strength and a weakness. The strength is in seeking out new ways of providing better service. The weakness is that in trying to meet all needs with limited resources, existing resources may be stretched too thinly and the quality of products/services suffers. Marketing is not just a matter of seeking out new product/service markets, it is also a matter of making choices and supporting those products and services the library/information center is best able to provide and that make the greatest impact on the largest number of individuals.

The purpose of marketing is to provide a product/service that satisfies customer needs and wants through an exchange process. Whether it is a product or service, the entity has a number of characteristics: a level of quality, distinguishing features, styling, brand name, and packaging.[17] The core product of the organization is the essential benefit to the customers. In the case of the library/information center, the core product is access to information. One can also describe the product by its desirability, its complexity, and its visibility. It can also be described by the extent to which it is familiar to the public. Services differ from products in that they can't be stored, the dissatisfied customer cannot return it, and customers may decide to perform the service themselves.[18] Products/services have life cycles and need to be reviewed regularly to ensure that they continue to meet customer needs. For example, a training program in Internet use needs to have up-to-date hardware and software, and the staff member conducting the training needs to be experienced in using it.

Most organizations have more than one product/service. They grow by increasing the share of the market for their product, by looking for new markets, or by developing new products.[19] Products/services differ in a number of ways. What differentiates your product/service from that of another organization? Products/services can be differentiated by tangibility; for example, they can be felt, tasted, read, or otherwise touched and explored. If it is a service, it can be differentiated from others by the level of quality and by the level of expertise of the professional providing the service. Products can be differentiated by their complexity. Computers are a complex product; a great deal of information is needed by the potential buyer in making a purchase and additional information is needed in using the computer. Considerable effort is needed to make complex services understandable to potential customers. Research services provided by the library/information center are complex and require an exchange of information between provider and consumer. Price, quality, and packaging also differentiate products/services. Each of these factors plays a role in identifying and maintaining products/services and the niche selected for them.

Launching a New Product/Service

Ideas for new product or service can come from anywhere:

- from staff working with existing products/services who see a new way to offer an existing service or who see the opportunity for an entirely new service
- from customers who would like to see a new product/service offered
- from developments in technology that make development of a new product/service possible
- from market research that identifies new needs and wants
- from out of the blue

Not all ideas are workable. Some are ahead of their time, some require resources not available, and others are of marginal value. Ideas are screened to determine those that will have appeal to a market or market segment and that can be developed within available resources.

Who screens ideas? In an organization in which the environment is collegial and staff work well together, the proposed idea would be discussed by those most involved in the area where the idea would be used. Outside experts would be asked for their views and suggestions. A good idea will grow stronger and weaker ideas will be put aside. The good idea will move up the hierarchy and, if promising, resources will be made available for further exploration. Taking new ideas seriously regardless of the initial proposer is a powerful means of maintaining a creative staff and a forward-thinking organization.

Once an idea has passed its early review, a concept will be developed to identify what makes it new and different, its benefits, and why it would appeal to the target market. A program on health information for retirees might be considered by the public library. Does it meet an unmet need? Is there a health information specialist on the staff to conduct the program? Are print and/or online resources available? Are there other similar programs available in the community? These are some of the questions that will be asked during the concept development stage.

The next step is concept testing.[20] Here a number of questions are asked:

- Is the concept clear and easy to understand?
- How is it positioned relative to competing concepts?
- Do individuals who are part of the test group show a preference for it enough to want to make use of the proposed product/service?
- Do individuals see that it meets a real need?

In addition, issues such as form, price, quality, and accessibility are explored.

The next step is to determine if the product/service is worth introducing. What are the costs of bringing it to market? Is there a better and more cost-effective way to achieve similar results? If all of the above tests have been passed and responses are positive, the product/service is then developed. Using the example of health information, a program would be outlined identifying kinds of information to be provided, where, when, and in what form. New materials would be developed if necessary. The program would then be tested by offering it to a small group representative of the market segment and this group would further refine the program with suggestions for improvement. At this point, the service is introduced to the market. It may be refined further to improve delivery, enrich resources, and ensure that it meets the needs and wants of the client group.

An organization cannot organize the consumer. Market research can tell us who the customer is and may give clues as to what the customer wants but it is the customer who decides if she or he wants the product or service. Service quality and reliability are high on the customer's want list. The excellent organization and the excellent product/service are the result of listening to the customer and responding with a better product and a better service.[21]

Price

Although in the nonprofit sector relatively few products/services have a direct cost to the consumer, all products/services have a cost. Each service provided by a library/information center has a cost that can be calculated by identifying the resources required to provide that service. Staff time, information resources required, technology access needed, overhead costs for use of space, and administrative overhead can be calculated for each service provided. (See chapter 16 for additional information on calculating cost.) Since libraries/information centers are paid for by taxes, tuition, grants, administrative overhead and similar sources, the cost of the service is deducted from the income received. As a library/information service has limited resources, choices are made about which products/services can be provided within limited budgets. To be continued as a service by the library/information center, the benefits of the product/service must be apparent.

A second way of paying for a service is for an outside agency to provide a grant. Many library/information services were started with grants from government programs or private resources. In some cases, external support was continued and in other cases, the library/information center was expected to pick up the cost. Some of the rationale here was that if a service was of apparent value to the community, the community would pay for it through increased budget resources. More often than not, grant-supported programs would tend to linger on after funding ended, be given limited funds, and then either be merged with a similar program or be discontinued.

Promotion of the Product/Service

Even the best product/service will not be used unless its availability is known. Promoting core services and new products/services is part of marketing. Promotion consists of five activities, each of which is used in making products/services visible. These are advertising, publicity, personal contact, incentives, and atmospherics.[22]

Advertising is the "paid form of non-personal presentation of ideas and goods by an identified sponsor." This can include paid announcements in newspapers, on television, on the Internet, or other communication medium. It can include the development of brochures, reports, videos, or other materials describing the product/service. Advertising provides a description of the product/service, any costs, where the service is provided, how often provided, and suggestions of the target audience.

Publicity is a means of stimulating interest in a product/service by placing or having someone place commercially significant news items in the media. Not only is it the most cost-effective means of bringing products and services to attention, it can highlight facets of the program/service of particular interest to a particular group. Publicity can be planned by the library/information center whose public relations officer identifies objectives for the publicity, identifies ideas to be stressed, and arranges for media cooperation. Publicity can take the form of an interview by the press of the director of a new service, it can be a news item describing the service, or it could be an interview with or letter to the editor from a satisfied customer. Publicity is not paid for by a sponsor. It reaches print or television because it is considered newsworthy by the press. Cultivation of good relations with the news media is an ongoing responsibility of the organization.

The library/information center's website is one of the best vehicles for informing the public about basic information such as hours open, location of branches, regular program offerings, and special events It can publicize new products/services. It can also link to the library's holdings, to specific reference databases, to community organization databases, and to many other resources. A well-designed website provides an image of the library/information center to the community. The website can also be used to poll citizens, asking their views on existing library programs and services and requesting suggestions for new ones. A well-constructed website that is information rich and easy to use provides an important public image for the library/information center

Personal contact is a particularly important means of promoting a product/service. The most important element here is the daily behavior of staff. Their positive, professional manner, not just in providing a particular service but in their overall performance, is the best advertisement a library/information center can have.

Incentives add something of value to the use of a product/service in order to introduce new customers, may be used. A new online service for business might be advertised by offering an initial discount for use of the service.

Atmospherics is the design of the environment in which the service is offered with the intention of producing specific positive responses. A bright, well-lit reading area with comfortable desks and chairs or a children's area with colorful walls, bright pictures, and big stuffed animals with places to curl up and read or listen to music provide advertisements in themselves that these are places to be.

FRIENDS OF LIBRARIES, LIBRARY ASSOCIATIONS, AND MARKETING

Friends of libraries (FOL) groups form a part of the community support structure of many libraries, particularly academic, public, and specialized libraries such as those located in museums or historical societies. Friends' groups are representative of the publics the library serves. Academic library FOL groups typically include a large alumni and faculty component as well as members of the community. Public library FOL groups represent a broad spectrum of the community; socially and professionally prominent members of the community are often well represented. Historical society libraries FOL groups typically include historians and local history buffs.

Friends' groups work with the library director and/or trustees to identify programs and activities that will in some way enhance the library's programs. This could include raising funds to purchase a special collection of materials, to underwrite a speaker or program series, to renovate part of the building, or to purchase furniture or equipment. Friends' groups have no administrative role in library activities. Activities put forward for program and/or fund-raising activities are subject to approval by library administrators. As a community-based group supporting library objectives, FOLs are good-will ambassadors in the community whose continuing support is important to the ways in which the community views the library and in this way are strong assets to the marketing program.

SUMMARY

An excellent summation of the purpose of marketing was provided by Blaise Cronin in which he stressed the following points. Marketing

- is user and client oriented and not product oriented,
- has primary concern for quality, not quantity,
- promotes effectiveness over efficiency, and
- emphasizes benefits to be gained by the user rather than the intrinsic value of the service.[23]

NOTES

1. Philip Kotler, *Marketing for Non-Profit Organizations* (Englewood Cliffs, N.J.: Prentice-Hall, 1975), x.

2. Robert H. Wilbur, ed., *The Complete Guide to Non-Profit Management* (New York: John Wiley and Sons, 2000), 56.

3. Kotler, *Marketing for Non-Profit Organizations*, 6.

4. Kotler, *Marketing for Non-Profit Organizations*, 17.

5. Kotler, *Marketing for Non-Profit Organizations*, 20.

6. Kotler, *Marketing for Non-Profit Organizations*, 30–33.

7. Valerie K. Tucci, "Information marketing for libraries," *Annual Review of Information Science and Technology*, edited by Martha Williams (Amsterdam: Elsevier, 1988), 62.

8. David J. Frieman, "The essence of marketing," in *AMA Management Handbook*, 2nd ed., vol. 6., edited by William K. Fallon (New York: American Management Association 1983), 11–16.

9. John L. Wood, "The markets and their effect on marketing," in *AMA Management Handbook*, 2nd ed., vol. 6, edited by William K. Fallon (New York: American Management Association, 1983), 17–35.

10. Kotler, *Marketing for Non-Profit Organizations*, 80.

11. Kotler, *Marketing for Non-Profit Organizations*, 56–62.

12. Kotler, *Marketing for Non-Profit Organizations*, 129–32.

13. Wood, "The markets and their effect on marketing," 18.

14. Wood, "The markets and their effect on marketing," 25.

15. Robert H. Wilbur, ed. *The Complete Guide to Non-Profit Management*, 2nd ed. (New York: John Wiley and Sons, 2000), 66.

16. Wilbur, *The Complete Guide to Non-Profit Management*, 66.

17. Kotler, *Marketing for Non-Profit Organizations*, 164.

18. Trudi Bellardo and Thomas J. Waldhart, "Marketing products and services in academic libraries," *LIBRI* 27, no. 3 (September 1977): 181–94.

19. Kotler, *Marketing for Non-Profit Organizations*, 165.

20. Kotler, *Marketing for Non-Profit Organizations*, 171.

21. Thomas J. Peters and Robert H. Waterman Jr., *In Search of Excellence* (New York: Harper, 1982), 157.

22. Kotler, *Marketing for Non-Profit Organizations*, 198–201.

23. Blaise Cronin, "Information services marketing," *South African Journal of Library and Information Science* 53, no. 3 (September 1985): 115–17.

ADDITIONAL READINGS

Cronin, Blaise, ed. *Marketing of Library and Information Services*. 2nd ed. London: Aslib, 1992.

Fine, Seymour. *Social Marketing: Promoting the Causes of Public and Nonprofit Agencies*. Needham Heights, Mass.: Allyn and Bacon, 1990.

Sass, Rivkah. "Marketing the worth of your library." *Library Journal* 127, no. 11 (June 15, 2002): 37–38.

Shontz, Marilyn, Jon C. Parker, and Richard Parker. "What do librarians think about marketing? A survey of public librarians' attitudes toward the marketing of library services." *Library Quarterly* 74, no. 1 (January 2004): 63–84.

Siess, Judith A. *The Visible Librarian: Asserting Your Value with Marketing and Advocacy*. Chicago: American Library Association, 2003.

Smith, Barry B. *Marketing Strategies for Libraries*. Bradford, U.K.: MCB University Press, 1983.

Unruh, Betty, ed. *The Information Marketing Handbook*. Philadelphia: National Federation of Abstracting and Information Services, 1989.

Walters, Suzanne. *Library Marketing That Works*. New York: Neal Schuman, 2003.

Weingand, Darlene. *Future-Driven Library Marketing*. Chicago: American Library Association, 1998.

———. *Marketing: Planning Library and Information Services*. 2nd ed. Englewood, Colo.: Libraries Unlimited, 1999.

Wood, Elizabeth J., and Victoria L. Young. *Strategic Marketing for Libraries*. New York: Neal Schuman, 1992.

Part III

MANAGING THE ORGANIZATION

Chapter Ten

Innovation and Planning

The environment within which we work and live is one of continuous change. Demographics change, the economic and political situation changes, and the ways in which we do business change. Since the 1980s, deregulation, privatization, globalization, and technological advances have altered the long-accepted boundaries between business and government and not-for-profit agencies. The need to reinvent one's organization and to look to new ways of providing services is essential to growth, and in many instances, to survival. Traditionally, ideas and impetus for change came from key leaders in the organization; they now also come from many additional directions: from stakeholders, from users of the services, from leaders in the information professions, from staff members, and, of course, from traditional leadership. With the availability of rapid cross-cutting communication through e-mail and other technology-enhanced channels, good ideas can come from any source quickly, as can the recognition of the need for change.

Community expectations of what a library/information center should change as well. Technological advances change the range of services one can provide. Internally, there are changes in staff and staff capabilities that may or may not be relevant to new expectations. Resource availability changes, service expectations change, and new opportunities emerge.

In an era of massive innovation in the ways in which information is used and can be used, fundamental questions emerge about the role of libraries in a digital age. Should they be innovators in working with their communities to use new ways of accessing information or should they merely serve as custodians of information? Should they follow the curve and thus potentially become peripheral to the action or should they be their community's proactive information resource? This question received mixed responses from those queried in a community survey by researchers from the Benton Foundation.[1] Many said that the library was not central to the digital age, that the library was a repository rather than a center for information activity, while others saw a more proactive role. It is evident from this investigation that libraries/information centers must find and build their competitive niche in the digital age, must look for "new life-forms" through collaboration with other agencies, and must be creative users of technology to enhance services to their communities.[2] The issues raised are too complex to assume that one can muddle through and hope for the best. We need to use all of our creativity, abilities, and resources to plan strategically to meet the future. This is an opportunity to reimagine ourselves and to meet the future with a fresh vision that, while it builds on known skills, abilities, and resources, goes beyond what we are doing today and reaches into an exciting tomorrow.

INNOVATION

Over the past decades, priorities in the management of organizations have shifted from those that keep the organization running smoothly toward those that ask, "Does our organization have the most appropriate current objectives?" "Does it meet those objectives in the most creative manner?" "Does the organization meet the needs and wants of the customer in ways most satisfying to the customer?" Questioning what we do and searching for better ways of doing it or doing new things is not only the right thing to do; for the long-term health and survival of the organization, it is a requirement.

Innovation is the means one uses to search for new ways of doing things and incorporates new activities into the organization. "Systematic innovation consists of the purposeful and organized search for change and in the systematic analysis of the opportunities such change might offer for economic or social innovation."[3] Innovation exploits the opportunities present in our environment, both inside the organization and external to it. Drucker lists among the sources of change internal to the organization the unexpected event that leads one to ask questions, or an incongruity that points out the differences between what is real and what we thought should happen.[4] Opportunities for innovation arise when a new activity is added and new ways of dealing with it must be developed. They also arise when changes in organizational structure, in the area served, or in the definition of those who are the primary recipients of a product or service occur. They may also occur when there has been a failure in the processes regularly followed and it becomes evident that new ways of operating are needed. External sources of change include changing demographics, change in how the organization is perceived by others, and changes due to the availability of new technology and new knowledge. Innovation is essential to the management of any organization and it is the responsibility of managers to create and encourage among staff an environment of "intelligent risk taking which then leads to creativity and innovation."[5] Augustine and Adelman reinforce this point by saying that more mistakes come from staying with the same thing too long than from jumping to the new too soon.[6] One must be ready to catch change and opportunity when it comes along. This assumes knowing your organizational mission and how innovation will further its objectives.

The availability of increasingly sophisticated communication and information technology tools has provided nearly unlimited opportunities to explore innovative ways of acquiring, organizing, storing, accessing, and delivering information to those who use library/information services and opens up opportunities to link with new suppliers and to serve additional segments of the community in new ways. The accelerating pace of the development and use of technology has increased the cycle of innovation so that new ideas are developed and implemented, often before the previous innovation has been fully incorporated into activities. Managers often find themselves responsible for dealing with partially implemented technical changes, initiating operational changes, closing down activities no longer relevant to goals and objectives, and at the same time being responsible for managing daily activities and making certain that the service levels remain high and the customer is satisfied.[7] Changing demographics (e.g., an increase in the number of immigrants in the community, the continuing increase in levels of education in the workforce, changing age levels in the community served) present opportunities for new services and the need to look critically at existing services. Today's successful manager looks at the constantly changing landscape as a source of opportunity.

Moving an idea for change to reality requires work. Many ideas never go beyond being good ideas, often because of an unwillingness to do the work needed to determine if they can be made to work. To take that next step, one must locate as much information as possible in order to analyze the social, perceptual, and economic factors that surround the idea. For example, an opportunity to provide information services to an off-site educational program has arisen. This would be an excellent means of extending services to a previously unserved group and would also have the potential to serve as a testing ground for a new type of service delivery. A staff member has been working on a plan for information delivery to the desktop and has been looking for a way to test that idea. What needs to be done to determine if this is an appropriate direction for the library/information center to move, and if so, to determine the best way to provide services? The library/information center manager would first appoint a team consisting of representatives of units who might be involved in the service and charge them to identify and analyze all relevant issues, make a recommendation, and if the recommendation is positive, to outline steps for implementation. If the library/information center is small, the director will conduct the analysis and make a decision. The timeline for this activity depends on the timeline of those who are developing the off-site educational program.

The team analyzes all available information on the educational program, including who the sponsors are, the content, external audience, resources available, and its duration. It determines what the sponsors expect from the library/information center, including types of resources, access to resources, on-site support, and other factors including the level of their willingness to pay for the service. And would they be willing to have the service used as a test bed for a new means of service delivery? The team also analyzes the library/information center resources to determine the extent to which they have the information resources and expertise needed and the ease of making them available. The social implications of the educational program being provided to a community and the potential benefits to the library/information center of supporting the program are identified. Is it perceived by the community to be served as positive and is it perceived by the library/information center as something it would be pleased to sponsor? Not all needed information will be readily available.

As the team assembles the information, gaps will appear. Some need to be filled before a decision is made while others are less important to the decision. Within this opportunity to provide added service is the opportunity to try out a new delivery system. Here again, the team analyzes the opportunity, working closely with the staff member who initially proposed the idea to refine the concept. The type of course being supported, the level of computer literacy of potential students, their access to computing, and the willingness of the instructor to support the proposed system are among the issues that need to be explored. The more information gained, the more questions asked, the more likely a workable plan for the innovation will be constructed.

All of this needs to be accomplished in a brief period of time. Innovation can be killed by being studied for so long that it is no longer new or the opportunity to test it has passed. The innovation itself has the best chance of success if it is simple, clearly described, and tightly focused. Innovations may fail if one tries to do too much at once, as one tends to lose focus. Innovations that are overly complex also tend to fail, as there are too many variables in play for one to manage. They also fail if they do not solve the problem or enhance the service as intended or do not lead to some form of improvement. The individual responsible for managing the innovation needs to pay close attention to the way it is implemented and to make changes along the way as needed. Even the failed innovation provides opportunities for learning, and today's partially successful effort may be the base for a revised success tomorrow. The only inexcusable reasons for failure are those that result from sloppy analysis or implementation. There is no such thing as a bad idea but there are ideas whose time has passed, whose time has not yet arrived, or where sufficient information is not available. The wise manager needs to know when to let go of an idea and to move on, just as he or she knows when to let go of an existing program that no longer contributes to the organization's goals.

The Innovator

The twenty-first-century organizational model, while based on a solid foundation stressing responsibility and accountability in the achievement of goals, is open to new ways of coming together to achieve goals and is not tightly tied at every level to earlier limiting hierarchical structures. This gives the individual greater flexibility and greater personal responsibility for carrying out tasks. In an environment that encourages and rewards innovation, each staff member has the opportunity to be an innovator.

Different individuals think differently. They bring different experiences and biases to an issue and they may have acquired habits of interaction with others that support or interfere with working together. Leonard and Straus caution that managers need to be aware that individuals have different styles of thinking and problem solving, and that putting a group of individuals together to deal with a problem or issue without managing the interaction can lead to chaos.[8] Individuals have varying approaches to perceiving and accumulating data, making decisions, solving problems, and interacting with others. These differences are often categorized as left-brain–right-brain thinking, with the left-brain thinkers seen as analytical, logical, and sequential in their approach while right-brain thinking is values based, nonlinear, and intuitive. Some individuals are comfortable with abstract thought while others prefer to experiment and collect reams of data before making decisions. The concept person has little patience with the person who focuses on details. While each has an important contribution to make, it often takes an outside voice to help each understand the other's contribution. The manager, when assembling a team, is aware of these differences and includes on the team a variety of thinking styles as well as individuals from different disciplinary backgrounds. Library/information specialists are particularly fortunate here, as most have undergraduate degrees in a specific discipline and many have advanced degrees as well. They thus bring a wide range of approaches to problem solving. Teams may also include customers or experts on the particular issue under discussion and they contribute different and useful perspectives to the mix. The manager clarifies the task for the team and sets a specific goal. Operating guidelines are set and an agenda is proposed that allows sufficient time on discussing the topic to accept divergent and convergent views to be expressed. In this way, all aspects of and views on an issue can be aired. Once this has been done, an action plan is set. When cognitive differences are understood, it is possible to manage interaction in such a way that creativity can be focused to support the development of ideas from the thinking stage to the plan and its application.

In the library/information center, much innovation is directed toward how one manages information resources and provides services. The staff members closest to the task are often the ones who see ways in which improvements can be made. They then share ideas with coworkers and supervisors, who discuss those ideas in relation to related activities. If the ideas are perceived to improve service and do not disturb other well-functioning services, they will most likely be implemented. This type of innovation is part of daily activities and often not recognized to be as important as the big new idea for services. The continuous honing of the organization to improve its operation is an essential aspect of innovation. Extensive innovation is directed beyond the incremental improvement of the organization and its services and is focused on building new programs and services or in making radical change. Each is an essential element of a healthy organization.

When organizational culture, personal loyalties, resistance to change, or other factors interfere with innovation, it is often difficult to move toward new directions. The long-established hierarchical organization can prevent members of the organization from bringing their full creativity to bear on issues and may even discourage creativity. It can also slow the rate of change and prevent the organization from responding to new opportunities. While social networks can be an asset to working together, they can become so strong that external information and divergent thinking does not get through. The success of innovative thinking in the organization is dependent upon a supportive organizational culture, an understanding of the unique contribution each individual makes, and the understanding that the process of innovative thinking, while creative, has structure and is not an idea free-for-all. While there is the need for the expression of many ideas, this is but one part of the process of finding ideas and turning them into action. Good ideas come from knowing what you do, knowing what you want to do, and finding the best connection.

PLANNING

Planning is the process by which "one makes the disciplined effort to produce fundamental decisions and actions that shape what an organization (or other entity) is, what it does, and why it does it."[9] Planning as a management tool is an activity that came to maturity during the last half of the twentieth century, although aspects of planning as we define it were present earlier. Initially focused on land use, planning activities received much of their early funding from the federal government. From the beginning, this type of planning was highly political as government-funded agency plans describing how a community should grow were subject to citizen input. During the 1960s and 1970s, planning activities matured and moved from decisions primarily related to land use and community growth to an activity focusing on policy and program innovation and the development of a process to achieve results.

Long-Range Planning

Early planning activities in many agencies resulted in long-range plans; for example, the five-year plan for economic growth. Long-range planning during its early development assumed a closed system in which change was limited. In long-range planning, mission, goals, and objectives of the organization are reviewed and any desired changes are noted. Data assembled for planning is largely internal data that is analyzed and from which quantitative models are built. Future decisions are extrapolated from existing data.[10] External data may be included in the planning activity. Often, but not always, long-range planning is the responsibility of a small group within the organization that determines what data, internal and external, is used. This group devises a structure for action and develops a plan for action that is to serve as the basis for future decisions. While useful in many ways, this form of planning lacks flexibility and does not hold up well in an environment of continuous change. It also carries the false promise that, if one carefully charts a future direction, the future has been predicted accurately and what one predicted will actually happen.

Many organizations require long-range plans and as libraries/information centers are often part of a larger organization, they will find it necessary to develop a long-range plan to satisfy this requirement. The limitations of this type of plan should be recognized. While it can serve as part of the library/information center's planning activity, it is too data driven and inflexible to serve as a daily action plan.

Strategic Planning

To compensate for the shortcomings of long-range planning, the strategic planning process was developed. While it builds on many of the elements of long-range planning, it is more dynamic in its response to changing circumstances. Its focus is on identifying issues, collecting information (both internal and external to the organization), and exploration of alternative strategies to respond to issues. It assumes an open, dynamic system, an external as well as an internal view, and qualitative as well as quantitative information. Current and future trends are examined to make current decisions.[11] It has been said that while long-range planning is the science of planning, strategic planning is the art of planning.

Developed in the 1970s and 1980s, the roots of strategic planning can be found in the literatures of policy, marketing, and effectiveness research as well as geopolitical theory, systems theory, and research conducted in leading schools of business. Peter Drucker, an early advocate of strategic planning, said, "First determine what your business is and what it should be and then set objectives and allocate resources."[12] He was one of the first (1954), if not the first, to ask the questions that are basic to the process of strategic planning. He stressed that strategic planning looks at effectiveness (doing the right things) over efficiency (doing things right) and that strategic planning requires looking at the whole organization to see how the parts interrelate rather than focusing on them as independent parts. He further stressed the need to look at elements external to the organization to determine their effect on the organization.

Elements of Strategic Planning

Strategic planning is a process focused on identifying and resolving issues. It recognizes the legitimate rights of many constituencies to participate in this process. To be successful, the process must have a champion—an individual of sufficient stature in the organization who will be able to conduct the process and ensure that the process will continue after its initial planning stages and that the actions based on the planning process will be taken. While, ideally, the planning process is initiated as a result of discussions among staff, stakeholders, and other interested parties concerning new opportunities arising from external and internal change, the process is often begun as a result of an impending emergency situation, such as budget cuts or the loss of key staff. Planning processes that are conducted in order to improve the organization's operations are preferred to those that emerge from a sense of crisis.

The leadership of the process must have an understanding of the whole organization and how it fits into the larger environment. What environmental conditions currently affect the organization, both internal and external? Strategic planners examine and reexamine issues and conditions in this iterative process, and stress is placed on identifying the right issues and in addressing them. There is an emphasis on changing conditions and the need to take advantage of shifting situations and opportunities. Strategic planners look at the special competence of the organization and its stated unique mission. This is an ongoing process based on internal and external data, participation by stakeholders, and an understanding of the organization and its mission. It is the act and art of selecting the appropriate decision or decisions from the several possible decisions that can be made to further the objectives of the organization.

"Strategic planning sets an institution's movement in a direction to travel."[13] It deals with the big issues of how to utilize resources to maximize opportunities. It is a way to help an organization think through what it is doing and identify the changes necessary to meet new circumstances and opportunities.[14] It is a process that can facilitate communication and participation, accommodate divergent values and interests, and foster orderly deci-sion making.[15] The planning process brings together representatives of all stakeholders to discuss mission and goals of the organization. Agreement on mission and goals helps articulate who you are as an organization and then helps develop a vision of what your organization can be. The direction this process provides brings a level of certainty to the organization. The image of the organization is improved, as there is a means of indicating what the organization is and what it stands for. This process requires effort on the part of all those involved; if common agreement on mission and goals as well as agreement to follow through with the planning process and its implementa-tion is not reached, the process stops at this point until a level of agreement is reached. Lack of agreement on mission and goals shows that the organiza-tion lacks common purpose and such an organization will not prosper.

Strategic planning is useful to the organization and helps it to:

- think strategically and develop effective strategies
- clarify future direction
- establish priorities
- make today's decisions with a view to future consequences
- develop a coherent and defensible basis for decision making
- exercise maximum direction in the areas under the organization's control
- make decisions across levels and functions
- solve major problems
- improve organizational performance
- deal effectively with rapidly changing circumstances
- build teamwork and expertise[16]

Models of Strategic Planning

An early model of strategic planning was developed by faculty at the Har-vard Business School and was intended to help a firm develop and fit within the environment. A pattern of purposes and policies was designed to define the organization and its business by analyzing internal strengths and weak-nesses and by gaining insights from senior management on these issues. External threats and opportunities were identified, as were social obligations of the organization. The assumption was that if such a model were adopted, the organization would achieve greater effectiveness.[17] The introduction of this SWOT analysis is an important element of this model. S(strengths), W(weaknesses), O(opportunities), and T(threats) provide a structure for looking at the organization and asking the right questions.

A second planning model is that of competitive analysis, in which one looks at the five forces that shape an industry: relative power of customers, relative power of suppliers, threats of substitute products, threats of new entrants, and amount of rivalry among players in the industry. One then analyzes these forces against the propositions that (a) the stronger the forces that shape an industry, the lower the general level of return; and (b) the stronger the forces that affect a unit, the lower the profit of the unit. Relevance of this type of analysis to libraries/information centers and other not-for-profit organizations is that all organizations, be they profit or nonprofit, compete for resources and it is essential to understand those forces that drive competition.

Strategic Planning Approach

Strategic planning is an organization-wide approach that includes the full range of stakeholder input, both internal and external. A major purpose of the activity is to promote understanding of the organization and to agree on a common purpose. This is both a political and a communications process that results in a common statement of who we are and what we do. The library/information center director is often given responsibility by the board or other governing body to take charge of the process and to name an individual or individuals respected both internally and externally to participate in the process. Alternatively, the governing body or the director may name a consultant to fill this role. If that is the decision, the consultant must interact closely with the director, with whatever committees are established, and with stakeholders to keep them informed of actions the consultant plans to take to gather information.

Agreement should be reached at the beginning of the process as to the purpose of the planning process, its membership, its responsibilities, and the resources needed to conduct the process. As the process and resulting documents and decisions have strong political and communication components, the structure and membership of the planning team named to lead the process is most important. One approach is to appoint department heads to the committee, as they will be responsible in large part for making operational decisions deriving from the plan once the planning process is in place. Professional and technical staff need to be represented, as do members of governing boards, advisory boards, and other relevant formal groups. One may wish to include representatives of users of services and perhaps suppliers. Technical experts may be named as advisors. Staff to the committee is also named.

The size of the committee is important; if it is too large, decision making becomes unwieldy and if too small, it is not representative. A useful solution is to name a steering committee of from ten to twelve individuals. This group will organize the process based on agreements reached earlier as to purpose and function and will have primary responsibility for getting the work completed and for producing documents. A larger advisory committee that includes the range of stakeholders will review and discuss decisions and make recommendations. It will also review and discuss documents produced. Ad hoc committees to investigate specific topics may be named as appropriate. If a consultant is part of the process, that individual will work with the steering committee to help design the process, develop any necessary data-gathering tools, and provide other expertise as needed. Timing of the process is important and a timeline for completing tasks should be agreed upon in advance.

Brown University Library's steering committee, representing several levels of the organization, set six strategic directions and named a task force with staff to deal with each of the directions. A coordinating group set four themes (focusing collections, designing user services, collaborating in learning, preparing for the twenty-first century) and then grouped recommendations from each of the task force recommendations under them. Each theme included forces for change, future expectations, and steps to the future.[18] This structure worked well for them.

Once the committee structure is in place, there should be an orientation session to educate committee members as to the purpose of the process and their roles and responsibilities. Those charged to lead the process are responsible for this activity. It can take half a day or more, depending on how well versed in planning the members of the committee are. Part of the orientation session should include the entire staff so that all are informed at the outset of the process as to what it is, its purpose, and the contribution they may be asked to provide. This could be presented via e-mail, although the best option would be for a face-to-face meeting followed by establishing a website detailing progress and providing opportunity for anyone to ask questions and receive prompt responses. A website also allows suggestions to be made and input provided when appropriate and keeps the process available to all staff on a real-time basis.

Concurrent with committee selection and education, those having staff responsibilities to the committee will begin collecting relevant data. Clarifying organizational mandates underlies all subsequent activities and is the first thing to investigate.[19] This includes legislation, administrative rules, polices, charters, contracts, or other documents defining roles and responsibilities. These documents identify what the organization can and cannot do under present regulations.

The first major task of the committee is to clarify the organization's mission and the values that undergird that mission. The present mission may need to be revised or completely rewritten. A stakeholder's analysis is conducted to determine who the stakeholders are, the power they hold, what they expect from the organization, and what the organization needs from the stakeholders.

The library/information center will also conduct a user analysis. Users are stakeholders and at the same time consumers of the service, hence a special study to determine their perspective is useful.

Each organization has its own culture and values that have evolved with the organization. They include professional values, personal values, and community values. As the mission is reviewed, it needs to be looked at in light of these values. Any mission statement for a publicly supported library/information center will support the values of free access and intellectual freedom.

The mission statement grows out of the discussion of the following elements:

- Who are we as an organization?
- What are the basic social or political needs we fill or problems we address?
- What do we do both actively and passively to address this?
- How should we respond to our key stakeholders?
- What is our philosophy; what are our core values?
- What is it that we do that makes us unique?[20]

Differing viewpoints will emerge and tensions will surface. With open and honest discussion, most of these can be resolved; from this, the committee will take ownership of the final product. Failure to discuss difficult issues

Table 10.1. External Environments of Libraries/Information Centers

Primary Environments	Public Library	Academic Library	School Media Library Center	Business/Industry Library/Info Center	Museum, Art, & Other Special Libraries
1. Users	General public Local gov't agency School/preschool groups Community groups	Students Faculty Researchers Alumni Employees Some members of the public	Students Faculty Employees	Company researchers Administrators Business colleagues	Researchers Students Employees Invited members of the public Association members
2. Suppliers	Vendors Jobbers Employment services Computing services Contractors	Vendors Jobbers Employment services Computing services Contractors	Vendors Jobbers Service contractors (as part of school system services)	Vendors Jobbers Computing services Contractors	Vendors Jobbers Employment service contractors Computing service contractors
3. Interfacing Organizations	Taxpayers Board of trustees Local gov't Labor unions Regulating agencies Consultants Professional societies Media Volunteer groups	Alumni University system governance Regulating agencies Labor unions Consultants Professional societies Media Volunteer groups	Taxpayers School district governance Regulating agencies Consultants Professional societies Media Volunteer groups	The business organization Governance Research community Competition market Regulating agencies Professional societies Media	Board of trustees Funding agencies Research community Professional societies Media Volunteer groups Interested public

4. Social	Community demographics Community attitude toward the library	Student demographics Attitudes toward higher education Status of the parent organization	Student demographics Attitudes toward K–12 schools Special needs of students Status of the parent organization	Attitude toward the particular business/industry	Attitude toward the particular library service
5. Legal/Political	Regulations Copyright law Laws regarding children's access to materials	Regulations Copyright law Legal decisions, e.g., affirmative action	Regulations Copyright law Laws regarding access	Regulations Copyright law Tax laws	Regulations Copyright law Tax laws
6. Economic	Local economic climate Market and its effect on public funding Interest rates Salaries Inflation	Effect of economy on level of funding Interest rates Salaries Inflation	Effect of economy on level of funding Salaries Inflation	Effect of economy on the business viability of products in the market Salaries Inflation	Effect of economy on funding sources Salaries Inflation
7. Technological	Computing and telecommunication technology developments	Computing and telecommunication technology Teaching/learning technologies	Computing and telecommunication technology Teaching/learning technologies	Product development and related technologies Computing and telecommunication developments	Computing and telecommunication developments

leads to development of a mission that is not representative of the organization and a mission that is only partially respected. The mission statement that emerges from discussion of the above issues is the foundation for planning and action. As such, it requires broad discussion. It is the responsibility of the steering committee to keep discussions on time and on target while ensuring that there is sufficient opportunity for all views to be heard.

Once there is general agreement on mission, the next step is to review the external environment. Many organizations conduct environmental scanning on a regular basis. If they do not do so, the steering committee may wish to name a task force to set up an environmental scanning task force to develop a process for gathering external data that will not only assist the planning process but can become part of the regular data collecting activities of the organization. In addition to general environmental scanning activities, it is important to identify particular areas of concern to stakeholder groups, as these tend to have a direct effect on the organization. Questions that can be answered by information from environmental scanning are those related to current and probable future directions of political, economic, social, and technical trends.

Environmental Scanning

As strategic planning was adopted by more and more organizations and as it became increasingly evident that the external environment within which the organization functions is critical to planning, the need to assess external trends in a systematic way became evident. The formal process of environmental scanning, begun in the 1960s and 1970s, emerged fully in the 1980s, and is now a basic component of the planning process. "The role of environmental assessment in strategic planning is to identify environmental factors relevant to the mission of the institution; to assess favorable or unfavorable impacts of events, conditions, and trends on priorities; to develop scenarios; and to devise realistic strategies for creating viable futures for the institution."[21]

Informal scanning, the process of looking around to see what is going on about us, is standard practice and something each of us does daily. While this informal passive scanning enriches our lives, it is not usually sufficiently rigorous to be applied to strategic planning and decision making in the workplace. Active scanning is a more structured and organized activity. It is the process of data collection following from the identification of issues critical to the organization. Examination of the external environment to identify emerging trends allows the organization to position itself in relation to an anticipated future and thus be more proactive in decision making.

One of the motivating factors for the formalization of scanning into environmental scanning was the recognition by planners that their organization needed to be more socially responsible, to identify trends in society that affected them, and to see where their organization impacted or did not impact the social environment in which they were positioned. While earlier planning focused on internal factors, environmental scanning provides information on the context within which the organization functions. Through scanning, trends can be identified and events monitored in relation to the organization's goals and objectives. The focus is on emerging issues and areas that appear to be changing rapidly from which issues may emerge.

A list of trends to monitor may emerge from discussion among members of the strategic planning committee. Each stakeholder (e.g., staff member, user of services, trustee, consultant, vendor) represented on the strategic planning committee will contribute different issues or different approaches to issues of importance to the organization. This list will include issues related to the economy and implications for future funding of services; demographic changes that may affect types and levels of services offered; social and political trends that may change attitudes toward information services, including concerns about universal access and intellectual freedom; and technical innovations that will affect both operations and services to patrons. The list will also include review of legislation to identify new regulations, changes in regulations, or new or changed responsibilities. Review of new media technology and its uses and the radical changes in the publishing industry that affect many aspects of information provision need to be included. Issues unique to the particular organization may also be included. One can use a standard scanning taxonomy that addresses political, economic, social/lifestyle, technology, and demographics/manpower topics and then adapt it to the individual organization, or one can develop a unique taxonomy. The advantage of adopting an existing taxonomy and adapting it to local use is that there is a greater possibility of locating data collected elsewhere and using that data to compare to data collected locally.

Typically, those collecting data find it easiest to locate data on demographic and economic trends, as this type of hard data is available from regularly issued reports; while projections using these data are still predictions, they have a solid statistical base. Technology trends are fairly easy to follow, as a great deal of information on developments and even some projections are widely circulated. Social trends are more difficult to identify and track because the data is softer and open to multiple interpretations. The organization will identify those areas of greatest interest and track and process information related to them. The list of areas to track will change as issues become more or less important to the library/information center.

Data for scanning is collected from many sources, including selected national, regional, and local newspapers, and national and regional news magazines. Some smaller circulation newspapers and journals that are noted for their cutting-edge ideas should be included, as well as these are often bellwethers that signal new trends and ideas. Also include a newspaper, newsletter, or journal outside but related to the core field of interest in order to gain new perspectives on trends. Inclusions should be selected carefully, as it is very easy to identify too many interesting resources and find oneself bogged down in retrieving information. Journals of relevant professional organizations are to be included as are relevant databases reflecting trends and ideas. Opinions vary on the number of sources to be regularly scanned. The number of individuals involved in scanning, the range of topics to be scanned for information, and how up-to-date the information needs to be will all be taken into consideration in deciding the number of sources it is feasible to select as a core.

Many organizations collect statistics on major trends and most of the data is available both electronically and in print. Many national and regional organizations produce strategic plans that include a section on their analysis of key trends. For example, the United Way of America is well known for its plans and scans. It is also helpful to identify strategic plans of other libraries/information centers to learn what trends they have identified. Needs surveys conducted for educational institutions by state governments, the federal government, by interest groups, or self-studies include environmental scanning elements. Questions are asked about what the school needs to do or be in the next year and about the expected years to meet anticipated challenges.

The list of possible resources to scan is lengthy; it is necessary to look broadly and select the most useful data while at the same time being prudent in the number selected. As one monitors the resources initially selected, some may be deleted as not useful while new ones may be added. This is a continuing process. The scan needs to be tailored to fit the niche the library/information center has identified as its own. And it needs to be continuously reviewed and refitted. The information resources selected for scanning are those most relevant to the organization and will vary depending upon the organization. Libraries/information centers in an academic setting, for example, will scan sources relevant to trends in higher education, demographics of potential students, and hiring patterns of graduates. Libraries/information centers in an industrial setting will scan resources related to market position, emerging products, and similar data. All organizations are concerned with technological change and will include key publications on this topic.

Questionnaires and interviews with key decision makers provide additional input. Computer-assisted decision making software is available to elicit ideas from groups of individuals and to rank those ideas and trends deemed most important. It is also important to scan several media as different emphasis may be placed on trends when expressed in different formats. Finally, look at what the media is saying about your library/information center. How many articles appear, on what topics, and with what frequency? Has the pattern of publication about your library/information center changed? How has it changed?

If one is not careful, scans can be skewed in any number of directions, depending on sources consulted. One may wish to use the delphi study, a technique used to gain consensus on likely outcomes. With this technique, knowledgeable individuals are asked for their opinion on a topic or series of topics. Their responses are summarized and the group is then asked to review the responses and to select the most likely outcomes from this summarized list. The process is repeated with an increasingly summarized list of responses until there is consensus on the most likely outcomes. Experts chosen to participate in delphi studies may represent a particular point of view or views. If this is so, the resulting information will reflect that view and be of limited usefulness. If one wishes to support a particular political or environmental philosophy or point of view, one can select newspapers, journals, and reports from organizations with a particular perspective. Here, too, the resulting information is of limited value. Biased results of scanning because of selection of specific sources are not useful inputs to planning. Environmental scanning is not a means of justifying personal bias on a topic.

Over time, patterns and trends will emerge from the data collected using environmental scanning. From the beginning of the activity, a database should be developed that can respond to questions about key trends. It will be added to regularly and reviewed to ensure that that the content is updated and that there is sufficient data available. This will provide a continuous source of information regarding external trends and issues deemed important by the library/information center and its stakeholders. Some of the issues of interest identified early in the process may be of short-term interest and will be dropped from the list and the database, while others may emerge and will be added to the list for monitoring.

Using the above inputs and relying on a smoothly working database, one can then ask questions such as "What is the likely budget picture for the next year(s) given the overall economic climate?" "What technical innovations should we expect to move toward?" "What new services will fit our plans and what existing services no longer meet community needs and interests?" It is also at this point that one can use the SWOT analysis (strengths, weaknesses, opportunities, threats) in looking at trends. One can further analyze the data collected in a number of ways, including probabilistic forecasting (the likelihood an event will occur), cross-impact analysis (how will an activity in one area likely affect other areas?) and policy impact analysis (the likely effect of a trend on policymaking).

Having identified the trends provided in the environmental scan, and having selected key questions, one can then develop possible scenarios of what the organization could do given a particular situation. For example, if it appears that the economy will dip, how should one respond? If demographic trends show an increase in the over–sixty-five age group in a service area, or an increase in Hispanic households, how should the organization position itself or reposition resources? At this stage, one has the luxury of thinking about situations before they become crises. It is possible to develop several strategies as possible responses and to be creative while looking for proactive solutions. While the scenario may never be played out, the discussion of possible future activities is an important forward-thinking process. Having alternative strategies already discussed and available prevents some of the errors that occur in last-minute planning and action. In scanning, one is looking at available evidence and projecting trends. Some of the evidence is reliable (e.g., data showing changing birth rates, which will affect growth in the student population thus requiring additional resources for education) while others (e.g., increasing popularity of a particular entertainment mode) are highly speculative. Environmental scanning provides good guesses of what can possibly occur, not what will occur.

Some organizations will assign responsibility for scanning to a committee while others will assign it to the office of institutional research. If a library/information center is in the academic setting, it will most likely rely on institutional research for basic scanning information and then research its own questions dealing with information-related issues. This may also be the case of library/information centers in industry, or scanning may be assigned to a marketing or planning unit. Some may also see it as part of the public relations function or may assign scanning to a separate committee. Legal counsel may be asked to scan for legislative and regulatory change. For the public library, it is most important to seek out strategic planning and environmental scanning documents of other local government agencies to see where coordination of effort can occur. It is important that the public library, regardless of size, conduct a level of environmental scanning as it is on the front line of social change and needs to know what the important issues are and may be. For those not wishing to assign responsibility to a committee or who lack access to an office of institutional research, a third approach is to affiliate in some way with organizations with similar interests and to benefit from collaboratively scanning sources. Or one can rely on existing organizations that do scanning and will, for a fee, share their findings.

Environmental scanning is a process that helps the organization respond to an unstable environment by using a process of continuous review, collection of data, identification of trends, and a review of one's activities in relation to those trends. Scanning is a continuous process and not an occasional dipping into the literature or asking others what they think the new trends are. Environmental scanning provides the external data needed by planners as they look at the challenges and opportunities facing the organization in the next planning cycle. The viability of the strategic plan and therefore that of the organization is directly related to the care with which one scans the external environment and keeps that process current.

Using information obtained from the environmental scanning process, from knowledge of the organization, and from views of committee members, one can list the strengths and weaknesses of the organization's operating environment. One can also list the threats and opportunities.

Internal Data Collection

Once external forces have been identified, the data collected from the internal environment covering such areas as services, use, staffing, and resource allocation is reviewed. If it is found that data is not being collected to respond to important questions, this is an appropriate time to set up the means to collect the data. A number of programs have been developed by and for libraries/information centers that can be adapted for use. In addition to data collection, current strategy is reviewed, as are performance and the ways in which performance is measured. Questions such as, "Can one look at inputs and determine outputs?" "Can performance be assessed?" and "Should measures be put in place to assess performance?" are asked both internally and of stakeholders.

Performance measures have been developed since the 1970s for public libraries, school library media centers, and academic libraries. These early guides have been reviewed and updated regularly and provide assistance in determining appropriate performance measures. The Association for Research Libraries has developed planning and assessment tools to assess the research library in self-review. (For further discussion of performance measures, please go to chapter 15).

Identifying Strategic Issues

At this point in the planning process, strategic issues can be identified. Using the mission statement as a guide and having assessed both internal and external environments, what issues emerge that the library/information center can influence and act upon? What factors make the issue important to the organization? What goals can be identified? What can be identified as success? How does it relate to SWOTs? What are the consequences of not dealing with the issue? If there are few or no consequences, this is not an issue and can be dropped from consideration. Goals will be identified for those issues of importance to the mission of the organization. Objectives that focus on specific activities are developed and from these, strategies are identified. In this process, goals, objectives, and strategies selected must meet the criteria of being realistic and measurable.[22]

After critical issues have been identified, the next step is to determine strategies with which one can manage the issues. This brings together what individuals have identified as issues with what they are willing to do to solve them. Bryson proposes a five-part management strategy.

1. Identify practical alternative solutions, ideal solutions, and so forth. This is an opportunity to think broadly and to be both creative and practical.
2. Identify barriers to each of the solutions proposed. Are there political, legal, technical, social, or economic barriers?

3. Develop proposals for achieving the most promising alternatives These proposals will address the following issues: steps to be taken, intended results, time frame, who is responsible for actions, resources required, costs, possible cost savings, flexibility, implications for other organizations or other individuals, and external effects. Is the strategy acceptable to stakeholders, decision makers, and the general public? Is it technically feasible?[23]

4. Identify actions to be taken in the next one to two years

5. Develop a six- to twelve-month working plan to guide actions. The strategy selected "must be technically workable, politically acceptable to key stakeholders, and must accord with the organization's philosophy and core values.[24] It must also address the issue it is supposed to address.

The final step in developing a strategic plan is to establish an organizational vision for the future. This ties mission to action and provides a guide to future decision making. It is a statement of mission and direction that can be disseminated. It identifies those issues the organization sees as most important for action. Conversely, it omits those things the organization will not at present take on. The steering committee is responsible for preparing the planning document, which summarizes all of these activities. Documents vary in length and need not be long. The document will include the mission statement and strategies formulated to achieve the mission. Alternative strategies and their positive and negative elements may or may not be included. The plan is intended to be a guide to current and future action. It is also a political statement and a communication tool. Once drafted, the plan is reviewed by the advisory committee and discussed among stakeholders and staff prior to being put in its final form. The plan should also include a process for regular review of strategies selected and the extent to which they are producing intended results. As traditional plans are not necessarily action documents, action should be built into the plan.[25]

The planning process, once in place, serves as the basis for continuing effort. The organization may make the planning committee permanent or may devise another means of regularly involving key decision makers in reviewing strategy and revising decisions when needed. Short-term strategies will be reviewed and revised as new information or new opportunities appear. Existing strategies may be discarded if they do not achieve desired results. The plan should not become a tool to stifle creativity. It should be a vehicle for promoting creative actions in accord with mission and goals.

Strategic plans for libraries/information centers are often part of a larger organization's plans and therefore need to be coordinated with them. Often, the larger organization dictates the form and timetable of the process, the resources available to carry out the plan, and the measures by which performance is to be evaluated. There may also be statewide plans that impose an additional level of control. Within this layering of plans, the individual library/information center will still identify its unique clientele, state its specific mission, and identify the ways in which it will carry out that mission, and at the same time meet the objectives of the larger organization of which it is a part.

SUMMARY

In sum, strategic planning is a continuing process of data collection and analysis, decision making, evaluation, and decision adjustments that include possible personnel and resource allocations. Strategic planning sets the road on which the organization travels.

NOTES

1. Benton Foundation, *Buildings, Books and Bytes: Libraries and Communities in the Digital Age* (Washington, D.C.: The Benton Foundation, 1996), 4–5.

2. Benton Foundation, *Buildings, Books and Bytes*, 38.

3. Peter Drucker, *Innovation and Entrepreneurship: Practices and Principles* (New York: Harper and Row, 1985), 36.

4. Drucker, *Innovation and Enterprise*, 35.

5. Richard Ferson and Ralph Keyes, "The failure-tolerant leader," *Harvard Business Review* 80, no. 8 (August 2002): 64–71.

6. Norman Augustine and Kenneth Adelman, *Shakespeare in Charge: The Bard's Guide to Leading and Succeeding on the Business Stage* (New York: Hyperion, 1999).

7. Jeffrey E. Garten, *The Mind of the CEO* (New York: Basic Books, 2001).

8. Dorothy Leonard and Susan Straus, "Putting your company's whole brain to work," *Harvard Business Review* 75, no. 8 (July August 1997): 111–12; Raymond J. Corsini, "Myers-Briggs type indicator," in *Encyclopedia of Psychology*, vol. 2 (New York: John Wiley and Sons, 1984), 414.

9. John M. Bryson, *Strategic Planning for Public and Nonprofit Organizations* (San Francisco: Jossey-Bass, 1989), xii.

10. Robert G. Cope, *Strategic Planning, Management, and Decision Making* (Washington, D.C.: American Association for Higher Education, 1981), 1.

11. Cope, *Strategic Planning, Management, and Decision Making,* 1.

12. Peter Drucker, *Management: Tasks Responsibilities and Practices* (New York: Harper and Row, 1974), 611.

13. Cope, *Strategic Planning, Management, and Decision Making,* 20.

14. Bryson, *Strategic Planning for Public and Nonprofit Organizations,* 21.

15. Bryson, *Strategic Planning for Public and Nonprofit Organizations,* 5.

16. Bryson, *Strategic Planning for Public and Nonprofit Organizations,* 11.

17. Bryson, *Strategic Planning for Public and Nonprofit Organizations,* 30.

18. Eric C. Shoal, "Fifteen months in the planning trenches: Strategically positioning the research library for a new century," *Library Administration and Management* 15, no. 1 (Winter 2001): 4–13.

19. Bryson, *Strategic Planning for Public and Nonprofit Organizations,* 49.

20. Bryson, *Strategic Planning for Public and Nonprofit Organizations,* 50.

21. Bryson, *Strategic Planning for Public and Nonprofit Organizations,* 52–53.

22. Robert H. Glover and Jeffrey Holmes, "Assessing the external environment," in *Using Research for Strategic Planning,* edited by Norman P. Uhl (San Francisco: Jossey-Bass, 1983).

23. Bryson, *Strategic Planning for Public and Nonprofit Organizations,* 59.

24. Bryson, *Strategic Planning for Public and Nonprofit Organizations,* 179.

25. W. Whan Kim and Renee Maudoigne, "Charting your company's future," *Harvard Business Review* 80, no. 6 (June 2002): 79–83.

ADDITIONAL READINGS

Innovation

Brown, John Seely. "Research that reinvents the corporation." *Harvard Business Review* 80, no. 8 (August 2002): 105–15.

Drucker, Peter. *Innovation and Entrepreneurship: Practices and Principles.* New York: Harper and Row, 1985.

Hamel, Gary. *Leading the Revolution.* Boston: Harvard Business School Press, 2000.

Martel, Charles. "The disembodied librarian in the digital age," *College and Research Libraries* 61, no. 1 (January 2000): 10–28.

Pearson, A. E. "Tough ways to get innovative." *Harvard Business Review* 80, no. 8 (August 2002): 117–24.

Randolph, Susan E. "The search conference: A strategic planning tool for a turbulent world." *Library Administration and Management* 15, no. 4 (Fall 2001): 230–40.

Sutcliffe, Kathleen M., and Klaus Weber. "The high cost of accurate knowledge." *Harvard Business Review* 81, no. 5 (May 2003): 75–82.

Thombe, Stefan. "Enlightened experimentation: The new imperative for innovation." *Harvard Business Review* 79, no. 2 (February 2001): 67–75.

Townshend, Barbara K., L. Jackson Newell, and Michael D. Wiese. *Creating Distinctiveness: Lessons from Uncommon Colleges and Universities.* ASHE/ERIC Higher Education Report no. 6. Washington, D.C.: George Washington University, 1992.

Planning

Charan, Ram. "Conquering a culture of indecision." *Harvard Business Review* 79, no. 4 (April 2001): 75–82.

Friedman, Roberto, and Warren French. "Beyond social trend data." *Journal of Consumer Marketing* 2, no. 4 (Fall 1985): 17–21.

Martin, Allie Beth. *A Strategy for Public Library Change*. Chicago: American Library Association, 1972.

McClure, Charles R. "Planning for library services: Lessons and opportunities." *Journal of Library Administration* 2, no. 2, 3, 4 (Summer, Fall, Winter 1981): 7–28.

Mintzenberg, Henry. *The Rise and Fall of Strategic Planning*. New York: Prentice Hall, 1994.

Palmour, Vernon E., Marcia Bellassai, and Nancy V. DeWath. *A Planning Process for Public Libraries*. Chicago: American Library Association, 1980.

Slater, David C. *Management for Local Planning*. Washington, D.C.: International City Management Association, 1984.

Tregoe, Benjamin B., and John W. Zimmerman. *Top Management Strategy: What It Is and How to Make it Work*. New York: Simon and Schuster, 1980.

Chapter Eleven

Organizing Work

"Organizing is the process of establishing an intentional structure of roles through the determination and enumeration of the activities that are necessary to achieve the goals of the enterprise and those of its component units. It also involves grouping activities, assigning personnel and delegating authority."[1] Additionally, "organization is the means by which all group enterprises are given socially acceptable purposes and made capable of efficient operation."[2] Since the latter part of the nineteenth century, the bureaucratic organization has become the defining organizing structure of much of our society, and a society of organizations has largely replaced communities as the major social unifying system.[3] Charles Perrow, in his study of bureaucracy, went on to say that "bureaucratic organizations are the most efficient means of unobtrusive control society has produced and once bureaucracies are loosed upon the world, much of what we think of as casual in shaping our society—class, politics, religion, socialization and self conception, technology, and entrepreneurship—become to some degree and to an increasing degree, and a largely unappreciated degree, shaped by organizations."[4]

Organizations are shaped by the culture in which they function. They also shape the culture of which they are a part. Most individuals work for an organization, small or large, profit or nonprofit, public or private, and they depend on it for their jobs and therefore their livelihood. They conform to the norms of their workplace as a condition of their employment. The organizational values become their social values. Within the larger organization, different groups—both social and work related—have their own interests, which may or may not conform to the larger organization's interests. The organization shapes the community in which it exists through the types of goods and services it provides as a result of the resources it consumes. The standard of living of a community is to an extent a result of the health of the many types of organizations that reside there.

Organizations are shaped by their purpose, their mission, goals, and objectives. Initially, they were highly centralized and were *machines of people* expected to be a resource in themselves and to use resources wisely in order to achieve objectives. This fit well with Frederick W. Taylor's scientific management theories, which were developed concurrently with the growth of bureaucracy in the United States. Most organizations continue to have highly centralized control although the workforce and its resources may be spread out over a wide area and connected through the use of information systems and telecommunications. Because of the pressure of public opinion, federal regulations, and social movements, organizations have found it necessary to become more and more socially responsible. These external pressures have resulted in equal employment legislation and requirements for diversity in the workplace.

THE PURPOSE OF THE ORGANIZATION

An organization is a means by which individuals can be brought together to work toward common goals and objectives. They are developed by individuals who have specific goals and objectives in mind. Depending on the mission and goals, different organizational structures may emerge. In all instances, the primary concern is getting the work done: what combinations of people and their interaction will accomplish this? Some organizations are very tightly structured while others are more flexible and open to new insights. In a fast-moving environment, the flexible organization is more responsive to changing approaches in order to achieve objectives. Organizations are rarely the result of systematic planning but evolve over time. While one would like to believe that organizations are shaped by policies, they are more likely to be shaped by the politics of the possible. As organizations develop over time, they continuously adapt to their role and to changing conditions. Gould and Campbell designed a series of tests (four *fit* tests and five *good design* tests) to help an organization build and refine its design through the identification of potential problem areas.[5] These nine tests, derived from the study of a large number of organizations, provide a structured approach to defining and analyzing those factors key to the building and success of an organization.

The authors' "fit" tests include:

1. Market advantage. In what market is the organization competing and what advantage does it have? Does the organizational design support what the organization is attempting to accomplish? Does it consider collaboration with entities with like interests?
2. Design for value. Does the organization's design help the parent organization by adding value to the overall enterprise? What does the organization do to further the goals of the parent organization? As an example, how does the academic library add value to the student's educational experience, to research activities?
3. The people test. Does the organizational design take into consideration strengths and weaknesses and motivation of staff? Is the right mix of skills present in the staff? What learning and hiring plans are available to ensure an appropriate mix of skills? Are there some individuals who may lose status if the organization is restructured? How will they be accommodated?
4. Feasibility. What constraints (e.g., financial, technical) in the organizational culture hinder implementing a new design or changing the existing one?

The five "good design" tests are intended to ensure an improved organization. They also outline the components of the well-functioning organization.

1. Refine the Design. Does each unit contribute to the organization's responsibility to get the job done? Are there units responsible for specific types of work that should be left alone to continue as they currently are? Archival activities and the management of special collections are examples of specialist cultures that are part of the larger organization but that operate under special constraints and with special expertise.
2. Does the design provide for easy coordination among units so that they can share experience and resources?
3. Is there redundancy? This test looks at the number and levels of groups responsible for managing functions to see if some can be eliminated. While some redundancy can be useful, too many layers of management slow the accomplishment of activities and can be costly.
4. Is there accountability? What control mechanisms exist? Do all

employees know what their tasks are in the organization and do they know how their performance will be evaluated?

5. Is there flexibility? This test looks at how adaptable the organization is to change.

This iterative process of looking at what you are doing, with the objective of continuous improvement, results in an organization that is responsive to internal and external change and is essential to its health and growth.

THE FORMAL ORGANIZATION

The formal organization has a clearly defined structure that can be described through organization charts, position descriptions, and communication flow. The formal organization tends to be a permanent structure in which change is slow and incremental. As organizations grow, they become more complex as functions become more complex. While the organization chart is not the organization, it is where one goes initially to understand how the organization is constructed. The formal organization is then divided into sections by function, by area, by product, by service, or by process. Functional division is based on the activity performed.

Figure 1. Organization by Function

In business, the three major functional areas are production, sales, and finance. Within each of these large functional areas, there are further divisions by subfunction. Within the library/information center, the standard large functional divisions are public services, technical services, and administration. Each function requires specialized education and experience. Individuals are hired into the functional division based on their ability to perform that specific function. Within each of these functional units are units providing more specialized functions; for example, within public services one finds units including children's services, reference services, and outreach services, The heads of the functional unit and the heads of the specialized subunits serve as the organization's experts in those particular areas and advise the director. As specialists, they have proven expertise in their area but may not have an understanding of other functional areas and the ways in which those areas interact. With the introduction of computing and telecommunica-

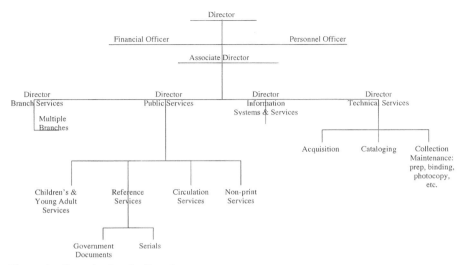

Figure 1   Organization by Function

tions technologies, elements of a virtual organization have appeared. These often fit within one of the functional structures and focus on activities that can be done remotely. For example, the individual who is responsible for ordering children's materials may do this from a remote location, or a reference specialist in a functional structure may do online searching for clients from a location other than the library/information center.

Figure 2. Organization by Geographic Location

Dividing an organization by area is often a response to geographic realities. A branch of the parent company may be opened to serve an area distant from the central location. Libraries/information centers of all types have branches that are geared to serve a particular area or clientele not easily served from the central library. The branch may be responsible for many of the same activities as the central library or may rely on the central library for a number of services. The director of a branch operation is usually responsible for its administration and its public services. Depending upon the size of the branch and the level of centralization/decentralization of the library, it may or may not be responsible for processing materials. Ordering, processing, and related activities are often done centrally for reasons of economy. A branch operation is closer to the customer and can provide more specialized and

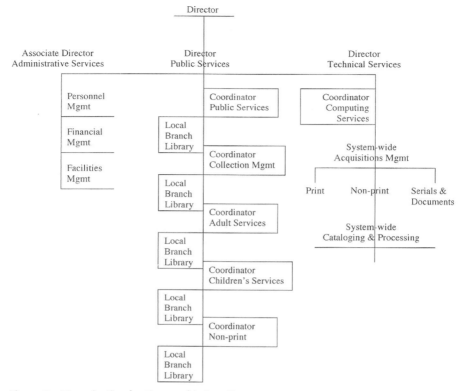

Figure 2   Organization by Geographic Location

more individual service. In many public libraries, branches specialize in collections reflecting the ethnic makeup of their community and may have staff who speak the languages that are in the community. With the availability of online catalogs and online reference services, a branch can be an important information source in the community and can provide service to individuals unable or unwilling to go to a central location. Common policies and objectives bind the branch locations to the central location. Because those in charge of branch locations are generalists and because they interact constantly with customers, the branches are excellent training grounds for those interested in assuming additional administrative responsibility.

Figure 3. Organization by Subject/Format

The organization may also be organized by subject or format. In this structure, content is the primary factor.

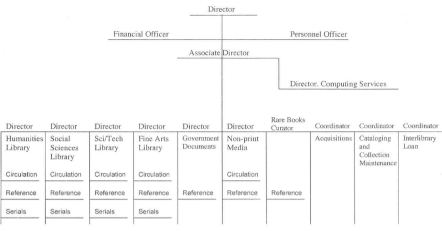

Figure 3   Organization by Subject/Format

Each of the above structures has links to other types of structures; in most cases, the structure of choice is a combination of more than one type of structure. It is important to strike a balance between overspecialized units and the unit that covers too many areas and is too large to operate efficiently. These differ for each organization. Although there are similarities among organizations, the structure of the organization needs to be tailored to the individual situation and to be reviewed regularly to ensure that it is meeting objectives in the most effective and efficient way. Regardless of the structure that emerges, its purpose is to provide a means for staff to work together toward common objectives. The total organization follows the same rules, regulations, and policies. Centralized guidance and authority and effective communication are required throughout the organization. Each member of the organization needs to feel a sense of belonging to the organization and a sense of personal importance in achieving objectives.

Coordination

Each unit in each of the structural formats has different areas of expertise and different priorities. It is the role of the manager to coordinate the unit's activities so that they focus on the priorities of the overall organization. In the traditional organization, this is done through department head meetings where discussion of organizational priorities and the contributions of each unit are discussed. Coordination is maintained through appropriate delegation of authority and through effective communication throughout the organization. Many organizations have moved to the use of cross-functional teams or committees to address specific purposes or to accustom individuals in different units to work together and to understand one another's perspective. Team members have the opportunity to work together to solve a problem that affects more than their unit. Another means of encouraging units to work together is to develop a matrix approach in which individual staff members are assigned duties in one or more departments on an extended basis—for example, a percentage of time in reference and a percentage of time in acquisitions or cataloging. This promotes a wider understanding of the organization and also promotes useful cross-training.

Along with each of the schools of management thought and organizational design, there has been much discussion of the span of control; that is, how many individuals should report directly to a single supervisor? There are those who assert that it should be no more than four to eight and one researcher advocated six. This rigid stance has been replaced by a more reasonable approach in which a number of factors influence the span of control. The ability of the manager to manage the situation, to know when to delegate and when to supervise closely, is particularly important, as are the skill levels of those doing the actual work and the complexity of the work. If the work is fairly routine and the staff members are well trained, one supervisor can manage a fairly large number of individuals (e.g., the circulation department in a large university library). If the work is complex and if continuous staff training and a great deal of individual consultations are needed, a narrower span of control would be appropriate. The culture of the organization may also influence span of control and attitudes toward delegation of work. The experienced manager will know how broad a span of control is appropriate in a particular circumstance.

Centralization–Decentralization

Centralization–decentralization is not a factor of geography but one of decision making. Regardless of the structure in place, where are decisions made? How much decision making comes from the top and how much is made at the various levels of the organization? This differs by organization and by how comfortable the manager is in delegating authority and how much trust the manager has in staff and their ability to participate in decision making. It is also affected by organizational history and culture. Some organizations are known for the willingness of managers to involve staff in discussions of issues and decision making while others are highly autocratic and all decisions come from the top. Policies and procedures are a means of controlling many activities in the organization, as they provide responses to many daily activities. The objectives of the organization, while not as strictly codified, also provide direction for daily activities. Dale used four criteria for determining the level of centralization-decentralization of decision making in the organization: the greater the number of routine decisions made lower down in the organization, the greater the degree of centralization; the more important those decisions made lower down in the organization are, the greater the decentralization; the greater the number of functions affected by decisions made at lower levels, and the less checking of those decisions, the more decentralized the organization.[6] In the most decentralized oganization, decisions made lower down in the organization are not checked on at all. In a rigid, slowly moving situation, decision making tends to be more centralized than in a situation in which the environment changes rapidly and new issues emerge that need immediate attention. The current environment of continuous change is one in which decentralized decision making is undergirded by policies that are regularly reviewed, which provides the best opportunity to function in today's world.

Dividing the Work

The responsibilities of the organization are typically divided into departments, each of which is responsible for an aspect or aspects of the organization's operation. These departments can be organized along functional, area, product, service, or process lines, and follow throughout the structural organization. All activities needed to carry out a particular set of goals are centered in one unit. The listing of these activities defines the specific responsibilities of the unit. Based on current objectives, this listing will change but will cluster around the primary responsibilities. A public service unit will include reference services and within that area, new programs may be initiated. New tasks may be required but they will require much of the similar expertise of other activities in the unit. Within the unit, each individual is assigned specific tasks based on the unit's responsibilities and based on the employee's expertise. The manager assigns individuals to each job and each job has its own description.

COMMITTEES AND TEAMS

Committees

Committees and teams are ways of grouping staff members and representatives of other stakeholders into groups responsible for accomplishing specific tasks. The *American Heritage Dictionary* defines a committee as "a group of people officially delegated to perform a function, such as investigating, considering, reporting, or acting on a matter."[7] Within an organization there will be several types of committees depending upon the needs of the organization. Standing committees are part of the formal structure of the organization and are responsible for specific tasks. Most organizations have standing personnel committees, finance committees, and planning committees. Each has an official responsibility, meets regularly, and advises the director on topics related to its area of responsibility. Membership depends on the structure of the organization, the expectations of the director, and the nature of the task. In some cases, membership on a standing committee is written into the individual's job description (e.g., the human relations director is a member of the personnel committee, the financial officer is a member of the finance committee). The work of the standing committee may be to study issues and make recommendations or it may have a degree of decision-making power. In a library/information center, members may represent professional, technical, and support staff. The composition of the committee, its power, and its responsibilities to carry out stated tasks must be clearly understood by committee members and by other members of the organization.

Ad hoc committees, or task forces, are formed to perform a specific task within a stated period; once the task has been completed, the task force is disbanded. Search committees, committees to advise on the purchase of technical equipment, or a committee to respond to specific community issues falls into this category. Membership is determined by the director with advice from staff, and will include the range of expertise and/or political representation to conduct and complete the task. Both standing and ad hoc committees maintain records of their activities, which then become part of the library/information center records. Should anyone question actions taken by these formal committees, a record is available for review.

Quality Circles

Several years ago, the quality circle was proposed as a means of sharing ideas. The quality circle consisted of seven to ten individuals "who meet regularly for the purpose of improving productivity, quality of performance, morale, and . . . product"[8] Quality circle members tended to represent similar units and levels of the organization but could be more far ranging. Each quality circle had a facilitator and a guidance committee that set clear expectations and targets for performance. The quality circle members would then identify a large issue, select a problem within it, then analyze the problem and recommend a solution. A further direction for quality circles was the development of possibility teams that would move beyond analyzing current issues to identify new threats and opportunities and suggest actions based on current and potential organizational strengths. Quality circles tended to be seen as a way for individuals with like interests to share ideas. The circles were advisory and had relatively little influence on operations. Lacking a strong connection to decision making, members of quality circles often lost interest in them and found other ways of sharing ideas. Quality circles have lost the interest of most managers and are only rarely used today.

Value of Committees

Committees have several important purposes beyond the subject matter of their charge or interest. They bring together individuals from different departments and thus strengthen the cross-functional network of the organization. They are important communication tools in that there is the opportunity for representatives of different units to share concerns. Committee experience in leadership and delegation within the committee is a valuable element in the professional growth of staff and may identify future leaders. The subject knowledge gained may be useful to an individual in other activities. While some administrators wish to use committees in a purely advisory role, others support a level of decision making by the committee. Participation in decision making by committees leads to a greater degree of "buying into" the organizational goals by the members. Not all decisions will be perfect, but neither are all administrative decisions. Some administrators see committees, if allowed to make decisions, as a threat to their power. They may be unsure of how to craft charges, select committee members, and ensure that a committee runs smoothly. Committees that are seen by staff as busywork devised by a director uninterested in the outcome or unwilling to consider recommendations are negative experiences. When the director shares information gathering and decision making with staff, then the committee structure reinforces the respect and trust staff have for one another.

Administrative leaders and committee members working together to reach the best possible solutions strengthens the organization.

In addition to formally structured committees, informal groups often appear. They can be formed by staff members, by clientele, or by some combination of stakeholders. Usually they form around an issue of current interest and exist so long as the interest continues. It is important for the director to be aware of these interest groups, as they can be early signals of emerging issues that will need additional attention.

Teams

"A team is a small number of people with complementary skills who are committed to a common purpose, set of performance goals and approach for which they hold themselves mutually accountable."[9] The purpose of a team is to respond to challenges in our rapidly changing environment that cannot be easily met within the existing organizational structure.

There are three kinds of teams: those that recommend things, those that make and do things, and those that run things. Teams that recommend things are charged with solving a particular problem and have a specific time frame within which to work. Members are carefully selected and are expected to involve those outside the team who will be responsible for implementing results. Teams that make things or develop new services are involved in ongoing activities. They involve those who perform the service or make the product. The focus is on better and better products and higher and higher levels of performance. Teams that run things are usually better defined as work groups, as managing an operation is more efficiently done when there is an identified leader.[10]

Teams differ from work groups or a project group in that a work or project group has a leader appointed by a senior administrator. Its task is assigned and roles within the task force are also often assigned. While a team is motivated by the charge assigned to it, the work group follows the instructions of its leader and produces the required result. The work group is more tightly organized than the team. In its meetings, members discuss, decide, and delegate, and then plan appropriate activities. The work group's effectiveness is measured by the influence of its activities on other units. Sometimes a team approach with its often more wide-ranging exploration of an issue is an appropriate structure, while at other times the single-leader work group is the better approach.

Teams take a cross-functional approach to an activity and use the skills of several functional units. All teams begin with the statement of a problem and a charge to the team from the director or other individual who has created the team. As a small group of individuals, the team has the skills to solve the problem. The team is given sufficient flexibility to discuss and develop its own view of the purpose, objective, timing, and approach to the problem.[11] Team members use all available information from both internal and external sources. They use as much current data as is available. From discussion of the available information, they develop multiple alternatives to solving the problem. The team spends considerable time and effort shaping and agreeing on its purpose and how it will approach the problem. The team continuously refines its purpose and translates it into specific performance goals. Performance goals then help the team define a set of work products, those activities that they will accomplish in order to fulfill their purpose. Having a specific set of work products facilitates clear communication within the team so that they focus on specific goals and on getting results. This helps each team member identify his or her best contribution to the collective purpose.[12] Team membership is often a full-time activity that involves a great deal of interaction and hard work to shape collective results. The team is motivated by its purpose and develops a synergy that makes the collective effort greater than the sum of the individual efforts.

A team does not have an appointed leader. Team leadership is shared and there is both mutual and individual accountability. At the outset, team members must agree on who will do specific tasks, how schedules will be set, what additional skills need to be developed, and how to continue to function as a team. Team members also need to agree on how they will make decisions. As members discuss and refine issues, each finds a unique contribution to make. The best teams spend a great deal of time shaping and agreeing on a purpose they own as a team. Team members listen and respond to the ideas of others. Performance is assessed directly by assessing the quality of the work product. One could call the team a structure for thinking and planning outside the organizational box. From these activities of working together toward a common goal, mutual trust and commitment arise.[13] The right skill mix is essential to team success and this includes not just technical expertise but also problem-solving and decision-making skills plus interpersonal skills.

In a distributed environment, team members may be scattered over a broad area. In this circumstance, team members must be able to coordinate their activities in support of team objectives. Numerous technical solutions are available to do this, but they work well only when individual team members have a shared understanding of the work to be done. Teams are a powerful means of solving problems through group effort. They are an "outside the organization chart" means of dealing with critical issues and they provide ways for members of the organization to think creatively. New technology (e.g., a new software package) may be adopted by a team to assist the team in problem solving and the team may then recommend its use to the larger organization. This means of testing new products and introducing innovation to the larger organization is an added benefit of using teams for specific activities.

Team Training

When someone is asked to join a team, that individual may have been selected because of expertise or because she or he represents a particular point of view or constituency, or because the experience may contribute to an individual's learning. New team members are given an orientation session so that each team member understands the charge and what the responsibilities are. The successful team is made up of team members who are self-disciplined and who value quality performance. Team members listen to one another, responding constructively to ideas and suggestions. While a general charge is given to the team, the team itself refines the charge and team members accept responsibility for specific aspects. Team members are accountable for their own performance and, collectively, for the team's performance.

  Not all individuals are team players. Some find it difficult to work in a relatively unstructured environment while others prefer to work alone. Team members need not agree on how to contribute but they need a common purpose or a common commitment to that purpose. Team members learn to manage the input of these individuals while not allowing them to damage the working relationships within the team. Team performance is directly measured by assessing the collective work product.

Team Evaluation

Teams are nearly always cross-functional with members representing different functions and different expertise, each area with its own terminologies and priorities. An early task for the team is to develop its own measures that incorporate the cross-functional issues of the task at hand. A small number of measures that can be tracked should be identified and used. These measures are to help the team conduct its work and to evaluate the result. Agreeing on cross-functional measures will allow the team to speak a common management language and allow it to assess team performance. These measures should help the team assess its performance and only secondarily assure top management of team progress.[14]

Management Teams

The literature and common practice often call the top leadership of an organization a management team. If one defines teamwork as working together, then there is validity to the definition. The management team is an executive council, not a team; it is a work group lead by a chief executive officer. Developing a real team at the senior level is difficult to accomplish and may not be the best approach. Each executive at the level below that of the chief executive officer is responsible for a specific area of the organization and for making decisions in that area. That individual is an advocate for his or her area and has responsibilities for and to it that may not be best expressed in a team situation. The chief executive officer is individually accountable to a higher authority and not to the management team. Katzenbach calls teaming at the top an unnatural act.[15] The management team leads a hierarchical organization and only in certain circumstances can it develop a collective work product, such as in supporting a fund-raising campaign for the entire organization. Senior management's role is to identify issues and appoint teams that can deal with those issues in creative ways and report back to senior management with recommendations.

THE INFORMAL ORGANIZATION

Informal organizations exist in most work situations and are parallel to the formal organization. The informal organization consists of "the unofficial and unauthorized relationships that inevitably occur between individuals and groups within the formal organization."[16] The informal organization supports the social needs of staff by providing a sense of belonging and affiliation. It also helps to socialize new employees by demonstrating what the organization sees as acceptable behavior and thus is an important source of learning for all employees. The formal organization has values and standards derived from the organizational culture, which it expects all employees to follow. The informal organization also has its expected standards of behavior that may or may not be the same as those of the formal organization; it, too, expects conformity. The informal organization leads by persuasion and influence. While it lacks the authority of the formal organization, it can use informal social pressure very effectively. In a hostile environment the informal organization provides protection for the worker. Poor management can create an environment in which the informal organization is perceived by staff as a needed support system. Leaders of the informal organization are not appointed but who, for one reason or another, are seen as leaders— perhaps because of special expertise, because of longevity in the organization, or because they have characteristics others appreciate. Ideally, the manager works with leaders of the informal organization to gain their support in meeting organizational goals. The informal communications network is particularly important, as it transmits information throughout the organization rapidly and usually accurately.

The informal organization can itself become a hostile environment for staff if its leaders insist on conformity to certain social or work norms that may be in conflict with the organizational culture. If individuals are hired who have backgrounds different from those of the majority and the informal leadership is not accepting, these individuals can find the workplace very difficult. This has often been the case when women and minorities have joined a previously all-white and all-male organization. The wise manager needs to be aware of the social environment within the organization and insist on fair and equal treatment for all.

POWER AND AUTHORITY IN THE ORGANIZATION

The organization is a structure for getting things done. Management and the manager provide the theory and practice for moving the structure and the employees are responsible for doing the work to meet objectives. Important to the functioning of the organizational structure, both formal and informal, is the set of components that helps the organization run smoothly. These include the ways in which power, authority, accountability, and responsibility are exercised.

Power

Power is the ability to do something. It is the basis for authority, accountability, and responsibility. It is necessary for the coordination of human effort, for example, the management of an organization. The alternative to power is chaos in which there is no direction. Adler said that power is the main motivator of the individual and is the way in which humans overcome feelings of inferiority.[17] Others say that power and the search for power is instinctual. Social and behavioral scientists have investigated the nature of power but, while it can be described fairly easily, it is difficult to study.

Hicks and Gullet discuss seven types of power:

- Physical power is the most basic type of power and relies on the threat of force. Intimidation of one person by another, the threat of destruction of property, and war are all manifestations of physical power. Physical power can also be used in positive ways, such as in protecting others and accomplishing feats of strength.
- Economic power is exercised by allocating resources. The individual in an organization who can promise to allocate resources or withhold or remove resources has a great deal of power. These resources need not be owned by the individual exercising the power but can be part of the individual's activities within the organization—for example, the dean of a college or the director of a project.
- Knowledge is power. The individual who has special expertise essential to the organization or who knows more about aspects of the organization and its plans than others has considerable power. Added useful knowledge that has power includes information on external forces such as market projections for service or information about an individual's personal life. With the advent of information and telecommunications technology, there is no longer the ability to hold information as closely as was once possible. The new power of information is that much of it is held by all those in the organization or can be found by them. This diffused nature of information changes the ways in which knowledge and power interact.
- Performance power is gained through special skills or talents. The basketball player or violinist has power through talent. Special skills on the job—for example, in doing a task or in relating to others—adds power.
- Personality can be powerful if the individual is charismatic or has good

people skills. If staff like to work for a manager because of her or his management style, that is a kind of power.

- Positions carry power with them. An individual hired as a manager has as part of the job description power over those below him or her in the organization chart.
- Ideological power is held by those who have a particular religious, political, or social belief that is of sufficient interest that others will willingly submit to the power of the individual with that belief.[18]

Usually an individual with power has a combination of these kinds of power, with that combination varying over time and in relation to the tasks at hand.

Berle suggests that there are a number of laws of power that are useful to know.[19] The first of these is that power invariably fills a vacuum. If there is a problem, someone will take charge. For example, if there has been a traffic accident and cars are backing up, someone will step forward and direct traffic until the police arrive; if the professor is very late to class, someone will suggest how the class should respond. Power is invariably personal. How you exercise your power is shown by how you manage yourself and how you interact with others. Setting objectives is a way of exercising power over one's self because it provides direction for action. Power is invariably based on an idea system or philosophy. This can be the way in which the worker is viewed, such as through that of scientific management or the human behavior school in which differing views of the worker will affect the ways in which the work is done. "An effective leader expresses the idea system and coordinates the members of the organization in activities designed to contribute to the system [and its immediate goal]."[20] Power is exercised through and depends on an institution, as the "institution confers, limits, controls, and withdraws power . . . power is invariably confronted with, and acts in the presence of, a field of responsibility."[21]

Power in the Organization

Managers are assigned power by those to whom they report to manage the organization or part of the organization. This may be the university president, the mayor or deputy in a public library setting, or a vice president for research in an industrial setting. Unless otherwise restricted, the manager is given the power to act in the areas of personnel, information access, allocating resources, and any other aspects of the organization. The manager will typically work with others in the organization to coordinate activities and resources. There may be individual agreements or interactions with power elements in the unit that change the power alignment within the unit and within the organization. For example, unions may insist on a particular way of assigning work and the manager will need to respond. The balance of power in the organization is always changing slightly with every decision, every assignment, and every personnel change.

When a manager is hired into an organization, that individual has a license to use the power that goes with the position. With every decision, the manager's power increases or decreases. If the decisions are good decisions, power increases and both those from above who hired the individual and those who work for that individual are pleased. Bad decisions have the opposite effect. If the manager abuses power by treating staff unfairly, by benefiting personally from interaction with vendors, or by other unwise activities, there is a decrease in power and in the willingness of employees to respond to the manager.

Authority

Authority, which is the right to do something, is a legitimate use of power. "It becomes legitimate when it is institutionalized by collective approval or by acquiescence by viable organizations."[22] Blau described the process in the following manner:

> Collective approval of power legitimates that power. People who consider that the advantages they gain from a superior's exercise of power outweigh the hardships that compliance with his demands on them tend to communicate to each other their approval of the ruler and their feelings of obligations to him. The consensus that develops as a result of these communications finds expression in group pressures that promote compliance with the ruler's directive, thereby strengthening his power of control and legitimizes his authority.[23]

Authority is the right to do something, the right the manager has to ask a subordinate to do something. The manager has the right to make decisions within the scope given by the higher authority, the right to assign tasks, and the right to expect and require satisfactory performance. How the manager exercises this authority determines to a large degree the level of satisfaction and productivity within the unit. The manager who discusses objectives to be met, indicates the tasks to be done, and then involves subordinates in aligning tasks with specific skills will have a much more positive environment than the manager who unilaterally assigns tasks. The extent to which subordinates can be involved in this activity depends upon the task and the level of work and the worker, but even the simplest of tasks, such as shelving books, can be assigned with some level of interaction.

In addition to top-down authority in which the manager makes the decisions, there is also a strong bottom-up authority in most organizations. Unless individuals are willing to be managed, the manager will have a difficult time meeting objectives. Those who are being managed are usually willing to grant top-down authority if the manager meets one or more of a number of criteria. If they agree with the manager's beliefs, such as his or her political beliefs, they may grant authority. If the individual has a higher rank in the organization, some will defer to that. The position itself, such as president of the university, or a tradition of deferring to a particular position may be sufficient to grant this authority. In addition, and of particular importance, are the personal qualities the manager brings to the position.[24] Does the manager have the intelligence and skills to do the job? What is the manager's personal style? Is it one of collegiality or is it an "operate by the book" style? The strength of the informal organization can be brought to bear on the manager who does not bring a level of knowledge and good interpersonal skills to the job. The successful manager knows how to exert authority in such a way that staff respect that authority and are willing to follow it.

Responsibility

Responsibility is the obligation to do something. If assigned a task, one accepts the responsibility for completing the task. Some staff members see accepting responsibility as an opportunity to learn new things, to grow on the job, and to work with others. The responsibility could be a request to serve on a search committee, to explore the feasibility of purchasing a new information product, or an assignment to complete an urgent task. Others may not appreciate being assigned added tasks, as they see it as a work overload, they have little interest in the job they are doing and don't want to do more, or they may be reluctant to accept the responsibility. It is part of the manager's task to counsel those who show a pattern of reluctance to accept responsibility, to determine its cause, and perhaps to reassign them. The manager should caution them that reluctance to accept responsibility could result in an unfavorable performance review.

Delegation

Delegation is the act of entrusting to another a portion of your responsibilities. The manager cannot complete each task in the unit alone and therefore delegates the responsibility for some tasks to others. If the manager does not delegate sufficient authority to accomplish the task, the individual assigned to the task has difficulty completing it and may need to return repeatedly to the manager before decisions can be made. It is essential that when a task is delegated, sufficient authority to complete it is provided. Delegation of authority is carefully structured so that it is tied to the tasks to be done. Tasks are assigned according to the basic job description of staff, taking into account their skills and abilities. Tasks can be assigned with the intention of providing opportunities for new learning experiences for staff and to see if the staff member is a competent leader or can work independently. In delegating tasks, the manager can delegate anything except the authority to perform management functions—for example, planning, motivating, communicating, and controlling.[25]

Learning to delegate is a skill the manager must learn. The manager may feel very responsible for his or her assigned activities and may have difficulty entrusting another to perform parts of those activities. What if the tasks are assigned to an individual who lacks the appropriate skills or the individual does not complete them in an accurate and timely fashion? Organizing the work to be done and assigning tasks to the appropriate individual is a learning activity. With regular monitoring of tasks and reorganizing and reassigning when necessary, the manager can ease this concern.

Accountability

When an individual is given the authority to do certain things, that individual is accountable for the outcome. Her or his success in performing assigned tasks is measured using performance appraisal methods that are discussed in chapter 14. Staff in a unit are accountable to the manager and the manager of each unit is accountable to the next higher level. In addition to this internal accountability, there are three types of accountability external to the organization: legal, legislative, and administrative. Organizations are required by law to meet certain criteria in their hiring practices and in their accounting procedures. Other laws at each level of government deal with issues such as handicapped access to buildings, access by children to Internet sites, and many other issues. Libraries are often required to present reports and requests to state and local legislative bodies, often at budget time, and may then receive directives for action. The library/information center must also comply with directives of the larger organization of which they are a part. This may include using a university-wide performance assessment measure or following system-wide purchasing processes. These types of accountability affect each level of the organization in one way or another.

PROBLEMS THAT OCCUR IN ORGANIZATIONS

A smoothly operating organization achieves goals and objectives in the least amount of time and with the greatest amount of satisfaction on the part of the manager, staff, and clientele. Problems may occur for a number of reasons. They may be inherent in the way the organization was envisioned and structured, or they may become apparent later on. The organization designed for a stable environment may not be easily adaptable to change. New rules, new social needs, or the need to develop new goals or adapt existing ones may be very difficult. The rigid organization is rule bound and will not survive long in a fast-changing world. The organization may be too impersonal, too focused on achieving certain goals and objectives, and may overlook the fact that it is individuals who do the work. Without their support, the organization does not function.

As an organization grows, it may decide to focus on narrower objectives, thus losing sight of the bigger picture. The manager who is focused on parts of the mission and goals and does not understand the interrelationships of activities will fail to adapt to larger, often external pressures. Those who insist on an organization that conforms to the organization chart may try to fit every activity and every employee into an existing slot, whether they fit or not. Over time, organization chart categories can be expected to shift, with some being eliminated and others being expanded or divided.

In this way, an organization remains viable and responsive to changing needs. If the same individual holds a position for an extended period, that individual may assume ownership of the position and try to decide what will or will not happen. If the individual is successful, the organizational structure may be adapted to that person's interests. Old jobs may be preserved beyond their usefulness, innovation may be discouraged, and change may be held back. Once that person leaves, the organization can then be reformed to meet changing needs, and a means should be put in place to prevent future similar occurrences.

The unsuccessful organization is one in which managers analyze everything and rarely innovate, as they are too busy studying the situation. This is a common means of preserving the status quo. It also discourages those who wish to innovate. Managers who dictate what is to be done and who insist on controlling all aspects of an activity may think they are in charge. Managers who have little respect for staff and expect that if they order something to be done, it will be done are ineffective managers. Such an environment in which staff are not appreciated for their skills and ideas, in which new ideas are discouraged or languish until they are no longer new, and in which analysis is a substitute for action leads to paralysis.

THE SUCCESSFUL ORGANIZATION

We have discussed the ways in which the organization is designed to accomplish work and have touched on those attributes of the unsuccessful organization: rigidity, impersonality, narrow focus, and an unwillingness to change. What are the attributes of a successful organization? In looking for answers to this question, Peters and Waterman studied a number of organizations defined as excellent to determine what made them successful.[26] They found that each excellent organization was outstanding in tending to the basics; its members thought about what they did, applied the wisdom of experience, and were sufficiently secure in themselves to allow a level of chaos in the organization. From their study, they identified eight attributes found in the excellent organization.

The excellent organization:

1. Has a bias for action. Rather than spending a great deal of time studying a possible action, managers would try it out and then fix any problems. This is what one manager called ready, fire, aim. Small teams acting quickly provide a flexible climate for getting things done.
2. Is close to the customer. The importance of learning from those the organization serves is essential. It provides consistent, high-quality

service and works with the customers to ensure that they are getting the services they need and want and at the level of quality they expect. When the organization is customer focused, changes in service can be made quickly.

3. Promotes autonomy and entrepreneurship. The organization has several leaders at different levels and in different areas who work in a climate in which new ideas are appreciated. The management provides the latitude to try new approaches.

4. Are productive through people. The organization recognizes that it is people who get the job done and it is the pride they have in their work and the quality of the work that results in high productivity. Respecting each individual's contribution to the enterprise is a key to success.

5. Is hands-on and value driven. The organization's basic philosophy and the values it supports are more important to success than carefully crafted organization charts or the availability of resources.

6. Sticks to its knitting. The successful organization knows its core skills and stays close to them. It does not try to diversify into areas where it lacks experience, even when it appears that there is an excellent opportunity to move into a new area.

7. Promotes a simple organization and lean staff. Organizational structures tend to grow and become increasingly complex. This complexity interferes with the need to get the job done. Keeping the structure simple so that it does not interfere with the work to be done requires continuous attention.

8. Maintains a simultaneous loose-tight organization. Some activities (e.g., adherence to core values) are held centrally while others (e.g., daily management of programs and services) are pushed as far down the organization chart as possible.

Peters and Waterman also found that the best organizations are soundly analytical and their managers make decisions based on fact and not assumptions. While their research was conducted some time ago, these attributes continue to define the successful organization.

THE LEARNING ORGANIZATION

Organizations at their outset are designed as a means of achieving goals and objectives. Then they grow and change as opportunities arise and challenges appear. The organization has a life cycle of birth, growth, and maturity, and if not tended carefully, it will decline. Leaders of the organization have the responsibility to keep it alive, lively and moving ahead. To do this, there needs to be a plan and a process, which is often referred to as the *learning organization*. Garvin defines the learning organization as one "skilled at creating, acquiring, and transferring knowledge and at modifying its behavior to reflect new knowledge and insights."[27] Learning organizations are skilled at systematic problem solving. They use the scientific method to investigate issues, focusing on data analysis rather than opinion and anecdotal statements. Learning organizations experiment with new approaches. In most cases, these new approaches are carried out in the existing organization. Therefore, experiments are usually small and incremental until tested and found useful. Larger innovations may be given to a special team; the team develops demonstration projects outside daily operations where the innovations can be tested and, if desired, then can be incorporated into the organization.

Learning organizations learn from their own experience and past history. What activities have been successful? Have failed? Why? What new approaches can be tried? A primary source of learning for the organization is from the stakeholders: staff, management, vendors, users of services, and other external colleagues. Data collected through environmental scanning and internal MIS systems add to the learning resource. Exposing staff to new possibilities through professional association meetings and trade shows also expands the possibilities for learning. Learning organizations also learn from the experience of others. They look for best practices that might apply to their own activities. They apply benchmarking where appropriate. And, finally, they transfer knowledge quickly and efficiently across the organization.

THE VIRTUAL ORGANIZATION

The term *virtual* describes a condition somewhere between fact and apparition. It is something that exists as if it were real. "What virtual technologies have in common is their ability to allow a powerful simulation of the physical world by electronic means."[28] Through the power of technology to reconfigure social space and social interaction, a work organization as a virtual system can be created. Davidow and Malone assert that new technologies are causing a revolutionary change in how organizations operate, in that information technologies have been instrumental in doing away with the time-space limitations of the traditional organization.[29] Nohria and Berkley describe the ideal virtual organization as having the following characteristics:

1. Written documentation that describes and guides the organization disappears and is replaced by electronic formats that are easy to revise and transmit and are readily available throughout the organization.
2. Replacement of face-to-face communication by computer-mediated communication for primary activities occurs. In order to maintain organizational coherence, there is at the same time an increase in face-to-face communication.
3. Issues of organizational structure are transferred from organizing humans to organizing information and technology so that "to an observer the functioning of the organization appears spontaneous and paradoxically *structureless*, while the functioning of the information system seems at once all pervasive and faintly magical."
4. The networking of individuals from technically separate organizations or units results in a blurring of organizational boundaries.
5. "The implosion of bureaucratic specialization into 'global' cross-functional, computer-mediated jobs, such that the individual members of the organization may be considered holographically equivalent to the organization as a whole."[30]

While the virtual organization appears new and different—and it is, in fact, technologically new and different—its underlying purpose adheres closely to the statements of Weber and Taylor of an earlier era, each of whom said that all organizations are knowledge organizations, and to control the organization, one needed to control the sources of knowledge. In 1947, Weber stated, "Bureaucratic administration means fundamentally the exercise of control on the basis of knowledge."[31] The objective of Frederick W. Taylor's study of scientific management was "to annex and control knowledge—both the savoir faire of the workers and the more systematic knowledge being produced by increasingly organized research and development—because the possession of knowledge and skill represent the possession of control and power."[32]

Because we can manage the interaction between information and people through information technology and do so more efficiently, we are strengthening control but we are putting it behind the scenes. The organizational structure does not disappear but has reappeared in a more efficient and technology-enabled form. The new structures are tied into real-time data and can respond rapidly to shifting environmental conditions. The virtual organization is just as controlling as earlier structures but has taken on technological form. Taylor's scientific management is alive and well in a new and more efficient form.

SUMMARY

"The reality of dynamic institutions today is not in the replacement of old structures and processes with new ones, but in continually adapting the old and integrating it with the new to optimize the range of choices at all levels."[33] While the ways in which work is organized have become more flexible and provide individuals greater latitude in the ways in which they do their work, the underlying hierarchy as described by Weber nearly a century ago continues to be in place in the organization. But as numerous experts have pointed out, hierarchy and the resulting bureaucratic organization is still the most efficient means of getting things done.

NOTES

1. W. Warner Burke, ed. "General management," *AMA Management Handbook*, vol. 1 (New York: American Management Association, 1983), 8.

2. Burke, "General management," 34.

3. Charles Perrow, *Organizing America: Wealth, Power, and the Origins of Corporate Capitalism* (Princeton, N.J.: Princeton University Press, 2002), 1–3.

4. Perrow, *Organizing America*, 3.

5. Michael Gould and Andrew Campbell, "Do you have a well-designed organization?" *Harvard Business Review* 80, no. 3 (March 2002): 117–24.

6. Ernest Dale, *Planning and Developing the Company Organizational Structure: Research Report 20* (New York: American Management Association, 1952), 105.

7. *The American Heritage Dictionary of the English Language*, 4th ed. (Boston: Houghton Mifflin, 2002), 372.

8. Joe D. Batten, *Tough-Minded Leadership* (New York: American Management Association, 1989), 92–105.

9. Jon R. Katzenbach and Douglas K. Smits, "The discipline of teams," in *The Work of Teams*, edited by Jon R. Katzenbach (Boston: Harvard Business School Press, 1998), 37.

10. Katzenbach and Smits, "The discipline of teams," 44.

11. Katzenbach and Smits, "The discipline of teams," 38.

12. Katzenbach and Smits, "The discipline of teams," 39.

13. Katzenbach and Smits, "The discipline of teams," 41.

14. Christopher Meyer, "How the right measures help teams excel," in *The Work of Teams*, edited by Jon R. Katzenbach (Boston: Harvard Business School Press, 1998), 51–52.

15. Jon R. Katzenbach, "The myth of the management team," in *The Work of Teams*, edited by Jon R. Katzenbach (Boston: Harvard Business School Press, 1998), 85.

16. Herbert G. Hicks and C. Ray Gullet, *Organizational Theory and Behavior* (New York: McGraw-Hill, 1975), 108.

17. Alfred Adler, *The Practice and Theory of Individual Psychology* (New York: Harcourt Brace, 1927).

18. Hicks and Gullet, *Organizational Theory and Behavior*, 24–27.

19. Adolph A. Berle, *Power* (New York: Harcourt Brace, 1969), 37.

20. Berle, *Power*, 37.

21. Berle, *Power*, 37.

22. Hicks and Gullet, *Organizational Theory and Behavior*, 266.

23. Peter Blau, *Exchange and Power in Social Life* (New York: Wiley, 1964), 23.

24. Herbert G. Hicks, *The Management of Organizations: A Systems and Human Relations Approach,* 2nd ed. (New York: McGraw Hill, 1972), 264–70.

25. Hicks, *The Management of Organizations*, 266.

26. Thomas J. Peters and Robert H. Waterman, *In Search of Excellence* (New York: Harper and Row, 1982), 13–15.

27. David A. Garvin, "Building a learning organization," *Harvard Business Review* 71, no. 7 (July–August 1993): 78–91.

28. Nitin Nohria and James D. Berkley, "The virtual organization: Bureaucracy, technology, and the implosion of control," in *The Post-Bureaucratic Organization: New Perspectives in Organizational Change*, edited by Charles Heckscher and Anne Donnellon (Thousand Oaks, Calif.: Sage Publications, 1994), 113.

29. W. Davidow and M. Malone, *The Virtual Corporation* (New York: Harper Collins, 1992).

30. Nohria and Berkley, "The virtual organization," 115–17.

31. Max Weber, *The Theory of Social and Economic Organizations* (New York: Free Press, 1947), 339.

32. Frank Webster and Kevin Robbins, *Information Technology: A Luddite Analysis* (Norwood, N.J.: Ablex, 1986), 339.

33. Jon R. Katzenbach, *The Work of Teams*, xi.

ADDITIONAL READINGS

Abbot, Andrew. *The System of Professions: An Essay on the Division of Expert Labor*. Chicago: University of Chicago Press, 1988.

Edmondson, Amy, Rochard Bohner, and Gary Pisano. "Speeding up team learning." *Harvard Business Review* 79, no. 9 (October 2001): 125–32.

Finholt, Tom, and Lee S. Sproull. "Electronic groups at work." *Organization Science* 1, no. 1 (1990): 41–64.

Galbraith, John Kenneth. *The Anatomy of Power*. Boston: Houghton Mifflin, 1983.

Grossier, Kerry. "Human networks in organizational information processing." *Annual Review* of *Information Science and Technology*, edited by Martha Williams, 349–400. Medford, N.J.: Learned Information, 1991.

Hambrick, Donald C., David A. Nadler, Michael L. Tushman, eds. *Navigating Change: How CEOs, Top Teams, and Boards Steer Transformation.* Boston: Harvard Business School Press, 1998.

Huber, George P. "Organizational learning: The contributing processes and the literatures." *Organizational Science* 2, no. 1 (February 1991): 88–115.

Kim, Daniel H. "The link between individual and organizational learning." *Sloan Management Review* 35, no. 4 (Fall 1993): 37–50.

Leavitt, Harold J. "Why hierarchies thrive." *Harvard Business Review* 81, no. 3 (March 2003): 96–102.

Martin, Lowell A. *Organizational Structure of Libraries.* Metuchen, N.J.: Scarecrow Press, 1996.

Nadler, David A., Marc S. Gerstein, Robert B. Shaw, and Associates. *Organizational Architecture: Design for Changing Organizations.* San Francisco: Jossey-Bass, 1992.

Presthus, Robert. *The Organizational Society.* New York: Random, 1962.

Ramesh, R., and Dee H. Andrews, ed. "Distributed mission training: Teams, virtual reality and real time networking." *Communications of the ACM* 42, no. 9 (September 1999): 65–84.

Travica, Robert. "Information aspects of new organizational designs: exploring the non-traditional organization." *Journal of the American Society for Information Science* 49, no. 13 (November 1998): 1224–44.

Tyre, Marcie J., and Oscar Hauptman. "Effectiveness of organizational responses to technological change in the production process." *Organizational Science* 1, no. 3 (August 1992): 301–20.

Victor, Bart, and Carroll Stephens. "The dark side of the new organizational forms: An editorial essay," *Organizational Science* 5, no. 4 (November 1994): 479–82.

Chapter Twelve

Decision Making

Decision making is what we do each day, as individuals and as members of an organization. It is not a special process but is integral to daily activities. The range and type of decisions one makes at work depends upon one's role and status in the organization and upon the availability of relevant information. Organizations use information to make sense of the external environment and to construct a shared understanding of the organization and its purpose. The organizational culture within which decision making takes place is nurtured by this flow of information and its connection to the external and internal environments, thus being continuously refreshed. Information is the basis for decision making. "In theory, this choice [a decision] is to be made rationally, based on complete information about the organization's growth, feasible alternatives, probable outcomes. . . . [A]ctually decision making is 'muddled' by competing interests, negotiations, personal choice, etc. . . . [A]ll organizational actions are initiated by decisions, and all decisions are commitments to action."[1] Many define decision making by saying that is the step one takes to turn policy into action, the way in which the organization's planning, goals, and objectives are moved from ideas to reality. Drucker separates decision making from problem solving by saying that decision making concentrates on what is important, that which is strategic and generic.[2] This process is conducted by top management. Those at lower levels in the organization use these decisions to address problems that occur at their level.

Decision making is guided by the organization's mission and its goals. That mission, which is derived from the organization's culture and values, is widely understood within the organization and each individual is expected to be familiar with it and to use it as the basis for decision making and problem solving at every level. The mission statement sets clear boundaries within which to act. In assessing competing demands, the demand most closely aligned with the mission gets priority. Using the mission statement as a guide, strategic directions are set and resources are allocated. In periods of rapid growth, organizational turnover, or other stressful times, the mission statement can provide continuity. The mission statement itself is reviewed regularly as part of the planning process to ensure that it reflects the values of the organization and specifically those aspects of the culture in which it exists that best exemplify those values.

Decision-making theory evolved from the study of patterns of actions of managers. Research studies conducted in the 1960s provided a basis for looking systematically at the ways in which executives make decisions. An example of these studies is the one conducted by Argyris, who studied the behavior of 165 top executives in six companies to observe how they made decisions.[3] He found that while they held one set of attitudes about how decisions should be made, in reality, they made decisions differently. While they said that they promoted risk taking and were open to discussion of issues, in actuality, they were more concerned with conforming to existing ideas and norms. In the 1960s there was still a strong "organization man" culture in which questioning proposed decisions was seen as contrary to being team players. The organizational culture favored getting the job done rather than on how the group performed, and the job usually got done through unilateral control from the top with subordinates being told what to do. The reward and penalty structure was the means by which performance was controlled. Information on which decisions were based was held by top executives who might or might not share it with subordinates. Argyris, in interviewing subordinates, found a high level of negative attitudes toward the executive decision makers. The decision makers were unaware of these feelings toward them and thought that they had good relations with subordinates as subordinates performed assigned tasks willingly. Subordinates lacked input into decision making and saw their managers as conforming to others in the hierarchy and to one another. They saw them as unwilling to listen to uncomfortable information, to take risks, or to deal with ideas different from their own. This resulted in a lack of trust of superiors.

This organizational environment in which decision makers thought that they were supported by their staffs has changed somewhat since the above study and related studies were conducted. The workforce has changed in the intervening years. It is better educated, less willing to submit to authoritarian structures, and more apt to question decisions rather than to follow orders. The workplace is more diverse; in grudgingly accepting diversity, the traditional workplace culture has become more open, more accepting of risk, and more accepting of individual differences and abilities. Additional major readjustments have occurred as the result of incorporation of information and communication technology into the workplace. More information and better organized information is available to more people and it is much more difficult to limit access to that information. Communication among all areas of the organization is now more likely to be the norm.

INFORMATION AND DECISION MAKING

Huber recognized that "a large part of what is known about the factors affecting organizational processes, structures, and performance was developed when the nature and mix of communication technologies were relatively constant."[4] Since then, computer-assisted decision-making technologies have developed and continue to be developed. Their impact on decision making is of continuing interest and concern. Organizations develop internal databases and access external databases. The ability to access information from related disciplines and professions and to locate information on specific areas of interest enriches one's own decision-making and decision-critiquing information base.

Information systems within an organization are designed to meet specific objectives. Of primary importance is the collection of data to assist in decision making. In the case of some routine decisions, the data is used directly to make decisions; in other situations, the data supports decision making. The information system is also used to monitor performance and to maintain records. "IT enables organizations to process decision relevant information in a more cost effective way, thus improving the quality and speed of upper management's decision making processes. This phenomenon may lead decision rights to move upward in the organizational hierarchy leading to more centralized management."[5] While hierarchical organizational structures may be weakening in some areas, information technology (IT) systems of data collection are centralizing decision making and reestablishing hierarchical control in others. IT provides the ability to monitor organizational and individual performance in new ways not previously possible, thus enabling managers in specific areas to make better local decisions. Gurbaxani and Whang suggest that IT systems do indeed provide operational data that can be used for local decision making.[6] They see that some decisions (usually strategic) are made at higher levels using input from management information systems (MIS) and others (operational) are made at multiple levels using localized data. While the technology allows us to collect and manage data for decision making, nearly half of executives in a study by Bonabeau indicated that they relied more on their instincts for decision making than on decision support systems, which they used to organize data in order to sort out options.[7] In general, managers tend to use what they know from their experience and that of colleagues and to use decision support systems as a secondary tool.

The Internet allows communication anytime, anywhere, with any mix of individuals one wishes to contact. And this is done in real time. More individuals with more information can now participate in decision making. While there is no substitute for face-to-face meeting among colleagues and with external experts, a large percentage of communication can take place electronically and thus allows participation by those at a distance. Decision making can now truly become a team activity, with participation limited only by the wishes of the decision makers. One advantage of this more open environment is that information at lower levels of the organization can move upward as smoothly as information at the upper levels moves downward. Local decision making can be done locally, using the decisions of top management as their guides. There is greater ownership of decisions when a greater number of individuals is involved in the process and this motivates individuals to be more interested in doing their best in their area of responsibility. While the free flow of information allows for discussion and participation in decision making, the reality is that while much operational decision making is being diffused throughout the organization, the important strategic decisions are usually made at the top with limited input from staff.

One should take care in the design and maintenance of internal databases to ensure that they collect data needed to make decisions and that the data collected is in a format that is easily usable. External databases used for decision making should be reviewed regularly to eliminate those that are marginally useful so that one does not suffer from unnecessary information overload. Additionally, one must be sure that databases are not skewed in the information they collect, which would result in a one-sided or limited picture of the area covered. Often a government agency or other entity will design and use a database for a specific purpose and, to make that data useful for that purpose, will tailor its content. That database may not be useful for other purposes as its content is limited. Decisions made outside the range of such a database have a high probability of being faulty.

ELEMENTS OF DECISION MAKING

Decision making requires that relevant information, quality information, be available. It also requires that appropriate decision-making processes be in place. "It is reasonable to believe that the quality of an organizational decision is largely a consequence of the quality of organizational intelligence and the quality of the decision making process."[8] Drucker outlined a multi-step process for decision making.[9] First, he *classifies* the decision to be made as to whether it is generic, unique, or a new kind of problem. Most decisions deal with recurring issues and are therefore generic. When one analyzes a number of recurring problems in an area, underlying causes may be seen and from that analysis a decision can be made. A unique problem may be one new to one's organization but may have occurred in a similar organization. While a merger may be new to one's organization, it has occurred elsewhere and there is information available to assist in decision making from those who have experienced that problem. While no two situations are the same, one can gain insights into one's situation by reviewing similar situations. The truly unique problem may be a symptom of something that is just beginning to happen but will happen more and more often in the future. Except for the truly unique problem, one can develop a generic solution and provide a rule, a policy, or a principle for guidance when encountering similar events. There is always the possibility that a generic event can have a kernel of something new and different. For this reason, one should always look for the possibility of the new and different in each situation. The second step is to *define the problem*, to identify all the issues involved. What facts are available to define the issue? Is there something new and different about the problem? Once the problem has been defined and we know what we are dealing with, it is necessary to specify *boundary conditions* for the decision. What do we wish to accomplish? What conditions must we satisfy? Then the *decision is made* based on what is right and not on what is acceptable. *Connect* the decision to action. Specify what is to be done, who will do it, and how success will be measured. Those responsible for the action must have the information, the ability, and the resources to carry it out. The final step is *evaluation*, the use of organized information and personal observation to determine if the decision was carried out and how successful it was. Throughout this process, one must continue to ask, "Is this the right thing to do? Does it support the organization's values and mission?" Choo cautions that many individuals in organizations " '*satisfice*' rather than maximize, that is, they choose an alternative that exceeds some criteria rather than the best alternative, and they follow *action programs* or routines that simplify the decision making process by reducing the need for research, problem solving, or choice." [10] The "good enough" alternative will deal with an existing problem but will not move the organization forward.

MODELS OF ORGANIZATIONAL DECISION MAKING

There are numerous models for decision making. Most fall under one of five general headings and some are combinations of models.

Rational Model

The rational model as described by March and Simon and by Cyert and March is goal directed and problem driven. [11] The choice of behavior is regulated by rules and routines intended to achieve procedural rationality. [12] These are in the form of work activities, specifications, or timing rules. They are agreed-upon guides to behavior and may or may not be written down.

The organization may have a standard operating procedure for decision making. By applying agreed-upon rules, one avoids uncertainty. There is a tendency in this situation to follow existing rules for as long as possible, perhaps beyond the point at which they are useful. Standard operating procedure also covers rules for performing tasks, rules for recording and reporting tasks, rules covering how information is maintained and disseminated (the formal communication structure), and rules for resource allocation. In this model, goals are set by negotiation among the dominant stakeholders. Negotiations set limits on what the organization can do within the diverse interests and concerns of the stakeholders. The decision must then fall within these agreed-upon boundary conditions. In order to reach acceptable compromise in determining goals, the following strategies may be pursued: avoid uncertainty and broad-based discussion by looking at short-term goals; attempt to control the environment; and use accepted standards and agreements to move ahead slowly. There is little opportunity for organizational change in this strategy.[13] The organization may look for possible solutions to a problem; once a solution—any usable solution—is found, the search stops. This may not be the only solution or the best solution. It may be a local solution or biased by personal interest. This strategy of *satisficing* rarely moves the organization forward. A further means of dealing with issues and setting goals under this model is to look at past performance and experience within one's organization and make comparisons with that of like organizations. The purpose of each activity is to reduce uncertainty rather than to take major steps forward.

Process Model

The process model of decision making focuses on stages, activities, and dynamics of possible behavior. Mintzenberg and his colleagues studied strategic decision processes in government and commercial organizations.[14] Despite the wide range of types of decisions, an underlying structure for decision making emerged. First, one had to determine that a problem existed. This would occur as the result of a build-up of events or other stimuli in an area to the extent that action was needed. The point at which action was needed would be dependent on individual assessment. In observing the situation, the decision maker would gather both internal and external information. Using actions the organization had taken in the past and using available new information, alternative solutions would be posed. The alternatives would be evaluated, looking carefully at the intersection of each alternative with other goals, as well as the possible consequences of each alternative. Using this information plus personal judgment, a decision is made.

These activities do not operate in a vacuum but are guided by existing routines that describe the limits of the problem, the individuals to be involved in discussions, and the resources available. Discussion of the problem moves it toward a decision. Information-gathering routines and communication routines already exist within the organization and play a role in the decision process. How fast this process moves depends on the urgency of the problem and the manager's ability to bring together relevant information and individual viewpoints to reach a decision.

Political Model

This model focuses attention on those who have authority to act in a situation. This authority may come from the position the decision makers hold and may be limited by the limits on that position. Their personal perceptions and perceptions of those they represent, as well as their relative power in the organization, can affect their ability to influence decisions. Issues are defined within existing action channels. Existing rules determine who plays and how. While this model is less directly applicable to the library/information center, it is important to consider, as the library/information center can by affected by decisions made by the larger organizational structure of which it is a part.

Anarchic Model

This model exists when there are ill-defined and inconsistent goals and the organization has a poorly organized set of ideas of what it is and what it does. Often these ideas are in the mind of an individual and vary with the interests and concerns of the individual. If processes and procedures exist, they are not well understood by others. There is little understanding of how one achieves desired goals. When decisions are needed, they are usually reactive in that they are made to correct dissatisfaction with activities or performance. The solution may or may not correct the problem as there has little or no information gathering or analysis. Also, in this environment, new ideas may be introduced without determining if they are appropriate to the situation. In an organization, one often finds an individual or individuals attempting this mode of decision making. If this occurs, the manager needs to apply corrective action.

Garbage Can Model

This phrase is used to describe the situation in which numerous issues are identified and much information is collected. Issues and information are thrown together in no particular order. Major policy decisions are the result of chance interaction among the following elements: choice, opportunities, problems, potential solutions, and participants.[15] "[L]ike the garbage in a trash can, the decision depends on the mix currently available. There are *collections of choices* looking for problems, issues and feelings looking for decision situations in which they might be aired, solutions looking for issues to which they might be the answer, and decision makers looking for work."[16]

Research has shown that this nonrational approach to decision making is typical of many organizations. As better information-gathering systems are put into place and as decision makers learn how to maximize their use, this ineffective decision-making process should fade away. However, when asked their method of decision making, many managers responded by saying that they just muddled through, hoping that a solution would appear. Unfortunately, many decisions or nondecisions made in this way continue to affect the daily activities of the organization. Some of this indecision may be due to lack of information or it may be due to an unwillingness by the manager to take responsibility for a course of action.

TYPES OF SOLUTIONS

Depending on the situation, decisions may be made for different purposes and for different lengths of time. The *interim* solution is a short-term solution and is intended to deal with a situation only until a permanent solution is provided. For example, if a department is short-staffed, it may be necessary for some individuals to work overtime until additional staff is hired. This short-term solution will be replaced by a permanent solution at some point. It is often the case, however, that once an interim solution is made, the problem it was intended to solve in the short term is forgotten and the interim solution becomes a permanent one. This is an example of poor management. The *adaptive* solution is not a solution but rather a temporary fix for a problem. Like the interim solution, it does not truly fix a problem but glosses over it. For example, a supervisor may be reprimanded for treating staff unfairly. The reprimand is an adaptive solution with limited expectation of success. The problem is not solved, it is deferred. Chances are that the problem will get worse rather than go away. The *corrective* solution fixes an existing problem. In the case of the supervisor who was treating staff unfairly, corrective action would not stop at a reprimand but could result in the removal of the supervisor or insistence that the supervisor participate in counseling to learn how to interact appropriately with staff and then to demonstrate that ability. The *preventive* solution is one in which a problem is anticipated and a solution is determined so that the problem will not occur. If there is a problem with the air conditioning unit in the building, the preventive solution is to have service performed on the unit during cool weather to ensure that the unit will not fail on the hottest day of the year. The *contingency* solution is developed by looking at issues that are expected to arise in the future and by discussing ways in which they can be addressed before they become problems. For example, if it is expected that there will be a budget cut in the next fiscal year, decision makers can discuss how that will affect services and will make tentative decisions to implement should the event occur.

DECISION-MAKING IMPLICATIONS

Each decision made affects several aspects of the organization. It is therefore important to look at the possible implications of a decision and to take them into consideration when making a decision.[17] Any decision always affects staff, as they will be the ones to turn the decision into action. Do they have the required skills and information to act? Is the area affected sufficiently staffed to carry out the decision? Will this cause an additional workload or require additional training, and will that affect morale and motivation? How much input into the decision-making process did staff have and how committed are they to the decision? On an organizational level, will the decision affect relationships between units? Will individuals in different units with different reporting structures need to work together? Will the reporting structures change? Given the history of cooperation among units, will this cause difficulties or is there a history of collaboration? Will the existing functions of the unit(s) be affected by the decision? Will the decision affect the quality and quantity of service provided by the unit(s)?

What are the external implications of the decision? Will it enhance the image of the library/information center? Will the decision affect other units in the community? For example, if a university library decision leads to cooperation with another unit, such as the university computing center, what operational issues need to be taken into account? As computing center and library staffs often have differing cultural values, how are these to be addressed? How do the staffs of the units look upon the cooperative activities that are proposed?

Decisions affect facilities and equipment. If the decision results in a reduction of space for one unit, what are the trade-offs that will make it acceptable to staff who are affected? If it is a reconfiguration of space or addition to space, how does this affect staff? Space and equipment are an important means by which staff determine the importance of their unit. Any changes in space have more than just square footage implications. If the decision is the result of downsizing or budget cutting, it is particularly important to include staff in the decision making. Every unit wants more space and if one unit gets more space, it is the staff outside the unit who did not get more space and may indeed have lost space whose attitudes are to be taken into consideration. There are fiscal implications beyond facilities and equipment, such as possible additional staff or fewer staff, or added or reduced communication costs. Are there cost savings? Will additional costs be incurred and where will the money come from? If it comes from shifting internal priorities, staff need to be part of the decision-making process and participate in the decisions leading to reconfiguration. Again, it is important to be sensitive to those whose resources are reduced and who see reconfiguration as a loss of value for their unit.

Does the decision implement a new process or idea? Where did the idea come from? Did it come from staff or from an outside consultant? Was it motivated by an external opportunity or need? How far from existing activities does the new activity lead staff? Decisions may add to the comfort level of staff if they solve current problems. They may also add to discomfort if they require new ways of doing things. In making a decision, decision makers need to weigh these factors as part of the decision-making process. There is also a hierarchy of decisions in that a decision at a higher level in the organization will limit the ability of those further down in the organization to make decisions.

DECISION-MAKING STYLES

Research indicates that when executives have to make important decisions, they tend to resort to a single style. Those providing input to decision makers are wise to understand the varying styles and to tailor the information or information product they provide to the ways in which decision makers prefer to receive them.[18] Do decision makers want a complete report? Do they want a one-page summary? A face-to-face discussion? One-fourth of executives describe themselves as *charismatic*. They absorb a great deal of information rapidly and tend to process it visually. They need facts to support proposals and want results-oriented proposals and arguments. They make methodical decisions based on balanced information. The *thinkers*, 11 percent of managers, want quantitative data to support arguments. They want to see all sides of the argument and are more interested in controlling situations than in innovation. They want to know the risks up front. The *skeptics*, 19 percent, are highly suspicious of each data point, particularly if it contradicts their particular worldview. They are "take charge" people who act primarily on their feelings. The *followers*, 36 percent, make decisions based on their earlier decisions or on decisions made by trusted colleagues. They fear making the wrong decision and are careful, responsible decision makers. They want solutions that are innovative but already tested somewhere else so that they can refer to another's decision making when making their own. The *controllers*, 9 percent, focus only on facts and see things from their point of view only. They tend to act unilaterally and, if wrong, blame someone else.

Another way to look at decision-making styles is to look at the speed of decisions. Eisenhart identified characteristics that differentiate slow deciders from fast deciders.[19] The slow deciders rely on planning and forecasting of tomorrow's probable issues. They consider few alternatives and seek consensus on their choice. They examine decisions in a vacuum and tend not to consult possible mentors. They are detached from daily activities. In contrast, the fast deciders rely on real-time information and consider a variety of alternatives. They thrive on conflict and welcome opposing views. They rely on older, experienced mentors. They integrate strategies and tactics and are immersed in the activity, moving fast to keep pace with events. Fast deciders rely on quality information systems and a dynamic management environment in which everyone has information and is involved in decision making.

DECISION-MAKING TECHNIQUES

Numerous quantitative techniques for analyzing the decision-making process have been developed. Several rely on mathematical formulae to order and analyze the many variables present in any decision. Simulation models may be developed using computer-based modeling. In the simulation model, variables in the model are changed to see what the possible effects may be. In addition to these quantitative approaches, qualitative techniques can also be used. These tend to focus on the human and social elements of a decision. Most decision makers employ both quantitative and qualitative analysis to decision making.

A recent model for decision making developed by Hammond and colleagues looks at the value of objectives in relation to one another and assesses the consequences of following each objective.[20] They set up a consequence table with objectives down the left side and alternatives listed in a matrix across the top. This provides an orderly means of listing objectives and the several ways of meeting each objective. It also forces one to define as many alternatives as possible and list relevant consequences at the outset. Once this is done, then one finds ways to eliminate alternatives. Perhaps they are too costly, too difficult to implement, or just not appropriate to the objective. The authors suggest that each alternative be ranked under its objective to see which alternatives rank higher than others. If there are still too many alternatives, which are most likely to achieve the objective? The difficult part of this exercise is in assessing probable consequences of each alternative and this is where subjective judgment is involved. Using this method, it is possible to look at the problem, identify objectives and alternatives, and gradually reduce options until the most useful alternative is selected. This method is somewhat reminiscent of Ben Franklin's method of decision making in which he took a sheet of paper, divided it in the middle and on the left side wrote all the reasons he should take a particular action and on the right side wrote all the reasons he should not take that action. He would add to each side for several hours or days depending on the time available and would then identify the objectives and alternative courses of action and then make a decision.

One can use software to model consumer behavior or project the likely impact of reorganization of space, of a management decision, or of a decrease in resources. One can build scenarios using information available from internal (MIS) and external (environmental scanning) systems to project a likely future and to outline decision options given a specific set of circumstances. The use of data in this way is one means of looking into the future. The error rate is high and as one manager commented, "How can you trust virtual people and situations?" but the exercise does give decision makers an indication of trends and the opportunity to look at possible futures for the organization and to be ready for likely opportunities should they arise. "Being prepared to make decisions against a background of rapid technological change, institutional plans, and static or declining resources has been key to achieving continuous evolutionary progress."[21]

DECISION-MAKING BARRIERS

There are two types of barriers to decision making: barriers that are the result of behaviors of decision makers and those that emerge from the decision-making process. Hammond and associates identify a number of ways in which the decision-making process can be flawed and they then provide suggestions for avoiding these traps.[22] In making a decision, it was found that the individual gives disproportionate weight to the first information received. This can be a comment on performance, a bias against a person, or an initial proposal for action. Any of these can set the context for a decision that can be a wrong decision. To avoid this trap, the authors suggest that the decision maker be open-minded and be wary of those who approach an issue from a particular point of view. Using alternative starting points to look at an issue differently will perhaps provide a different perspective. For some, the status quo is a comfortable nonresponse to having too many choices. Before settling for the status quo, ask if the status quo is the best alternative. Then choose the best alternative. If a poor decision has been made, it is often difficult to change it, as there are those who have invested in the decision. But throwing more resources at a poor decision is in itself a poor decision. Consider why admitting that a decision was a poor one is distressing. Pulling a poor decision may be the best decision. When that decision was made, it may have been seen as the right decision. Situations change and there is no negative aspect in recognizing that a changed situation may require a revised decision. Some decision makers collect only the evidence that confirms their decision and ignore any other information. It is important to examine all evidence and look at it objectively. Throughout the decision-making process it is essential that one has asked the right questions. Are you looking at the relevant issues and their relationships? Return to the initial question and be sure that it is still the right question to ask. One needs to have a healthy distrust of forecasting information; it is rarely as accurate as one would like and is actually a set of educated guesses. A healthy mistrust of one's ability to make decisions is also helpful. Are we too overconfident and think that we know more than we do or do we lack confidence to make decisions? Discussions with one's peers or mentors are excellent ways to evaluate one's decision-making prowess.

As decision making becomes increasingly complex in our increasingly complex environment and as the rate of change accelerates, individuals have developed a number of ways to avoid making timely, rational decisions.[23] They may approach decision making by not making any major decisions. They will muddle through by making small decisions that avoid or correct local difficulties. They have no overall plan or goals except to move away from trouble. Their need for information is limited as their decisions are local and limited. Others may choose to make decisions based on their intuition and experience rather than spend time analyzing information and reflecting on possible courses of action. They see action, any action, as of primary importance. Some find comfort in analyzing and overanalyzing a set of data and perhaps even applying it to a problem. They may hope that the problem will go away while they are enmeshed in analyzing data.

SUMMARY

While we are more information-rich than ever, individuals still need and want to interact with one another to discuss issues of concern. Information systems, while data-rich, cannot address values held by individuals or a group, nor can they provide political nuances for an issue. Human experience and intuition provide important additional elements to the decision-making process. Brown and Duguid say that "the human and digital are significantly, and usefully distinct. Human planning, coordinating, decision making, and negotiating seem quite different from automated information searches and following digital footsteps."[24] Humans make connections not possible electronically and move in directions automated systems would not. Brown and Duguid stress the social value of working as a group and sharing expertise. In this context, information is a critical support to decisions that are made by people. As with communication in the organization, both formal and informal channels and structures have an important role in decision making. Information systems cannot replace interpersonal discussion and the need to understand why decisions are made.

NOTES

1. Chun Wei Choo, *The Knowing Organization: How Organizations Use Information to Construct Meaning, Create Knowledge, and Make Decisions* (New York: Oxford Press, 1992). 2.

2. Peter Drucker, "The effective decision," *Harvard Business Review on Decision Making* (Boston: Harvard Business School Publishing, 2001), 1–19.

3. Chris Argyris, "Interpersonal barriers to decision making," *Harvard Business Review on Decision Making* (Boston: Harvard Business Review Publishing, 2001), 59–95.

4. George P. Huber, "A theory of the effects of advanced information technologies on organizational design, intelligence, and decision making," *Academy of Management Review* 15, no. 1 (1990): 47–71.

5. Vijay Gurbaxani and Seungjin Whang, "The impact of information systems on organizations and markets, " *Communications of the ACM* 34, no. 1 (January 1991): 66.

6. Gurbaxani and Whang, "The impact of information systems," 69.

7. Eric Bonabeau, "Don't trust your gut," *Harvard Business Review* 81, no. 5 (May 2003): 116–23.

8. Huber, "A theory of the effects of advanced information technologies," 63.

9. Drucker, "The effective decision," 2–17.

10. Choo, *The Knowing Organization*, 165.

11. James G. March and H. A. Simon, *Organizations* (New York, John Wiley, 1958), 162–63; R. M. Cyert and James G. March, *A Behavioral Theory of the Firm* (Englewood, N.J.: Prentice Hall, 1963).

12. Choo, *The Knowing Organization*, 170.

13. Choo, *The Knowing Organization*, 175.

14. H. D. Mintzenberg, D. Rasingham, and A. Theoret, "The structure of unstructured decision processes," *Administrative Science Quarterly* 21, no. 2 (April 1976): 246–75.

15. Kerry Grosser, "Human networks in organizational information processing," *Annual Review of Information Science and Technology*, edited by Martha Williams (Medford, N.J.: Learned Information, 1991), 383–84.

16. Michael D. Cohen, James G. March, and Johan P. Olsen, "A garbage can model of organizational choice," *Administrative Science Quarterly* 17, no. 1 (January 1972): 1.

17. Charles H. Kempner and Benjamin B. Tregor, *The Rational Manager* (New York: McGraw-Hill, 1965).

18. Gary Williams and Robert B. Miller, "Change the way you persuade," *Harvard Business Review* 80, no. 5 (May 2002): 65–73.

19. Kathleen Eisenhart, "Speed and strategic choice: How managers accelerate decision making," *California Management Review* 32, no. 3 (Spring 1990): 39–52.

20. John S. Hammond, Ralph L. Keeney, and Howard Raffia, "Even swaps: A rational method for making trade-offs," *Harvard Business Review on Decision Making* (Boston: Harvard Business Review Publishing, 2001), 21–44.

21. Rebecca R. Martin, "Restructuring the University of Vermont libraries: Challenges, opportunities, and change," *Restructuring Academic Libraries: Organizational Development in the Wake of Technical Change*, edited by Charles A. Schwartz (Chicago: American Library Association, 1997), 177.

22. John S. Hammond, Ralph L. Keeney, and Howard Raffia, "The hidden traps in decision making," *Harvard Business Review on Decision Making* (Boston: Harvard Business Review Publishing, 2001), 143–67.

23. Amitai Etzioni, "Humble decision making," *Harvard Business Review on Decision Making* (Boston: Harvard Business Review Publishing, 2001): 51.

24. John Seely Brown and Paul Duguid, *The Social Life of Information* (Boston: Harvard Business School Press, 2000), 61.

ADDITIONAL READINGS

Bonabeau, Eric. "Predicting the unpredictable." *Harvard Business Review* 80, no. 3 (March 2002):109–16.

Cronin, Blaise. *Library Orthodoxies: A Decade of Change*. Oxford: Taylor Graham Information Press, 1991.

Gadush, Orit, and James L. Gilbert. "Transforming corner office strategy into front line action." *Harvard Business Review* 79, no. 5 (May 2001): 73–79.

Kaufmann, Arnold. *The Science of Decision-Making: An Introduction to Praxeology*. New York: McGraw Hill, 1968.

Malone, Thomas W. "Is empowerment just a fad? Control, decision making, and IT." *Sloan Management Review* 39, no. 1 (Winter 1997): 23–25.

Peters, Tom. *Liberation Management: Necessary Disorganization for the Nanosecond Nineties*. New York: Knopf, 1992.

Chapter Thirteen

Staffing Systems

This chapter focuses on staffing systems, including positions, position descriptions, and compensation. Diversity, recruitment, interviewing, training, and evaluation are discussed elsewhere in the text.

Within the organization, staff are organized in a variety of ways depending upon the objectives to be met, the skills of the worker, and the flexibility of the organization. All organizations have both a formal and informal structure. The formal structure, as laid out in the organization chart, provides the skeleton on which the activity areas of the organization are placed. By looking at the organization chart, one can determine how the organization is structured and the extent to which it follows a hierarchical organizational format. Does the administrative staff dominate the top half of the organization chart? Is the organization divided by function so that, for example, public services and technical services report to different managers? Is there a divisional organization in which separate units serve a subject or geographical area and within that unit a range of services is provided?

The organizational structure adapts as the organization grows, as new tasks and responsibilities are added, and as others are removed. A useful way to plot the changes in staffing in an organization is to review the organization charts over time. In most cases, change is slow and incremental; only rarely will one see radical changes. Some say that an organization chart should reflect the strengths of current employees and should be adapted to provide them maximum ability to grow their talents while others say that individuals must conform to the role(s) indicated by the chart. In reality, the relation between individual skills and the chart depends on circumstances and the expectations of the director.

Those who expect that an up-to-date organization chart improves orderliness in the organization are only partially correct. The chart is the skeleton on which positions and activities are placed. From this structure, a variety of combinations and cross-functional activities emerge. The days of the organization chart showing the director at the top, department heads and specialized staff (e.g., the financial officer) reporting to the director, and everyone else slotted in positions of descending responsibility has gone the way of the completely hierarchical system when all power and information came from the top and flowed downward. Today's organizations are more flexible, even fluid; power, responsibility, and information flow both up and down. The dictatorial library director who fancied himself king of the library and treated staff as drudges is an artifact of an earlier era.

TYPES OF POSITIONS

Individuals in the organization are defined in a number of ways: by their educational level, their tasks, and their levels of responsibility. One major division is that between line and staff employees. Line employees have direct authority over those units and individuals below them in the organization chart and report directly to a supervisor or agency member above them. They have the responsibility for meeting objectives assigned to them and those who report to them. In the organization chart, their position is connected to other positions by a solid line. Staff employees do not have direct authority over others and their role is to advise line employees. Staff employees tend to be specialists such as personnel officers, fiscal officers, or public relations specialists and often have educational backgrounds different from line employees, whose backgrounds are more directly tied to the product or service that defines the organization. These individuals are expert in a particular area and are relied upon to recommend the best way to deal with issues in their areas of expertise—for example, implementing affirmative action requirements, launching a fund-raising campaign, or dealing with budget issues. While they do not have line authority, they have the ability to persuade based on their special expertise and the reputation they have built in the organization for fair and reasoned advice. In the organization chart, their connections to other positions are identified by a dotted line. Line officers may have administrative assistants who occupy staff positions. Staff officers such as the fiscal officer may have their own staffs who report to them as part of their operations.

The organization is also divided into professional, technical, and clerical staff. Individuals are hired into the organization at one of these levels based on their education and experience. Typically, the organization has a relatively small number of professional employees, a larger number of technical employees, and an even larger number of clerical staff. At one time, there were formulas for what percentage of each group should be represented on the staff of a library/information center but one seldom sees such percentages in the current literature.

Hughes defines a professional as one who "delivers esoteric services—advice or action—to individuals, organizations or government, to whole classes or groups of people or to the public at large."[1] There is an intellectual basis for the problems the professional handles. The professional has special expertise that is used to deliver services and the professional asks to be trusted when delivering these services. Barber identifies four characteristics of professional behavior: a high degree of generalized and systematic knowledge, primary orientation to community interest over self, a high degree of self-control through codes of ethics and voluntary self-administered associations, and a system of rewards.[2] He goes on to say that the university professional school, in addition to providing the expertise on which the professional's career is based, leads in inculcating these attitudes.

Professional employees direct operations and provide the expertise needed to meet objectives. In a library/information center, they direct operations, provide expertise in the management and use of information resources, are responsible for the intellectual content and the development and maintenance of the collection, provide specialized services to groups, manage the ways in which technology impacts the collection and its use, and maintain strong contacts with external groups. They have advanced degrees in library/information science and often have additional advanced degrees in a subject area, in business, or in public administration.

The educational background of technical staff ranges from the associate degree in a community college to advanced degrees, depending on the type of work they do. Technical staff can include fiscal officers, personnel officers, rare book curators, and other highly educated individuals. It also includes a large percentage of those involved in maintaining the information systems, both those used for library operations and those intended for use with the public. Technical staff work throughout the library/information center. They may manage the circulation department, reproduction department, carry out much of the nonoriginal cataloging, and perform a wide range of technical duties. This group has increased in the past several years in response to additional demand for expertise in computing technology and to the revision of librarian position descriptions to eliminate many of the routine activities librarians once performed.

Clerical staff are the individuals who perform the routine operations of the library/information center, such as staffing circulation desks, doing data entry, processing orders, and providing the many secretarial functions that must be maintained, such as correspondence and filing. They also provide support to managers throughout the organization. The quality of work and the attitude of clerical staff are extremely important to the smooth functioning of an organization. In many respects, this is the group most responsible for the success of the organization as their efforts make the operation run smoothly and their lack of support places roadblocks in every area. Clerical staff typically have secondary school educations and often have additional preparation.

Additionally, there is a maintenance staff that is responsible for keeping the building in repair, keeping it clean, and maintaining the grounds. In a university, school, business, or other situation where there is a maintenance staff for the whole organization, the library/information center is part of the larger organization and relies on that staff. In a public library that does not rely on a municipality-wide service, the maintenance staff reports to the director or her or his deputy. In either situation, the condition of the building and grounds sends a message to employees and to the public about the attitude of the larger organization and of the library staff toward where they work.

Part-time workers are present in most libraries/information centers. Part-time positions may be held by individuals not wishing, for personal reasons, to work full time. The library/information center may not need a full-time individual in some areas, as the workload is insufficient or the workload may be seasonal. The part-time employee may be part of the professional, technical, or clerical staff. That individual's position description and necessary qualifications are the same as those for full-time employees. Only the number of hours worked and the level of benefits differ.

Other categories of employees include the part-time student worker who is a staple of the university or college environment. This individual most typically does routine tasks such as shelving materials, filing hard-copy materials, and checking materials in and out. Student workers can also perform specialized tasks depending upon their individual skills and these may include tasks such as keeping computing equipment in working order or translating materials for a patron. Student workers typically report to a clerical or technical staff member.

Many libraries also welcome volunteers who perform specific tasks depending upon their expertise and interest. They can enrich the staff by bringing special expertise to it or by providing extra support for routine activities. When working with volunteers, it is important that they understand their role and what the library's expectations are. Conversely, the library staff needs to understand that they are volunteers who have personal expectations of their role. Volunteers are not paid except in the satisfaction they have in their work. They determine how many hours they will work and should have some input into deciding which tasks they will perform. Their schedule should be set in discussions with their supervisor and they have the responsibility to adhere to it. While volunteers can be major assets to an operation, they can also cause stress. Some volunteers do not keep the hours they have promised. Others may wish to bring their expertise from a former position into their work, which may not be relevant to the current situation, and this may cause difficulties. Volunteers are a valuable means of connecting with the larger community and can be helpful in numerous ways. It may also be difficult to remove a volunteer who does not wish to fit into the existing situation. A clear statement of expectations, mutually agreed upon at the start of the volunteer's work, protects both parties. (See chapter 15 for further information on volunteers.)

Each position in the organization has a position description that has been written with that position and all other positions in the unit and the organization in mind. These position descriptions are reviewed regularly to ensure that they are up-to-date and that they are designed to serve the objectives of the organization. Typically, the position description specifies the knowledge, skills, and abilities the individual should bring to the position, the scope and complexity of the tasks for which the individual is responsible, and the level of supervision required. The position descriptions are then brought together into a position classification system.

DEVELOPING OR REVIEWING THE POSITION CLASSIFICATION SYSTEM

The position classification system is based on the jobs currently in the organization and the extent to which the jobs reflect actual activities. Each position is an important part of the entire classification system and is subject to the following rules: one cannot change the classification level of any system until a current job description questionnaire and the relationship of that position to other classification levels have been reviewed; positions can be identified in only one classification level; and when a vacancy is to be filled, the position's job description and classification level should be reviewed. As part of a review, existing job descriptions are reviewed to determine if they accurately reflect what individuals do. A questionnaire to each employee asking his or her view of the job description, the job as he or she performs it, and what he or she might suggest to revise it is an important activity. Not only does it elicit valuable information for reviewing positions, it also involves each member of the organization in the classification activity. The next step of the process is to review classification systems in like organizations to identify ways in which they have designed their systems. It is sometimes valuable to contact those organizations to ask how well the system works and if they have advice on how to make the classification system work even better. As libraries/information centers are usually part of a larger organizational structure, it is essential to be aware of position classification systems within which the library/information center's system must fit. Civil service systems for municipal and state governments tend to be rigid and it is often difficult to mesh them with the requirements of library positions. This may also be true of university-wide classification systems or those of school districts. It is also most important to know if one can develop a library position classification system to be used within the larger system and, if so, what adjustments must be made to ensure conformity. It may be the case that the library/information center is not allowed to develop its own system and must use the general classification system even if it does not fit the situation. A consultant who is an expert in job classification is often brought in to direct the development of a new or revised position classification system. An external consultant is not limited by being part of the organization and is unlikely to have a bias or two about how the system should be constructed. The consultant will have worked with similar organizations and can bring that experience to bear on the issue.

Assuming that the library/information center can develop its own classification system, the position descriptions, as updated by the questionnaires, are arranged into levels depending upon the mix of education, experience, and supervision required. For a medium-sized public library, for example, the levels identified begin with the director at level I and continue through each level until one reaches that of page/shelver. (See chart on the following pages). There is a set of levels for professional/technical, for administrative support positions, and for operations maintenance. Each classification level is described by a general statement of duties; distinguishing features of the class; required knowledge, skills and abilities; and minimum qualifications. Some levels have only one position (e.g., director), some include unique descriptions within the class (e.g., business manager), and others have several positions with differing assignments (e.g., librarian I and library assistant II). Each position within each level has its own description. A staff committee, often working with a consultant, will have reviewed the system and made recommendations in accordance with their perspectives and that of those they represent.

A compensation plan can then be mapped against the classification system. The lowest level on the chart, that of page/shelver is pegged at the current minimum wage. In suggesting compensation at other levels, the best approach is to look at salary levels at comparable institutions, look at current in-house salaries at these levels, and assign salaries that reflect both local reality and the market. Look also at salaries in other municipal units to see if library salaries are comparable. If the local library salaries are well below the market or below those of other local units, this is the time to adjust them upward. There should also be the ability to adjust for cost of living increases and to provide merit increases for outstanding effort. Assigning salaries has political implications in any environment. There may be an unwillingness by the funding agency to pay appropriate salaries, or there may be insufficient funds to do so. Priorities in the larger environment may not include libraries and there is an unwillingness to fund them if it means taking resources from other priorities seen by governing officials as more important. The compensation plan should be reviewed annually. If the library/information center is part of a university, a school system, or a business organization, compensation rules are dictated by the larger organization, with the possible exception of merit increases, which are often given in a lump sum to be distributed according to very specific rules.

The following job classification summary and selected position descriptions are illustrative of position descriptions and the ways in which they come together into a classification system. The classification system should be available to all staff so that they know their responsibilities and the ways in which these responsibilities mesh with those of other positions and fit within the overall system. The compensation levels change annually and a chart of these levels is usually available to staff as well. In private institutions such as private universities or in business-related information centers, the system, particularly the compensation plan, may not be as open for review as in publicly supported institutions.

The following information is included:

    Job Classification System Summary

    Classification of Positions by Compensation Level

    Sample Position Descriptions

        Library Director

        Librarian III

        Librarian I

        Personnel Administrator

        Library Assistant II

        Senior Clerk

JOB CLASSIFICATION SYSTEM SUMMARY

Professional/ Technical	Administrative Support	Operations/ Management
1. Director		
2. Deputy Director		
3. Librarian IV		
4. Librarian III		
5. Librarian II	Personnel Administrator	
6. Librarian I		Operations Supervisor
7. Library Assistant III	Public Relations Officer	
	Administrative Secretary	
	Bookkeeper	
8. Library Assistant II	Computing Manager	
9. Library Assistant I		
10.	Senior Clerk	Operations Assistant
	Senior Technical Assistant	
	Clerk Typist	
	Receptionist	
11.	Business Office Assistant	
12.	Clerk	Custodian
13.	Page/Shelver	

CLASSIFICATION AND POSITIONS BY
COMPENSATION LEVEL

Compensation Level	Classification/Position
Level 1	Director
Level 2	Deputy Director
Level 3	Librarian IV
	Head, Extension Services
	Head, Adult Services
	Head, Technical Services
	Head, Children's Services
Level 4	Librarian III
	Coordinator, Info. Services
	Coordinator, Collection.
	Development
	Supervisor, Regional Branch
Level 5	Librarian II
	Supervisor, Large Branch
	Periodicals Librarian
	Senior Info. Services Librarian
	Senior Tech Services Librarian
	Senior Adult Services Librarian
	Senior Coll. Dev. Librarian
	Other Positions
	Personnel Administrator
	Business Manager
	Circulation Supervisor
Level 6	Librarian I
	Supervisor, Med. Branch
	Children's Librarian
	Cataloger
	Info. Services Librarian
	Other Positions
	Operations Supervisor
Level 7	Library Assistant III
	Supervisor, Small Branch

Compensation Level	Classification/Position
	Staff Assistant III
	Acquisitions Manager
	Other Positions
	Public Relations Manager
Level 8	Library Assistant II
	Periodicals Asst. II
	Tech Services Asst. II
	Circ. Asst. II
	Branch Library Assistant(in a med to large branch)
	Bookmobile Assistant
	Other Positions
	Admin. Secretary
	Bookkeeper
Level 9	Library Assistant I
	Ch. Services Asst. I
	Tech Services. Asst. I
	Circulation Asst.
Level 10	Other Positions
	Senior Clerk
	Operations Asst. I
Level 11	Clerk Typist
	Receptionist
	Operations Asst. I
Level 12	Clerk
	Custodian
Level 13	Page/Shelver

SAMPLE POSITION DESCRIPTIONS

Library Director

General Statement of Duties

Serves as the head of a large library system.

Distinguishing Features of the Class

This administrative position involves responsibility for all library functions. The work includes carrying out broad policy as determined by the library board. General supervision of personnel is expected.

Examples of Work

(illustrative only)

Recommends policies and necessary library services to the board
Establishes and maintains good working relations with local government agencies
Directs and supervises expenditures of library funds
Directs maintenance of building and grounds
Evaluates library service effectiveness in meeting community needs
Attends professional meetings and keeps informed of professional developments
Conducts staff meetings
Responsible for hiring, transferring, promotion, dismissals

Required Knowledge, Skills, and Abilities

Knowledge of library services, comprehensive knowledge of administrative practices, ability to carry out policies and to plan and coordinate the work of others; ability to exercise leadership and motivate others, ability to evaluate situations and make decisions, good oral and written communication skills, ability to work with the public and to represent the library.

Minimum Qualifications

1. Degree recognized by the American Library Association
2. Eight years of satisfactory professional service in a library of recognized standing, five of which have been in a responsible administrative capacity.

Librarian III

General Statement of Duties

Serves as department head, may coordinate aspects of special projects. Duties as assigned.

Distinguishing Features of the Class

Responsibility for professional supervision of the work of a specific library service unit. Work is performed under general supervision.

Examples of Work

(illustrative only)

> Analyzes community and identifies user needs
> Recommends materials for acquisition
> Supervises a regional branch
> Develops and conducts programs for community groups
> Initiates, plans, and coordinates programs within the department
> Plans and recommends new services
> Makes administrative decisions for the unit
> Assigns and supervises staff duties
> Attends professional meetings, keeps informed of professional developments

Required Knowledge, Skills, and Abilities

Thorough knowledge of library activities of the unit, good knowledge of library administrative practices, ability to carry out library policies, ability to comprehend users' needs accurately, ability to plan and coordinate the work of others, good interpersonal skills, good oral and written communication skills.

Minimum Qualifications

1. Degree recognized by the American Library Association. Subject specialization or second master's degree may be required
2. Four years of satisfactory library experience

Librarian I

General Statement of Duties

Performs professional library duties under direct or general supervision. Does related work as required.

Distinguishing Features of the Class

Has completed the MLS or other degree approved by the American Library Association. Applies education by performing specific duties under the supervision of a higher-grade librarian. Employees in this class are assigned progressively more challenging tasks as they gain experience. They may be assigned the direct supervision of a unit or program.

Examples of Work

(illustrative only)

    Provides bibliographic instruction and/or reference service
    Assists administrative officers in their activities
    Compiles bibliographies, conducts programs
    May supervise a medium size branch
    May supervise the work of clerical staff
    May provide interlibrary loan services
    Keeps informed of professional developments

Required Knowledge, Skills, and Abilities

Basic current knowledge of library/information service practices and principles, basic knowledge of organization, procedure, and policies of information services, initiative, good communication skills, good interpersonal skills.

Minimum Qualifications

1. Degree approved by the American Library Association
2. Specialized subject knowledge or skills developed through work experience elsewhere where appropriate.

Personnel Administrator

General Statement of Duties

Coordinates and manages all personnel activities including development and direction of employee training and development programs.

Distinguishing Features of the Class

Individual is expected to monitor all personnel activities, to exercise initiative in improving existing personnel practices and to make personnel suggestions to the director. Position requires considerable discretion and independent judgment.

Examples of Work

(illustrative only)

Coordinates recruitment
Schedules and maintains records of annual and sick leave
Interviews prospective employees
Develops, maintains, and upgrades personnel policies
Plans and executes employee training activities
Counsels with staff supervisors on personnel problems
Keeps up to date on current developments in personnel administration

Required Knowledge, Skills, and Abilities

Extensive knowledge of personnel administration principles and practices; ability to relate in confidence and sensitivity to all employees; ability to work with minimum supervision; have excellent communication skills.

Minimum Qualifications.

1. Bachelor's degree in Personnel Administration
2. Two years experience in personnel related activities
3. Knowledge of library/information services

Library Assistant II

General Statement of Duties

Performs library functions under general guidance. Supervises clerical personnel or library pages. Does related work as required.

Distinguishing Features of the Class

This is a paraprofessional position involving responsibility for technical applications of professional library/information services, initially under day-to-day supervision but ultimately with latitude to operate independently within the context of prescribed responsibilities.

Examples of Work

(illustrative only)

    Assists head of medium or large size branch, may supervise in absence of branch head
    Assists administrative supervisory officer
    Prepares displays
    Orders supplies
    Performs specialized tasks depending upon specialized background and skills

Required Knowledge, Skills, and Abilities

Aptitude for library/ information work, initiative, resourcefulness, good judgment, accuracy, ability to make decisions and direct the work of others, good communication skills.

Minimum Qualifications.

1. Bachelor's degree
2. Additional course work where appropriate

Senior Clerk

General Statement of Duties

Responsible for clerical operations requiring prior training or knowledge. May supervise one or more subordinate clerical employees. Does related work as required.

Distinguishing Features of the Class

Those in this class have prior training or experience in performing library clerical operations or a knowledge of them. Persons in this class work under supervision when beginning new tasks but once the task or procedure is adopted, they require little or no supervision. Persons in this class may be required to assist in duties listed in subordinate classes. They may also be required to train and supervise one or more clerical employee.

Examples of Work

(illustrative only)

> Prepare forms and reports
> Perform circulation duties
> Reserve rooms for meetings
> Maintain records
> Enter data into MIS system
> May supervise circulation, filing or other duties
> May be responsible for aspects of program planning

Required Knowledge, Skills, and Abilities

Knowledge of word processing systems and experience in working with them. Ability to understand and carry out directions, ability to supervise the work of others, ability to prepare reports, accuracy, neatness, tact, interest in library/information work, good interpersonal and communication skills.

Minimum Qualifications

1. Graduation from High School
2. Two years of college, university, or secretarial training

3. One year of library clerical experience
4. Additional skills as required by the job

PERFORMANCE ASSESSMENT PLAN

A performance assessment plan can also be developed using the position description as a beginning point. For each task in the position description, one can determine the extent to which the employee completed the task. This information then feeds back into the compensation plan to be used to determine salary increases and merit allocations.

The complete classification system should be reviewed every five to seven years, as technical and organizational changes affect the tasks and responsibilities assigned to positions. Regular incremental changes over time may have skewed positions, and changes in the overall system may be called for. Some positions are relatively stable and can be used as benchmarks against which other positions can be reviewed.[3]

STAFFING IN A CHANGING ENVIRONMENT

The development of position descriptions and classification schemes assumes a hierarchical organization in an environment of relatively slow and steady change. While these systems provide stability in the workplace, they may also prevent the organization from changing as rapidly as it may need to in light of what Battin calls the transformational age.[4] The strengths of a stable classification system and job descriptions may become liabilities in that they may hamper the ability of the organization to have sufficient flexibility to meet changing demands. In an environment in which each staff member is urged to learn and stretch to meet new challenges, a narrow job description may be a hindrance if management or staff adhere too closely to it. The most useful job description is the one that outlines responsibilities and leaves the specifics to the supervisor and the staff member to determine, given the current situation.

What workers do and how they perform tasks has changed radically in recent decades.[5] Working in an era of advanced information technology, the workplace has been dramatically restructured, continuously adopting new processes as all staff learn new skills. Their interaction with each other changes as new skills are added. Some positions will expand while others will contract. Workflow patterns may change. Individuals have a stake in reviewing their job descriptions and what is expected of them in the workplace to see how they have changed.

The key to implementing change in the workplace is training and retraining—in new computing skills, in new uses of information systems, in new configurations of the work and the workplace. Regular training sessions of all staff are a constant in today's workplace. The workplace is a renewable asset, renewable through the application of new technology and through continuous training of staff. While the purpose of the library/information professional (to acquire, manage, and provide information) has not changed, the ways in which this is done have changed and will continue to change. The organizational structure and its staffing must be sufficiently flexible to adapt to change in order to serve its publics at the highest level.

The new workplace is outwardly seen as more diverse and more casual than earlier organizations. Individuals work in a more self-directed fashion and as long as they are productive and accomplish their tasks well, they have flexibility in how they do them. Not all positions lend themselves to this flexibility; for example, individuals dealing directly with the public are expected to be in a particular place for a specified time period. Those responsible for other tasks (e.g., building a database, ordering materials, or researching an issue) may set their own work hours and work location. Their performance is assessed by the quality and timeliness of their work. This outward flexibility is, however, firmly grounded in the position description and expectations.

Job sharing among individuals who, for personal reasons, may not wish to work full time has become an option in the workplace. With the supervisor's approval, the position description is reviewed and its component tasks are divided. Pay and benefits, care of shared workspace, and the means of performance evaluation are negotiated. To be successful, partners in job sharing must be compatible, have excellent communication skills, and be sufficiently flexible to assist the other by assisting with the other's tasks if needed.

SUMMARY

Today's environment is one in which the only constant is change. While for some this is an exciting challenge, for others it constitutes a continuous threat. For some, testing new ideas, exploring new technologies, and daring to move in new directions provides exciting opportunities While library/information center managers were initially slow to recognize the impact of technology on the workplace, they soon became convinced of the potential of information technology to manage activities and have in many instances become leaders in managing change in the workplace. Most incorporated new ways of integrating technology-enabled activities into existing work activities while others radically restructured the entire organization. In nearly all libraries/information centers, innovative ways of working are in place. Cross-functional teams are commonly used to solve specific problems. The virtual workplace enabled by communications technology allows individuals to be in widely separated areas and yet meet their responsibilities to the position and the organization. For those who are unsure of their ability to learn new skills and adapt to new environments, change may be stressful and they may resist it as best they can. The individual who has built a power base within the existing system fears losing that power if the system becomes too flexible or changes. All of these options come together in the position classification process in which each position's role in relation to other positions is identified. The classification scheme expands the organization chart by specifying the roles and responsibilities of each individual.

NOTES

1. Everett Hughes, "Professions," in *The Professions in America*, edited by Kenneth S. Lynn et al. (Boston: Beacon Press, 1965), 1–14.

2. Bernard Barber, "Some problems in the sociology of the professions," in *The Professions in America*, edited by Kenneth S. Lynn et al. (Boston: Beacon Press, 1965), 15–34.

3. Laine Stambaugh, "Are your library support classifications ready for the 21st century?" *Library Administration and Management* 14, no. 3 (Summer 2000): 167–71.

4. Patricia Battin, "Leadership in a transformational age," in *Mirage of Continuity*, edited by Brian Hawkins and Patricia Battin (Washington, D.C.: Council on Library and Information Resources and the Association of American Universities, 1998), 271–73.

5. Shoshana Zhuboff, *In the Age of the Smart Machine: The Future of Work and Power* (New York: Basic Books, 1988).

Chapter Fourteen

Performance Appraisal

Today's workplace is in a state of continuous change. The organization is increasingly sensitive to internal pressures of financial constraints, expectations for new service directions, the phasing out of some activities, the incorporation of information technology and communications technology into all facets of the operation, and the increasing diversity of the workforce. External pressures include demands for accountability by taxpayers of not-for-profit organizations and by stockholders in the for-profit sector. Each group of stakeholders wants more and more productivity from the organization while at the same time providing access to fewer and fewer resources. These and related issues have placed increasing pressure on managers to ensure that the workforce functions at a high level of productivity. Since approximately 70 percent of the budget of a not-for-profit organization is in salaries, increased workforce production is the most important area for cost savings.

The organization responds to these pressures by maintaining a database inventory of current staff: their skills and abilities, the nature of the job they fill, their years on the job, and the age at which they will most likely retire. At the same time, and in a companion database, the organization maintains up-to-date position descriptions for each job based on the position description system in place. As new services and new technologies are adopted, new types of positions that may be needed are projected and positions that will probably be phased out are identified. The database that includes this information can be utilized in a number of ways to project future needs. While most inventories of current staff describe current employees and their status, they often do not answer questions such as "How many staff do you need?" "Do you have sufficient staff in all areas, or too many or too few in some areas?" There is a tendency for managers to take the current situation and plan from that base rather than asking what the right number and appropriate mix of staff may be. As organizations move toward management by objective or some variation thereof or toward team management, they can look at their resources in different ways and identify staff to meet an objective or to conduct a project.

INTERVIEWING AND SELECTING STAFF

Interviewing is the first step in performance appraisal. In today's workplace which is more diverse and at first glance more casual than in the past, the prospective employee is less willing to be molded into the culture of the organization than may have once been the case. While the organization's style and culture play an important role in determining the environment, the new kind of employee exerts a strong influence, and the interaction between new hires and those already in the organization can set a tone. Today's new employees anticipate that the new ideas they bring to the workplace will be heard and respected. The new dot-com world has produced an attitude toward work and working that is based less on seniority or authority and more on what one knows and can do or thinks one can do. While this may not be a completely realistic attitude, it exists and does require that potential employers take it into account. Today's prospective employees are more often apt to take pride in their creativity and their ability to contribute to the objectives of the organization than wishing just to fit in. Prospective employees are looking for positions that promise interesting work, economic stability, and the opportunity for personal growth.

The search, interview, and hiring process provides the organization with an important means of renewal. New ideas and new talent can be added to the organization. Ideally, managers are always looking for promising new talent that might become available. Usually, one does not start looking for prospective employees until a position becomes vacant or will soon become vacant or if new positions have been allocated. While the human resources professional will deal with the logistics of a search, the manager will be involved in all aspects of the process. If the library/information center is part of a college or university, a school district, or a business, an institution-wide manual with procedures, standards, forms, and so forth will be available and will guide the process. This is also true of searching and hiring in the public library where procedures are under the control of a municipal or county human relations department. Because of the extensive legal regulations that affect hiring, almost no library/information center has the independent authority to determine how searches are conducted.

In many library/information centers, a search committee will be named and will represent not only the department in which the position is available but other units as well. It may also include stakeholders (such as students or clients) and staff from all levels of the organization. The makeup of the search committee will be as representative of the staff and stakeholders as possible and will have gender and minority representation. If the search is for a technical or clerical position, a search committee is not usually formed. The department manager will conduct the search within the unit and involve those staff with whom the new employee will work. All procedures, standards, forms, and so forth for these positions are used to guide the process in the same way as for professional positions using a search committee.

Once formed, the search committee may wish to review the existing position description with the manager and other staff members to discuss ways in which it might be revised to meet new needs. If the position has become skewed over time to fit the talents of the previous incumbent, it will be necessary to recraft the description to ensure that it reflects the skills and abilities now needed. In some instances, a revised and up-to-date description is provided to the committee while in other cases the search committee participates in the review of the position description. In this way, the classification system is kept up-to-date. Once there is an acceptable position description, the position is advertised in relevant locations. If the position is for a clerical or technical position, most of the advertising will be within the library/information center and the larger organization of which it is a part, as well as in the local press. If the library/information center has, or is part of, a union or other staff organization, specific procedures for advertising positions may be required. Professional positions, in addition, receive national postings in appropriate journals and job lines. Professional associations are contacted and the postings are placed in their services. Particular attention is given to ensuring that minority journals receive job postings. If the position is a high-level position, an executive search firm may be contacted. In all searches, it is a responsibility of the members of the search committee to contact likely candidates they may know personally. Every effort is made to ensure a large and diverse pool of candidates.

A deadline for receiving applications is set; as applications arrive, they are filed and made available to the search committee. They should be treated as confidential documents and the names and qualifications of applicants are not made public at the early stages of a search. Once the application deadline has passed, the applications are reviewed to ensure that they are diverse in terms of gender and ethnic components. Applications are reviewed initially to identify those who meet the basic job requirements as stated in the position announcement. Those applications that do not meet the basic requirements receive a letter thanking them for their application and notifying them that their application will not be considered further. If a sufficient number of applications remains in the pool, they become a smaller pool that receives greater scrutiny. If there is an insufficient number of qualifying applications or the pool is not sufficiently diverse, the search may be extended and additional efforts will be made to attract additional qualified candidates. To provide flexibility in the search process, application deadline dates are often given as "Deadline is [date] or until sufficient applications have been received." This allows the committee to extend a search rather than begin anew.

Applications that meet job requirements are reviewed a second time. References are checked and further review of credentials in relation to the job description is conducted. It is important for the search committee to know any skills and competencies beyond the basic job requirements. The committee may be looking for someone who likes to solve complex problems or is very comfortable with new technology but may not need a high level of interpersonal skills. Or it may be looking for someone who enjoys working with others and may or may not be highly skilled in specific technological areas. Perhaps creativity in developing new programs is desired. In any case, the individual needs to be able to fit not just the duties of the position but also to fit into the culture of the organization and its expectations. Ream cites the Human Relations Consulting Group statistic that "[n]early 80% of turnovers is the result of mistakes in hiring," with the most often cited failure being directly related to a mismatch with the culture.[1] A person's behavior and attitudes will usually determine their level of success as a new member of the organization.

Once applications are checked and references contacted, the search committee will rank the applications by the extent to which they meet the expectations of the job. Typically the top three to five candidates are contacted and arrangements are made for personal interviews and an opportunity to meet members of the organization. In a high-level search, there may be preliminary private interviews of a larger number of applicants from which three or more individuals are invited for a more extensive interview. Each of these steps is reviewed by human resources staff to ensure that EEOC (Equal Employment Opportunity Commission) guidelines are met and that each applicant is treated with equity and fairness.

Interviewing is a two-way activity between applicant and the search committee. The applicants are looking at the position and the extent to which it fits their desire for growth. The applicant will have researched the organization and will have a good idea of what its objectives are and how its culture functions and will have prepared a series of questions to ask during the interview process. The interviewers know the skills and competencies required by the job and the attributes they wish to see in a new coworker. If more than one person is conducting the interview, those involved should discuss ahead of time what questions should be asked. It is useful to assign questions to a particular team member who will then be responsible for that line of questioning. Interviewing is an acquired skill that improves with experience. The primary skill of interviewing is to listen to the candidate. In the interview, some beginning key questions are asked about the candidate's interest in the position, how she or he sees the fit between personal skills and the position, and what contribution(s) she or he can make to the organization. Creth identified a number of types of questions that can be asked:

- Factual questions: These are used to obtain specific pieces of information or to clarify items in the application that may not be clear.
- Broadening questions: These are used to elicit new information. Questions that refer to personal management style or attitudes toward public service can elicit information not evident in the factual information but the information is very important.
- Justifying questions: These give the applicant the opportunity to challenge existing or proposed practice and to offer reasons for the stand taken. For example, one could ask how the applicant would deal with filtering information on the Internet or charging fees for services.
- Alternative questions: These provide the applicant an opportunity to express opinions about a particular type of practice.
- Hypothetical questions: These are a useful means of exploring new and untried activities and give the candidate the opportunity to be creative.[2]

Other questions to be asked relate to how the candidate functions on the job; does he or she work well independently or is there a need for supervision and how much supervision? Is the candidate comfortable in a flexible environment or is there a desire for a highly structured environment? Is there a wish to perform a variety of activities or would the candidate prefer to specialize in a limited number of areas? Does the candidate work well as a member of a team or is there a preference for working alone?[3] The interviewer should not rely heavily on first impressions, as some candidates may be nervous and may need to become comfortable before they are at their best.

Interviews can be stimulating activities for both interviewers and the candidate. New ideas are discussed and challenged and the different experiences that are brought to the table can broaden the knowledge of both. The interview situation is not the time to critique the candidate or disagree with ideas put forth by the candidate. At the conclusion of the interview, and after the candidate has left, there is an opportunity to review the interview and to assess how closely the candidate meets the predetermined criteria for the position. Once all candidates have been interviewed and additional references or points checked, the search committee completes a report and gives it to the director or other individual to whom the search committee reports. Depending on the wishes of the director, the candidates may be ranked or may be listed with comments. The search may also have no candidates to recommend. In that case, it calls in more individuals who are in the final pool or it may report that the search has resulted in no viable candidates. At the point at which a slate of candidates is sent to the director or it has been reported that no viable candidates have been interviewed, the task of the search committee has been completed and it is disbanded.

The individual responsible for making an offer to hire reviews the information provided. During the search process, the director will most likely have had the opportunity to meet and interview each candidate. If the director wishes to make an offer, it is done at this point. In the meantime, the candidate has received information regarding benefits and other materials relevant to the position and the organization. The interview process is the first, and in many ways, the most important performance evaluation. It sets a benchmark for the individual's progress in the organization once hired. It is also the most intensive evaluation the individual will receive relevant to the job and attitudes toward the job. Later evaluations will use this as a take-off point for evaluating job performance and personal growth.

Interviewing and Hiring Part-Time Employees

Part-time employees usually hold permanent positions but work fewer hours than are in the standard work week as defined by the organization. They may be responsible for specialized tasks for which the organization needs only a limited amount of service, such as cataloging local history materials, writing press releases, or managing a special purpose program. Part-time employees may also request that status because of non-job-related responsibilities that make it difficult for them to meet the requirements of full-time employment, such as caring for family members or personal physical limitations. Part-time employees provide the organization a certain flexibility as they can divide positions or fill partial positions. Hiring part-time individuals is often not done as carefully as hiring of full-time employees. Part-time employees are important members of the staff and may become full-time employees at some time. Equally rigorous standards in hiring should be followed. Often today's full-time employee may become tomorrow's part-time employee because of changing personal or organizational needs. Part-time employees are regular members of the staff and should have access to and be a full partner in the organization. Their salary and benefits will be subject to external rulings; for example, health benefits may be available only if the employee is on the job more than 60 percent of the time.

Temporary employees are usually hired full time for a short period. They may be hired to fill in for a full-time employee who is away from the job for a limited period (e.g., for health reasons) or they may be hired to assist in a high-peak work period, such as the installation of a new computer system. Temporary employees may be part of a pool held by the larger organization (e.g., a university or municipal work pool). They are interviewed and hired by the larger organization and then are assigned, upon request, to a particular unit for a short period. The library/information center does not have a role in hiring but is routinely asked to evaluate the employee's on-the-job performance. Temporary employees can also come from agencies that specialize in providing temporary services; in this case, the agency controls hiring and other procedures. Should the library/information center do its own hiring of temporary employees, those hired should meet specific job requirements.

Other types of support personnel include students who are paid by the parent organization or by work-study programs. Students are assigned to the library/information center and it is the responsibility of the library/information center to train and supervise them. The savvy supervisor makes sure that the jobs they hold are more than routine tasks and that there is an element of learning about new things in the job. For example, the student assigned to shelve and maintain stacks may be asked to comment on the physical quality of the materials or the student at a circulation desk may be asked to suggest alternative work routines. While each of these suggestions may make additional work for the supervisor, new ideas may result and the student may learn something new. It is the role of the educational institution to educate students whenever and wherever possible. Students are often assigned for an academic year and may not be reassigned the next year to the same position so the relationship may be a short one. While the student is at work, it is the responsibility of the supervisor to assess the quality of the student's work.

Volunteers

Volunteers may be retired staff members, retired members of the larger organization, or individuals in the community who are looking for a way to contribute. Many retirees make valuable contributions, particularly when they have desired skills that do not fit into the budget. The retired French literature faculty member may be invaluable in reviewing the French literature collection and evaluating it in relation to a new degree program in French language and literature. The retired elementary school teacher may be a born storyteller and the star of the children's literature hour. Others may enjoy shelving materials and just being around books. Volunteers require special attention in that they are not paid employees and are dedicating time to service. While they agree to do a certain task, they may not meet the hours agreed on or they may not complete a task during the agreed-upon period. They may or may not perform the task at an acceptable level. The supervisor will quickly learn what to anticipate from each volunteer. It is necessary to identify tasks to be done and a means of evaluating them so that volunteers know what is expected. If expectations are not met, there should be a means of gently releasing the volunteer from any agreements. It can be useful to accept a volunteer's services for a period of time, such as three to six months, and then if the experience is mutually satisfactory, to renew it if desired. Volunteers can be a valuable connection to the wider community and can be positive spokespersons for the organization. They can also be of marginal value and create difficulties if their efforts are less than useful.

THE APPRAISAL PROCESS

The organization responds to internal and external pressures for productivity by ensuring that its employees are working productively to accomplish organizational objectives. There has always been an element of appraisal by managers and peers in the job situation. As management theory has moved from scientific management to the human relations approach, so has the appraisal methodology. One will find an appraisal component in nearly all management theories.

The culture of the organization also places pressure on individuals to conform to existing norms. If the organization's culture supports high levels of productivity, workers will strive toward that goal in order to be accepted by peers; conversely, if there is a culture of low productivity, that will also place pressure on the individual.

While many managers are uncomfortable with the task of assessing performance and may go to considerable lengths to avoid it, assessment is an essential element of organizational productivity and individual growth. Levinson identified seven purposes for performance appraisal and review.

1. To measure and judge performance
2. To relate individual performance to organizational goals
3. To foster the increasing competence and growth of subordinates
4. To stimulate the subordinate's motivation
5. To enhance communication between superior and subordinate
6. To serve as a basis for judgment about salary and promotion
7. To serve as a device for organizational control and integration[4]

All performance appraisals derive from the job assigned to the individual. The job description is the basic definition of responsibilities upon which specific tasks are placed. When individuals are hired by the organization, they have demonstrated through resumes, letters of recommendation, and similar documents that they have the skills and ability to do the work and the potential to grow in the job. Regular reviews provide feedback of individual progress. Most evaluation is informal and continuous as the supervisor observes the work being done. Individuals responsible for routine tasks are observed regularly by the supervisor and corrections are made as needed. For higher-level and professional positions, the individual typically requires less constant supervision than do individuals in beginning positions or positions that are unique to the organization and require specialized learning. In addition to regular relatively informal supervision, a formal appraisal system is in place in most organizations. Appraisal is an essential component of organizational and individual growth and is important to all involved.[5]

The appraisal process itself is an interaction between supervisor and employee. As indicated earlier, the process is based on the individual's job description and the expectations of the organization and the individual. Most organizations have a highly structured process of assessment in which a rating form has been developed by human resources experts that specifies areas to be covered and questions to be asked. As library/information centers are typically part of a larger organizational structure, these forms will have been developed at the university, the municipality, the school district, or other higher level and are intended for use by all units in that larger organization. These forms will have been reviewed to ensure that they focus on performance and not on individual traits, that they are in compliance with federal and state regulations, and that they do not include questions that may be considered biased. Rating forms will differ in their content depending upon the type of position being rated. Clerical positions that have highly specific job descriptions will have forms that address the elements of the job description and measure the extent to which they have been performed well. In professional and administrative positions where there is more flexibility in the job description and an expectation for a level of independent thinking and decision making, the rating form is sufficiently flexible to take this into consideration. Employees at each level of the organization receive the same rating form for that level to ensure that the evaluation is uniform across the level and that employees at that level receive the same depth of review. The centrally devised rating form provides a general assessment but does not address differences in activities or applications from unit to unit. Different organizations deal with this differently, but most ask additional questions specific to that unit's activities. When additional questions are asked, they must conform to federal and state guidelines and in most cases may not be included in the formal assessment that goes into the personnel file. The library/information center will typically include items specific to its activities in addition to the generic review. For those library/information centers that are not required to use a generic assessment form, they develop their own forms, which must, of course, conform to federal and state guidelines and be consistent with organizational objectives. Performance standards and the means of establishing ratings are also set.

In setting performance standards for library/information service, standards set by similar organizations or documentation from professional associations may be reviewed to ensure that standards reflect more than local practice. Useful appraisal forms are difficult to devise. They must measure performance in specific areas, they must meet a variety of standards, and they must be simple and straightforward. And they must be reviewed regularly to ensure that they continue to mesh with organizational objectives. Most importantly, they must measure what they are supposed to measure. An excellent guide to developing and assessing one's performance appraisal forms is to look at those of comparable organizations and to seek assistance from the professional associations.

The appraisal process itself consists of four steps:

1. A common understanding between employee and supervisor on what the employee's responsibilities are, the work to be done, and the means of evaluation.
2. Ongoing assessment of performance and progress, continuous feedback to clarify or modify behavior.
3. Formal documentation of performance through the completion of appraisal forms
4. Formal appraisal discussion based on the appraisal form but not necessarily limited to it.[6]

When salary is dependent on the results of the appraisal, discussions on this topic is the final step.

Timetables for formal assessment are set centrally for the organization. Typically, the assessments take place a few months before the next year's budget is due so that salary increases that may be set after the assessment process is completed can be factored into the budget. As soon as the timetable is set, the manager completes an appraisal form for each individual in the unit. The manager reviews individual performance and assesses the extent to which each performance objective has been met. There should be sufficient performance data to make the assessment. If not, the assessment is limited in its usefulness. If a gap in available performance data is found, it should be corrected in the data-gathering process so that adequate information is available in the next assessment cycle. On most forms, a rating scale is provided to indicate the extent to which a performance measure has been met and ranges from *exceeds expectations* to *meets expectations* to *below expectations* to *unsatisfactory*. There should also be an opportunity to record specific incidents that support the manager's assessment; for example, (positively) "The reference specialist provided additional support to an undergraduate history course when the professor introduced new assignments requiring the use of hard-to-locate primary source materials, thus contributing to student learning," or (negatively) "The supervisor of circulation had not, on several occasions [give dates] prepared a work schedule for staffing the unit in the evenings and on weekends, thus preventing employees from knowing when they were expected to work."

Creviston and Freed warn that managers, in reviewing performance, should avoid making general statements or giving an employee an average rating because their performance is generally satisfactory.[7] In reviewing an individual's performance, the manager should not judge one or two recent events but should review the entire year and place those events into perspective. Some managers may look at two or three areas of performance, find them acceptable, and then assume that other areas are acceptable as well. This halo effect may cause real deficiencies to be overlooked. Ratings based on how likable a person is or how closely that person's work style conforms to that of the manager contribute little to the process. The manager must be thoughtful, thorough, and careful in making assessments. Another person's self-image is involved and any unfairness or bias harms that individual, destroys any feeling of trust in the manager, and destroys the positive aspects of the assessment.

Once the manager has completed the forms, a time is set to meet with the employee to review the form and any issues arising from the job situation. One technique that has proved useful is for the supervisor to give the employee a blank assessment form to be filled out as a self-assessment. When completed thoughtfully, this serves as a basis for discussion during the assessment interview. Most employees know their strengths and have suggestions on how to deal with areas where help is needed. This activity also reminds the employee of the content of the rating form and the areas covered. Another technique is to ask employees to be prepared to respond to questions such as what could the supervisor have done to help the employee achieve an objective or ask other questions to show that the supervisor recognizes that success is a shared activity.

The Assessment Interview

When the work environment is good, the employee's performance positive, and when there are no clouds caused by budget cuts or the threat of downsizing, the performance review can be relatively nonstressful. In less positive circumstances or when the supervisor has the task of discussing difficult issues with the employee, the interview can be stressful for both supervisor and employee. Therefore, the logistics of the interview should be structured with care. An uninterrupted hour scheduled well in advance in a neutral location such as a small conference room should be arranged. Preparation on the part of both the supervisor and the employee is essential. Each should have certain points to discuss and each should be specific in the comments made, citing events or data and avoiding general statements that are hard to support. Each should also take notes. In order to clarify progress or lack thereof in both organizational and personal objectives, discussions should be open and candid within the interview but confidential.

Managers have a number of styles in conducting interviews, not all of which are particularly useful. Some may do all the talking, telling the employee what was done well, where improvement is needed, and what those improvements will be. To the employee, this style is not satisfying as there is no opportunity to correct errors, to ask questions, or to respond in any way. A second style is to tell the employee all of the above and then provide an opportunity to respond. With discussion of the points made, a mutually agreed-upon direction for improvement can be reached. A third method is for the supervisor to ask open-ended questions, identify a problem, move to problem-solving discussions, identifying specific issues and specific solutions.[8] The final step of the interview is to develop a plan that will improve the employee's performance within the organization, provide individual growth, and strengthen the ties between the individual and the organization. During the interview, issues may be raised about organizational problems that may interfere with performance. The supervisor should record these and discuss them at a future date as appropriate. The supervisor then summarizes the discussion, indicating future steps to be taken. The appraisal form plus any notes are placed in the employee's file. The employee and the supervisor will sign off on the appraisal form to indicate agreement with the content. If there is disagreement, the employee should have the right to state that in writing for the file. In many organizations, the employee also receives a copy of the completed rating form. The personnel file will include each year's assessment and provides information over time about the employee's contribution to the organization. Should difficulties arise, this file provides essential information for both employee and employer.

The Personnel File

Each employee of the organization from the director to part-time clerical staff member has a personnel file, which is a record of that individual's employment status. It includes the following items:

- the employee's current address, phone number, and person to be contacted in case of emergency
- the initial job application plus references received (If references were confidential, they may be in a separate file.)
- a copy of the letter offering employment and the employee's acceptance of employment
- a copy of any contract or employment agreement
- copies of letters showing salary increases, changes in job status, performance reviews, and any comments regarding the reviews
- letters of commendation, honors, awards
- information regarding benefits (e.g., retirement programs, health insurance, accumulated leave status)
- copies of any correspondence from a supervisor and to a supervisor
- record of courses taken, workshops attended
- record of special assignments, committee membership, etc.
- notices of unsatisfactory performance, records of grievance hearings, etc.
- letter of resignation or termination

Personnel files are kept for an extended period of years after the employee has left the organization as questions may arise about benefits, requests for references may be made, or other data may be needed to verify records. Personnel records continue to be confidential as long as they are held.

Problems with the Appraisal Process

Appraisal has problems, "many of which stem from the appraisal system itself—the objectives it is intended to serve, the administrative system in which it is embedded, and the forms and procedures that make up the system."[9] The goals of the organization may be unclear and therefore there can be a mismatch between goals and ratings. An institution-wide form may not be directly relevant to a library/information center and may be too general in stating areas to be rated to be useful, or the forms may be out-of-date. The supervisor may not be experienced in conducting appraisals and may try to avoid giving honest feedback by making general statements such as "You had a great year" or "That program was a disaster." Neither statement provides any helpful feedback one can use to build on success or correct errors. Some supervisors focus only on the negative, assuming that if nothing is said regarding an objective that the employee will understand that performance was good. This is a dangerous assumption. Most likely, the employee sees that there is only negative feedback on some things and therefore assumes that the overall performance must be negative. Employees need overt positive statements when a job has been well done. And then there is the pro forma review with little input by the supervisor and little or no feedback that results in the average rating. Managers are not usually psychologists and while they can date and measure performance (e.g., the number of titles cataloged), they lack the skills to measure personality; when they try to do so, misunderstandings often result. Those employees who hold negative attitudes about performance evaluation have probably interacted with a supervisor who is not skilled in this area of management.

An important element in appraisal is how to evaluate without harming the individual. The forms used and the interview process should minimize negatives to the extent possible. One should always evaluate the job and job-related activities, not the individual. The supervisor should know the job, what good performance in that job is, and focus on that. The key to getting the greatest benefit from performance appraisal is in the nature of the ongoing relationship between employee and supervisor. If there is trust and good communication, the formal appraisal reflects the ongoing relationship; if there is mistrust, that is reflected as well.

Peer Appraisal

Informal peer appraisal occurs each day as individuals work with one another to achieve objectives and make comments and suggestions to improve activities. Some organizations have instituted a formal appraisal in which peers rate peers. This is a difficult process for several reasons.[10]

Peiperl sees a number of paradoxes in this method. There is the paradox of roles in that the peer is also a judge. The peer may particularly like or dislike an individual and may hesitate to speak openly and fairly. The assessment can then be distorted. The paradox of group performance is that the focus on the individual within the group fails to address group performance. The group will either pull together and evaluate one another very positively so that the group looks good, or those in the group who may have become disaffected may see the process as a way to place blame on certain individuals for poor group performance. The paradox of rewards is that when peer appraisal counts most, it helps least. When appraisal is for rewards, it may provide honors but does not help the individual grow. Peiperl stresses that for peer appraisal to work, the individuals involved must know the purpose of peer appraisal and the specific ways in which it will be used. Since it is very difficult for peer appraisal to be anonymous, there is reluctance to speak honestly. While some see the employees who rate their peers as being empowered, most workplaces hesitate to move very far toward this type of rating system.

The tenure and promotion process is a peer evaluation in which the faculty member's teaching, research, and service record is reviewed by members of the faculty member's department and by external experts who work in the same field. In those university libraries in which there is faculty status, this type of review is a standard activity. When carried out fairly, it provides faculty members with a thorough assessment of their work.

Team Appraisal

When teams or work groups are reviewed, a different appraisal method is needed. If the team is the primary "home" of the employee, the job description should reflect team membership and should include components related to how one is expected to perform as a member of a team. If team membership is a secondary responsibility and the employee has a home departmental supervisor who is responsible for appraisal, the time spent as a team member should receive separate review.[11] Mohrman, Mohrman, and Lawler recommend that all members of the team discuss the team and its goals and agree on "objectives requiring one another's support, and renegotiate as conditions change."[12] Peer evaluation is important in team review because each individual contributes to the success of the entire team. The team and its individuals can be rated on the basis of the extent to which goals were met. Individual performance on the team is more difficult to determine and it is usually through a form of peer evaluation that this activity is rated. Todaro suggests that managers survey team leaders and ask them to assess the contribution of team members and then ask team members to assess their leader.[13] The areas easy to assess include the following:

- Did the team create workable goals and can they be measured?
- Did the team follow and complete goals and were they achieved in a timely manner?
- Did the team meet and how often and were these meetings productive?
- Did the team have a communication chain and did it work?
- Did team management communicate and was communication clear? Were conflicts resolved?
- Did the team report regularly and maintain a record of activities?

Todaro then listed the following areas as more difficult to assess:

- Was there an even distribution of work and did each team member do his or her share?
- Did the team produce quality work? Enough work? Were expectations met?
- Did the team leader guide the group well?
- Did the team leader follow guidelines and ensure a climate of participation?
- Was the team well organized?

Team members are individuals and need individual attention despite membership on a team. Team members often have concerns about the uneven distribution of work, they may distrust the work of others, or they may not often be satisfied that others understand their personal contribution. Some team members dominate the group and cause discomfort in the group while others stifle discussion and progress and thus frustrate other team members. These issues are often difficult to include in assessment but need to be addressed. While team participation needs to be reviewed, individuals should also receive personal time to look at personal contributions and ways in which they can grow personally.

Appraisal as Evaluation

Appraisal has two distinct goals: that of evaluation and that of development. Evaluation focuses on the organization while development focuses on the individual. Some see these two goals as conflicting. Evaluation for improving performance is specific and job related. The system is used to track progress or lack thereof and to provide regular feedback. Promotion decisions and salary increases as well as separation decisions are made based on performance. Those who perform well receive positive feedback. They will most likely continue to work well within the organization. Those who are marginal performers or whose conduct requires disciplinary action need to be dealt with fairly but dealt with nevertheless. Some employee's job performance is barely adequate. They tend to be tolerated by the supervisor because they are not overtly damaging to the organization. They are often long-term employees who have stopped growing in their job, are unwilling to do a different job, or because of their longevity have loyal friends who protect them.[14] Axelrod and colleagues say that the barely adequate worker has a negative effect on staff, as others have to compensate for that individual's lack of activity. Every barely adequate worker is holding a position that could be assumed by an excellent worker and therefore is a negative effect on productivity. They recommend that these low performers be identified through regular, clearly defined assessment. An action plan should be devised by the low performer and the supervisor that could move the individual to better performance. Not all low performers will respond. For those who do not, one may need to move them to another position or ask them to leave the organization.

Appraisal for Development

The second goal of appraisal is to identify ways in which employees can grow in their work. In this desire, both individual and organizational goals mesh. Individual development on the job assumes that new learning is essential to performing the job as it evolves. It is the role of the organization to provide access to means of increasing job-focused learning and personal improvement.[15] Staff members, as adult learners, must be involved in determining what they need to learn and in "planning, executing, and evaluating their training and development and in assessing their progress."[16] Educational programs work best when they are tailored to the individual and move from what the staff member actually knows to what the staff member wants and needs to know. The educational program must relate directly to what the employee wants to learn and must have applicability to the job. Learning programs can range from workshops to formal courses. They can be at conferences, at a university, provided in house, or available online. More and more programs are available online, which gives employees the flexibility to take courses at home, at work, after work, or at some other convenient time and place. Learning opportunities can be used for management training or for organizational development to inform the supervisor and employees how a new appraisal system works, to provide new insights into resource allocation, or to introduce new ways to market library/information services.

The new employee will have had an orientation session shortly after joining the organization and at that point learned about the organization and its goals as well as about employee benefits and responsibilities. Programs geared to working within the organization, including information on how to work in teams or how to assess changes in the environment, are a continuation of the orientation sessions and keep staff current with new techniques and new directions for their organization. This is also an opportunity to hold guided discussions on cultural differences and interpersonal relationships within the organization, and ways in which to serve the customer with courtesy and efficiency. In order to gain maximum benefit from programs such as these, they must be led by skilled instructors and have the support of management.

The supervisor can often serve as a mentor to staff as they look toward building their careers. Career planning and the support of further education by the organization results in staff who are better prepared to perform their present roles and to gain satisfaction from personal growth. Career workshops held by professional organizations or within the library/information centers are often available. For employees reentering the workforce, it is important for them to know what additional education they will need to prepare them for today's world of work; for current employees, it is important that they know the next steps they need to take to move up in their chosen area.

The concept of the learning organization is that the organization is continuously looking at its activities and its environment and encouraging new ideas.[17] Senge said that the ability to learn faster may be the only sustainable competitive advantage. "A learning organization is one that is continually expanding its capacity to create its future." To develop the individual and the entire organization, he sees five technologies: systems thinking in which one looks at the entire organization and not just one aspect, personal mastery in which the individual continually clarifies the personal vision, mental models that identify the ways in which we think the world works, the building of a shared vision for the future that will guide the organization, and the development of the team as a basic learning unit. Individual development, career development, and organizational movement toward the learning organization are all part of the same activity. The organization that learns—individuals who learn both to support the organization and to support personal development—are better equipped to face the future and have the tools to do so.

Appraisal and Rewards

While not the primary purpose of appraisal, the formal appraisal is usually tied to salary increases. It also provides the opportunity to discuss promotion within the organization or the assigning of new tasks. There is some question about the appropriateness of tying salary increases to appraisal ratings as there may be the assumption that money is available to reward excellent performance and that excellent performance will result in an increase. In years in which the economy is good and money is available, the connection is easy to make. Merit increases for outstanding performance may be added to incremental increases. In years when there is little or no money for salary increases, those who see appraisal largely as a means of allocating increases may be frustrated when they go through the process and receive little or no reward for quality service.

Salary increases are but one, albeit the most visible, means of rewarding performance. Additional rewards include providing funds to attend a conference, allocating additional resources to support a staff member's special project, or recognizing performance through awards. Rewards go to individuals or groups of individuals to recognize their superior performance in finishing a difficult task on time, on designing a new work process, in providing outstanding service, or similar outstanding activity. Recognition is a broader term and can include everyone in a unit or in the organization and recognizes quality performance by the group. Recognition for a job well done need not be tied directly to the appraisal process and in some cases it might be useful to keep the two separate. Simple, flexible, creative ways to say thank you are morale boosters as well as public recognition of work well done.[18]

Performance Appraisal as Renewal

Once performance appraisals have been conducted for a unit, certain patterns may emerge. It may be found that all aspects of the unit's responsibilities are matched by staff competent to carry them out. It may be found that some areas lack sufficient staffing or expertise. The solution may be to provide staff training or it may be found that an area of responsibility has grown more rapidly than current staff can handle. If the latter, the solution may be to reallocate or retrain staff internally; when this is not a solution, additional staff may be requested. If new clienteles or new technologies are anticipated, new or revised job descriptions may be necessary. Redundancy in completing tasks may be identified. If a staff member has expanded duties in a nearby area, overlap may have resulted. If this results in better performance, it may be continued. If it duplicates efforts, it should be discontinued. Through the appraisal process, changing ways of working may emerge. Appraisal is a powerful means of continuous improvement.

Union Involvement in Appraisal

In those institutions in which employees are unionized, the union provides a voice for the employee in matters of employment, which includes appraisal. Librarians are often part of municipal unions, teachers' unions, and in some colleges and universities they are part of faculty unions. When not part of the faculty union, universities that are unionized have specific agreements with librarians. Technical and clerical staff usually belong to other unions that support the concerns of support staff. These unions may encompass all support staff in an institution or a municipality or other larger unit. The purpose of the union is to form a bargaining unit, "a defined group whose community of interest allows them to be represented by a single exclusive bargaining agent [the union]."[19] Unions, through collective bargaining with management, develop agreements relating to the conditions of employment and the responsibilities of both management and worker. For example, unions may negotiate the conditions of overtime and overtime pay, leave policies, and other conditions in the workplace. They often provide oversight of appraisal activities and, in those instances where retrenchment is necessary, will serve as advocates for union members. Management is wise to have cordial working relationships with the union and to keep them informed of organizational issues that will affect union members.

CONFLICT MANAGEMENT

All employees in the organization have their own view of the organization and its objectives and have their own view of how they contribute to the larger effort. In the ideal situation, these views mesh. In those situations in which the employee has one view of the organizational culture, of the specific job, or of the evaluation process and other employees or the supervisors have a different view, conflict may arise. Conflict may arise because of a differing understanding of assignments, because of cultural differences, because of insufficient training to apply requisite skills to the job, or for other reasons. Conflict can grow from one incident to become a global issue (e.g., "You aren't listening to me" to "You never listen to me."). The larger the area of conflict grows, the harder it is to manage. When a person's ego or integrity or other part of the self is involved, the individual becomes defensive and does not look beyond the *me* in the issue. If conflict continues to grow, others may join in, harsh words are said, and the manager has a large-scale problem. It is important to resolve the conflict as quickly as possible. Conflict that is not resolved continues to grow and to dominate the organization until it is resolved.

Individuals tend to deal with conflict in a number of different ways.[20] Some deal with conflict by avoiding it. They try to prevent conflict and if that is not possible, they withdraw. The issue is not resolved and they tend to hold their resentment inside. Others try to seek a solution through compromise and are willing to live with the compromise. Some see the conflict as a competition and seek to dominate the discussion and to impose their own views. Those who do not like conflict will often accommodate to the situation and go along with the views of others. Still others will try to find a mutually satisfactory solution through collaboration. Those who collaborate discuss the issues that have led to the conflict. A solution that takes into account the attitudes and feelings of all involved and that is reached through open discussion of issues will have the best chance of success. Conflict can be positive if it motivates the employee to question assignments, to learn new ways of interacting with others, or to learn new skills. It can also bring to attention activities that may need to change. Conflict can be a tool for continuous improvement of the organization. It can also be negative if conflict produces stress and disrupts productivity.

Some organizations have a culture of complaint in which staff appear to enjoy dwelling on real or assumed wrongs. If this is present, the supervisor listens to concerns, finds out what is troubling employees, and looks for ways to work together to fix the situation. Perhaps one or two people are unhappy in their lives and the discontent spills over into the workplace. They might need counseling or a leave of absence. If there is evidence of unfairness or of problems the supervisor has not addressed, these should be resolved. Many organizations have an ombudsperson who will hear staff concerns and then work as their advocate when situations have not been dealt with by the supervisor to the staff member's satisfaction. Morale is an important element in the workplace and it flourishes in an environment of fairness. It cannot be taken for granted and requires constant attention.

DISCIPLINARY ISSUES

From time to time, the supervisor will find it necessary to deal with disciplinary problems. The individual may not be performing well on the job, may be chronically late in reporting to work, or may be disruptive in the workplace because of lack of courtesy to fellow staff members or to the public. Before taking any action in situations such as these, the supervisor would contact the human resources department in the larger organization to determine what university, municipal, business, or other organizational policies cover the disciplining of employees. Each employee has a personnel file that includes copies of performance evaluations, commendation letters, letters of complaint, and other information relevant to the individual's performance. If the concern is poor job performance, the evidence will be in the file. The supervisor is responsible for counseling the employee and, within guidelines set by the human resources department, for working with the employee to devise a plan to improve performance. In some cases, external pressures (such as serious illness in the family) may cause an employee's job performance to deteriorate. Counseling to find a means of providing support during a temporary situation may be the solution. If poor performance is chronic, a warning that continued poor job performance will result in separation from the organization is appropriate. If there has been a complaint by a staff member or a member of the public, the supervisor needs to respond. Depending upon the severity of the complaint, a review of the situation and some counseling in private with the employee may be a sufficient response. If the complaint is more severe, the supervisor may need to contact the human services department or the institution's attorney for advice in how to proceed.

There are a number of actions by employees that warrant immediate separation from the organization. These include gross insubordination or threat of force, theft and destruction of property (including computer hacking), falsifying information on one's application for employment, bringing guns or drugs to work, altering official records for personal gain, or being absent without leave. The employee who believes the supervisor is unfair or is treating the employee in an illegal manner has the right to file a grievance on the procedure or action in question. Usually the first step is for the supervisor to contact the human services department to which the complaint will be forwarded. The employee is given an opportunity to present her or his case. Both employee and supervisor will be informed of the process for resolving the situation. If the situation cannot be resolved within the procedures of the organization, a lawsuit may result.

RETRENCHMENT

Not all terminations are the result of poor performance or unacceptable behavior. An employee may be terminated for other reasons: downsizing the organization, reorganization, or fiscal cutbacks. When an organization is involved in these situations, it is essential that management keep staff regularly informed of impending changes and the impact those changes may have on the individual. If a budget cut requires a 10 percent reduction in staff, management should announce this and then indicate the criteria to be used to effect the reduction. Perhaps the reduction can be accomplished through early retirement or by not filling existing vacancies. If staff need to be reassigned or terminated, they need to be reassured that they are not being let go because they are poor employees. In these instances, most are not. When reassigned, staff should receive appropriate retraining to ensure the best experience in the new job. When terminated, staff should be assured that efforts will be made to help them find other employment. These actions are traumatic for those involved as they affect feelings of personal worth and directly affect the individual's economic stability. Regular performance assessment with the opportunity for both supervisor and staff member to discuss the job and one's performance provide the long-term basis for individuals to assess their contribution to the organization and to understand if termination is in any way the result of poor performance.

MANAGEMENT BY OBJECTIVE

In the past decades, additional means of organizing work and of evaluating employees have become popular. Probably the most well known of these is management by objective (MBO). MBO is both an organizing tool and an assessment tool. Although its assessment aspects have received more attention in recent years, it was initially seen as a means of organizing work. When first discussed in the 1930s, it was tied to Taylor's scientific management approach and was seen as an efficient means of redesigning work. It was also tied to Fayol's emphasis on planning, organizing, and controlling work. This approach resulted in a top-down decision-making process in which the objectives of the organization were set at the top and each descending level of the organization was given a set of tasks to complete. Enhanced productivity was the purpose of this approach. During the same period, McGregor saw MBO as a means of performance appraisal, a way of providing guidance for individual activity and for assessing progress. The two uses of MBO tend to merge and most MBO systems in place are combinations of control and assessment.[21]

A major reason for the development of MBO was that planning models set on past performance do not work well in a changing environment. Looking backward to plan for the future does not take into account the fact that demands on the organization are changing. MBO looks at what the desired future results of organizational activity are and then plans for that future. MBO became popular in the public sector in the 1970s and was adopted by the federal government in 1973. After a period of active use, it gradually faded to become just one more approach. Drucker was an early champion of MBO and much of its popularity can be traced to his writing on the subject.[22] Drucker said that turning good intentions into real objectives forces the manager to see that there are multiple objectives and that there is a need to set priorities among them. The manager must communicate the objectives of the organization widely and then indicate those objectives selected for priority action and the reasons for the selection. Resources would then be allocated to the selected strategies. If these activities are performed at the top of the hierarchy and decisions given to employees, the result is different than if employees are involved in setting objectives or in discussing their role in meeting them. When given to employees as work targets, the objectives are little different from scientific management approaches. Granvold said that while performance objectives are an attempt to ensure productivity, they can also be tools for growth and development.[23] If written by and with the staff members, they can be used for performance appraisal and as a guide for personal growth.

MBO is a systems approach to managing the organization. Those responsible for the organization's activities, and this can include members of the community when a nonprofit organization is involved, decide what they want to achieve over a period of time; from this, they establish goals, objectives, and priorities. All units of the organization have a role in achieving those goals and each unit and each individual is assigned a role. The extent to which each individual accomplishes the assigned role provides a high degree of accountability.[24] In the not-for-profit organization, this approach is a response to the demand for greater accountability. With MBO, the organization can show what it plans to contribute to the community, and then can show what it has contributed. It is also a means of showing that the success of many objectives is directly tied to the availability of resources.[25]

When it is used as a means of performance assessment, the employee and supervisor work together to set goals that will further the objectives of the organization and also take into account the employee's desire for personal growth. Each of these goals lists resources needed to achieve them, a timeline to chart progress, and a means of measuring progress on the goals. Each goal must mesh with the goals of the organization. When involved in the setting of one's personal goals, the individual has a greater motivation to accomplish them. In this situation, the individual has more self-direction in working to meet goals. In addition to periodic review during the year, toward the end of the fiscal year when salary increase decisions are made, the supervisor meets with the employee and reviews the year's objectives to discuss the extent to which they have been met. If they have not been met, the reasons for this are discussed. It may be from lack of promised resources, additional workload that has been placed on a particular objective, external circumstances beyond the employee's control, or some other factor for which the employee was or was not responsible. The supervisor and employee then discuss what went right and what went wrong during the year and a report of the session is prepared by the supervisor, signed by the employee, and becomes part of the employee's file. At this session, discussion of the next year's goals is begun. Personal goals supporting employee growth are discussed and growth opportunities are built into the goals. This may include taking a course, adding a set of responsibilities to the job that will allow for growth, or attending a professional meeting or trade show.

MBO is a powerful tool for assessing individual activities and progress. It allows the employee to work independently, using the objectives as guides to what is to be done and with what priority. For those working in virtual organizations where their physical connection to the organization may be limited, MBO provides a guide. MBO is not for all employees. Clerical and many technical staff whose jobs are routine and for which there is a job description outlining their duties are better evaluated on their performance of those duties. Professional staff who have a wide range of duties that change in response to external pressures and who need to prioritize tasks, find MBO useful. MBO is a very time-consuming activity. The one-on-one time spent between supervisor and employee in setting objectives, in checking progress, and in annual reviews is considerable. In addition, the supervisor needs initial training in how to apply the system. It takes a year or more for most employees to understand how the system works and to become comfortable with it. Despite the time-consuming nature of the activity, over time it can help the organization become more self-directed in pursuit of organizational goals and can help employees gain greater job satisfaction through greater independence in carrying out objectives and in the opportunity for personal growth.

SUMMARY

Performance review and appraisal plays a key role in maintaining the quality of the workforce. It responds to society's demands that individuals contribute to their organizations. It provides the organization with an ongoing review of employee performance and it provides the individual with a personal evaluation that can serve as the basis for growth and development on the job.

NOTES

1. Richard Ream, "What's my hiring line?" *Information Today* 19, no. 5 (May 2000):18–19.
2. Sheila Creth, "Conducting an effective employee interview," *Journal of Academic Librarianship* 4, no. 5 (November 1978): 356–60.
3. Creth, "Conducting an effective employee interview," 5.
4. Harry Levinson, "Management by whose objectives?" *Harvard Business Review* 81, no. 1 (January 2003): 107–16.

5. Michael Beer, "Making performance appraisal work," in *Managing People and Organizations*, edited by John J. Gabarro (New York: McGraw-Hill, 1992), 195–212.

6. Robert L. Creviston and John W. Freed, "Performance appraisal," in *AMA Management Handbook*, 2nd ed., vol. 7, edited by William K. Fallon (New York: American Management Association, 1983), 81–93.

7. Creviston and Freed, "Performance appraisal," 80.

8. Beer, "Making performance appraisal work," 195–212.

9. Beer, "Making performance appraisal work," 196.

10. Maury A. Peiperl, "Getting 360 degree feedback right," *Harvard Business Review* 79, no. 1 (January 2001):142–47.

11. Allan M. Mohrman, Susan Albars Mohrman, and Edward E. Lawler III, "The performance management of teams," in *Performance Measurement, Evaluation, and Incentives*, edited by William J. Bruce Jr. (Boston: Harvard Business School Press, 1992), 217–41.

12. Mohrman et al., "The performance management of teams," 233.

13. Julie Todaro, "How am I doing?" *Library Administration and Management* 14, no. 1 (Winter 2000): 31–34.

14. Beth Axelrod, Helen Handfield-Jones, and Ed Michaels, "A new game plan for C players," *Harvard Business Review* 80, no. 1 (January 2002): 80–88.

15. William R. Tracey, "Career development and training," in *AMA Management Handbook*, 2nd ed., vol. 7, edited by William K. Fallon (New York: American Management Association, 1983), 65–93.

16. Tracey, "Career development and training," 67.

17. Peter Senge, *The Fifth Discipline: The Art and Practice of the Learning Organization* (New York: Doubleday, 1990).

18. Linda Musser, "What we say when we reward: Valuing employees through recognition programs," *Library Administration and Management* 15, no. 2 (Spring 2001): 85–90.

19. John W. Weatherford, *Librarians' Agreements: Bargaining for a Heterogeneous Profession* (Metuchen, N.J.: Scarecrow Press, 1988).

20. Kenneth W. Thomas, "Conflict and conflict management," in *Handbook of Industrial and Organizational Psychology*, edited by Marvin D. Dunnette (Skokie, Ill.: Rand McNally, 1976), 889–936.

21. Peter Drucker, "Management by objective: What results should you expect?" in *Management Systems in the Human Services*, edited by Murray L. Gruber (Philadelphia: Temple University Press, 1981), 74–87.

22. Drucker, "Management by objective," 74–87.

23. Donald K. Granvold, "Supervision by objective," in *Management Systems in the Human Services*, edited by Murray L. Gruber (Philadelphia: Temple University Press, 1981), 96–107.

24. Dale D. McConkey, "The future: Its challenges and promises," in *Managing the Nonprofit Organization*, edited by Diane Borst and Patrick J. Montana (New York: American Management Association, 1977), 199–206.

25. William K. Fallon, ed. *The AMA Management Handbook*, 2nd ed., vol. 1 (New York: American Management Association, 1985), 26.

ADDITIONAL READINGS

Burns Jr., William J. *Performance Measurement, Evaluation, and Incentives*. Boston: Harvard Business School Press, 1992.

Campbell, John P., Marvin D. Dunnette, Edward F. Lawlor III, and Karl E. Weick Jr. *Managerial Behavior, Performance and Effectiveness,* New York: McGraw-Hill, 1970.

Flanagan, Robert J. *Trade Union Behavior, Pay Bargaining, and Economic Performance.* New York: Oxford University Press, 1993.

Foster, Richard N. *Innovation: The Attacker's Advantage.* New York: Summit Books, 1986.

Hambrick, Donald C., David A. Nadler, Michael L. Tushman, eds. *Navigating Change: How CEOs, Top Teams, and Boards Steer Transformation.* Boston: Harvard Business School Press, 1998.

Johnstone, Ronald L. *The Scope of Faculty Collective Bargaining: An Analysis of Faculty Union Agreements at Four-Year Institutions of Higher Education.* Westport, Conn.: Greenwood Press, 1981.

Jones, Phillip J. "Individual accountability and individual authority: The missing links." *Library Administration and Management* 14, no. 3 (Summer 2000): 135–45.

McLain, Gary, and Deborah S. Romaine. *The Everything Managing People Book.* Avon, Mass.: Adams Media, 2002.

Pfeffer, Jeffrey, and Alison Davis-Blake. "Unions and job satisfaction: An alternative view." *Work and Occupations: An International Sociological Journal* 7, no. 3 (August 1990): 259–83.

Chapter Fifteen

Program Measurement and Evaluation

"Measurement is the collection of data representing the state of the library, its services, and users. It provides objective data on efficiency and effectiveness to assist decision making." It compares what is with what ought to be.[1] Libraries came relatively late to the understanding that their services needed to be measured—indeed, that they *could* be measured. For many old-line professionals, the mantra was that library service is special, is unique, and that trying to quantify it in any way would destroy what made it special. Since the 1960s, this attitude gradually began to fade for a number of convergent reasons. After a period of increased funding for libraries/information centers from local taxes and from federal programs, resources became less available and libraries found themselves in competition with other publicly funded activities for the funding that was available. Using techniques developed in the for-profit sector, library managers and other not-for-profit organization directors began to utilize measures of effectiveness and efficiency to justify their budgets. Measurement of services gradually moved beyond being seen as a necessary evil to being seen as a useful, if still somewhat suspect, tool for justifying support. During this same period, library management was becoming increasingly professionalized. This was a period of growth in PhD programs in library and information science and these research-trained PhD scholars were assuming responsibility for the education of new librarians. The shift from the library practitioner as faculty member to library researcher with practitioner experience as faculty member changed the nature of the curriculum and infused it with a research orientation. Similar changes were occurring in public administration and related not-for-profit management fields. It became standard practice to apply strategies developed in business contexts to library/information center management, adapting as necessary for the not-for-profit environment. Faculty who combined research competence and operational experience had the expertise to conduct research dealing with ways in which to plan for and evaluate programs, thus providing managers with tools to measure organizational performance. Library staff members became increasingly aware of the need to justify their programs by evaluating the services they provided and to show that they were using resources wisely in support of the needs and interests of those who use or might use their services.

An additional component in the move toward more professional management was the leadership provided by the professional associations. The American Library Association (ALA) and its divisions have long been leaders in these activities. During the 1970s and continuing to the present, professional associations have provided a number of guides to management, including the Public Library Association's (PLA) *A Planning Process for Public Libraries* (1980), the development of standards for school library media centers by ALA's American Association of School Libraries (AASL), and regular revision of standards for university libraries and college libraries by the Association of College and Research Libraries (ACRL). Leadership also comes from the Association of Research Libraries (ARL) in developing and testing new management strategies, from the efforts of the Council on Library and Information Resources (CLIR) to support new management strategies and to provide educational seminars for next generation library management leaders, the work of the Special Libraries Association (SLA) and the Medical Library Association (MLA) to develop standards for quality service, and many more. Each of these associations has been in the forefront of supporting research, conducting continuing education programs for library/information center staff, and leading their members to higher levels of performance.

PLANNING

During this same period, and for many of the same reasons, the need for planning library services was a primary theme. To plan for service, it was necessary to know something about services and potential users. The Public Library Inquiry (PLI), a series of studies of public libraries, their services, and users, funded by the Carnegie Corporation, was conducted in the late 1940s and early 1950s and laid much of the foundation for later study. Of particular importance was the fact that the PLI was conducted by the Social Science Research Council. The social science approach to these studies contrasted dramatically with the view of the field as reported in the library press of the period, and provided a solid research base for future study and action. One of the volumes in the study, Berelson's *The Library's Public* asked the question, "Who is the library's user and what does he want?" and focused on an overview of demand.[2] This approach to library service from the user's perspective continues as a core element of planning and evaluation. The development of planning processes specifically for libraries developed concurrently with similar efforts in the for-profit sector. With the business sector leading, the not-for-profit sector moved rapidly to adopt the new business practices involved in planning and evaluation.

Drucker defined planning as "the continuous process of making current entrepreneurial decisions systematically and with greatest knowledge of their futurity; organizing systematically the efforts needed to carry out these decisions; and measuring the results of these decisions against the expectations through organized systematic feedback."[3] He went on to say that systematic planning requires evaluation of current activities to ensure that objectives are appropriate to the situation and that those appropriate objectives are being met. Objectives that had become less important over time and those that gained in importance could be identified and resources allocated according to perceived importance.

A major event in library management was the publication in 1980 of *A Planning Process for Public Libraries.*[4] Underlying the process, the purpose of which was to evaluate current library services as the first step in planning and then to plan for future service, was the collection of appropriate data. The authors stressed that "[l]ibrary management requires a system of data, or statistics to provide information for decision making, to meet the reporting requirements of local, state, and federal authorities, and to allow for comparison with other libraries."[5] They further emphasized the need for a coordinated system of data collection based on a determination of what is needed, how it is to be used, the collection interval, and reporting frequency, how the data is to be collected and who is responsible.[6] Once a decision has been made as to the types of data to be collected, it is relatively easy to put into place a good management information system that allows for continuous online collection of data that one can access on demand.

Much of the data required to review accomplishment of goals and to monitor programs are in the form of performance measures. Library statistics are not performance measures but contribute to them. Library statistics—including number of books, number of borrowers, questions answered, program attendance, and other input-output measures—have been collected since libraries were established. Little thought was usually given to how they were to be used to evaluate the library. When library managers began to look at traditionally gathered statistics and to decide which ones were useful to determine performance, they tended to measure what was easiest to quantify (e.g., circulation statistics or number of books processed) rather than to ask the question "What do I need to know to make decisions?" The real questions about performance and the use of data to answer those questions were rarely asked.

The purpose of measurement is to provide objective data on library operations that can be used to determine how well that library has performed in relation to its objectives and to make decisions about allocation and reallocation of resources. Performance measures focus on output and effectiveness. They are "an analytical tool which provides a manager with the means to evaluate the activities of his/her organization as to the results produced an the extent to which these results fulfill pre-designed objectives."[7]

Service can be evaluated to determine

- Effectiveness: How well does a service satisfy demand?
- Cost effectiveness: How efficient are the internal operating systems?
- Cost benefit: Is the value of the service worth more or less than the cost of providing it?[8]

In his research, Kantor developed four objective performance measures that were then tested in five ARL libraries.[9] The purpose of these measures was to provide feedback to management on the extent to which organizational objectives had been met and to measure quantity or quality of service. Data was collected to describe current operations with the expectation of highlighting areas where objectives had not been met. Identification of services that perform below intended levels is useful in a number of ways: to staff who can then review the activity and adjust as needed, and to managers who may need to reallocate resources to support an underperforming program or perhaps to discontinue the program. Collection of objective data over time provides a longer range view of the degree of success of a program in meeting long-range goals. Drucker makes the point that service groups within the for-profit sector (e.g., special libraries) are paid from overhead.[10]

To continue to be supported, they must be well managed and be able to show how they contribute to the organization.

Output Measures for Public Libraries builds on *The Planning Process for Public Libraries* and focuses on ways to collect data "representing the state of the library, its services and users."[11] A range of data-collecting tools is presented from which a library can select those that answer the particular questions about what they do and how well they do it. The criteria the authors provide to guide the selection of measures are applicable to any selection of measures for evaluation. They include the following:

- Validity: Does the tool measure what we want to know?
- Reliability: Are the results of the measurement consistent?
- Comparability: Can we compare the results of the measure over time and across like situations?
- Usefulness: Are the results of the measurement activity useful for decision making?
- Precision: Many measures, particularly user surveys, have a margin of error. Is that margin of error such that results are not useful?
- Cost to gather: Is the data collected worth the effort made to collect it?[12]

Van House and associates next applied the use of performance measures to the academic setting.[13] They stressed that the reason for developing objective data on an organization is to determine how good it is and how it can be better. Through objective measures, one can quantify performance in relation to goals achieved and services delivered. Feedback on performance and the evaluation of service is possible. One can also demonstrate the value of a service. The data collected supports decision making and "as libraries become more and more complex, management needs objective, standardized data on which to make decisions."[14] Measures describe the existing situation and these are placed against goals and objectives to determine the extent to which they were met. This is a cyclical process in which one sets a level of expected performance (goals) and develops broad-based criteria from which measures are developed. Specific operations and services are identified as those critical to meeting goals. Measures are applied to these operations and goals; data is collected and analyzed to determine the extent to which goals were met to see how closely actual activities match the goals set forth for it. Goals are then reviewed and revised as appropriate, and the cycle begins anew. Measures typically include measures of user satisfaction, materials availability and use, quality of facilities, use of library facilities, and the use and quality of information services.[15] While it is relatively easy to measure inputs (e.g., materials purchased) and outputs (e.g., materials circulated), it is more difficult to measure outcomes (e.g., level of user satisfaction with a service) and the impact the service had on the individual's activities. While output measures are objective and straightforward, outcome measures have an element that is subject to interpretation.

In collecting data, one should be aware that it is easy to skew measures, thus providing an incomplete or inaccurate result. Collecting a single measure relating to a service or program provides data on only one aspect of that service or program. For example, circulation statistics measure items checked out but do not provide a full picture of the use of the collection. They are a limited measure of use and additional data is needed. How many items did the individual review before checking out some items? Were the items checked out the ones the individual wanted or were they what was available? Analysis of use requires a set of related measures that provide a fuller picture of how individuals use their library. Another limitation of objective measures is that they reflect the use of services provided but do not address other roles of the library such as its archival role or its socioeconomic role in its community. Measures can also be manipulated to provide an inaccurate picture. One might measure attendance at a particularly well-attended program in a series otherwise poorly attended and thus say that the series was successful when it actually was not. The selection of a possibly nonrepresentative sample will not provide accurate information. Care should be taken to ensure that data collected tells the full story accurately. Inaccurate data, whether collected by accident or on purpose, casts a pall on the data-collecting activity and makes the data unusable for decision making because it will be seen as untrustworthy.

In addition to measuring the levels of service provided by an organization, one can also measure the effectiveness of the organization and its climate.[16] With the use of questionnaires, interviews, and observation, one can learn how an organization makes decisions and what the outcomes of those decisions were. One can also learn how well various units in the organization interact, how well they communicate, and how well they support one another. The success of a particular management style and the enthusiasm and loyalty of staff can be measured. Each of these, as well as related elements of the way in which the organization functions, can be measured, the data analyzed, and adjustments made to improve the operation of the organization.

During the 1970s and 1980s, numerous studies of library services and users were undertaken. The result was a large number of interesting independent studies from which few generalizations could be made, even though methodologies in collecting data differed from study to study. In addition, these studies tended to focus on output (i.e., what the library accomplished) but did not tie to input (the resources needed to accomplish tasks). Their usefulness for resource allocation was therefore limited. An additional limitation of these individual studies was that the library or unit in the library being studied was studied in isolation. Libraries as interdependent units within a system must be reviewed and evaluated within the context of the relationships with other units and organizations. Libraries that are part of larger systems have had a role identified by that larger system for them. Their success in meeting goals is directly tied to the expectations of and support by the larger organization. Individual studies conducted out of context provided an opportunity to test various methodologies and how well they answered specific questions.

MEASURES

Performance measures were implemented in the 1960s as a means of evaluating service. The most often asked question was, "Did users get what they wanted?" DeProspro and his colleagues aimed at developing simple, usable measures.[17] At the same time, a number of researchers using operations research methodology were developing complex mathematical approaches to measurement. While some very innovative research was carried out using operations research methodology, it was often done by those unfamiliar with the library setting and the results were not easily assimilated by library managers.

There are no right or wrong measures. There are poorly designed measures or measures that are not carefully and consistently applied. Van House stresses that measures alone do not diagnose causes of problems. They do indicate possible problem areas that require further investigation. "[The results of output measures] reflect the interaction of users and library resources constrained by the environments in which they operate. The meaning of a specific score on any measure depends on a broad range of factors, including the library's goals, the current circumstances of the library and its environment, the uses and the users, the manner in which the measure was constructed and how the data were collected."[18]

EVALUATION

Evaluation is part of the organization's planning process. One sets goals and objectives, allocates resources, and works to meet those goals and objectives. Evaluation is the process of measuring the extent to which goals have been met. The measures demonstrate "effectiveness" or the extent to which a service or activity meets stated objectives and the extent to which the service or activity meets user expectations and the extent to which users are satisfied. One can also determine if library activities are managed efficiently, if relationships with external groups (including the parent organization) are positive, and if the needs of the library's multiple constituencies are being met. Effectiveness carries evaluation one step beyond "Are we doing things right?" to "Are we doing the right things right?" Both terms—evaluation and effectiveness—relate to an information-gathering, analysis, and reporting process. Both reflect quantitative and qualitative elements, and each carries an element of value judgment. Both assume that evaluation is a permanent element of the planning process and that data collection and analysis will be carried out on a regular basis. There is also the assumption that evaluation will contribute to an environment of continuous improvement.

DuMont stressed that the library is a system and there are trade-offs in evaluating it.[19] If the primary emphasis is on physical input (e.g., staff, materials, or equipment), one set of measures is used. If the emphasis is on the dynamics of the organization, another set of measures will be used. A different set of measures is applied to collect data on user satisfaction, and yet another set to assess the library's role in its social context. Each set of measures focuses on a particular area and provides a view from that perspective. It is essential to select measures carefully, ensure that they are directed toward the areas of particular concern, and verify that they provide a full picture of that area. The library is also part of a larger system, which may be an academic institution, a school, a business, or municipal government. When one is looking at relationships between the library and the larger system, another set of measures is applied. There is no consistent definition of what constitutes an effective library. Criteria for assessment change depending upon circumstances. Measures taken to assess short-term activities may vary from those reflecting long-term performance. In determining what and how to measure, one must be aware of the trade-offs, which are as much political as managerial.

One can evaluate effectiveness from a number of perspectives. Early measures focused on how well the organization was meeting its goals of providing service. As evaluation became a standard part of the planning, operating, evaluating cycle, greater attention began to be placed on the quality of service as perceived by users. Nitecki applied the SERVQUAL instrument to academic library service to determine if this tool designed in a business setting could be used to measure "the discrepancy between customer expectations or desires and their perceptions."[20] While most measures of service focus on information-seeking behavior, Nitecki wished to go a step further and measure perceived service quality in greater depth. SERVQUAL is a five-dimensional construct and includes tangibility, reliability, responsiveness, assurance, and empathy. Twenty-two items were identified that would measure these dimensions across all industries.[21] The purpose of Nitecki's research was to determine if SERVQUAL could be used by library managers to see if there was an effect on users over time regarding efforts to improve service. The consumer evaluates service by how that service affects her or him and this is largely subjective. SERVQUAL provides a way to measure how well customer expectations are met on a consistent basis. How a service is delivered affects the perception of quality. While the technical quality of a service may be excellent, much of the evaluation of the service comes from subjective perceptions of how it was delivered. Nitecki found that SERV-QUAL can be used to gain the user perspective, particularly user expectations of service. The identification of expectations can be used to tailor services more closely to expectations. While most user surveys ask the users what they wanted and whether they were satisfied with the result, SERV-QUAL goes a step further to ask what users expected and the extent to which those expectations were met.

Heath at Texas A&M built on SERVQUAL and introduced LibQUAL+ as a tool to identify service area needs and to fix them promptly.[22] This joint Texas A&M and Association of Research Libraries project was designed:

1. "to provide information of 'sufficient granularity' to have meaning at the local level [for library administrators] to identify strengths and

defects across the dimensions of library service quality, and with this information to be able to do a better job of allocating resources."

2. by placing local results in a normative context, administrators can see their activities in a peer perspective, and
3. by achieving a normative perspective, administrators can identify best practices among their peers that have satisfied users."[23]

LibQUAL +, which is based on the research conducted on SERVQUAL, used a web-based survey instrument to measure expectations, desired service levels, and gaps across the dimensions of affect of service, which includes library as place, personal control, and information access. It also measured attitudes toward responsibility, assurance, empathy, and dependability. Library users were asked to respond promptly regarding their experience in using the library. Feedback is rapid and adjustments in service can be made quickly. Heath champions the inclusion of the user of services in evaluation and adjustment of services as it provides an additional and direct measure of effectiveness.

Some have labeled effectiveness as evaluation with value added. We evaluate services, programs, and the organization to determine if they are doing what we expect them to do. Evaluation provides a means of fine-tuning existing programs and thus contributes to organizational improvement as well as program improvement. It provides information on where funding allocations may need to be revised to improve services and programs. It provides both the organization and its parent organization a means of monitoring how resources translate into programs, services, and satisfaction. It also provides staff with an understanding of how those programs and services for which they are responsible are functioning and how those taking advantage of those programs and services view them. External constituencies can see how well library managers are managing resources and the level of satisfaction on the part of users. Evaluation provides continuous information on the status of the organization and its programs and services. It must lead to organizational improvement. If programs and services do not meet expectations, they should be revised or perhaps eliminated. If the organization itself is not functioning efficiently, changes are to be made. Evaluation provides a means of fine-tuning the library and its programs and always working to improve them. The emphasis on continuous improvement sends a strong message to all stakeholders: that excellence is a way of working, that when problems occur they are dealt with quickly, and that resources are being used wisely. There is no better long-range public relations statement than this.

An additional measure, in addition to effectiveness, is efficiency—a measure of how carefully resources are being used. Efficiency measures relate to how much it costs to perform an activity and is a measure of internal productivity. For example, what is the cost of processing a book? Has the cost increased over time? Why? How do cost figures compare to those in a similar library? If the costs are too high, efforts are then made to restructure the activity with a view to bringing costs in line. Efficiency measures are used to ensure that internal processes support delivery of services at the least cost. They are not used for priority setting or program planning.

As measures of effectiveness are refined and as new measures are developed, their use will doubtlessly be extended. New services and programs are being developed and provided, particularly in the area of electronically delivered services and with new services, new or revised measures will be needed. Evaluation of services is a growing and changing area that library managers and library staff need to monitor and to apply those elements most useful to their situation as they become available.

TOTAL QUALITY MANAGEMENT

Total Quality Management (TQM) was developed in Japan in the latter half of the twentieth century under the leadership of W. Edwards Deming.[24] TQM focuses on quality of services and customer needs. Deming defined quality as a process that results in a product or service one can sell to customers who will ultimately be satisfied with the product or service. Thomas Shaughnessy said that as most library services are processes and not products and vary from producer to producer and from customer to customer, it is therefore difficult to evaluate them using this technique.[25]

TQM has grown to become another format for planning and evaluation that includes the standard elements of planning and evaluation as described earlier. The TQM organization has the management of quality as its central theme. This changes the organization itself from a hierarchical structure to a series of interconnected service teams with the end user at the center and all services focusing on the user. In this organizational structure, the needs of the user are paramount. The service teams are responsible for the processes by which services are delivered and are also responsible for continuously improving those processes so that users receive the highest possible level of service.[26] Teams monitor service using those measures most appropriate to the particular service, determine the extent to which the services are meeting goals or targets for performance, and adjust performance when necessary to improve service delivery. Those who champion TQM say that the focus on the customer and quality changes the dynamic of the organization from one concerned with process to one concerned with the customer. In reorganizing the staff into teams, there is a focus on services as they impact the user and the user is thus involved in determining quality. Communication goes from team to team, to library management and back to the user. While the major differences with TQM are in organizational structure and communication patterns, the overall measurement objective of determining if goals have been met, if problems exist, and then analyzing problems and making adjustments that lead to an improved program, service, or organization are the same.

STANDARDS

For many years, all types of libraries and information centers, within their professional organizations, have developed and updated standards for performance. Early standards tended to be very brief and to be quantitative (e.g., number of books per capita, per capita funding, size of staff). These standards were often used as targets for support by funding agencies and once a target or standard had been met, one was assumed to have a good library. While the professional societies saw the standards as bare minimums, funding agencies often saw them as goals. Nevertheless, these standards did set a baseline. As library management became more professionalized, as the professional societies continued to study and develop services, and particularly as planning processes and output measures were made widely available in the 1970s and 1980s, simple and generic standards gave way to a more individualized approach. Each library is seen as unique; within the framework of standards and measurement required by its parent organization or the municipality of which it is a part, it should determine its own criteria for performance and how it will evaluate that performance.

Standards are a means of measuring achievement. Using agreed-upon criteria, the library manager establishes identifiable outcomes (both quantitative and qualitative) and thus arrives at a clearly stated set of expectations for the process of planning, budget adequacy, collection adequacy, and building and equipment adequacy. Outcomes are also established for the level of use of collections, resources, and services. Standards provide a benchmark against which measures can be viewed and provide additional information to those responsible for determining priorities and evaluating performance in terms of mission. In the case of college and university libraries, standards revised and adopted for university libraries in 1989 and adopted for college libraries in 2000 provide a segue to outcomes assessment, which has become the evaluation process for higher education.

ASSESSMENT

Beginning in the 1970s, state agencies and coordinating boards were created to develop and implement assessment measures for higher education, and by the 1980s had become a politically popular tool for reporting on the quality of higher education. Assessment activities have been driven by state legislatures who want to give assurances to the taxpayers that their tax dollars are being used wisely. This follows from a growing attitude on the part of the public that higher education wastes money and does not educate their children. Assessment is a means of assuring students, parents, and the public at large that colleges and universities are indeed providing a quality product and that the quality can be measured.

Assessment joined accreditation as a program review tool. Accrediting agencies have always been concerned with institutional and program improvement. They look at the goals of academic programs and the extent to which stated goals have been met. The institution or specific academic programs are reviewed according to a set of external standards that have been developed by accrediting agencies or, in the case of professional programs, by that profession's professional society. Each is considered unique and programs are not compared to one another but are reviewed in relation to the standards. Assessment is a state-level activity that looks for common measures that can be applied across programs: overall cost of a program, number of graduates of the program, what they learned while in the program, or the market demand for graduates, for example. A third level of review may be conducted by the college or university itself for its own planning purposes. This third level of review often results in programs being prioritized in relation to their centrality to the mission of the institution. For example, a research university may place a low priority on professional master's degrees or a college may place a high priority on business degrees because the demand is high and they bring in needed revenue. Each of these activities—assessment, accreditation, and internal review—requires the identification and collection of relevant data. A requirement of assessment is that permanent programs of data gathering and review be put in place so that data can be collected and reviewed on an ongoing basis.

In the past decades, colleges and universities have reviewed their curricula to determine each program's centrality to the academic mission, its relevance to society, the cost effectiveness, the demand in the workplace for graduates of the program, and their political viability. During this period, programs that failed to meet a certain level of performance as measured by student leaning, efficiency of program management, or social/economic value were merged with a similar program or discontinued while other programs received additional support. This is a continuous activity with colleges and universities; academic units regularly review their programs.

From the perspective of many outcomes-assessment directors, libraries are peripheral to student learning and are grouped with administrative and educational support services along with computing and student counseling or with environmental factors such as classroom quality and the quality of the student center. Students might be asked if they use the library and, if so, their level of satisfaction. From the planning perspective, libraries and all other support units are expected to develop goals and objectives that further the overall academic program. However, this does not mean that the library is not part of overall assessment activities. The standards under which accrediting bodies operate include sections on libraries and their role in supporting students and faculty. Internal program reviews usually include similar sections. These tend to focus on output measures (e.g., number of books and periodicals) rather than on services provided or learning outcomes. Individuals responsible for developing assessment tools are not yet fully aware of the sophistication of measurement now present in academic libraries, nor are they aware of the range of outcome measures that are available. It is the responsibility of the library manager to educate those developing assessment tools by ensuring that library faculty or staff serve on committees that devise and implement assessment tools and by providing information beyond that requested when there is no opportunity to revise an assessment tool. Library managers should also have a voice in determining the types of data collected by the library so that measures of service and measures of learning outcomes are included along with the standard output measures. As assessment is a political as well as a planning tool, library faculty and staff need to be represented on university- and college-wide assessment committees to present and interpret information about the library's contribution to learning outcomes.

The present standards for university libraries and college libraries support the trend toward self-evaluation and the review of library goals within the context of the parent institution and its planning process. The standards recognize that each library is different, that it exists within a unique institution, and that it should set goals appropriate to its needs. Standards that encourage self-evaluation provide useful support to campuswide outcomes-assessment activities. Library managers need to be sure that their ongoing data-collection program provides the information relevant to answering the questions of how effective library programs are and how they contribute to student learning, to research, to the overall campus learning environment.

SUMMARY

The development and implementation of measures to evaluate the success of library programs in meeting stated objectives provides a continuous opportunity to adjust and improve programs. It responds to questions by stakeholders regarding the ways in which resources are used and serves as a basis for planning future services. Program review and evaluation meets the library/information center manager's responsibility to be accountable.

NOTES

1. Nancy Van House, Mary Jo Lynch, Charles R. McClure, Douglas L. Zweizig, and Eleanor Jo Rodger, *Output Measures for Public Libraries*, 2nd ed. (Chicago: American Library Association, 1987), 1.

2. Bernard Berelson, *The Library's Public: A Report of the Public Library Inquiry* (New York: Columbia University Press, 1949).

3. Peter F. Drucker, *Management: Tasks, Responsibilities, Practices* (New York: Harper and Row, 1973), 125.

4. Vernon E. Palmour, Marcia C. Bellisari, and Nancy De Wath, *A Planning Process for Public Libraries* (Chicago: American Library Association, 1980).

5. Palmour, Bellisari, and De Wath, *A Planning Process for Public Libraries*, 84.

6. Palmour, Bellisari, and De Wath, *A Planning Process for Public Libraries*, 84.

7. Sandra Parker, "A conceptual framework for the performance measures of a Canadian

federal government health sciences library network," in *Quantitative Measurement and Dynamic Library Service*, edited by Ching Chi Chen (Phoenix, Ariz.: Oryx Press, 1978).

8. Ching Chi Chen, "Statistical systems application in library management," in *Quantitative Measurement and Dynamic Library Service*, edited by Ching Chi Chen (Phoenix, Ariz.: Oryx Press, 1978), 4.

9. Paul B. Kantor, *Objective Performance Measures for Academic and Research Libraries* (Washington, D.C.: Association of Research Libraries, 1981).

10. Drucker, *Management: Tasks, Responsibilities, Practices,* 132–45.

11. Van House et al., *Output Measures for Public Libraries*, 1.

12. Van House et al., *Output Measures for Public Libraries*, 5.

13. Nancy Van House, Beth Weill, and Charles McClure, *Measuring Academic Library Performance: A Practical Approach* (Chicago: American Library Association, 1990).

14. Van House et al., *Measuring Academic Library Performance*, 3.

15. Van House et al., *Measuring Academic Library Performance*, 5.

16. Michael Nash, *Managing Organizational Performance* (San Francisco: Jossey-Bass, 1983).

17. Ernest R. DeProspro, *Performance Measures for Public Libraries* (Chicago: American Library Association, 1983).

18. Van House et al., *Measuring Academic Library Performance*, 7.

19. Rosemary Ruhig DuMont, "A conceptual basis for library effectiveness," *College and Research Libraries* 41, no. 2 (March 1980): 103–11.

20. Danuta Nitecki, "An assessment of the applicability of SERVQUAL dimensions as customer based criteria for evaluating quality of service in an academic library," PhD diss., University of Maryland, College Park, 1995.

21. V. A. Parasuraman, L. Zeithani, and L. Berg, "SERVQUAL: A multiple item scale for measuring customer perception of service quality," *Journal of Retailing* 64, no. 1 (Spring 1988): 12–40.

22. Carolyn A. Snyder, "Measuring library service quality with a focus on the LibQUAL project: An interview with Fred Heath," *Library Administration and Management* 16, no. 1 (Winter 2002): 4–7.

23. Snyder, "Measuring library service quality," 4.

24. W. Edward Deming, *Out of Crisis* (Cambridge, Mass.: MIT Press, 1968).

25. Thomas Shaughnessy, "Search for quality," *Journal of Library Administration* 8, no. 1 (January 1987): 5–10.

26. Irene Owens, "The impact of change from hierarchy to teams in two academic libraries: Intended results vs. actual results using total quality management," *College and Research Libraries* 60, no. 6 (November 1999): 571–84.

ADDITIONAL READINGS

Buckholtz, Thomas J. *Information Proficiency: Your Key to the Information Age.* New York: Van Nostrand, 1995.

Clark, Philip M. "New approaches to the measurement of public library use by individual patrons." *Occasional Papers.* Urbana: University of Illinois, Graduate School of Library and Information Science, 1984.

Ewell, Peter. *Assessment and the "New Accountability": A Challenge for Higher Education Leadership.* Denver, Colo.: Education Commission of the States, 1990.

Gray, Peter J., ed. *Achieving Assessment Goals Using Evaluation Techniques.* New Directions for Higher Education no. 67. San Francisco: Jossey-Bass, 1987.

Hoadley, Irene B., and Alice S. Clark, eds. *Quantitative Methods in Librarianship: Standards, Research, Management.* Westport, Conn.: Greenwood Press, 1972

Middle States Association of Colleges and Schools. *Handbook for Institutional Self-Study.* Philadelphia: Commission on Higher Education, 1984.

————. *Characteristics of Excellence in Higher Education: Standards for Accreditation.* Philadelphia: Commission on Higher Education, 1981.

Mock, Theodore J., and Hugh D. Grove. *Measurement Accounting and Organizational Information.* New York: John Wiley and Sons, 1970.

Nichols, James O. *A Practitioner's Handbook for Institutional Effectiveness and Student Outcomes Assessment Implementation.* New York: Agathon Press, 1991.

Willard, Patricia, and Viva Teece. *People and Libraries: A Study of Why People Visit a Public Library and the Library's Response.* Kensington, Australia: University of New South Wales School of Librarianship, 1981.

Chapter Sixteen

Financial Management

Financial planning underlies financial management and is conducted in a complex and ever-changing environment. External trends (political, economic, and technical) affect planning and budgeting as much or more than internal data. The structure within which the library/information center is located, as well as local, state, and national government policies and actions, directly affect what the library/information center can do. One must consider additional variables in planning, those that reflect the demands and expectations of the user community. The library/information center manager studies these and related aspects of the external environment and anticipates their effects on internal activities.

Taking into consideration this range of variables, the library/information center manager makes decisions based on past practice and current activities as they relate to educational and/or service objectives and to the success of current programs. Often, staff are more focused than the director on internal activities. It is the role of the manager to bring the external and internal worlds together and to build plans for the library/information center future on information from the combined sources. It is also the role of the manager to ensure that external constituencies are aware of the bases on which decisions on programs and expenditures are made.

Except for the library/information center in for-profit agencies and those that are in privately managed organizations (such as foundations, some art galleries, think tanks, and other similar locations), the major resources for libraries/information centers derive from the tax base through allocations. They are therefore sensitive to the condition of the economy. Those in the for-profit sector or private sector are equally sensitive to the economy but in different ways. After the rapid growth experienced by educational institutions, including libraries, in the 1960s and early 1970s, there came a period of retrenchment and then slower growth when the economy prospered, as in the mid-1990s, and cutbacks when the economy cooled. Much of the funding for public, school, and academic libraries comes from state and local sources; when those sources are diminished due to a lower level of revenue, so are the budgets of those agencies that depend upon them. While long-term predictions of the economy are not possible, the library/information center manager should be aware that the cycle of good years and difficult years exists and it is essential to have a long-term financial view.

PLANNING AND BUDGETING

Planning

The ways in which the library/information center provides service have changed dramatically in recent decades, due in large part to the application of technology to the organization of, storage of, and access to information. One must also take into account the increased access by individuals to information over the Internet and the changes this has made in what is expected of libraries. While the service and philosophical goals are still strongly user focused, the ways in which these activities are carried out have changed. The role of financial planning is to provide a high level of service in an ever-changing economic and technological environment, and funded from resources that change as the economy changes. This activity is carried out in a highly political atmosphere in which other units of government, the university, the school district and other not-for-profit agencies are in competition for the same dollar.

As management has become increasingly professionalized in the nonprofit sector, there has been an increased emphasis on strategic and long-range planning. As government, too, has become increasingly professionalized, nearly all organizations that rely on tax dollars for support are expected to have a planning process in place. In some cases, the process is limited to a single unit, but more commonly the process will encompass a number of units. In the academic setting, a state's public universities will be charged by the legislature to develop a plan to accomplish certain goals. Each university in the system builds a plan that supports the system plan and that is compatible with the plans of other universities in the system. Within this overall planning activity, the library's plan will be developed for each university.

The private academic institution's plan serves as the umbrella for its library. School (K–12) plans operate similarly depending on whether they are public or private. Public library plans may appear to be stand-alone but should connect to other municipal agencies and to regional and statewide library systems. The for-profit library/information center derives its charge from the expectations of the parent company. The library/information centers develop long-term goals based on their missions and that of their parent companies. The goals reflect the wants and needs of client groups and the expectations of the parent organization, and focus on core activities. Upon this base, the library/information center develops annual plans for the organization. While individuals in the organization may change and levels of funding may vary, the fundamental purpose of the library/information center—to provide access to information—does not change. The planning process provides stability to the organization as it develops a budget to pursue its goals.

Budgeting

Budgeting is the allocation of scarce resources to meet specified objectives. In the public sector, the government determines the resource available to the library/information center, having determined from its perspective the level at which it wishes to support information services. Decisions on how to spend public monies are influenced not only by economic factors but also by noneconomic values that emerge from social, political, and cultural considerations. Information service provided by libraries is a public good in that it is an activity with high social benefit over a long period, it enhances our quality of life, and it does not stop at political boundaries. Its benefits are difficult to measure but it is agreed that the activity is worth public support. Other examples of public good include education and the national highway system. In the private sector, the marketplace determines the amount of money available for information services and the value placed on information services by each business/industry determines the allocation.

The budget is where planning and funding come together. Dollar figures are allocated to the plan. Thus, the budget should be seen as the library/information center's plan of action for the year with dollar figures allocated based on priorities set forth in the plan. Integral to the planning/budgeting activity is evaluation. What level of service is expected from a program given a specific allocation? Have objectives been achieved and were resource used wisely? Resources that must be managed are capital, critical physical assets, time, and knowledge. Their use should follow guidelines so that one can determine how they are used and can measure the extent to which each contributes to the goals of the organization. Decisions for action are based on data gained through regular evaluation of use of resources. Decisions made without careful review of data can be damaging to the organization and its objectives.

As a planning and decision-making device, the budget has a number of functions. Primarily, the budget is a plan of action for the budget year and is based on a realistic assessment of the resources it can hope to receive. The budget is linked to performance evaluation, as there is an implied contract between the organization and the funding source that if a certain level of funding is received for an activity, a certain level of service will result. As with any planning process, the budget process highlights the ways in which different activities and programs are related and are mutually dependent. Wildavsky describes the budget as a political act in that resources are requested from a funding body.[1] It is a plan of work in which activities for the ensuing year are listed and costs of objectives stated. The budget is a prediction of what staff wishes to accomplish. It can highlight or hide objectives depending on the personal interests of the planner and the perceived political climate. It is a means of control, as the level of funding per program will, to a large extent, determine the level of activity. The budget is a type of agreement between the organization and the funding body that outlines priority needs, sets objectives, and promises to meet those needs and objectives to the degree possible with funds allocated. Once accepted by the funding body, the budget sets a precedent on which the organization can build in later years. The budget is a planning tool and a political document. In financially difficult years, it is particularly important for the library/information center to have a reputation for careful planning and for responsible stewardship of funds.

The planning process has more than one horizon; long-range projections of three to five years indicate what needs to be done over the long term to achieve desired goals. The annual budget focuses on the upcoming year and what needs to be done in that period to further the long-term goals. Special projects or capital budgets may have time frames that vary depending on the activity. These plans and their related budgets are part of the planning/ budgeting process but are separate from the annual budget. They are interrelated in that the purpose of each is to meet long-term goals.

The Budgeting Process

Budgeting is a continuous year-round process and not a flurry of activity that occurs prior to deadlines for submission of documents. It is also highly political and requires continuous communication, both internally and externally, to set the necessary context for decision making. A budget committee, which is a standing committee chaired by the budget officer or library manager if there is no budget officer, represents both internal and external stakeholders. While two or three members of the committee do much of the data gathering and budget building, other members of the committee serve as reviewers and critics and ensure that the document best represents the library/information center and its objectives. Members of the committee include library staff, and may include members of the board of trustees, external library advisory committee members, and others whose input is essential to the fiscal health of the library.

Data gathering, which provides the foundation for the budget, is conducted regularly, using data from management information systems (MIS) in the library/information center and other internal data such as book stock, access to electronic information services, the current value of equipment and buildings, and the anticipated rate of growth of services and population served. In the case of equipment, how up-to-date is it and when should it be replaced? Looking at services, what is the size of the staff? What are their duties and how might the duties change? What fiscal implications might this have? Has the governing agency imposed standards for service that will change current work patterns and staffing needs? Results of reviews and evaluation of current programs and recommendations for increased support, steady support, or reduced support are considered. The environmental scanning process (see chapter 9) is used to identify trends and issues that may affect services. Many libraries/information centers regularly conduct a community analysis, which describes the current population served according to factors such as age, education, and ethnic background. When collected annually or on another regular basis, it is possible to identify changes in clientele and to project possible need for changes in services. These data, both internal and external, while based on statistical information, include subjective elements as well: How much emphasis should be placed on staff development? What are the expectations concerning legislation governing filtering of information for minors? What are the implications of a new academic program in the university for information services? Each of these questions is answered by a combination of objective and subjective input. Additionally, the budget committee will look at recent advances in technology to identify promising new software or delivery systems that will enhance the ability to bring client and information together. The long-range goals and objectives of the previous year are reviewed in light of the above information and are revised as appropriate to meet the anticipated needs and resources of the new budget year. Projections for spending are set so that the cost of each objective can be determined at any time throughout the year to see if anticipated and actual costs are similar. This information is useful when, later in the budget year, one wishes to determine if an activity is costing more or less than anticipated and may wish to adjust allocations to meet the new situation.

Building a budget based on extensive data gathering is time consuming, even when one relies on well-designed and efficient information systems. At times, during the year, decisions may need to be made quickly and resources allocated to meet a crisis; for example, because of a difficult financial situation where the funding agency has recalled part of the allocation it made for the budget year. Goals, objectives, and priorities have been set through the planning process, and the budget officer in discussion with the library/information center director will indicate those areas of lower priority where cuts can be made, keeping in mind that core activities must be protected. Particular programs may be reduced or, if they do not damage core activities, may be cut. It may be necessary to rethink goals and objectives for the year and revise them. Whatever the decisions, they should be based on the data used for planning and budgeting, should be sensitive to the political climate, and should be carried out carefully so as not to damage the long-term viability of the organization. The planning/budgeting process provides the structure for budget adjustments throughout the year.

Types of Budgets

There are two general types of budgets: the operating budget and the capital budget. The operating budget specifies how funds will be expended during the next year and its income is provided annually, largely from the funding agency. The capital budget is separate from the operating budget and is typically used to support large-scale activities such as building improvement, land purchase, and major technological investments. It is not tied to annual budget activities and its income can come from various sources: endowments, contributions, fund-raising campaigns, and similar non-tax-supported sources. In some cases, the capital budget is used as a vehicle for accounting for income from sources not intended to be part of the operating budget. Either way, it is used for expenditures not covered by the operating budget. If special-purpose grants are awarded under a government program or from foundation or other source, they are handled separately and are not part of either the capital or operating budget.

The operating budget has several variations, three of which—the line item, program, and performance—are most commonly used or discussed. In addition, one may encounter other less often used budget formats including lump-sum budgets, formula budgeting, and zero-base budgeting.

Lump-sum budgeting is the most primitive type of budget. Funding agencies ignore long-range plans and budget proposals in making this type of allocation. They might look at the previous year's allocation and add a small increase, or in a difficult year, might decrease the allocation. No goals, performance assessments, or plans for the next year(s) are reviewed in this method. Such an approach reinforces the status quo and reduces the time and attention the funding agency give to the decision. Unfortunately, in some situations, incremental changes and lump sum allocations continue to be the funding pattern for libraries/information centers. In such a situation, the library/information center director has the responsibility for developing and following an internal budget process, allocating funds internally based on internal planning.

At one point during the latter half of the twentieth century, some academic libraries experimented with formula-based budgets, which allocated funds based on a complex formula that took into account factors including size of collection and anticipated growth by discipline, size and type of student body, and faculty size. They would then calculate a budget figure that served as the basis for allocations. It projected a certain level of growth based on the formula and from this, a level of funding was proposed. As often happens with overly complex methods, formula budgeting collapsed under its own complexity and is no longer considered a useful tool.

The zero-base budget (ZBB) received considerable attention during the 1970s as a new planning and budgeting tool. The initial step in this process was to ask if the program under consideration was essential to meeting stated goals and objectives. If essential, a continuum of support from bare bones support to full support was devised. A continuum was developed for each essential library program. Once all programs had been developed along a cost continuum, programs were prioritized and the level of funding per program was determined by their priority level. If budget cuts occur during the year, one could reduce levels of funding or eliminate programs because priority decisions had already been made as to which programs were low priority. While a helpful planning tool in some instances, ZBB was too complex and too time-consuming for regular use.

Traditionally, most budgets were developed as *line item* or *object of expenditure* budgets. Each element of the budget—staff, books, periodicals, equipment, and so on—is listed and a dollar amount placed next to the item. The prior year's budget was often used as a guide to ensure that all items were included and that funding percentages were generally the same. In building the budget, each category is typically increased slightly to account for anticipated increases in such items as salaries, book prices, and overall inflationary increases. The line item budget is easy to construct, as it is based on the prior year's expenditures. It is also easy to cut, as the funding agency cannot see the effect of cutting a line such as salaries has on specific programs. The line item budget is not a planning document. Goals and objectives may be stated but it is difficult to envision how they will be carried out when allocations are presented in a line item format. It is a bit like describing a cake by listing the ingredients.

With the movement toward greater emphasis on planning for services, one of the tools developed for budgeting was the *program budget*. This type of budget begins with the identification of mission (who are we, why are we here, what do we do) and the formulation of goals and objectives to carry out the mission. These goals are then broken down into annual goals and objectives, and the budget is developed around library programs and functions aimed at meeting those goals and objectives. Reference services, circulation services, electronic information services, children's services and other functions are listed and for each function or program, a detailed line item budget is prepared. The same process is followed for technical services, maintenance support, and administrative overhead, which includes items such as staff training and public relations as well as salaries for managers. Maintenance support and administrative overhead can then be allocated to each program area based on the use of these services. To achieve a true program budget, library/information center programs are listed and are tied to goals and objectives. Then all costs related to that program are listed: staffing for the program; print and nonprint materials, including the costs of processing, storing, and circulating materials; administrative overhead; and any other costs. Many libraries/information centers cost out activities by function and then cost out particular programs more finely depending on the importance of the program or need, to determine if continuing the program is a good use of resources. The initial development of a program budget takes time, as one must determine the cost of staff, information resources, and other costs and then assign them to the program or function. Once prepared, the program budget provides a clear understanding of the programs and services the funding agency is supporting and a clear picture of what the library/information center does and what it costs. When funds are added to the budget, one can see what they are supporting; when funds are cut, the funding agency knows and the public knows what is being cut. More and more libraries/information centers are moving toward this budget format, partly because it is a much better indicator of what they do and what their priorities are. Most agencies require a standard format for submitting budget requests and it is most likely the line item format. It is not difficult to derive line item figures from a program budget, as each program has its line item budget and they can be combined to produce a traditional line item budget. Because the program budget is a much better indicator of what the library/information center actually does, the library/information center manager often prepares two budget presentations, one to meet the line item requirement and one to describe library activities.

The *planning program budgeting system* (PPBS) or *performance budget* is an extension of the program budget. Here, each library program or function must be justified to show how it contributes to the fulfilling of stated goals and objectives. A plan for continuous feedback and evaluation is developed so that library/information center managers can at any time determine the extent to which a program is meeting its objectives. Output measures (e.g., numbers of online searches, number of books circulated, number of attendees at a program) are developed and used to determine program effectiveness. Outcome measures that look at the ways in which library/information center programs and activities have changed attitudes, have increased educational levels, or otherwise affected the larger environment are being introduced as a means of determining the value of information services. As funding agencies move toward greater emphasis on outcomes that will indicate the extent to which a funded program has met expectations, more and more library/information centers will adopt measures that consider this question. While they may not move all the way to performance budgeting, they will develop assessment measures of some kind.

Budget Approval Cycle

The budget cycle can be divided into five parts: preparation, submission, approval by the legislature or other administrative body, execution, and audit. Each step consists of a set of formalized procedures, and formal models have been devised to carry them out. Budget preparation, as indicated earlier in the chapter, is a yearlong activity beginning with a review of existing goals and objectives. After desired modifications are made, a general statement of anticipated costs for the new year, a proposal for funding, is developed.

The budget year may not coincide with the calendar year. The federal government's budget year begins October 1; state budget years begin April 1, July 1, or some other date. Many academic institutions begin their budget year July 1. The library/information center year begins the same date as that of its parent organization. Using the appropriate date as the beginning of the budget year, library planners develop a budget calendar to guide their activities during the year. Dates assigned to specific activities should be compatible with other internal activities and should be in compliance with external regulations and guidelines. Libraries/information centers that receive federal funds such as those for special projects will need to set a separate calendar that is in compliance with federal budget dates for those funds. The same is true for any other funds received from agencies with calendars different from the calendar of the primary finding agency.

Prior to the beginning of the budget cycle, planning has taken place, goals and objectives have been reviewed, the budget document has been developed in its general outline, and necessary coding and analysis have been done. The budget director prepares estimate forms for each department so that each may report its request for support for the new year in a consistent manner. When the forms are completed, the budget director consolidates data and prepares a budget estimate for the organization. Once this has been done, a series of departmental hearings is set up so that department heads can discuss their budget estimates, justify costs, and present the case for funding the unit at a particular level. The budget is revised, based on information gained in the hearings, and the modified budget is submitted to the library/ information center director who reviews it and if needed revises it further, with the assistance of the budget director. It is then submitted to the next higher authority. In the case of the academic library, the budget would go to the institution's fiscal officer. In the school library media center, the budget would go to the building principal or, if part of a school district in which there is a library supervisor, the budget proposal would go to that individual who would prepare a systemwide budget and submit it to the district budget officer. The building principals and the district library supervisor would discuss the proposed budget prior to its submission. The public library budget would be submitted to the board of trustees who review it, make any changes they might wish, and then it is passed on to the municipal government fiscal officer. In other nonprofit environments, the budget would be sent to whatever body or individual is responsible for the library/information center. In the for-profit environment, it would go to a designated business officer.

The next step is usually a hearing in which library/information center representatives are given the opportunity to discuss their budget, the ways in which it carries out stated goals and objectives, and how it meshes with the overall university, municipal, school district, or corporate budget. For those whose funding comes directly from the tax base, there is usually a closed hearing and then a second open hearing in which citizens can question budget items, can support or object to library programs, and can exercise their roles as citizens. After the hearings, the budget is again reviewed and perhaps revised and an allocation is determined based on anticipated revenues. If revenues fall below expectations, budget figures may be reduced at a later date to comply with actual revenues.

The wise library administrator maintains continuing cordial relations with government officials, with budget officers, and with others in the governing agency who make financial decisions. A consistent effort is made to represent the library and its purpose, needs, and accomplishments. It is most important to have a good working relationship with those who make funding decisions and to know how to work with them. When making budget presentations, a carefully planned presentation includes an overview of goals and objectives, a mention of new programs and reporting on any programs to be deleted, plus some information on past performance. A brief statement of resources requested completes the formal presentation. Those conducting hearings will have heard or will hear similar presentations from other units. They will appreciate well-organized, to the point, brief presentations. Library/information center representatives should be prepared to answer any specific questions. Hearings are partly informational, partly political, and only in small part financial. The process provides an opportunity for open discussion of ways in which the library/information center contributes to the good of its community. Libraries are at some disadvantage in this process in that they are rarely the top priority of those allocating funds. In the public sector, fire and police protection and some social programs receive more attention; in the academic sector, direct faculty and student teaching and research needs have strong advocates; and in the private sector, activities that have a more direct impact on the bottom line usually prevail. On the other hand, libraries/information services are seen by most funding agencies as important to a community and they will do their best to provide support.

Throughout the year, the budget officer prepares regular reports indicating how funds are being used. At the end of the fiscal year, a summary statement is provided that includes both fiscal information and a statement showing the extent to which goals and objectives were met. An audit of records by an outside agency on a regular, not necessarily annual, basis ensures that appropriate accounting principles and practices have been followed. The auditor, who should be experienced in conducting audits in the nonprofit sector, may also make recommendations for improving the way in which records are kept. Regular audits ensure that the organization conforms to accepted standards and that it can account for monies entrusted to it.

The planning cycle, often called the management control cycle, is a continuous process running from planning and budgeting, on to operating and accounting, and ending with reporting and analysis before moving again to planning. Getting and spending money in support of a complex set of services requires both political and managerial skills that are learned over time. Success in these activities ensures the viability and growth of the library and its services.

Consortial Agreements

Libraries of all types have found it financially beneficial to band together in consortial agreements with publishers and other information providers in order to negotiate prices for online databases and other services. Libraries can negotiate a better price for online service when they work together with a single vendor and the vendor gains a wider market for the service. In working together, libraries share information on the prices asked by publishers and are in a better position to negotiate a fair price. This is particularly helpful to the small libraries that cannot, on their own, afford the range of databases and other resources their users expect to access. Some libraries have developed consortial arrangements to negotiate subscription services. As a stop-gap solution to deal with rising prices of periodicals and databases, consortial agreements made with vendors is providing libraries with time to deal with the underlying problem of rising costs and increasingly tight budgets. In addition to arrangements with publishers, libraries have joined together to provide such services as centralized cataloging or to manage a book storage facility. These arrangements may be suggested by an already existing library grouping, such as public library systems within a state or region, academic libraries within a system, or other organization, or may be suggested by library directors in a region. The arrangements are fluid and may last for the life of a contract or for several years. In the budgeting process, each arrangement must fit into the planning for the library and must show that it contributes to the goals of the library.

Planning and Budgeting in a No-Growth Environment

Depending on the economic conditions, planning and budgeting takes place in a growth environment in which resources are available and programs can thrive or in a no-growth environment in which programs are cut and some may be eliminated. It is for this reason that libraries/information centers must identify their core activities. When budgets must be cut, decisions are made that preserve core activities such as maintaining the information resource and providing specific services. Any budget cut will affect people and services and therefore library/information services managers need to anticipate to the extent possible the implications of any budget cut. Library managers should, in their planning, identify programs that can be reduced, put on hold, or eliminated if adequate resources are not available. The library/information center, as part of a larger institution, makes its own strategic planning decisions but makes them in the context of reduced or realigned goals of the parent institution. This reinforces the fact that library/information center managers must have a wide understanding of the interdependence of information services with other aspects of the institution of which they are a part.

Funding for public higher education has to a large degree shifted from state support to support from the institution, family, and the student. This shift began in the late 1990s and continued to accelerate with changes in student loan and other support criteria. Funding for academic support services including library service comes less and less from governmental sources, a trend that appears as if it will continue. There has been a conscious decision by state governments to move from state-supported higher education to state-assisted higher education, a move that has resulted in steadily increasing tuition. The extent to which these changes limit access to higher education by those unable to pay is still in question.[2] At the state level, when the economy is tight, there is a great deal of emphasis on how to cut state spending. In the case of higher education, one can no longer rely on the high level of support once provided. Legislators tend to support programs based on political interests of their party or those of their immediate constituency rather than considering overall programmatic concerns. While a strong residual support for higher education continues, many conflicting needs such as those for health care and safety are in competition with the same limited resources.[3]

Internal Budget Management

The internal budget management process, like the external process, has its own political interactions. Within the organization, there are individuals with specific ideas about the organization and how its services should be funded. Each may have a constituency and it is often necessary to discuss issues with these internal leaders until a satisfactory decision is reached. Each individual involved in decision making is influenced by a number of factors: social interaction with peers and those outside the organization, the ever-present concern for the availability of sufficient funds to conduct an activity as one would like, and attitudes toward building and maintaining the increasingly interactive electronic information environment. These and other variables are processed through the individual's personal and professional value system. Each individual has a different view of change and has a different level of power in the organization. Discussions are often influenced by personal factors rather than data.

DATA ANALYSIS

As library management has become increasingly participatory and as goal setting has become more and more a group activity rather than the decisions of the director, there is an increased need for all staff to be knowledgeable about data needed for decision making and the ways in which it can be used. Basic planning data is available from library records; data is gathered from management information systems, for example, circulation statistics, library attendance, status of the book stock, and financial records. The data gained in this way is mostly in the form of raw data and it must be analyzed in order to answer questions such as how much does it cost to put a book on the shelf or to answer a question from print resources or from electronic sources. A number of techniques have been devised that take data and turn it into information to answer questions.

Unit Cost

One of the most heavily used of these techniques is unit cost. Cost is defined as a monetary measure of the amount of resources needed for a particular purpose. A unit cost is the amount of resources used to produce one unit for a particular purpose. To calculate a unit cost, one divides the total cost of producing a specified number of units by the number of units produced. The resulting figure represents the average cost of production per unit.

$$\text{Unit Cost} = \frac{\text{Cost of Producing N Units}}{\text{N}}$$

Using the unit cost, for example, of processing a book in year one, it is then possible to see if the cost increases in year two. One can also compare one's unit costs with those of similar agencies to see if one's costs are in line with practices elsewhere. It is also possible to vary the ways in which a book is processed to see if there is a less costly way of doing the job. Unit costs are also the basis for cost analysis.

In developing unit costs, it is necessary to identify all costs involved in an activity. Because an information service is highly labor intensive, personnel costs are typically the largest component of unit costs. To identify the salary component of an activity, both wages and benefits are factored in. Of the approximately forty hours per week for which an individual is paid, time is used for vacation, sick days, and for time used during the day for non-job-related activities. Unit costs are therefore more accurately calculated based on the actual number of hours worked plus benefits. The actual productive hourly cost may be as much as one-third higher than the hourly wage when all other considerations are factored in. If the hourly wage of a reference specialist is $40.00, the resulting wage may be closer to $50.00 per hour when benefits, taxes, and other considerations are included in the calculation. The costs of supervision, training, staff meetings, meetings with vendors, and other job-related activities are added to the labor cost.

To obtain this type of data, it is necessary to conduct cost studies in which each staff member indicates how she or he spends work time each day. Being asked to report activities for each fifteen-minute period over a specified period, usually a week, is time-consuming. Staff may resent the added activity and may also assume that they are being observed by a manager suspicious that they are not doing their job. It is important to show staff that a time study is beneficial to them in that it may answer their questions about why they are working so hard and accomplishing less than they would like. The time study may show that a staff member has been given too many tasks to complete or is doing tasks that could be taken over by a lower-paid employee. The job description the staff member is working under may be out-of-date and no longer as relevant as it once as. It is often the job analysis aspect of the time study that is most directly useful to staff. While a level of assessment is present in the time study, it should be downplayed and time on task and the average time it takes to complete a task should be emphasized.

Depreciation

In addition to staff costs, depreciation is an important component of unit costs. All equipment—from desks and chairs to workstations—have a usable lifespan. Workstations and their related software have a brief lifespan while furnishings last longer. For accounting purposes, a percentage of the replacement cost of an item should be part of the cost of performing a task. A number of models to calculate depreciation exist with, straight line and declining balance the most common. The simplest is straight line depreciation, which is calculated in the following manner:

$$\text{Annual amount} = \frac{\text{purchase price minus salvage value of item when replaced}}{\text{number of years between time item was purchased and when replaced}}$$

For example, a laptop computer when new cost $2,000 and will be replaced in three years. Assuming a salvage value of $200, annual depreciation is $600.

$$\frac{\$2,000 - \$200}{3} = \frac{\$1800}{3} \text{ or } \$600 \text{ per year}$$

Straight line depreciation assumes that the laptop will decrease in value an equal amount each year when actually it declines in value faster in the first year. Automobiles are an example of items where the declining balance approach is the appropriate approach. Depreciation is high the first year or two, then declines slowly and levels off toward the end of its useful life. In neither case is the cost of inflation factored in, nor is the declining cost of computing and telecommunications technology. The cost of replacing equipment or book stock will usually be more than the original purchase price. Hence, depreciation figures are used as estimates rather than as firm figures.

Other Program Costs

When identifying the total cost of a program, the cost of leased equipment and subscription services are included in the cost if they are used to perform the service under study. Any parts of a service that have been contracted out are included in overall costs. Costs of supplies—paper, pens, discs, and so on—are added, as is the cost of storing supplies. The building or part of the building in which the library/information center is located is an additional cost item. Cost per square foot of replacing the building, assuming a twenty-five-year life span, plus per square foot costs of insurance, maintenance, heating and cooling, and all other building-related costs are calculated to reach an annual per square foot cost. This cost is calculated annually and used for a variety of purposes. If the building is leased or rented, per square foot costs are based on annual rental and any costs not included in the rental agreement. For the unit cost of an activity, the number of square feet used is multiplied by the maintenance cost per square foot. When one is calculating the cost of housing a book collection, this is a major component.

Administrative overhead is a combination of administrative salaries, staff training, public relations, and other aspects of administrative activity that affect the organization. A portion of overhead is assigned to each program depending on the size of program and any special attention the program may receive.

Fixed and Variable Costs

Costs can be fixed or variable. A *fixed cost* is one that does not change regardless of the amount of use of an item or service. For example, having a library open for a specified number of hours will have a fixed cost regardless of the number of people using its services. Showing a movie has the same cost whether ten or a hundred people view it. *Variable costs* are those that change depending upon the number of activities involved or the number of people using a service. For example, a student training lab activity in the use of a new software package would be a fixed cost as the lab and terminals are available and have the same cost regardless of the number of users. But if the trainer charges a fee per registered student, that is a variable cost as it is dependent on the number of users.

It is stressed in accounting literature that valid unit costs must be derived from sufficient information to permit statistical analysis. This data is collected within the normal operating activities and not from a test situation. Further, the cost of the activity must be related to the actual product resulting from the expenditure, and this can be done only when real situations are studied. Calculating unit costs allows us to determine the actual and full cost of an activity. In collecting cost data, the manager reviews each element of the cost and may find that some inputs need to be revised—for example, too much staff time is devoted to the activity or too many supplies are being used. These staff and resource allocation issues are positive side benefits of conducting the cost study. The manager revises the staff time allocated to the activity and enters the cost of the appropriate amount of time. Once a unit cost is developed based on the appropriate level of inputs and the actual cost of components, it can serve as a figure against which comparisons can be made over time and across similar organizations. If the manager wishes to vary the way in which a task is performed by changing a routine or adopting new software, the original unit cost can be used as a benchmark against which unit costs of the innovation can be compared.

A basic premise of calculating unit cost is that all elements of a task can be identified and costed. While this may be true when one costs out a product such as the unit cost of a chair or a tool, how an activity or how much of an activity is performed during a period calculation is less specific in a service environment where customer demands may change. Unit costs are a good approximation of actual costs—good enough to be used in budget calculations and good enough to be used to make decisions about the preferred way to conduct an activity.

Cost Accounting

Cost accounting is the identification of the cost of providing a specific service. Although its focus is financial, cost accounting is a management tool for the entire organization, the purpose of which is to connect effectiveness to cost in order to make comparisons between and among similar activities so that the manager can select the best approach. Studies to determine the actual cost of programs and services have long been a staple of the for-profit sector and for a long time were resisted by many in the not-for-profit sector who argued that one could not put a price on the interchange between client and professional. This attitude was gradually eroded as it became necessary for service agencies to start determining the cost of their services. While the value of interpersonal interchange cannot be costed, personnel and resource costs can be identified.

The development of a cost analysis program for a library/information center follows generally accepted accounting guidelines but requires adjustment to the specific situation. Because of the need to develop a program on site to meet the specific situation, a staff member or someone else who knows the organization well, assisted by an external consultant, will most likely provide the best mix of expertise. Within the organization, one person should be responsible for cost analysis activities. To conduct a cost analysis, the first step is to identify all current library activities. Activities are then grouped into major task categories and broad functions are identified. Tasks are then assigned to appropriate functions. Organizational units for which costs are to be calculated are established. Production units produced by the library are defined and equated to standard units. A computer program is developed using the above categorizations in order to generate and provide data regularly.

As an example, Mitchell and associates identified four units within the academic library:

- The *processing production unit* in which the basic unit was volumes added. The tasks and times involved in adding one volume can be calculated. The resulting processing time figure can be converted to volumes added figures. Other items being processed (such as film, tapes, and documents) received similar attention and are then converted to volumes added equivalents.
- The *reference service production unit* is based on the average time for each traditional question category: directional, consultation, and equipment.
- Additional production units include *interlibrary loan* and *circulation*, which have the cost of one unit circulated as the basic unit.

- The *bibliographic instruction production unit* used the number of individuals instructed as the basic unit.

Although the work was done some time ago, it continues to provide a useful guide.[4] Within the units, tasks will have changed due to changes in technology and approaches to the activity but the units themselves still work well.

When one groups activities under tasks, variances between tasks are described and the actual performance expectation for the task becomes apparent. Tasks are written down as static and their performance may change over time in response to changing needs and personal preferences. The tasks as initially envisioned may be too theoretical to translate into performance. A great deal of adaptation is usually needed to merge activities and tasks. As noted earlier, cost activity has major implications in other management areas such as job descriptions and work flow patterns. Conducting cost studies has been seen by many libraries and information centers as a useful management tool. A number of academic libraries have conducted cost studies either to identify costs or to develop cost-flow studies to build the case for increased budget support. The cost study is a means of more precisely identifying the effects of inadequate funding.

The library/information center is a cost center within the larger organization and has the same requirements for accountability as all other cost centers. Because approximately two thirds of the library/information center budget is typically spent on personnel, the bulk of the data needed to justify cost is related to staff costs. Cost studies may identify activities with unusually high costs and these activities may be adjusted to reduce costs or eliminated if of low benefit. If tasks are redesigned to reduce costs, workloads may then change, departmental organizations may be revised, or other personnel decisions may be made with the intention of streamlining activities and thus cutting costs. Information derived from cost studies is also useful in forecasting; with an analysis of current economic conditions and possible trends, this provides useful financial planning data.

Cost-Benefit Analysis

The primary objective of cost-benefit analysis is "to determine the economic feasibility of developing alternatives to the current system. It insures that the user receives the best possible return for the investment."[5] Cost-benefit analysis is a method by which one can identify the costs of a program or activity and the benefits of each alternative. Responding to the question "Is the product or service worth the price?" is objective in terms of dollar figures and subjective in terms of values. The question is answered in terms of cost input and benefit output. A number of intangibles are part of the cost-benefit process and though they cannot be assigned a direct dollar value, they represent aspects of the financial health of the organization as well as the image it projects.

Financial decisions made by a library/information center can have an impact on the image it projects. Does the library seem to favor unduly one client group over another? How rapidly does it bring technological innovation to public services? Is the building well maintained or does it have an unkempt appearance because insufficient funds are spent on maintenance? There may well be valid reasons for making specific decisions. Whatever they are, the decisions themselves and their collective impact will label the library/information center as innovative and forward thinking, traditional, or somewhere in between. Financial decisions affect staff morale. For example, the staff member who has worked hard to design a program or to support and improve an existing program will respond positively if the program receives additional support. The impact of staff satisfaction or dissatisfaction contributes to a general staff attitude that affects both internal services and attitude toward and treatment of patrons. When funding decisions are made that staff recognize as wise allocations of funds, they will support that allocation even though they may wish more funds were available. When decisions are made that appear to be based on favoritism or in support of a pet program, staff will rightly object. The library/information center manager needs to have cost figures available that show the reasons for specific decisions so that those reasons can be shared with staff or other stakeholders who are concerned about specific allocation decisions. The extent to which funds are allocated in a fair and businesslike manner will, in large part, determine the extent to which staff support the administration. One of the ways the library's priority in the larger organization is determined is by the level of resources it receives. Similarly, within the organization, staff will assess their program's priority by the support it receives.

Because information service results are largely intangibles (the quality of information, the intellectual effort required, the uses of the information acquired, and the client's level of satisfaction), they are difficult to measure in dollars. But it is possible and necessary to use dollar figures as one way of measuring information services and setting priorities. Measuring the cost of traditional services may put some at risk as being too costly for the benefit obtained while others will be seen to be economical. Cost-benefit studies are also useful in identifying levels of service. How much information does a client want or need? Do different categories of clients require different levels or types of service? Cost benefit has been defined as "the ratio of the amount of money collected from customers to the total funding for the information service."[6] This definition assumes that some sort of charge is attached to each service, and if the system is to be self-supporting, income must equal cost.

In the nonprofit sector, cost benefit is calculated differently. The costs of an activity are identified and a decision is then made as to whether the cost to the taxpayer or other funding source is too high. If so, reductions in cost are considered or the program may be eliminated. Or because of overriding social or educational benefit, the program may be continued regardless of cost. Remedial educational services are often in this category. They are very expensive, as there is a great deal of individualized attention but they are a necessary component of educational services and are supported regardless of cost.

In the for-profit sector, libraries/information centers must justify their presence based on their contribution to company profits. In this environment, information service is typically classified as overhead and its services are generally available rather than being tied to a particular project. Those who have conducted studies identifying the project cost of information for a specific research activity have provided cost estimates. Although estimates of specific projects for information support can be made, combining them does not necessarily provide an accurate picture of the library/information center and its overall benefits. As current cost decisions are carried out in future environments, projections must attempt to take into account environmental factors over which one has little or no control, such as declines in state appropriations that could reduce budgets already approved or inflation in book and periodical costs that exceed projections. Declines in college enrollment or a move of population from the public library's service area would change its support base as well as its user workload.

Mason differentiated between the private and social costs of an activity.[7] A private cost is what a person or organization gives in order to receive a good or service. A social cost is what society must give up to permit the individual to receive the good or service. In many cases, the private and social costs are similar. For example, the cost of a book to a buyer may be equivalent to producing the book—the consumer has paid full price for the item. In other instances, such as federal health care programs, society subsidizes the program and the consumer pays for only part of the service. Information services in the not-for-profit sector are in the second category; they are subsidized by taxes and only a small amount (if anything) is directly paid by the user. This is a reflection of the definition of the library as a public good in that it is something society is willing to subsidize in order to enhance the social environment. Costs associated with providing information services through publicly supported libraries/information centers are the resources given up by society so that the service can be offered.

Benefits are measured by willingness to pay. There is little data on what society or the individual is willing to give up in order to have information service. The ability and willingness to pay can be determined in part by the priority level library services receive when budgets of the university or college, the school district, the municipality, or other agency are determined. A high value may be set on the service but there may be an unwillingness to pay. When fees are charged to cover partial costs of making information available, there is typically a sharp drop in use. In developing this cost model, Mason indicated that it is difficult to separate the value of the service that provides information from the value of the information. He concluded that there is no way to measure the actual social benefits of either information or information services, although it is generally accepted that those benefits exist.

In allocating resources for libraries and their information services, who benefits? Does one group benefit more than another? Is the group that benefits the group that pays? In the case of public library service, the typical user is described as middle income, middle class. Since most of the support for the public library comes from the local tax base, is the middle-income family paying its share? What about residents who are taxed but do not use the service? The response to these questions is that the taxpayer derives general benefits from taxes but not in equal measure from all services. Library service is a collective good; once available, it is available to all to use as little or much as each wishes.

Cost Effectiveness

Cost benefit seeks to measure the benefit of a particular activity to an individual, an organization, or society and to relate this benefit to the actual cost of a service. Decisions are then made based both on the cost of the service and on its benefits. The library manager selects the option that best balances the two. Cost effectiveness is a measure of the extent to which the service objectives of the organization are met. For example, if the library manager is concerned by the level of book circulation and its cost, a cost-effectiveness approach would focus on increasing circulation and reducing unit costs. The cost-benefit approach would have similar objectives but would pay greater attention to staff and clientele attitudes and to how the service is performed. Cost and effectiveness are objective statements that can be measured. Benefit is subjective and does not lend itself easily to measurement.

Model Building

A model is a simple version of a complex reality. Information services and the organizations that provide the services are very complex and it is often helpful to design a model so that one can see what the major components are and how they interrelate. In designing a model, major components are identified and secondary elements are set aside. In this way, the basic elements are highlighted and it is easier to see how they are organized. Planners who use models as a way of educating their staff and others they work with often use models as analogies. For example, the teamwork needed to win a basketball game can be a useful way of demonstrating the need to have a plan and a leader and to carry out the plan, in order to achieve an objective in the library setting. Or the listing of ingredients needed to make a cake can be a useful analogy for developing a line item or program budget. As long as the analogy is understandable to the audience, it is a beneficial tool.

The model is also a useful framework for developing a checklist of factors to be considered in decision making. The model itself can be in the form of a flowchart, a matrix, or a narrative. Software for model building is available that makes it easy to manipulate the variables in the model. In this way, one can see the overall effect of changing one or more variables.

Cost-Behavior Analysis

Cost-behavior analysis is the projection of cost behavior into the future. What will be the likely cost of operating a branch in a particular neighborhood? Where will the money come from? Will the projected branch meet community needs for five years? For ten years? To do this, one must project client needs, income expectations, and the range and projected costs of services to be provided. A computer-based decision package allows one to input current costs, current community demographics, and a listing of services that will be offered when the branch is opened. Using this and related data, one can anticipate expected first-year costs. If one projects the next year's costs using the same variables and applying data from trends such as inflation and economic growth projections, an estimate for the next year(s) can be determined. Libraries, as with other service activities funded by the larger organization of which they are a part, typically manage their activities based on past performance rather than on the present activity or future projections. "If libraries are to do the best job of managing information in the public interest, they must know the costs of strategies designed to pass on this information, they must be prepared to identify, measure, and control costs so that the results they want can be afforded, and the quantity and quality of information they believe is appropriate to their clientele is available given the financial resources available."[8]

FINANCIAL CONTROL

Reporting expenditures and accounting for the funds entrusted to the library serves a number of purposes: financial, evaluative, and political. These activities complete the planning cycle in that results are used to evaluate, modify, and refine the plan as represented by the budget. It sets the stage for the next planning cycle.

The Reporting System

The financial information system is designed to meet a variety of needs. Budgeting systems—program budgeting, performance budgeting—developed in recent decades have the improvement of management of resources as a primary objective. Long-range planning for services, estimation of cost of programs, and development of line item budgets for each program are required. Evaluation in relation to objectives is built into the system. Once the budget is approved, the funding authority sets an appropriation level that is then adopted and serves as the upper limit at which the library can spend money. The financial management system is set up to ensure that funds are spent on the goods and services for which they were allocated, and that those individuals spending public funds are doing so responsibly. The financial management system is set up to maintain control of expenditures and to facilitate evaluation. Evaluation data is then used to modify the long-range plan and can also be used to modify objectives in the current budget cycle. The financial management system should also provide data in a form to be shared with external groups. The format of reports will vary in amount and complexity depending on the audience. In all instances, reports must be accurate, clearly written, and easy to understand.

Accounting practices and reporting systems have similar components regardless of the environments in which they function. They are regulated by standards imposed by groups responsible for uniform accounting practices such as the Financial Accounting Standards Board of the American Institute of Certified Public Accountants. There are different emphases in application to the profit and to the nonprofit environments. A nonprofit is "an economic entity that provides *without profit to the owners* a service beneficial to society and that is financed by equity interests that cannot be sold or traded by individuals or profit seeking entities."[9] Nonprofit organizations may be privately supported and may or may not be self-sustaining. Those that are involuntarily supported by government entities include public colleges, public libraries and other public information entities, and public schools. These are not self-supporting and require government subsidy. Depending on their governance structure, libraries can fall in either category. Nonprofits may be controlled by a voting membership or by representatives of the taxpayers. Decisions made in all nonprofit organizations are intended to meet the general needs of the community. The function of the reporting system is to keep the public regularly informed as to how resources are being used and what the results are.

Reporting Standards

Accounting principles have been published for several types of nonprofit agencies and they tend to be fairly consistent. State statutes governing reporting are less so. Several states have either no practices prescribed by law or practices inconsistent with those approved by the American Institute of Certified Public Accountants (AICPA), or by the National Council of Governmental Accounting. A number of audit guides have been published by federal agencies to be used for reporting on federal funds received. The result of this less-than-clear set of directives is that a number of nonprofits have financial systems that developed outside approved standards. Some are rarely audited by certified public accountants who understand the nonprofit environment. While this situation is steadily improving, there is still some divergence.

Users of the Reporting System

Users of reporting systems are interested in knowing the extent to which objectives have been achieved. To the extent possible, both accounting and reporting systems should be designed and developed to make information on the financial condition of the organization available and to serve as a means of monitoring it. The amount of information presented and the format used can depend on the audience.

Tax-supported agencies are required to complete standardized report forms that may or may not reflect their categories of expenditure. The forms may have been in place for decades and may not reflect current expenditure categories or may lump many items under one category—for example, a line for books but no reporting space for discs, periodicals, documents, online information resources, and other information materials. In the income section, there may be a category for gifts but none for government grants. When the library's income and expenditures are locked into pigeonholes that do not fit, it is impossible to report with any accuracy. The only viable solution is to report twice—once to reflect actual income and expenditures and once to meet the requirements of the parent organization.

Regardless of the final product or audience, all reports contain similar information. An introductory section describes the organization and how it reports its activities. The financial section provides a summary comparison of operating budgets over several years so that expenditure and income trends can be seen. A statistical section includes a review of income and expenditure from all sources, changes in level of support, and the degree to which levels of support meet any stated standards.

External groups (city manager, board of trustees, board of education, university administration, etc.) as policymakers need to know the overall health of the organization in general terms. What has been accomplished with funds provided? What was not accomplished due to limited funds? What could be accomplished in specific areas with additional funds? This audience expects information in measurable terms indicating how funds were used and what was accomplished. Reports should show relationships between effort and resources and between expenditures and their results. The amount of information provided is limited to what is needed for policy decisions and planning. These groups expect brief reports and are not well served by reports that are long and detailed.

Internal managers need the same information and, in addition, they require detailed data on daily operations. Each department head needs full information on how resources in that department were used and what the results were. The reporting activity and evaluative process are integral parts of the program and performance budgeting systems, and the resulting detailed reports are useful to this group. This information in a slightly generalized form for each department and program provides the director and administrative staff with what they need to plan and monitor services.

Taxpayers and other constituent groups, including those who do business with libraries such as jobbers and contractors, have a right to know how funds were spent. The library must continually demonstrate that it is worthy of support, and one way to do so is to publish annual reports showing the ways in which resources have been used to provide information services. Data provided to this group should respond to policy questions in terms that are as quantifiable as possible. How many people were served? What kinds of services were provided? What is the size and composition of the information resources and how are they kept up to date? What is the level of professional expertise available to users? Specific programs lend themselves to specific answers of who was served, with what resources, and how much did it cost. Overall questions of levels of service for money spent can be answered more generally, yet sufficiently for the purpose. This form of reporting is intended to inform the general public. It is accurate, informative, and is used both for reporting and as a public relations document to show the public the value to them of library service.

Accounting

Accounting is the technical aspect of recording quantitative data about income and expenditures of an organization, a way of recording its assets and liabilities over a period of time. It is "an information system for maintaining financial records of an organization and for communicating significant fiscal events both within and without the organization."[10] Financial accounting is the basis for developing reports. Financial accounting has been called scorekeeping—keeping track of where money comes from and where it goes. A number of terms are used in accounting practices, some of which have been mentioned previously in the chapter, but a review here is useful.

- *Cost accounting* is the art of determining the cost of a product, a service, or activity. It is used for budgeting, cost analysis, comparison with standards, and general comparisons with actual and historical costs.
- *Historical cost* is the cost of an item or service at the time of purchase for use and is the basic figure used to record assets and expenditures.
- *Standard cost* is the determination of what costs for an identifiable output or activity should be. It can be the result of detailed study or an informed estimate. It serves as a measure against which to review historical costs.
- *Unit cost* is the cost of providing a specified unit of service or product and is the most common way of expressing cost.

Accrual and Cash Accounting

The use of accounting data to identify actual costs, evaluate services, and compare costs in delivery of service over time and among units is essential to both planning and decision making. Accrual accounting, a way to report liabilities such as accounts payable and assets in addition to cash, gives a more accurate statement of worth than cash accounting, which records cash transactions only. In accrual accounting, when an item is ordered or service contracted, an obligation or encumbrance is placed against the appropriate line in the budget. Funds are obligated through a purchase order or the signing of a contract. As tax-supported organizations typically operate under an annual appropriation, obligations are made so that they can be paid within the fiscal year. An encumbrance becomes an expenditure when goods are received, billed, and paid for. Liabilities are amounts owed as a result of expenditure activities. Whatever is owed outside the organization is a liability. Long-term debt such as building renovation is usually recorded separately from short-term liability, which is recorded in the general operating budget. Long-term liability is usually part of the accounting for the capital budget.

Agencies funded on an annual basis may not be allowed to save funds from their budget in one year and hold them over to another year to purchase expensive items with long-term use, such as equipment or furnishings. Fiscal policy in many government units states that expenditure must equal income and tax rates are set with this in mind. The enforcement of this requirement prevents the organization from saving resources to make expensive purchases that don't fit in the annual budget. In some states, this has been relaxed and agencies are allowed to carry over a portion of their budget so they can save for expensive items.

Depreciation Accounting

This process takes into account the wear and tear on equipment, buildings, and other long-term items. It reports their worth in relation to decreasing value. While experts agree that there should be an informal record of the declining value of equipment and other long-term use items, some do not see that depreciation accounting is useful for nonprofits. They say that since service operations do not make a profit, depreciation accounting has no purpose. Since depreciation is a means of charging the use of fixed assets against revenues, and since libraries do not produce revenues beyond charges for some specific services, they see this as a pointless activity. Nonprofit agencies are recorded as operating on a year-to-year basis. Trying to mesh year-to-year funding activities with multiyear depreciation is difficult. Those who support depreciation accounting contend that there is the need to report accurately the organization's assets so that one can plan for replacement in an orderly fashion. If this is not part of formal reporting, an informal record of depreciation should be kept.

Inflation Accounting

Accounting and reporting are based on the principle of historical cost (cost at time of purchase). The effects of inflation on purchasing power or current value of assets is not reflected in this type of reporting. There are a number of ways to deal with the differences between historical costs and current costs. The first is to adjust historical dollar amounts to reflect changes in general price levels. Changes can be stated in terms of units of money or in general purchasing power spent for a particular item such as a book or journal. Adjustment of historical dollar amounts is based on the assumption that there is relative stability in the size of the measurement unit, but this may not be the case since the purchasing price of the dollar may not be stable. One way to deal with this is to report historical costs in terms of general purchasing power rather than in dollar costs.

A second way to account for inflation is through current pricing of specific items. This is less satisfactory than calculating a general price at the same rate, and pricing of specific items can skew results. Books and periodical costs have increased rapidly during some periods while the costs of some computing equipment has decreased. Reporting individually on some items does not provide a usable overall view.

A third type of inflation accounting is to record the current price of specific items and adjust for changes in the general price level. This method is based on the premise that money has value in relation to what it can buy and the historical amounts need to be adjusted to reflect current purchasing power. In order to restate historical dollars in dollars of uniform purchasing power for the current reporting period, adjustments are made in relation to an index that reflects changes in the purchasing price of the dollar. The historical amount and the date it was fixed must be known. The historical amount is then multiplied by a fraction, the numerator of which is the index for the date of the historical amount. The cost of an asset acquired for $10,000 during year five can be adjusted to reflect year fifteen dollars in the following manner:

$$\frac{\text{Index at end of year 15} \times \$10,000}{\text{Index at date of acquisition (year 5)}} = \text{cost of asset in end of year 15 dollars}$$

The most regularly consulted index is the Gross National Product (GNP) Implicit Price Deflator. If it is not available for the period under review, the most recent index is used. The reporting sheet resulting from this exercise will show both historical costs and adjusted costs reflecting current value. There is general agreement that inflation distorts reporting and that some form of supplemental reporting is needed to reflect the effects of inflation on both income and expenditure.

Fund Accounting

Income is typically derived from a number of sources. For many libraries, tax revenues are the major source. Other sources include involuntary contributions (fines and fees) and voluntary contributions (gifts and grants). Income from federal and state sources is listed separately, as is any income from investments. Each source of income must be listed and if there are limitations on use, that is noted. If there are no limitations on income; those funds go into the general operating fund. Special purpose funds that cannot go into general operating are treated separately, with income and expenditure reported in accordance with terms of the fund. A fund has been defined by the National Committee on Governmental Accounting as "an independent fiscal and accounting entity with a self-balancing set of accounts recording cash and/or other resources together with all related liabilities, obligations, reserves, and equities which are segregated for the purpose of carrying on specific activities or attaining certain objectives in accordance with special regulations, restrictions, or limitations."[11]

A fund can be a special purpose grant, a bequest, a gift, or other income. All funds have specific requirements governing expenditures. Some are to be used for specific purposes while others are to be invested and the interest made available for use. The manager is legally and morally committed to spend the funds only for the specified use. Each fund has separate accounting and reporting and its identity is maintained at all times. Federal or state program grants are treated in the same manner. The income statement for the library consists of two sections: one listing income that goes into the general operating budget and the other listing all special purpose funds and any income derived from them during the period of the income statement. If the library has a capital fund, its income is credited to it and it is maintained separately from the operating budget.

Accountability

Boards of trustees, library directors, and other managers are accountable to their larger organization and through them to the legislative bodies that provide funds. They are required to comply with all laws, regulations, and policies. Managers are also accountable for the ways in which they use resources. Efficiency in the use of resources can be measured through output (increased output with stable input), through input (vary input until the least amount of resources is required to achieve desired output), through a mix of the two, or through the concept of optimal efficiency. Optimal efficiency is the level of efficiency where the quality and quantity of benefits are at the highest possible level given the limitations on available resources. Optimal efficiency is program oriented and thus useful to planners.

Libraries are also measured by levels of performance. Criteria for performance are often part of the goals set for the organization. Three types of indicators of accomplishment are set: operations, impact, and social. Operations indicators are output measures stating in nonfinancial terms what was produced as a result of money spent; for example, circulation data, materials acquired and processed, or reference questions answered. These indicators show the amount of work that has been done. Program impact indicators are directly related to the extent to which the program has met a public need. They are a combination of operations indicators and measures of accomplishment and are therefore both quantitative and qualitative. The availability of added reserve materials to support a course for undergraduates may have increased test scores, or special instruction in the use of a database may have increased student learning, which is then reflected in test scores. Social indicators are even more qualitative and reflect changes in social conditions resulting from a library program. Managing activities with a view to their value often requires an attitude change. Managing to get the best use of the dollar is part of the manager's responsibility. Managing for value and impact is also important.

One use of measures of effectiveness is to compare one's data with that of similar organizations. While this may be helpful, the resulting comparisons should be viewed with skepticism. Too many variables in the way data is collected, ways in which programs are funded and administered, and the differing environments for service are barriers to a set of data that can have useful comparisons.

ALTERNATIVE SOURCES OF FUNDING

As tax-based support of libraries becomes less and less assured and as costs continue to increase, nonprofits have moved steadily toward greater emphasis on seeking alternate sources of funding. Deans of academic units within the university—including the dean of libraries, directors of public libraries, managers of information programs, and others involved in providing information services—are expected, as part of their job, to seek funds for their programs. Library managers have found themselves in the role of fundraisers. In the small library, this may consist largely of identifying members of the community who have an interest in library programs and activities and in maintaining close contact with them. It may also include the need to work with established community groups willing to work with libraries. Directors of all sizes and types of libraries will seek out foundations, representatives of industry in the area, and other potential sources of funds. Larger libraries, and often academic libraries, will often have full-time fund raisers to assist in presenting the library's programs to the public and in identifying potential sources of funds.

Many libraries have a Friends of the Library association consisting of members of the community who wish to support the library. Friends promote the library and raise money for the library through special events and other community activities. The library/information center director, as part of regular duties, maintains good relationships with the Friends and other support groups, keeping them informed of library activities and indicating specific activities that they might wish to support. Fund-raising is a positive activity, stressing the benefits of contributing to the library.

Gifts from Business and Industry

Typically, businesses that reside in a community support selected local community programs as part of the cost of doing business. Companies such as IBM or Microsoft have established philanthropic units that announce areas of interest and concern they are willing to support. Some companies have developed national and international foundations, such as the Ford Foundation or the Gates Foundation, while other companies have a more informal structure. While at one time companies gave to their local communities to show that they were good citizens, they have become more directing in their activities. Many now see the role of the company as one that will design programs, fund them, and seek community groups to support the objectives they have set forth.[12] In this environment, the library/information center will need to know what these programs are and to join in if a compatible niche occurs.

Foundations

Numerous foundations have been established by corporations and individuals to support social, economic, or scientific activities of particular interest to the donor. Each foundation has a set of priorities for giving. Some foundations support particular national programs while others give locally or regionally. Foundations are administered by a designated individual or group that reviews proposals, makes decisions, and awards grants in accordance with the wishes of the donor. Information on foundations, their priorities, and grant patterns is available online through the efforts of the Foundation Center, which "gathers, analyzes and disseminates factual information on philanthropic foundations." Libraries have received one-time grants to support special programs and building construction. Funds received are used for activities that add to the services of the library. They are not used to support core activities, as that is the role of the primary funding source.

Endowments

Libraries, and most often academic libraries, are often recipients of endowments from alumni or for former faculty in their honor. Typically, endowments are managed as part of the overall university or college endowment pool. Earnings from endowments, depending upon the terms of the endowment, may be used to enhance a particular activity for which the endowment was set up, or may be used for other purposes if so stated. Income from endowments is uncertain and it is unwise to rely on earnings to support ongoing costs.

Federal Grants

Since the 1950s, the federal government has provided funds for library programs through legislation. Seeking government grants that provide start-up funds for new programs, specific support for improving access to collections, or similar special purpose funds is a continuing activity. Knowledge of programs that provide funds for libraries and an ability to write grant proposals that are innovative, can be replicated elsewhere, or meet a specific need is an essential part of library management. Activities such as preservation of a unique archival collection or the development of a program for an underserved population may receive funding from this source. Federal funds are one-time, single-purpose grants that further federal objectives. If the program they have funded is a success, the library may find itself obligated to continue the program with library funds. When library managers are developing long-range plans and identifying core activities that must be supported, they also identify programs and activities that would enhance the library's ability to serve in special ways or would preserve and protect valuable parts of the collection. These activities are most appropriately identified as opportunities to write proposals for federal funding.

Fees

Charging for specific library services has been a topic of often heated discussion for a long time. Discussion is focused to a large extent on the public library, as it has the responsibility of serving the entire community and is supported in large part by tax revenues. Academic and special libraries/ information centers have a more limited clientele that may pay for part of its library services through tuition and other means, and may provide a broader range of specialized services. Many libraries have charged fees for particular noncore services for many years and continue to do so. Some argue that all library services should be freely available while others argue that basic services should be free and that specialized services should carry a fee. Services such as photocopying, use of certain online services, and in-depth consultation on a research topic could be for a fee. Depending on the type of library environment and the kind of clientele, there may be a role for imposing fees for some services. This is a highly charged political and social issue and needs to be approached carefully. An added caution is that in some areas, fees charged do not go to the library but to the general fund of the parent organization.

Added sources of revenue may include publications of bibliographies, local histories, or other materials. It may also include services in kind donated by groups or volunteer activities by individuals or groups. Each of these resources can be useful to the library provided that the cost of acquiring them is less than the cost of supervising the volunteer or administering a donated program.

SUMMARY

Financial management paired with planning sets the context for achieving goals and objectives. Looking at today's situation and projecting tomorrow in terms of changing client needs, programs, resource needs, resources available, and the changing nature of resources is all part of financial planning and management. Of equal importance is to demonstrate, through regular reports to funding agencies and the public, that the library/information center is a responsible steward of funds and a provider of quality service.

NOTES

1. Aaron Wildavsky, *The New Politics of the Budgetary Process*, 2nd ed. (New York: Harper Collins, 1992).

2. Patrick M. Callum and Joni E. Finney, eds. *Public and Private Financing of Higher Education: Shaping Public Policy for the Future* (Phoenix, Ariz.: Oryx Press, 1997), 75.

3. Daniel T. Layzell and Jan W. Lyddon, *Budgeting for Higher Education at the State Level: Enigma, Paradox, and Ritual* (Washington, D.C.: George Washington University School of Education and Human Development, 1990).

4. Betty Jo Mitchell, Norman E. Tanis, and Jack K. Jaffe, *Cost Analysis of Library Functions: A Total System Approach* (Greenwood, Conn.: JAI Press, 1978).

5. Virginia Beach Department of Public Libraries, *Cost Benefit Analysis of a Catalog System for the Virginia Beach Department of Public Libraries* (Virginia Beach, Va.: Virginia Beach Department of Public Libraries, 1978), 5. (ED 153675)

6. B. T. Stein, *A Cost Benefit Technique for Research and Development Based Information* (Kent, U.K.: Wellcome Foundation, August 1970), 7.

7. Robert M. Mason, "A lower bound cost benefit model for information services," *Information Processing and Management* 14, no. 2 (February 1978): 71–83.

8. Helen Drinan, "Financial management of on-line services, a how-to-guide," *ONLINE* 3, no. 4 (October 1979): 14–21.

9. Emerson O. Henke, *Accounting for Nonprofit Organizations* (Belmont, Calif.: Wadsworth, 1977), 1.

10. United Way of America, *Accounting and Financial Reporting: A Guide for United Way and Not-for-Profit Human Resource Organizations* (Alexandria, Va.: United Way of America, 1974), 3.

11. National Commission on Governmental Accounting, *Governmental Accounting, Auditing, and Financial Reporting* (Chicago: Municipal Finance Officers Association, 1968), 161.

12. Morino Institute, *Venture Philanthropy: The Changing Landscape* (Washington, D.C.: Morino Institute, 2001).

ADDITIONAL READINGS

Abels, Eileen G., Paul B. Kantor, and Tefko Saracevic. "Studying the cost and value of library and information services: Applying functional cost analysis to the library in transition," *Journal of the American Society for Information Science* 47, no. 3 (March 1996): 217–27.

Blecke, Curtis J., and David L. Gotthilf. *Financial Analysis for Decision Making.* 2nd ed. Englewood Cliffs, N.J.: Prentice Hall, 1980.

Crego Jr., Edwin T., Brian Deaton, and Peter Schiffren. *How to Write a Business Plan.* 2nd ed. New York: American Management Association, 1986.

Cummings, Martin M. *The Economics of Research Libraries.* Washington, D.C.: Council on Library Resources, 1986.

Hasperslaugh, Phillipe, Tomo Noda, and Faras Boulos. "Managing for value: It's not just about the numbers." *Harvard Business Review* 79, no. 7 (July–August 2001): 65–73.

Irvin, Hal, and Rosalind Meyers. "Can your auxiliary services compete?" *NACUBO Business Officer* 35, no. 11 (May 2002): 29–31.

Lindquist, Jan. "A complete transformation: activity based costing represents a business revolution." *NACUBO Business Officer* 29, no. 12 (June 1996): 31–39.

Matzer, John J., ed. *Practical Financial Management: New Techniques for Local Government.* Washington, D.C.: International City Managers' Association, 1984.

Prentice, Ann E. *Financial Planning for Libraries.* 2nd ed. Lanham, Md.: Scarecrow Press, 1996.

Schauer, Bruce P. *The Economics of Managing Library Services.* Chicago: American Library Association, 1986.

Shim, Wonsik, and Paul B. Kantor. "Economic approach to the evaluation of academic research libraries." *Proceedings of the 61st ASIS Annual Meeting* 35. Medford, N.J.: Information Today, 1988, 400–10.

Smith, G. Stevenson. *Managerial Accounting for Libraries and Other Not-for-Profit Organizations.* 2nd ed. Chicago: American Library Association, 2002.

Turock, Betty J., and Andrea Pedolsky. *Creating a Financial Plan: A How-to-Do-It Manual for Librarians.* New York: Neal Schuman, 1992.

Van House, Nancy A. *Public Library User Fees: The Use and Finance of Public Libraries.* Westport, Conn.: Greenwood Press, 1983.

Chapter Seventeen

Planning and Managing Physical Facilities

The space within which the library/information center is located and the way in which it is configured says a great deal about the attitudes of the parent agency, the community, and the staff toward their view of the role of information services. And it is a public statement for all to see. Many communities have libraries that are vital centers of community life. The Enoch Pratt Free Library in Baltimore, Maryland, and the New York Public Library are libraries that serve as symbols of service to the community and are at the same time architectural landmarks. Columbia University Libraries, the Newberry Library in Chicago, and the Library of Congress are active monuments to learning. Each is in a building or buildings that makes a statement about our culture. Many communities have new and modern libraries that are statements reaffirming the value placed by the community on its libraries. Many have been designed by leading architects who understand the dual needs of a library building: "[to address] the unpredictable future proliferation of new technologies that the new library would need to encompass and the new social functions that it may have to serve."[1] Academic libraries are also symbols of their role in academic life. The location and design of an information center in a business, an industry, or a not-for-profit agency is a statement of the centrality or lack thereof of information services to its operations. Is it located centrally? Is it technologically current? Is it a pleasant place for staff and customers to work? The library/information center management needs to be sensitive to the image the physical space and location projects and to ensure that that image enhances the ability to provide service. An architecture critic, in reviewing the new Seattle Public Library building, called its groundbreaking design "the first library of the twenty-first century."[2] The architects and the library director received the ultimate accolade "that they did not reinvent the library, they reaffirmed it."

The library building or space is an important part of its community; as such, it attracts the interests of groups who support its objectives and groups who wish to exert pressure on some aspect of the library or its services. The location of the library in its community is a political statement and the result of political decisions. While long-established libraries typically occupy a central location in the community, the establishment of branches in communities is subject to the competing needs and wants of those communities desiring services. With the growth of suburbs and the increase in size of existing communities, the demand for the establishment of branch libraries has grown. At the same time, school systems have expanded and new schools are needed to support the needs of growing communities. Community colleges in their expansion to serve new areas develop new campus facilities. Community planners and local political leaders often suggest that some sort of joint facility could serve more than one constituency. Perhaps a joint school/public library branch or a joint community college/public library branch would provide desired service and the pooling of resources would result in a larger and better equipped facility than if there were two smaller facilities with overlapping collections and services.

JOINT USE FACILITIES

There has been considerable discussion, both pro and con, on the issue of joint facilities. For it to work, a number of preliminary steps are required. Recognition that the community is changing, that pressures for increased services will grow, and that existing facilities are inadequate and additional resources are needed is the first step and must be taken by those contemplating a merger solution. Conversely, a community with aging facilities and a shrinking population might see a joint facility replacing two or more libraries as a cost-saving means of providing quality service. The second and highly important step is for each library to determine its primary mission: who does it serve, what services are provided, and what are its priorities? Then each library reviews its mission and looks at its level of convergence with the mission of the other library and the extent to which the staff would feel comfortable in merging activities. In the case of joint facilities between a community college and a public library branch, there can be considerable convergence in parts of the collection and in reference services. While the community college needs seminar rooms and study carrels, the public library needs public meeting space and ample room to support children's services. If the level of convergence is sufficient and there is a clear understanding of both convergence and differences, an interagency contract is proposed. What often happens in these discussions is that staff whose experience was focused in serving one clientele find that there are large areas of common interest and services when looking to serve another clientele. Discussions within the libraries and with political leaders in both municipal government and college or school administration begin early in the process, as do meetings between staffs of both libraries. Issues are discussed and possible solutions posed. Existing libraries may also provide service to the constituents of the other.

In the case of St. Petersburg (Florida) Junior College, the public library near the newly established junior college agreed to provide reference service to students; in return, the college provided resources to augment the reference collections.[3] Staffs of the two libraries met regularly to oversee the activity and to discuss mutual concerns, which provided a good foundation for further interaction. Using its interagency contract proposal as a guide, the community college and the community library developed plans for a new joint use facility and held public forums involving the entire community. Concerns were raised, suggestions put forth, and the initial plan was revised to respond to the added input. A vote was then taken and the plan was approved. The design of the new joint-use facility provided for areas of convergence (collections, reference service including access to workstations) and for those unique to each; children's services, meeting rooms for the public library, and seminar rooms and study area for students.

Once agreement on the building is reached, an operational agreement can be negotiated to deal with daily activities such as hours of service, and specific building use. Often a college and a public library will have different classification systems—Library of Congress for the college and Dewey Decimal Classification for the public library. Decisions should be made as to which will prevail, if there will be two separate collections, or if all new purchases will be given one of the classification system numbers, thus over time resulting in one system. Regular joint staff meetings are required to ensure that issues are resolved to mutual satisfaction. In the case of a public school/public library joint use facility, there may be issues of access to sections of the collection or use of computer terminals for certain purposes.

Over the past fifty or more years, there have been numerous examples of joint use facilities in small communities or developing communities. In California, San Jose State University, an urban, nondoctoral university, and the public library entered an agreement to build a major joint use facility. Both the university and the public library serve an urban clientele and considerable client crossover had long existed. The joint use facility provided a much larger, more technologically sophisticated facility that benefited both constituencies. The new library focused on *library as place* and enhanced the concept so that it is also *library as technology place*. The library technology, its collections, and services are greater than would be possible in separate facilities. And the facility is open more hours and thus more accessible to the public. Again, the areas where problems may arise if not carefully addressed early on is in attention to unique mission and services, the building of one staff from two staffs, and decisions concerning classification systems.[4]

ORGANIZATION OF INFORMATION SPACE

In the academic setting, decisions to maintain existing departmental libraries, to fold them into the central library, or to establish new departmental libraries are often hard-fought political decisions. They include elements of cost and academic program concerns, but are essentially political. The increased availability and use of technology to locate and access information provides flexibility in where and how resources can be located and accessed. Changing attitudes toward the relative roles of teaching and research in the university, changing curricular emphasis, changing teaching/learning philosophies, in addition to changing technologies all play a role in the location of resources on campus or among campuses.

In the 1960s and 1970s, many academic planners advocated the building of libraries devoted to service for undergraduates. Over time, it became evident that this was not an overwhelmingly successful concept. Dividing collections required either that multiple copies be purchased or that users would have to go to more than one library for resources. Services were duplicated in each library, requiring added staff and space. And many undergraduate students resented being relegated to what they saw as special (and therefore inferior) facilities. As academic libraries reviewed space in ensuing years, the undergraduate library tended to disappear and space was reassigned.

Where questions of joint use of facilities in communities where convergence of interests lead to a decision, where questions of how to spread or centralize services in an academic institution, or where questions of if and where to locate a new public library branch are raised, these are political decisions and must be treated as such. Financial concerns; concerns dealing with quality of service, staffing; and related concerns are components of the basically political decision that will be made within the political arena.

Because technology plays an ever-increasing role in how information is acquired, stored, and retrieved, a second area of convergence is that in which a university, a municipality, a school system, or a business proposes combining information technology systems. While this is an organizational issue, it is also a building and space issue. Definitions of information technology in support of teaching and research and how that differs from information technology in support of business operations must be agreed upon. While a library's personnel management system may operate on a city, district, or university-wide information management system and while technicians can manage these systems, they typically lack the skills and understandings to manage access to online information systems. Careful attention to what should be managed by information professionals (librarians) and what should be managed by information technology professionals is essential. The storing and maintaining of very large information databases, such as the U.S. Census, may be a jointly managed activity. Convergence in this area, again, is a space issue, a political issue, and a management issue.

In the academic setting, it is also an issue of how one plans the entire campus to integrate learning and research in an information-rich society. The computer center and the library are components of a larger plan to map an information technology infrastructure onto the existing facility. Typically, the information technology infrastructure has evolved from telephone lines, to administrative needs such as payroll systems, to campuswide connections that involve college business and academic needs. There is often a plan to for taking the next steps in infrastructure development. The base structures usually grew without a comprehensive plan and responded to need and existing technology. In revising the information technology infrastructure to meet teaching and research needs, computer center administrators need to be sensitive to the academic needs of the institution and involve faculty, students, and particularly librarians in the activity to ensure that the resulting structure reflects the best of current practice and actually meets student and faculty teaching and research needs. Developing the new configuration requires coordination between the library and the computing center. Each has different purposes, objectives, uses, and values and each is equally essential to the business of the university, which is providing the optimum teaching/learning environment for students and supporting high-quality research.

THE LIBRARY ENVIRONMENT

The library is a place and its "placeness" is an important aspect of what a library is. It engenders a certain unique set of images: a place to go to gain information, a place in which one is comfortable as one works, or the center of the school, the university, the community. How does one build and maintain a library/information center that preserves and enhances the sense of place while ensuring an efficient, safe, attractive environment? In the 1960s and 1970s, anthropologists and sociologists became particularly interested in the spaces people inhabit and the relationship between the individual and space. Hall noted that individuals in different cultures have different attitudes toward what makes the space they inhabit comfortable.[5] Not only does this apply to differences seen among ethnic cultures, it also applies to the environment in which one lives. The individual growing up in a rural environment has different ideas about space than does an urban dweller. An individual from a large family sees space differently than does the individual who lives alone. Each individual has a sense of what his or her personal space is and how close or distant he or she prefers to be from others. All individuals need sufficient space in which to work and live so that they feel they can move freely without interfering with others. Architects and designers, says Hall, need to design work, study, and living environments to take this into consideration.

Among the questions included in the LibQUAL+ Assessment Tool (www.libqual.org) (See chapter 15 on Program Measurement and Evaluation) are several questions asking about the quality of physical space as perceived by users. Students completing the web-based tool have the opportunity to comment on their environment and the way in which it impacts their work time in the library. Their comments are useful inputs to configuring spaces. Despite the increase in online access to information, the concept of the library as place continues to have an important impact. The library as social space for study and as an intellectual center for the campus has not changed. While the range of information access activities is distributed between on-site and off-site activities, the library is still *the place*.

Robert Sommer goes further to say that the best buildings are designed with the functions they are to support in mind and that functionalism is based on user behavior.[6] He includes regional planners, city planners, architects, engineers, and interior designers in the list of those whose responsibility is to ensure that the location of a building and the uses to which it is put (its function) are more important than the form.[7] It appears that, just as in the case of hardware and software design, professionals who design spaces and places risk becoming overly involved in form and forget function and forget that someone has to live and work in the spaces designed. Many beautiful building plans are works of art to the eye but are difficult workplaces. The library with all-glass exterior walls may be a beacon of light at night. It may also be an oven during sunny days. Form should not only follow function, it must assist it. With the use of computer-assisted design (CAD), architects can plot many of the functions intended for the space and ensure that the spatial layout supports those functions.

Design of a building is subject to political decisions. If it is to be a centerpiece of an urban area, those living in the area—political leaders and funding agencies—want input into the location and the design. Many of those involved have specific interests; they want the building to be a monument, a building similar to its surroundings, an example of the latest architectural fashion, or they have a particular architect or architectural style in mind. They are concerned about the finances and want to build a building that will fit in the budget, want the best building and will look for donors, or perhaps want specific program areas in the building. Others look to the future and want a building that will not be highly expensive to maintain. The Americans with Disabilities Act (ADA) specifies how buildings are to comply with access needs of those with disabilities. Additional legislation and/or regulations may also affect the building design.

With all of the above considerations in mind, the bottom line is still that building design should center on how individuals will use the building. What do staff want in building design that will make it a pleasant and efficient place to work? What do users want—convenience, comfort, and ease of use? How do people actually use library space and does this vary from library to library? Potthoff and associates asked library patrons to identify relevant areas in a given space and then asked them to make forced choices about the similarity and/or differences of triad groupings in these areas (what elements should go together).[8] This resulted in preferences for specific groupings of materials and for activities. Two additional studies of the same space focused on impressions of library space use. A floor plan was designed and respondents were asked about its usability. Other methodologies for gaining information on how staff and patrons utilize current space and how they would like to see it improved can be used to determine user behavior in particular spaces. Different clientele may have differing ideas on the preferred configuration and use of space. It is important for those planning space utilization know how their clientele envisions the spaces they use or would use.

In designing space, individuals need room in which to work comfortably. A public reading room should provide sufficient space and seating for user comfort, both psychologically and in terms of the task at hand. Color of furnishings, walls and carpets affect the environment as do floor tile or wood patterns, lighting, noise levels, and temperature. While fast food restaurants design their environments to prevent patrons from getting too comfortable and staying too long by installing uncomfortable furniture, keeping lighting very bright, and the noise level high, libraries are designed to support an individual's need to work quietly and privately for extended periods. While studies have shown that there is often little relationship between productivity and the environment, as the individual committed to a project will overcome a difficult environment to do the work, there is still a major effect on individual comfort levels.[9]

With the incorporation of technology into building plans, one's space is further enhanced. While there was initial concern that technology would reduce the individual's privacy, this need not be the case.[10] Supervision varies depending on the configuration of terminals and the uses to which they are put. Some libraries/information centers have provided areas where many computer terminals are in one place thus making it easier for either technical or information staff to provide service. Others have placed terminals around the building in smaller configurations. In other cases, outlets are provided at the desk or tabletop and individuals can use their personal computers from there. While there is the possibility of loss of privacy, this can be alleviated with careful design.

Underlying the ways in which people use space and respond to their environment are basic issues of territoriality and dominance, how much space a person needs to control or to have around himself or herself when at work. Space can also institutionalize power and bureaucracy. Administrative offices may increase in size as the administrator moves up the bureaucratic ladder; there may be an administrative suite in a choice part of the building. The departmental supervisor, on the other hand, may have a small office in a crowded or noisy area. We have all heard tales of administrators who move to other offices; as soon as they leave, remaining staff race to see who will take the wooden wastebasket for their office space and replace it with the less-prestigious metal one, or who traded the better desk chair for their older one. In a bureaucratic environment, all items and spaces hold status.

THE BUILDING PROGRAM

Once one has taken into consideration the political, social, technological, and behavioral aspects of building planning, one can then begin to plan the structure. At this point, the decision will be made as to whether to renovate the existing structure, add to the existing structure, or build a new structure. The choice made will depend on the condition of the existing structure, the space available for expansion at the location, and resources available. A library building is an expensive outlay and planning its construction requires great care to ensure that it is well designed for its purposes and that it will serve those purposes for a number of years after its initial construction. Despite expectations that information technology would slow the growth of print collections or that collaborative arrangements among libraries would reduce purchasing of new titles, library collections continue to grow. Uses of the facility change as needs change. A good building plan takes these and related factors into consideration.

The building planning process involves many groups, each of whom needs to be involved from the outset.[11] Major decision-maker (e.g., university president, the mayor or city manager, school superintendent, CEO, or other leader) approval of the process and plans is essential to success. These individuals have specific concerns about what the library will do for their specific community, how it will impact other projects, and what it may cost. They also want the project to be a success, to come in at budget, and to be a source of pride for their administration. A library building planning committee representing library administrators, users (faculty, students, staff, the public, researchers) provide input on how they use space, what they want in new space, and what they don't want. The library director and staff provide input on how they see the building being used to provide optimum service.

The architect and any consultants take the input received, add their expertise, and develop the building program, which outlines the functions that will take place in the building, the physical requirements of the building, any legal requirements, plus an early concept of what the building will look like. This is both a political document and a planning document that is continuously revised by the stakeholders until any outstanding concerns and issues are resolved. It then forms the basic document from which the building design is developed. The extent to which library staff and the director are involved in the process is dependent on the individual circumstances, but the wise director maintains careful oversight of the process. There are numerous books and articles available from both library and architecture professional organizations and journals describing library and architecture practice. (See the suggested additional readings at the end of the chapter.) The administrator and staff involved in a building program would be well advised to read widely in the current literature, discuss the process with others who have been involved in similar activities, and select an architect who understands libraries and who approaches the challenge with a creative yet realistic mind. Where appropriate, the library administrator will bring in consultants who can address specific problems and issues. The process of building a library is complex; once one gets past the basic concepts and planning steps, it is continuously changing.

The new library/information center is a projection of what its role(s) will be in the next decade. The challenge to the planning team is to build a beautiful, functional structure that can adapt to changing needs while at the same time protecting the collection and providing users optimal access. How do users use the library/information service? How will this change? Will staff do their work differently? How should space be configured to support new uses? Bazillion and Braun stress that the future needs of information technology are unpredictable and that architects should plan for flexible space, infrastructure, and functionality so that buildings can accommodate the changes that will occur.[12] Buildings are to be designed so that they can be adapted to new uses with a minimum of difficulty. Libraries will grow and evolve in response to technology and its needs but more importantly in response to the vision of librarians and users. They are "likely to be local, incremental, and opportunistic rather than a grand plan."[13] Sannwald summarizes tomorrow's building:

> In order to serve the customers of today and tomorrow, library buildings need a flexible layout so that space can easily be modified as service requirements

change. The building design must be responsive to these changes, allow for ease of movement for users, staff, and collections; make supervision of staff and patrons easy; and allow for a high degree of unmediated patron services. The building should be easily accessible from the exterior, and once inside, navigation should be intuitive and aided by a wayfaring system that is obvious but not obtrusive, providing access to other portals inside the building. The design of the building must be expandable to permit future growth with minimum disruption. Whenever possible, planning for expansion should be incorporated into the initial phase.[14]

He goes on to say that:

In the future, the library buildings will be different. They will be flexible in order to accommodate an ever-changing variety of activities and functions over their life cycle of approximately fifty to one hundred years. They will need to be energy efficient and employ sustainable design to conserve the planet's scarce nonrenewable, and expensive resources. Library designers also will need a better understanding of why and how people use libraries because the behavioral and programmatic aspects of space need to shape the form and function of the building. Libraries will continue to exist because they are the tangible link between people and the information they need, and people will always need information.[15]

Shill and Tonner, recognizing concern over the "increasing student reliance on the Internet and electronic resources, along with growing administrator awareness of declining usage patterns in some physical facilities, . . . [wished to determine if] a verifiable relationship between capital investment and student usage [exists]."[16] They identified academic institutions that between 1995 and 2002 built new libraries, renovated and/or built new additions, or underwent major redesign, and asked library administrators about the type of improvements made and subsequent usage. They found that there was a significant increase in the size of buildings and a dramatic upgrading of technology and communication technology. The significant increase in seating capacity with online access was in direct response to student information-seeking patterns. Provision for collection growth was mixed, with some libraries projecting space problems in five years or less while others anticipated a ten-year window before space for collections became a problem. The new and/or redesigned library places its focus on today's student patterns of access to information and creates a pleasant, electronically connected study atmosphere. The academic library has become a leader in campus technology innovation and a different type of library is emerging, one that is still a library but one that infuses new technology and user requirements into traditional structures to become a "hybrid print/electronic library." The new and evolving library is designed to address teaching and learning needs well into the future.[17]

FACILITIES MANAGEMENT

Maintenance

While building a new facility or the completion of a major renovation is not an everyday occurrence, maintaining the facility is an ongoing responsibility. From the day it opens, something in the building will need repair—a leaky pipe, torn carpet, malfunctioning electrical systems. The heating, ventilating, and air conditioning system (HVAC), which is essential to a comfortable working environment and one in which the collection is protected from excessive heat, moisture, or dryness, requires constant attention. Depending upon the size of the facility, one may have a supervisor of a maintenance staff who clean and maintain the building and grounds on a regular basis and who are responsible for maintaining all systems. In smaller facilities, one or two individuals may have this responsibility. In larger organizations of which the library/information center is a part, maintenance may be part of the larger organization's responsibilities. In an academic setting, maintenance may be a responsibility of physical plant staff. A number of their employees may be assigned to the library as their area of responsibility. Or the physical plant staff specialists may deal with HVAC, lighting, and so forth as the need arises. The library may have a cleaning staff assigned to it by the physical plant. In the public library, the library might have its own maintenance staff, might contract with the municipality for service, or might contract out maintenance to a private firm.

In addition to the daily maintenance of building and grounds facilities, managers are aware of changing space and use needs. If a computer lab space becomes crowded as use increases or if new services require new space, they are responsible for reorganizing existing space to accommodate the changes. If the building has been designed with potential changes in mind (e.g., a modular design with ample telecommunications and electrical outlets), minor interior renovations can be made without undue difficulty. As the collection grows, shelves become crowded and decisions about whether to add new shelving in existing stacks, relocate less-used materials to another on-site location (perhaps in a compact shelving area), or to place rarely used materials in off-site locations need to be made. Ideally, in the original building plan, such decisions will have been made so that when overcrowding occurs, a plan is already in place.

A well-cared-for building and grounds is a statement by all staff members of the level of respect they have for the workplace and those who visit it to read, write, conduct research, or attend programs. Maintenance is much more than emptying trash and mowing lawns.

Safety and Security

Each individual working in and around the library/information center has the right to know that his or her safety and security is ensured. This is done in a number of ways, beginning with high-quality maintenance. To ensure that every effort is being made to provide a secure environment, managers of public buildings often conduct a security audit. This can be done by an insurance company, a consultant, or by local fire and police officers. These audits determine the level of physical safety within a building; the number and location of emergency exits in case of fire, that the exits are well marked, that emergency exits open promptly, and that working fire extinguishers are present at strategic locations. While emergency exits, if not locked, can provide opportunity for theft of materials, they are usually equipped with alarms to alert building maintenance or other staff to unauthorized use. Safety hazards or impediments to use by those with disabilities are identified and a checklist of items to fix is prepared. The audit includes library parking lots and any other exterior areas for which the library/information center is responsible. The auditors may recommend better lighting in garages, trimming hedges around the building, or other tasks to improve visibility and safety.

Within the context of the larger organization of which they are a part, libraries/information centers are insured against accidents to the public and to staff. While excellent building maintenance and quality security systems and activities to ensure safety eliminate the possibility of most events that might cause harm, one cannot anticipate all problems. It is essential that appropriate insurance be in place and that the library/information center administration knows what it covers. In publicly supported libraries, insurance policies are determined by the state and administered centrally. Having a policy in the file locally is not enough. Knowing what the coverage is so that decisions can be made quickly in case of emergency is essential.

As libraries are usually public buildings, some who use them may make others uncomfortable. While personal attributes of some individuals may be distasteful to others, they do not necessarily constitute a safety hazard. If individuals become irrational or harass others in the library, security guards (if available) need to be called. If not available, library/information staff should be trained in how to deal with difficult patrons and those whose actions create an unsafe environment. Individuals using libraries rarely become a risk, but library staff should have a plan in place should the need arise. Such a plan is also useful should someone become ill and require medical attention.

Theft is always a problem in libraries. One public library director estimated that 10 percent of the collection is stolen in any one year. While much of the theft is accounted for by books not being returned by borrowers, theft from shelves is also a serious problem. Some may steal rare materials while others may take materials required for class assignments. Many libraries/information centers have installed security systems to prevent unauthorized removal of materials. There are a number of security systems on the market and while expensive to purchase and install, they may be less expensive than the annual cost of theft. Other problems include the mutilation of materials and destruction or theft of computing equipment. Depending on the severity of the problem, surveillance cameras may be installed or staff may regularly monitor key areas. While most problems of theft involve theft of materials, patrons and staff should be alerted to the danger of leaving personal items unattended. Safety and security is the responsibility of all those using the facility.

Maintaining an environment in which people are safe and feel safe is essential to daily activities. Reviewing insurance policies, updating security audits, and maintaining a general level of oversight so that unusual or inappropriate behavior is noted and acted upon are all elements in ensuring a safe and comfortable workplace.

Disaster Planning

Disasters rarely occur. When they do, the prudent organization has a plan in place that can be used to direct actions both in the immediate crisis and in the recovery phase. Fire and flood are the most common disasters. While the best disaster prevention is a quality building maintenance program and security system, additional planning needs to be in place in case of hurricanes, earthquakes, and other severe situations. The disaster plan outlines a series of actions to be carried to deal with the immediate crisis, including agencies and individuals to be contacted immediately; identification of core staff to be called in; and a statement of tasks each staff member is expected to do. The safety of people is the first priority followed by the safety of the collection and equipment. When the collection has been damaged, what is to be saved? Water-damaged materials need to be moved for preservation within seventy-two hours and if damage is extensive, decisions on what to save first need to have been made in advance so that valuable time is not used in discussion at that point. In the case of computing files, there should be off-site backup as part of day-to-day business activities. The plan should include directives on identifying priority activities and determining what can be left until later. Staff training using a simulated disaster can bring together all elements of the plan to see how well it works and to make modifications where needed. Not only does this improve the plan and alert staff to their roles, it is often a very useful team-building activity.

The Recovery Plan

The recovery plan outlines steps to be taken to repair damage and to restore services in the shortest possible time. Fire and police officers need to determine the safety of the building, insurance adjusters need to assess damage and the cost of repairs, workmen need to do the repairs, and if the entire building is not at risk, plans need to be in place to carry on business as usual where possible. Also, discussion of costs and where funds may come from are part of the plan. Many libraries/information centers have experienced disasters and have recovered from them. A number of them have been reported in the press, and case studies of disaster and disaster recovery programs are available. They provide an excellent guide of what to do and what not to do when disaster hits. No one can be ready for all eventualities but one must anticipate those that are likely to occur so that in that eventuality, one is prepared.

SUMMARY

The library building—the care with which it is designed and how well it is maintained—is a public statement of the role of the library in its community.

Members of the community who see the library as a symbol of access to learning in a democratic society take pride in their library. Staff who provide services to the community and take pride in their work maintain a library that is the most inviting place around. Patrons who enjoy using their library for research, for recreation, and as a place to be reflect the attitudes of the community and library staff. The library building is a social and political statement of the value placed on free access to information. Technology has changed many of the ways in which information is accessed and space within the library is used, but it has not changed the role of the library as *the information place*.

NOTES

1. Richard Lacayo, "One for the books," *Time* 163, no. 17 (April 26, 2004): 137–39.

2. Paul Goldberger, "High-tech bibliophile," *New Yorker* 80, no. 13 (May 24, 2004): 90–92.

3. Susan Anderson, "Planning for the future: Combining a community and college library," *Library Administration and Management* 13, no. 2 (Spring 1999): 81–89.

4. Ilene Rockman, "Joint use facilities: The view from San Jose; An interview with C. James Schmidt," *Library Administration and Management* 13, no. 2 (Spring 1999): 64–67.

5. Edward T. Hall, *The Hidden Dimension* (Garden City, N.Y.: Doubleday, 1969).

6. Robert Sommer, *Personal Space: The Behavioral Basis of Design* (Englewood, N.J.: Prentice Hall, 1969).

7. Sommer, *Personal Space,* 3.

8. Joy K. Potthoff, David L. Weiss, Dale S. Montavelli, and Matthew M. Marbach, "The evaluation of patron perception of library space using the role repertory grid procedure," *College and Research Libraries* 61, no. 3 (May 2000): 191–204.

9. Sommer, *Personal Space,* 161.

10. Stuart Shapiro, "Places and spaces: The historical interaction of technology, home, and privacy," *Information Society* 14, no. 4 (1998): 275–84.

11. Keyes D. Metcalf, *Planning Academic and Research Library Buildings* (New York: McGraw Hill, 1963).

12. Richard J. Bazillion and Connie L. Braun, *Academic Libraries as High-Tech Gateways: A Guide to Design and Space Decisions.* 2nd ed. (Chicago: American Library Association, 2001), vii.

13. Rob Kling, "The Internet and the strategic reconfiguration of libraries," *Library Administration and Management* 15, no. 3 (Summer 2001): 144–51;

14. William W. Sannwald, "To build or not to build," *Library Administration and Management* 15, no. 3 (Summer 2001): 156.

15. Sannwald, "To build or not to build," 160.

16. Harold Shill and Shawn Tonner, "Creating a better place: Physical improvements in academic libraries, 1995–2002," *College and Research Libraries* 64, no. 6 (November 2003): 431–36.

17. Harold Shill and Shawn Tonner, "Does the building still matter: Usage patterns in new,

expanded, and renovated libraries, 1995–2002," *College and Research Libraries* 65, no. 2 (March 2004): 123–50.

ADDITIONAL READINGS

Bazillion, Richard J., and Connie Braun. *Academic Libraries as High-Tech Gateways: A Guide to Design and Space Decisions.* 2nd ed. Chicago: American Library Association, 2001.

Klasing, June P. *Designing and Renovating School Library Media Centers.* Chicago: American Library Association, 1991.

Lueder, Dianne C., and Sally Webb. *Administrator's Guide to Library Building Maintenance.* Chicago: American Library Association, 1992.

Lushington, Nolan. *Libraries Designed for Users: A 21st Century Guide.* New York: Neal Schuman, 2002.

Lushington, Nolan, and James M. Kusack. *The Design and Evaluation of Public Library Buildings.* Hamden, Conn.: Shoestring Press, 1991.

Martin, Ron G., ed. *Libraries for the Future: Planning Buildings That Work.* Chicago: American Library Association, 1992.

Chapter Eighteen

Knowledge Management

Knowledge management (KM) is a natural outgrowth of today's working environment, a working environment increasingly populated by individuals more highly educated than in earlier years, who are more comfortable working in teams than in a hierarchical environment, and who expect to make many of the decisions in their area of expertise. They place value on what they know and, in a supportive environment, are willing to share their knowledge. The human capital of an organization—its people power—has become recognized as the single most valuable asset of the organization. Knowledge management is a way "to create a process of valuing the organization's intangible assets in order to leverage knowledge internally and externally . . . to create a sharing environment where 'sharing knowledge is power' as opposed to the old adage that "knowledge is power."[1] Knowledge management is a means of using what people know (human capital) and combined with databases and other formally organized information (structural information) developing new knowledge that can then be communicated.

Knowledge management emerged during the early 1990s as a new way of looking at the organization and what the people in it know, plus a recognition that what people know is an important asset. It encompasses not only management theory and practice but also sociology, psychology, and anthropology as applied in innovative ways to the workplace. Emerging first in the corporate world, KM soon moved to the public and nonprofit sectors. The first knowledge management conference in the public sector was held in 2000 by the Foundation on Electronic Government and drew a large and varied attendance, including representatives of higher education and libraries.[2]

The impact of KM on organizations continues to grow so that its elements are evident throughout many organizations.

The institutional memory of an organization—who worked there in an earlier time, what projects were successful or not, how decisions were made, problem areas, special knowledge about how to deal with particular long-standing problems and many other facts and perceptions great and small—undergirds the organization's culture and forms part of the organization's identity. Organizational culture is also influenced by factors such as the ethnic mix of employees with the unique perspectives each brings, the environment in which the organization operates, the people it serves, and the kinds of services it provides. The organization's response to change, its level of technology, and the kinds of people it hires all contribute to what the organization is and how it functions. Organizational culture thus consists of shared experiences, shared values, and accepted norms of behavior.

Davenport and Prusak ask the questions: What happens to corporate knowledge? How do you retain it and use it to grow the organization? Which technology can best be used to collect and analyze data and to communicate findings?[3] They stress that human intelligence is required to use what is collected and analyzed to make decisions. They further state that "the only sustainable advantage a firm has comes from what it collectively knows, how effectively it uses what it knows, and how readily it acquires and uses new knowledge."[4] This holds true regardless of whether the organization is profit or nonprofit. Knowing what your organization knows, knowing how to use it, and using it to further organizational objectives is the crux of knowledge management.

DATA TO KNOWLEDGE

Knowledge management is not putting operations manuals, the organization's calendar of events, or the personnel manual online. Making these kinds of information widely available is helpful to members of the organization but is not organizational knowledge of the type and level with which knowledge management is concerned. KM is concerned with data, information, and knowledge, both tacit and explicit, that are central to the organization's functions. Data, the structured records of transactions, is usually managed through an information technology system and is available on demand. It can be used to determine costs, time taken to perform tasks, or the level of activity of a department as defined by the volume of service. Data is the collection of facts with no interpretation. Data—when collected and organized manually—took a great deal of time; analysis of the data, once collected, could take weeks or months. By the time it was analyzed, the results were so dated that they were largely of historical value and did not contribute measurably to decision making. Today, data can be collected, organized, and analyzed in a very short time and thus can have a direct impact on decision making.

Information is data that is organized for a purpose and is moved around the organization both formally and informally. Some information can be organized, sent, reviewed, or revised using technology, but most activities must be completed by humans who organize it for a particular purpose. Converting data into information to support decision making requires specialized knowledge about the data. The specialized knowledge needed to do this is scattered throughout the organization among those who work with certain data on a regular basis. If one were to identify the data to information specialists and their locations, a very different chart would result than the hierarchical organization chart.

Knowledge "is a fluid mix of framed experience, values, contextual information, and expert insight that provides a framework for evaluating and incorporating new experiences and information. It originates and is applied in the minds of knowers. In organizations, it often becomes embedded not only in documents or repositories, but also in organizational routines, processes, practice, and norms."[5] Within the organization, much of the knowledge available is found in departments where the work is done, where learning about the work takes place, and where standards of practice and productivity are known and observed.

INFORMATION TECHNOLOGY AND KNOWLEDGE MANAGEMENT

Information technology is essential to the collecting and storing of data, to providing rapid analysis of data and then communicating it to the appropriate locations. An efficient management information system is basic to the operation of any organization. Some managers equate a good technical system with good information and do not take into account the importance of the ways information is used by people. If a system is organized according to a particular information architecture plan that technical designers have devised to ensure that all the relevant information in an organization is collected and made available, that architecture may look good conceptually but may be unusable by the people for whom the system was designed. Without input from the users or an understanding of how data is to be used, a system is of limited use. If an off-the-shelf turnkey system to manage information is selected, there are risks. These systems have a particular structure and this imposes specific ways of collecting data on the organization. It will impose its data-gathering structure on the organization, a structure that may or may not mesh with the organization's existing structure. Turnkey systems tend to reinforce a hierarchical structure and often do not take into account an environment in which information of many types is distributed widely throughout the organization. Data is collected according to the rules of the system and only secondarily in response to the questions the organization needs to have answered. The economies achieved in buying an already developed system are often lost in the cost of adapting the system to the organization or in dealing with a system that does not respond to organizational needs. Elaborate systems take a long time to design and are expensive; while they are being designed, the information and its uses may change. When the overall information management system does not respond to information needs in ways staff can use, there is a tendency in larger organizations to set up local shadow systems that will provide staff with the information they need in a timely fashion. This is costly, as it duplicates effort but may be less costly than trying to use a grand system that does not work.

The information technology system that does work begins with the question "What does the system user need to know to make decisions?" The system must meet the needs of those who use it and it should be easy to use. The more complex the system, the fewer the number of individuals who will use it. Many managers stress that information technology systems should be managed, not by a technical expert, but by a manager who understands the ways in which information is used to further the goals of the organization. The information system should be integrated so that there is one place to go to gain a unified view of the organization and its data. And again, it should meet the needs of the organization rather than being a thing of technical beauty.

WHERE ORGANIZATIONAL KNOWLEDGE IS

Much of the information in the organization that people want is not in the information technology system. Managers typically ask others for information first and then refer to online sources to confirm or deny what they have heard. Studies have projected that up to two-thirds of decision makers follow this procedure.[6] How does one discover what people know, where this knowledge is located, and how to gain access to it? Davenport and Prusak identify a number of sources of knowledge.[7] Knowledge develops over time from our experiences—what we read, learn, do, and see. And this provides a context or new information. Knowledge also derives from learning what really works and what does not work. One learns that simple answers rarely exist and that each problem is different. Refining what you know through judgment and knowing the limits of one's knowledge are part of knowing.

Tacit Knowledge

Tacit knowledge is what individuals know. It is highly personal, hard to communicate, and is rooted in action. It includes both intuitive knowing and learned technical skills. Tacit knowledge is gained through everyday experience on the job—how to fit the key in the faulty lock so that the door will open on the first try, which lights not to turn on, how to deal with a cranky patron, or how to interact politically and socially with one's peers and the public. It can also include insights, intuition, and serendipitous knowledge— the beginning elements of new knowledge not yet well formed. The essence of this knowledge cannot be captured on paper but it can be discussed and shared so that others can benefit. Tacit knowledge cannot be given a particular dollar value although it adds value through customer satisfaction, personal satisfaction, and positive attitudes toward the organization by those who work in it and those who benefit from its services. It is this kind of knowledge that leaves the organization when staff members leave. It cannot be replaced. In a number of instances of organizational downsizing, individuals who had essential tacit knowledge were let go and the organization found itself lacking important information it could not recover.[8] A healthy organization is not defined just by the leanness of the organization chart but also by the efficient flow of essential information.

Much of our knowledge, modified as it is by experience as well as personal and organizational values and beliefs, is intangible and thus difficult to measure. Intangibles, such as special understanding of a customer's need, an awareness of cultural differences, or a sensitivity to political nuances, are based on knowledge gained by staff in working in a particular environment. These add value as they add to customer satisfaction. These elements are not captured in information systems but are shared among staff.

Explicit Knowledge

Explicit knowledge is that which has been documented and organized for access. This includes manuals that outline processes, informal how-to guides, and similar reports. As processes are always changing, this knowledge requires constant updating. Explicit knowledge is relatively easy to manage and to update. It relies only partially on the presence of specific individuals and can usually stand alone based on the information therein.

Sharing Information

How does an organization bring people together to share what they know? Expert systems based on experience have been designed to guide others doing similar work. Others have developed notebooks describing processes and how to do them and include cautions about what not to do and why. Numerous other methods to bring together what people know have been tried. The most effective methods continue to be those that support face-to-face interaction. Individuals will seek out others with similar concerns and build informal networks to share information. Often, in an organization, communities of practice will emerge. These self-organized groups focus on a common issue or set of responsibilities. They could be centered on a problem related to the redesign of an information system or the best way to provide services in a new branch library. The focus could be on the best ways to use volunteer services in a library. Members of the community of practice come together to share expertise in order to find the best solutions. While most members of the community of practice will be from inside the organization, it may also include people with special knowledge who are outside the organization. A member of the group may ask a friend who is a software specialist for advice. An individual in the community who is knowledgeable about working with volunteers may offer advice. In this community of practice, knowledge management is taking place. Existing knowledge is being used to create new knowledge that can be used to further the objectives of the organization. Communities of practice may be part of a larger network or in addition to smaller networks.

The professional organization can play a major role in knowledge sharing, as it provides a larger external network for sharing specialized information. With librarians/information professionals working in many types and sizes of libraries, the external network provided by the professional organization may be the best—and in some cases, the only—link for knowledge sharing. The learning, both formal and informal, provided by the professional organization is of value to the individual and to the organization.

What motivates individuals to share what they know with colleagues? There is a general awareness that special knowledge has value. One brings in external knowledge by hiring consultants. Internal knowledge when recognized as having value, can be bartered ("You tell me what you know, and I'll tell you what I know"), or can be given to another depending on the relationship of the asker and the knower. Some share information because it contributes to the general good of the organization. Others take pride in their knowledge and want to be recognized for their knowing. In some organizations, information sharing is a component of personnel evaluation and part of the incentive/reward process. Whatever the motivation to share, a level of trust is essential. Individuals want to be recognized for sharing and need to know that someone else will not take credit for their special insights. To build an environment of trust, which starts at the top, individuals need to get to know one another and to work together. A negative aspect of telecommuting and the growing popularity of the virtual workplace, where individuals are scattered in many directions with technology as their sole link, is that there is little or no personal time together to build the interactivity so essential to trust. People need consistently available informal time to build the level of trust essential to sharing.

Information is best shared in an environment in which there are no barriers and in which value is placed on information sharing. One must trust that one's colleagues are willing to share and to assist in a situation needing their special expertise. In such an environment, staff see that their expertise is valuable and that they are important to the success of the organization. The quality of the communication medium used is also an important factor. In an environment of openness and trust where issues are discussed so that there is a general understanding of problems and possible solutions, there is a stronger loyalty to the organization. Also, in this type of organization, ideas are respected, as is knowledge. There is respect for and appreciation of knowing and sharing and it is understood that it is a good and positive activity in which to participate.

KNOWLEDGE GENERATION

"[A]ll healthy organizations generate and use knowledge. As organizations interact with their environments, they absorb information, turn it into knowledge, and take action based on its combination with their experiences, rules, and cultural values."[9] Some of the information used is acquired externally and put to internal uses. This can be done individually through networking or may occur when one organization or department merges with another. Existing information is sometimes adapted to solve new problems or to approach old problems in new ways.

To be useful, knowledge in the organization needs to be put into a form that is easily accessible. Davenport and Prusak set the following principles for organizing this type of knowledge.[10] The first is to determine the goals of the organization that will be addressed by this type of knowledge, much of which will be tacit. Evaluate the knowledge for its usefulness and appropriateness, and identify an appropriate medium for organizing and disseminating it. Knowledge management will not succeed unless there is an organized effort to identify relevant knowledge, to organize it, and to make it available. This requires approval and acceptance by top administration as well as leadership by someone able to work with others to build a system. From the outset, the system should include data on the value of knowledge management: the duplication of effort avoided by learning of similar activities, the money saved by not repeating a costly error, and the benefit to the organization of dealing with a political issue in a way that was informed by tacit knowledge held by staff members.

Tacit knowledge cannot be organized in a database but it is possible to identify the person or persons who know. Some organizations have produced a directory of names of individuals who have specialized information. While it may focus on internal staff members, it may also link to external individuals who may have important insights. Here again, the expertise of the professional organization, networking, and consultants enriches local knowledge. How one interacts with the knowledge knowers varies depending on the local culture. For some, informal interaction is desirable while others may want a more structured interaction.

While everyone in the KM-focused organization is expected to contribute his or her special knowledge and to learn from one another and from external sources, specialized skills are needed to obtain knowledge from those who have it, to put it in a structured form, and to maintain and refine it over time.[11] This is a role the librarian/information professional, particularly in the corporate world, has developed and has become skilled in performing. The librarian/information professional has skills, abilities, and professional experience plus an overall knowledge of the organization, its records, and its products, and is strategically placed to guide the process and advise others in its use.

When a library/information center uses knowledge management to enhance its own management practices, there is a strong reservoir of experience and understanding of the value and uses of knowledge. Libraries are managed for the most part by professionals who are proud of their education and professional status. They know how to do their job as they have the underlying educational preparation to do so (*know-how*). They have applied their cognitive knowledge to develop advanced skills (*know what*), they understand the cause-and-effect relations that underlie their discipline (*know why*), and they are self-motivated to do their best to achieve success for their organization and for themselves (*care why*).[12]

Townley describes how academic libraries can combine transactional information residing in databases, knowledge embedded in processes, and tacit and explicit knowledge held by staff and clientele to make informed decisions.[13] While librarians are information experts, he makes the point that they have not necessarily utilized their own management information to the extent possible and that there is an opportunity here not to be missed. The librarian/information specialist has applied the skills necessary to process information for knowledge management purposes to the processing of scholarly information. They know how to select and use what is most important to support library goals. They are experts at organizing information for use and in communicating it. Townley cites Davenport and others who identify four knowledge management processes and then shows how those processes are essential to the library in its knowledge management activities.[14] He says that the library/information center needs to:

- Create knowledge repositories to provide useful information about internal operations and user activity, which can be used "to create

explicit organizational knowledge, to inform services, to guide operations, and to measure goal attainment,"
- Improve knowledge access through expert networks, encouraging communities to practice building "Yellow Pages," and connecting to virtual
  libraries to expand on internal knowledge,
- Enhance the knowledge environment by encouraging sharing of tacit
  knowledge, and
- Manage knowledge as an asset, including both tacit and explicit knowledge.[15]

Townley goes on to say that much of knowledge management has been in
practice in libraries and information centers for some time. What is different
now is that knowledge management focuses on goals and the ways in which
staff contribute to those goals. There is also a more proactive approach to
sharing information than has been true in the past.

KNOWLEDGE AUDIT

Some consultants recommend that the organization conduct an information
or knowledge audit to review knowledge assets and their associated knowledge management systems: human capital, structural capital, and customer
capital. Using this information, one can assess the strategic position of the
organization in relation to its environment, its customers, and its resources.
Using the data, one can identify the information needs of the organization,
the unit, and the individual. Existing expertise and knowledge assets are
identified and gaps noted. Information flow and any bottlenecks can be
detected as well. The result of this activity is a knowledge map of the organization showing where the knowledge is and where it flows. A limitation of
the knowledge audit is that it describes internal assets and assigns value to
those that exist. It is possible to shift the assets, looking for new combinations. There is little emphasis on looking at what might be or in taking large
leaps forward. The audit may be a means of institutionalizing yet another
aspect of the organization.[16]

NEXT STEPS FOR KNOWLEDGE MANAGEMENT

Malhotra urges that knowledge management be used not just to support
existing organizational goals with existing knowledge.[17] He stresses that

with the accelerating rate of change, the need to be creative is ever more essential. It is important to "keep the centralized knowledge base and its custodians (managers) continuously current with the discontinuously changing external environment . . . while at the same time continuously updating employees on changes in their outputs (goals) plus any changes in procedure to achieve those outputs."

Knowledge management is more than developing and recording *best practices* that focus on how the individual/organization did something in an excellent way. That excellent way may not really be the best practice. It might have been yesterday's solution, which is no longer relevant. Knowledge management—which he calls *minds at work*—functions best in a dynamic setting. How can we work in a dynamic setting when we have to deal with approved goals, objectives, structured information, best practices, and approved communication links? Malhotra proposes that we apply social, creative, innovative, and intuitive thinking to the available information. Go beyond specific problem solving to the *what if* questions. Interpret and reinterpret data, rethink the premise, and evaluate possible outcomes. Rather than trying to avoid errors, look to see where they might occur and anticipate them. Look to see where discontinuities exist. Goals and objectives are a useful structure for thinking and operating but should not box one in if new and promising possibilities appear. The role of the leader/manager is to see the vision of "what can be" beyond the goals and objectives and to ensure that the vision on which planning is based and goals and objectives are set is carried out. Management of the organizational vision is a balance of organizational structure with individual knowledge input that furthers the vision. "These characteristics of the proposed model integrate the sense making capabilities that are human and social with the information-processing capabilities of archival, retrieval, and dissemination, which are the forte of the new computer based technologies."[18] His model respects the creative elements of tacit knowledge input.

Managers have few tools that can be used to capture institutional experience, disseminate its lessons, and translate them into useful action. With this concern in mind, a group from the Massachusetts Institute of Technology developed a tool called the *learning history*.[19] Members of the team prepared a written narrative of a recent critical event identifying both positive and negative aspects. They recorded the information and placed it in two columns: column 1, using direct quotes, listed relevant episodes described by participants, those affected by the events, and observers; column 2 recorded comments by trained outsiders and knowledgeable insiders who looked for recurrent themes and raised questions and issues. Column 1 (with its wide range of responses) and column 2 (with its analysis and commentary by trained observers) were used as the basis for discussions. It was a particularly useful tool to see an event from many perspectives and to identify questions and concerns no one had been sure how to raise. Tacit information and explicit information were gathered and analyzed to further learning.

THE LEARNING ORGANIZATION

Bringing people together to share knowledge promotes learning and adds to organizational knowledge. Many individuals think narrowly about their role in the organization and what they need to learn. In a learning organization, they are expected to grow and to think more broadly. Continuous improvement of the organization requires that it commit to learning and to seeing the world from new and changing perspectives. Garvin says that the learning organization follows three activities: meaning, management, and measurement.[20] To have meaning, "a learning organization . . . is skilled at creating, acquiring, and transferring knowledge, and at modifying its behavior to reflect new knowledge and insights"; the learning organization translates new knowledge into new ways of believing.[21] To operationalize learning, one begins with systematic problem solving, use of the scientific method as a process, and the application of organized data to the problem. One then goes on to test the new information gained from systematic review of the data, to learn from past experience and the experience of others, and then to report findings. These learning activities are continuous and are the major source of new knowledge. Managing both the learning process and putting the learning used to use is critical to successful operations. Measuring the amount of new knowledge gained, identifying the uses to which it is put, and finally measuring benefits gained completes the cycle.

SUMMARY

The practice of management is to an extent organic in that it builds on existing systems, takes into account changes in those systems, and adapts to the changed environment. In this way, management is a learning organization and is prepared for today's and tomorrow's challenges.

Knowledge management is a way of looking at the entire organization and providing continuous renewal and improvement. It can reinforce the current organizational culture through the sharing of knowledge. Networked employees use their shared knowledge to develop solutions that reflect experience and that are responsive to the organizational culture. This type of activity is not new. It has always been a component of the healthy organization. Managing the knowledge one has, applying technology to providing access to information, and providing a means of communicating it rapidly and broadly, is the best means of keeping the organization healthy and moving forward.

NOTES

1. Jay Liebowitz, *Building Organizational Intelligence: A Knowledge Management Primer* (Boca Raton, Fla.: CRC Press, 2000), 1.

2. *Knowledge Management Conference Proceedings* (Washington, D.C.: Foundation on Electronic Government, 2000).

3. Thomas Davenport and Laurence Prusak, *Working Knowledge: How Organizations Manage What They Know* (Boston: Harvard Business School Publishing, 1988).

4. Davenport and Prusak, *Working Knowledge*, vi.

5. Davenport and Prusak, *Working Knowledge*, 5.

6. Davenport and Prusak, *Working Knowledge*, 6.

7. Davenport and Prusak, *Working Knowledge*, 7–12.

8. Ikujiru Nonaka, "The knowledge creating company," *Harvard Business Review on Knowledge Management* (Boston: Harvard Business Review Publishing, 1998), 26.

9. Davenport and Prusak, *Working Knowledge*, 52.

10. Davenport and Prusak, *Working Knowledge*, 69.

11. Davenport and Prusak, *Working Knowledge*, 110.

12. James B. Quinn, Philip Anderson, and Sydney Finkelstein, "Managing professional intellect," *Harvard Business Review on Knowledge Management* (Boston: Harvard Business Review Publishing, 1998), 181–205.

13. Charles T. Townley, "Knowledge management and academic libraries," *College and Research Libraries* 62, no. 1 (January 2001): 44–57.

14. Townley, "Knowledge management and academic libraries," 49–50.

15. Townley, "Knowledge management and academic libraries," 48.

16. C. Marshall, L. Prusak, and D. Spilberg, "Financial risk and need for superior knowledge management," *California Management Review* 38, no. 3 (Spring 1996).

17. Yogesh Malhotra, "From information management to knowledge management; beyond hi-tech hidebound systems," in *Knowledge Management for the Information Professional*, edited by Kanti T. Srikantaiah and Michael D. Koenig (Medford, N.J.: Information Today, 2000), 37–61.

18. Malhotra, "From information management to knowledge management," 53.

19. Art Kleiner and George Roth, "How to make experience your company's best teacher," *Harvard Business Review on Knowledge Management* (Boston: Harvard Business School Publishing, 1998), 137–51.

20. David A. Garvin, "Building a learning organization," *Harvard Business Review on Knowledge Management* (Boston: Harvard Business School Publishing, 1998), 47–80.

21. Garvin, "Building a learning organization," 51.

Index

About the Author

Ann Prentice brings to management a combination of teaching, research, and application. For several years, she taught management courses and presented workshops and in-service programs in the United States and abroad. She has written numerous articles on management based on her research, particularly in the area of financial management and planning. She is the author or editor of fourteen books, many of them dealing with management issues. She has been involved in the management of libraries and academic programs at various levels and from differing perspectives: as a school library media specialist and public library director and as a public library trustee for a small public library, for a metropolitan public library and as a trustee for a public library system serving sixty-five libraries.

Dr. Prentice was director of the School of Information Sciences at the University of Tennessee and from there went to the University of South Florida as the associate vice president for information resources where she worked with the university libraries, the computing center, and related information services to coordinate the information activities of a multicampus university. At the University of Maryland, College Park, in addition to her tenure as dean of the College of Information Studies, she was the acting assistant vice president for information resources for four years. Her experience in bringing research to practice on a daily basis in complex information and management environments has been the motivation for writing the text *Managing in an Information Age*.

Ann Prentice has a BA in political science from the University of Rochester (New York), an MLS from the School of Information Science and Policy from the State University of New York at Albany, and her doctorate in library/information science from Columbia University. She holds an honorary doctorate from Keuka College (New York). She is currently professor emerita of the College of Information Studies at the University of Maryland.